THE RELATIONSHIP RIGHTS OF CHILDREN

This book presents the first sustained theoretical analysis of what rights children should possess in connection with state decision making about their personal relationships, including legislative and judicial decisions in the areas of paternity, adoption, custody and visitation, termination of parental rights, and grandparent visitation. It examines the nature and normative foundation of adults' rights in connection with relationships among themselves and then assesses the extent to which the moral principles underlying adults' rights apply also to children. It concludes that the law should ascribe to children rights equivalent (though not identical) to those adults enjoy, and this would require substantial changes in the way the legal system treats children, including a reformation of the rules for establishing legal parent–child relationships at birth and of the rules for deciding whether to end a parent–child relationship.

James G. Dwyer is Professor of Law at the William & Mary School of Law. He received his J.D. degree from the Yale Law School and a Ph.D. in Philosophy from Stanford University. He has worked as an attorney in law firms in Washington, DC, and as a law guardian representing children in family court in the Albany, New York, area. He has published numerous law journal articles and book chapters on children's rights. His two prior books are *Religious Schools v. Children's Rights* and *Vouchers Within Reason: A Child-Centered Approach to Education Reform.*

The Relationship Rights of Children

James G. Dwyer
William & Mary School of Law

CAMBRIDGE UNIVERSITY PRESS
Cambridge, New York, Melbourne, Madrid, Cape Town, Singapore, São Paulo

Cambridge University Press
40 West 20th Street, New York, NY 10011-4211, USA

www.cambridge.org
Information on this title: www.cambridge.org/9780521862240

© James G. Dwyer 2006

First published 2006

Printed in the United States of America

A catalog record for this publication is available from the British Library.

Library of Congress Cataloging in Publication Data

Dwyer, James G., 1961–
The relationship rights of children / James G. Dwyer.
   p.   cm.
Includes bibliographical references and index.
ISBN 0-521-86224-8 (hardback)
1. Parent and child (Law) – United States.   2. Children – Legal status, laws, etc. – United
States   3. Guardian and ward – United States.   I. Title.
KF540.D89   2006
346.7301'7 – dc22   2005037956

ISBN-13   978-0-521-86224-0 hardback
ISBN-10   0-521-86224-8 hardback

To my daughters, Anna and Maggie

Contents

Acknowledgments

One part of the process of writing a book that leaves a strong and lasting impression is receiving feedback from excellent scholars who generously sacrifice their time to review drafts. I will be forever grateful to Matthew Kramer and Brian Bix for helping me improve the rights analysis in Chapter 1 and the Appendix; to Jonathan Herring for reviewing Chapter 2 and clarifying several points of English law; to Alan Fuchs for aiding me with the philosophical analysis of Chapters 4 through 6; and especially to Peter Vallentyne, for very thoughtful comments on the entire manuscript. I owe a debt of gratitude as well to colleagues at William & Mary who participated in colloquia on several aspects of the book and to family law scholars from several other universities who joined in a conference on this topic that I held at William & Mary in spring of 2002: Emily Buss, Naomi Cahn, June Carbone, David Meyer, Elizabeth Scott, and Barbara Woodhouse. Those conversations did much to advance my thinking. A former student, Briordy Meyers, offered valuable insights on several aspects of the analysis, both while he was at William & Mary and during his employment in the Public Guardian office of Cook County, Illinois.

The book reflects a massive research undertaking, principally because Chapters 2 and 3 present descriptions of the law in numerous countries on numerous issues affecting children, parents, and incompetent adults. That research was pulled together by a legion of extremely capable law students: Katherine Aidala, Emily Anderson, Andy Befumo, Elizabeth Bircher, Sarah Cane, Brendan Chandonet, Natalie Collins, Sarah Edmonson, Carolyn Fiddler, Peter Flanigan, Caroline Fleming, Katheryn Mckinlay Hamrick, Emily Jones, Kelly Kumpula, Sarah Lenet, Briordy Meyers, Pia Miller, Ruth Nadeau, Gina Pereira, Andrea Phelps, Emmy Salig, Chris Seacord, and Kelly Street. Research librarian Fred Dingledy provided crucial assistance both to those students and to me in obtaining the more difficult sources.

Another law student, MaryBeth Wysocki, did superb editorial work on the final manuscript.

Completion of this project was made possible by research grants from the College of William & Mary and from the Marshall-Wythe School of Law at William & Mary.

THE RELATIONSHIP RIGHTS OF CHILDREN

Introduction

C hildhood ordinarily entails numerous personal relationships. We do not often recognize it, but the fact is that the state determines, to a large extent, what those relationships are. In some ways, it does this directly, most crucially by deciding who each newborn child's legal parents will be. The state also influences children's relational lives indirectly by conferring on legal parents some measure of control over children's associations with third parties. This book aims to develop a general theory of what principles should guide the state in making decisions about children's personal relationships, whether the issue is paternity or custody after divorce or termination of parental rights or grandparent visitation.

This topic is of profound importance for the well-being of individual children and for the health of society. The state's decisions as to who will raise and associate with a child are largely determinative of whether the child's life proceeds positively or poorly, and the aggregate result of good or bad state decision making is a citizenry that is happy and flourishing, mired in dysfunction and conflict, or something in between. And there is good reason for examining rigorously the appropriateness of current practices, because on many occasions in many contexts, the state in western society and elsewhere today makes decisions about children's relationships that are injurious to the children involved.

There can be reasonable disagreement as to precisely which state decisions are bad for children and about how often they occur, but every scholar of family law could point to some legal rule or established practice that he or she believes contrary to the welfare of children. Some of these occasionally capture the public's attention – for example, the dramatic "botched adoption" stories of the 1990s in the United States, such as the Baby Richard case, in which courts removed children from the custody of long-term adoptive parents and handed them over to previously absent biological fathers, solely because the adoption process did not comply with technical requirements for terminating the biological father's legal rights. Others receive less attention, even though, or perhaps because, they are more routine. For example, the prevailing rules for parentage create legal parent–child relationships for newborn children solely on the basis of biological connection, with no regard for the preparedness of particular biological parents to raise a child, and as a result cause a significant percentage of children to suffer abuse or neglect at the hands of parents who are manifestly unfit for child rearing. The state's response to abuse and neglect – that is, its child protective rules and agencies – has many critics, including both those who believe the state removes children from their homes too readily and returns them too late and those who believe the state is too deferential to parents. Increasingly, we hear about custody and visitation disputes between legal parents and persons who are not legal parents but who have helped to raise a child, such as a former same-sex partner or stepparent, and the law governing such disputes in many jurisdictions empowers legal parents completely to sever a child's bond with those "de facto" parents.

Of course, sometimes children suffer simply because the state has limited information and resources rather than because the legal rules are indifferent to their welfare. The proper response in that case might not be legal reform but rather greater commitment of resources and acceptance of the unavoidable imperfection of human institutions. However, in many situations, children appear to suffer because the legal rules governing particular decisions about their relational lives do not require state decision makers to act with a single-minded focus on the welfare of the affected children. Instead, the law encourages state actors to protect interests of other persons or to advance broad societal aims, and those interests and aims can conflict with the interests of the children.

In particular, the rules governing many state decisions about children's family relationships are designed to protect interests and perceived rights of biological parents. Less commonly, rules are explicitly crafted to serve progressive causes such as gender or racial equality. For example, with respect to postdivorce custody decision making, courts in many jurisdictions are resistant to treating even as a relevant consideration in postdivorce custody disputes a mother's decision to move with the children far from the site of the marriage to pursue a career, despite the substantial disruption this can cause in a child's life. Judges express concern for the freedom and social advancement of women and on that basis are willing to limit application of the general "best interest of the child" standard for custody decision making. In the United States, the Supreme Court has ruled out consideration of any stigmatization that might befall a child as a result of being in the custody of a parent who has entered into an interracial intimate relationship, based on the premise that states should be counter-acting rather than giving effect to racial bigotry. In contrast, most lower courts in the United States that have addressed custody disputes involving a parent in a same-sex relationship have been willing to consider the poten-tial effect of stigmatization on a child. Arguably, the two situations should be treated the same, but whereas from the adult-centered perspective that most family law scholars take the correct approach is to exclude consider-ation of stigma in both types of cases, from a child-centered perspective the correct approach might be to consider it in both. Scholars and social workers also perceive a conflict between child welfare and the claims of racial minorities in the adoption context; many adoption agencies remain resistant to placing minority-race children with white adoptive parents, in part because of concerns that such placements weaken or undermine minority communities, even when this means that a child might not be adopted at all.

To say that the law compromises children's well-being to some degree in some situations, to serve interests of individual adults or broad societal aims, is not equivalent to saying that the law is bad and should be changed. Any detriment to children might be outweighed by benefits to the children immediately involved themselves, or to children generally, or to other persons, and it might be morally appropriate to sacrifice the welfare of some children to some degree for the sake of other individuals' welfare or for the betterment of society as a whole. The European Court of Human Rights has in fact consistently taken the position that, when interests of children and parents conflict in family law controversies, the interests of one should be balanced against the interests of the other, thus allowing for the sacrifice of children's welfare in some cases to serve interests of adults. I do not presuppose that that is improper but rather aim in the course of this book to analyze whether it is so. The starting factual assumption of this book is simply that the state sometimes does cause detriment to some children when it makes decisions about their relational lives and that it does so in many cases because its decisions are based at least in part on supposed rights and/or interests of people other than the children immediately involved. Knowing precisely when that is true as a factual matter is not necessary to the normative analysis of this book.

The overarching question that this book addresses, then, is whether and to what extent it is morally permissible for lawmakers to create any legal rules for decision making about children's relationships that by design compromise the welfare of children to serve interests of other individuals or general societal aims. Conversely, it asks whether legislatures and courts should reform the laws governing children's relationships to ensure that all decisions are based exclusively, or simply to a greater degree than at present, on the welfare or rights of the affected children.

To point to the welfare or rights of children as a potential basis for state decision making raises numerous questions that have been the subjects of debate among legal scholars and philosophers, questions conceptual (e.g., what sort of rights, if any, can a child possess?), procedural (e.g., who should determine what is good for children and who should possess the power to assert any rights children have?), and substantive (e.g., does procreating give rise to rights or only to responsibilities?). The analysis of this book touches on many of those questions. I cannot, of course, attempt a resolution of all relevant debates. What I hope to accomplish in this book is to advance discussion of several broader philosophical issues and to present a fundamental challenge to existing assumptions about what aims are morally legitimate in the legal contexts addressed – in particular, the increasingly popular view that it is appropriate for state decision makers to balance children's interests against the interests and rights of others in crafting statutes and in rendering individualized decisions that determine certain aspects of children's relational lives. Doing so will leave unanswered many important empirical questions, and as I proceed I endeavor to identify the questions of law and policy whose ultimate answer must depend on having not only a better theoretical understanding of the topic but also better factual information than I can muster or than is currently available.

The central aim of the book, then, is to develop a general theory of what children are morally entitled to as against the state, and correlatively what moral duties the state owes to children, when the state takes it upon itself to make authoritative decisions about the legal family relationships children will have and about which of a child's social relationships will receive legal protection. Before embarking on the normative analysis, though, in Chapter 1 I clarify what I mean when I speak of children having rights and explain why I examine the topic through the lens of rights, and in Chapter 2 I describe the current state of the law in some detail to document just how far short of a children's rights model existing rules fall. The remainder of the book then analyzes whether the state's decisions about children's relational lives should be governed to a greater extent, and perhaps exclusively, by rights of the children.

In developing a theory of the relationship rights of children, I assume for the sake of analysis that in every case the other persons whose relationship with a child is in question do wish to have that relationship. As it happens, and as explained in Chapter 2, the law in western society currently does not force unwilling adults into social relationships with children, and the well-known reality is that some adults decline to associate even with their biological offspring. That adults are legally free not to associate with children is itself significant in considering what rights children should have. Whether the law should ever force any adults to associate with certain children is worth considering, but I do not do so here.[1] My aim is to construct a general theory of what legal rights children ought to have in connection with their personal relationships with willing others.

My approach to developing such a theory is applied moral and political philosophy. It is "coherentist" in style, meaning that it first looks for widely agreed on general moral principles relating to intimate human relationships and then considers whether those principles ought to apply in state decision making about children's relationships and, if so, whether existing rules and practices in this area are inconsistent with those general principles. A basic premise of coherentist reasoning is that insofar as moral persons strive for rational consistency or coherence in their moral beliefs, they should want to change any specific rules and practices that are inconsistent with their general principles, unless they are prepared to abandon the general principles. In the context of children's relationship rights, this approach entails the following three-step process.

The first step, in Chapter 3, is to describe the legal rights competent adults now possess in connection with their personal relationships, which I treat for the sake of analysis as paradigmatic of human relationship rights. It shows that competent adults have a nearly absolute legal right to establish and maintain mutually voluntary relationships of their choosing with other competent adults. They also possess an absolute legal right unilaterally to terminate, or to avoid in the first instance, a relationship with any other person if they so choose. Chapter 3 also considers the extent to which this model of relationship rights has been extended in the law to incompetent adults. Chapter 4 then plumbs moral and political theory to discern the normative foundation on which the existing rights of adults to freedom of intimate association rest. It principally examines strands of modern political philosophy and popular moral discourse that treat human welfare or autonomy as ultimate values. From this examination it is possible to develop a fairly robust account of why we adults have the relationship rights we do.

Next, Chapter 5 examines whether the prevailing moral justifications for adults' relationship rights provide any support for attributing rights to children. On the surface it appears that they do not, at least not for younger children, because each invokes adults' capacity for rational self-determination. But a deeper examination of welfare-based and autonomy-based moral reasoning about rights in personal relationships reveals ample support for children's rights as well – not, for the most part, rights identical to those which we adults enjoy, but rather rights that are analogous and equally effective – "equivalent rights," one might say. Those minors who are capable of mature decision making as to their personal relationships should have the same right that competent adults have to effectuate their choices, but in the more common case of children not yet capable of mature decision making, the law should afford them in every context a right to effectuation of "imputed choices" – that is, to what it is most reasonable to assume they would choose if capable of mature decision making, which will generally mean what is in their best interests, all things considered. Doing this would require transforming much of family law in most western nations.

Importantly, attributing to children rights equivalent to those held by adults would not entail that adults have no rights as to relationships with children. It would entail, though, that adults' rights to form and maintain relationships with children are no greater than their rights to form and maintain relationships with other adults. Adults would still be entitled to be considered for relationships with children, just as they are entitled to make known their interest in having a relationship with other adults. But the law would fully satisfy this right by permitting adults to petition for a relationship with a child to whomever – a court, a child's legal parents, or a child himself or herself – the law properly treats as the decision maker for the child. If the child's actual or imputed choice, as appropriate, is not to have the relationship, then that should be the end of the matter, just as would be the case where an adult rebuffed the efforts of another adult to form a relationship between them. If, however, the child's actual or imputed choice is to have the relationship, then the adult would possess an additional right against the state's or other private party's interfering with the relationship.

My analysis of the theoretical underpinnings of adult relationship rights and of their applicability to the situation of children raises many subsidiary questions, and subsequent chapters endeavor to address the more salient ones. Chapter 6 responds to objections that giving children rights equivalent to those enjoyed by adults would result in a substantial welfare loss for biological and legal parents and/or would infringe on, or undermine the basis of, parents' autonomy. It then addresses some novel and intriguing theoretical questions regarding constitutional and policy constraints on, or bases for, state decision making in this context. As revealed by the survey of existing rules in Chapter 2, there are situations in which a single-minded focus on the welfare of children could produce outcomes that conflict with legitimate and important societal aims, some of which are embodied in "constitutional" restrictions on state action. I treat "constitutional" in this context as encompassing non-U.S. analogues to the U.S. Constitution, such as the European Convention on Human Rights. On what basis, then, may or must the state make decisions in such situations? Is the state's role in these cases a purely *parens patriae* one – that is, one of acting as agent for, or protector of, a private, dependent individual? Or does the state also or instead act here in its more common "police power" role, as agent for society as a whole? And if the state is acting to some degree in a *parens patriae* role, is it as constrained by constitutional provisions as it is when it acts in a purely police power role? Even if not compelled to do so, may the state nevertheless use its power over children's relational lives to promote the progressive societal aims underlying certain constitutional provisions, or does this amount to illicit instrumental treatment of children?

Chapter 7 then tackles the several difficulties said to plague application of the best-interests standard, responding to family law scholars who have taken the position that this standard is unworkable or incoherent. Chapter 7 also considers some perplexing questions not addressed by others writing about this area of law but that arise when one understands a best interests inquiry in terms of imputing choices to children. For instance, should children be assumed to have only self-regarding interests? Or should they instead have imputed to them altruistic concern for the happiness and well-being of, or a debt of gratitude toward, certain other persons, such as their biological parents? If we ask, for example, whom a newborn child would, if able, choose to be his legal mother, between a biological mother who is addicted to drugs and an available adoptive mother, should any sympathy for the biological mother enter into our reflections, on the grounds that people who can feel sympathy generally do so with respect to their biological parents' sufferings, or given that the child might later in life actually feel sympathy for his biological mother? Should we impute to the newborn child a "choice" to show gratitude to the biological mother for giving the child life rather than having an abortion? Or should we think only about the child's developmental needs?

Last, Chapter 8 reassesses a few of the existing legal rules governing decisions about children's relationships, by reference to the general theoretical conclusions arrived at regarding children's relationship rights, and indicates how the legal rules might be modified to comport with these conclusions. I focus in particular here on the legal rules governing initial assignment of children to parents, because they are the most crucial to children's lives and because they are arguably the most divergent from a children's rights model. I proffer a model statute to govern creation of legal parent–child relationships and discuss its main features in light of the book's theoretical analysis. I do something similar with respect to termination of parental rights and third-party visitation. This exercise lends greater concreteness to the analysis of the book, illustrating some of the real-world implications of taking a children's rights approach to state decision making about their family lives.

Still, some readers might resist the predominantly theoretical approach I take to these issues. Some might believe that, because each child's situation is unique and family interactions are so complex, the best we can hope for in this area of state decision making is good empirical information and reasonable intuitions, and general theories are out of place. They might be correct, but until a theory is developed, it is not possible to assess its utility.[2] Even legal pragmatists must concede that decision making is paralyzed absent initial judgments about which principles and ideas have some validity or usefulness and that those judgments must in turn rest on some theory about what makes a principle or idea valid or useful.

Moreover, there is good reason to be suspicious of any claims that theory has no place in the complex business of structuring children's lives. Adults are far too willing to give up on trying to act in a principled way toward children. It is implicit in much of the scholarship relating to children's relationships that the fact of children's lesser competence means that nothing true of adult lives can be extended to children's lives, that it is not worth thinking about how the theoretical premises of adult rights could be applied to children, and indeed that it is not necessary to appeal to any general principles at all. The situation of children is unique, many seem to believe, so ad hoc reasoning is entirely appropriate. But there is no good argument for concluding from the fact of lesser competence that no general moral principles apply to children. Children are today viewed as persons, and many of our social practices reflect moral beliefs about what people are owed simply by virtue of being persons – for example, the belief that each person's interests should receive equal consideration in state decision making, and the belief that all persons should be viewed as "ends in themselves" and not merely as means to advancing the ends of others.[3] In addition, children are not alone in being incompetent relative to normal adults and in presenting complex problems for those who must make decisions about their lives. Many adults are also relatively incompetent, and their situations also give rise to perplexing legal and moral issues. Yet with any group of adults, we insist on being as principled as we can be. To not insist on that with respect to children fails to accord them the equal moral respect they are due as persons.

Yet to date there has been little theoretical writing about the moral claims of children in these core family law matters. Increasingly, legal scholars, advocates for children, and state actors have embraced the idea that the primary, perhaps even exclusive, aim of state decision making about children's relationships ought to be promoting children's welfare,[4] but that is typically mere assertion. Proponents of a child-centered approach might have little to say to someone who simply disagrees and asserts in response that interests of adult individuals or of society as a whole should be balanced against, and perhaps override, children's interests. In fact, as we will see, many family law scholars do not take the position that children's interests should dominate law and policy in these areas, but instead emphasize the interests of adults in writing about these issues. A general theory of children's relationship rights would provide a substantial foundation for conclusions as to whether exclusive emphasis on children's welfare is appropriate or whether instead other interests and aims ought to influence decisions as well.

A final preliminary point: The easy response to a theoretical account that emphasizes children's rights and the best interests of children will be to think of practical impediments to implementing any principles it generates. A common response to arguments for greater rights for children from defenders of parental prerogative is to conjure a massive government bureaucracy taking over family life. For many people, perceived practical concerns provide an excuse for quickly shifting back to a focus on adults' rights and interests, where the practical and conceptual difficulties are thought to be less daunting. This, too, happens with great regularity in discussions of the law governing children's lives; many people are all too willing to find that any practical obstacle or conceptual difficulty is sufficient justification for abandoning a focus on the child. They are somehow less willing to do so when the lives of adults are at stake, even though practical impediments can be just as great – for example, with incompetent adults' rights – and even though the law governing adults' personal and business relationships is replete with nebulous standards. There are, to be sure, practical obstacles to implementing almost any right children have, precisely because children are generally unable to exercise and effectuate their rights independently and because there is no perfect substitute for self-determination in exercising and effectuating rights. Determining what is best for a child is hindered by conceptual and evidentiary difficulties and by institutional shortcomings.

I proceed on the assumption, however, that the most appropriate way for us adults to reason about children's lives, prior to exercising the awesome power we have over them, is first to figure out what basic rights children ideally should possess, stated at whatever level of generality is necessary to bracket conceptual or empirical uncertainties. And then we should think about which legal rules those rights would dictate if certain assumptions are made about what children's interests are or about what counts as evidence of interests, departing from the ideal set of legal rules only insofar as is necessary to deal with practical problems created by children's dependency and lesser capacities or by institutional limitations. The ideal theory must be done first if we are to have any clear sense of what the legal system should be aiming at, of what is lost when we make compromises to political and practical realities, and of what conceptual or empirical questions we should be trying to answer.

1 Why Rights for Children?

The analysis of the book is couched largely in terms of rights – what moral rights children have in connection with state decision making about their relationships and what legal rights they should have, as well as what rights any other persons should have in connection with such decision making.[1] Most people in western society are, I think, quite comfortable with the idea of children having rights and with moral reasoning about what legal rights they should have. But some have reservations of one sort or another about thinking in terms of rights when discussing child welfare policy, and I want to try to remove that obstacle up front.

One concern can be eliminated very quickly. There is some tendency to assume that any argument for children's rights must amount to an argument for empowering children to run their own lives without adult interference. If one had that understanding of rights, one would be understandably resistant to the idea of attributing rights to young children in connection with, for example, termination of parent–child relationships. A claim that five-year-olds should be entitled to choose to "divorce" their parents would suffer from a seemingly insurmountable facial implausibility. Let me emphasize at the outset, then, that I am deploying an understanding of rights, consistent with common usage, whereby rights can be protections of persons' interests independently of any choices they make. In fact, we can attribute to children certain rights to protection of their interests even against choices they make. Just as infants might be said to have a right to be restrained from running into the street, five-year-olds might be said to have a right against the state's terminating their legal relationship with their parents even if they say they want different parents, if doing so would be contrary to their interests. I consider the possibility that some minors should have choice-protecting rights in some relationship contexts, but for the most part the rights I consider in this book are

interest-protecting rights rather than choice-protecting rights. The understanding of rights I employ also presupposes that persons can have rights
even if they are incapable of effectuating the rights themselves but rather
must have someone act in their behalf. Some philosophers object on conceptual grounds to the idea of nonautonomous persons having rights, but
existing practices – both as to children and as to incompetent adults –
reflect a widespread acceptance of the idea. I explain in an appendix to the
book why those conceptual arguments are, in any event, flawed, for the
benefit of those who take an interest in that philosophical debate.

Other concerns merit a somewhat fuller response here, and this opening
chapter briefly addresses two. First, some readers might believe that rights
are appropriate to human interaction in the public sphere but out of place
in the private sphere of the family. Second, some might fear that any new
rights for children would entail an unwelcome expansion of government
power. After responding to these concerns, I briefly describe the various
forms that rights of children can take in connection with state decisions
about their relationships, as a prelude to Chapter 2's descriptive account
of children's rights today.

I. Rights Discourse and Children's Lives

Western culture, and particularly American culture, appears already
plagued by an obsession with rights. Rights-talk, it is said, promotes hostility and litigiousness and weakens harmony and community spirit. It is
symptomatic of a collective failure to foster virtues and a sense of responsibility. Rights proliferation is, for some people, particularly troubling in
the context of families, because they believe individuals should not be
encouraged to view their intimate relationships in terms of individual
entitlement. That only weakens the emotional bonds that should characterize family life. Rather, the law and public morality should speak in terms
of familial responsibility and love and should emphasize the interconnectedness and nurturance that characterizes family life.[2] Rights-talk fosters
self-centeredness, whereas talk of duties fosters more socially desirable,
other-regarding attitudes.

Insofar as this critique is leveled against adults' rights in connection
with their dominion over children, I wholeheartedly agree. Talk of parents'
rights encourages an entitlement view of parenthood that makes parents
more resistant to guidance from others, more preoccupied with their own
desires, and less concerned with the interests of their children.[3] Parents'
rights rhetoric and legal doctrine also cause state decision makers to lose

sight of the moral claims of children, who typically do not have forceful advocates in legal proceedings concerning their lives.[4] But this critique of rights-talk in relation to the family almost never is directed at parents' rights. It has almost exclusively been directed against rights for women within marriage and rights for children with respect to their upbringing. What is sought is effectively a unilateral disarmament of the weaker parties in intimate relationships.

But putting aside the perverse asymmetry of the typical criticism, let us consider its substance. Some commentators express the view that talk of children's rights is inappropriate, because talk of rights suggests conflict between disconnected persons, whereas children's lives are or should be marked by interconnectedness and harmony between them and their care-givers. One concern appears to be that rights-talk will encourage parents to become detached from their children or will cause adults generally to overlook children's dependency and need for intimate nurturance. Thus, Ferdinand Schoeman writes:

> The danger of talk about rights of children is that it may encourage people to think that the proper relationship between themselves and their children is the abstract one that the language of rights is forged to suit. So, rather than encouraging abusive parents to feel more intimate with their children, it may cause parents in intimate relationships with their infants to reassess the appropriateness of their blurring the boundaries of individual identity and to question their consciousness of a profound sense of identification with, and commitment toward, their families. Emphasis on the rights of children might foster thinking about the relationship between parent and child as quasi-contractual, limited, and directed toward the promotion of an abstract public good. Such emphasis unambiguously suggests that the relationship is a one-way relationship aimed almost solely at promoting the best interests of the child.[5]

Others might worry that children raised amidst a discourse of children's rights will become selfish and belligerent rather than community-spirited and obedient. The alternative form of discourse typically suggested is to speak in terms of good and bad ways of treating children, of our moral obligation to care about the well-being of children, or of the responsibilities parents and other adults bear with respect to children. This would encourage both adults and children to adopt more other-regarding dispositions and so foster harmonious communal life and nurturing family life.

The counterargument is now quite familiar: rights-talk is in western culture today a necessary, or at least uniquely effective, instrument by which to improve the situation of historically mistreated groups. Rights have a particular force in our society and so have been vital to the advancement of groups whose interests society has long undervalued or disregarded. Rights-talk emphasizes the moral standing of the beings who are the objects of duties – that is, to whom duties are owed. The result of doing so is in part to inspire some such persons whose moral standing has previously been underestimated or ignored to demand greater respect for themselves and to resist oppression, but it is also in part, perhaps principally, to grab the attention of those in power in a way that talk of good and bad or of their moral responsibilities does not. Rights-talk impresses upon moral agents the bindingness of their obligations and the wrongfulness of failing to carry out their obligations, because it vividly presents to them the moral or legal standing of the persons to whom the duties are owed. Talk only of fulfilling responsibilities suggests a perfectionist outlook, appealing to a moral agent's desire to be a good person, whereas talk of rights directs the attention of moral agents outward to other beings and to their moral deservingness. Attribution of rights also suggests a more severe sanction for failure – namely condemnation rather than just a denial of respect. Michael Freeman writes: "Who would wish to beg or grovel, to be the recipient of noblesse oblige or charity when they can demand what is their due?"[6] Certainly no group of adults.

Children, who are arguably the least powerful group of persons in any society and the least well represented in any political system, have much to gain from their advocates' asserting in public fora that they have rights that are being violated. As Tom Campbell explains, "rights are the language of priority in modern society, so that to exclude or limit rights for children is to render them vulnerable to the counter-claims of those who have rights."[7] Thus, to the extent one believes significant change in treatment of children is morally requisite, one will find rights-talk useful, even necessary, in a practical sense. Although a legal right for a three-year-old obviously cannot mean precisely the same thing as a right for a battered spouse or for an adult African-American who suffers employment discrimination – in particular, in terms of what it protects (e.g., interests vs. choices) and how it is effectuated (e.g., by proxy vs. directly), it can nevertheless serve the same function of limiting the ill effects of power imbalance within relationships and focusing the attention of moral agents on others' deservingness.[8] There is much to be gained in rhetorical impact from talk about rights for children, just as there is with talk about rights for women and minorities. It can elevate the standing of children in the eyes of adults and dissolve the still-prevalent proprietary conception of parenthood.

Beyond this familiar response to the concern about excessive rights talk, I would add that concern about the effects on adults' attitudes implicitly assumes that the attitudes adults currently have toward children either are ideal or already involve too much thinking of children as separate persons rather than as needy, dependent persons, so that any movement in the direction of greater treatment of children as separate persons would be bad. But not only do those who object to rights-talk in this context, such as Schoeman, fail to make this assumption explicit, they also provide no empirical support for the assumption. It might well be that current adult attitudes toward children are not ideal and that parents now generally have too little regard for the distinct personhood of their children and are too inclined to view their children as their property or as appendages of themselves. If that is the case, then more talk of children having rights might move attitudes closer to the ideal, if it is possible at all to say what the ideal is. (And if it is not possible to describe an ideal set of attitudes, then this complaint has no foundation.)

Moreover, children's perceived moral standing can be elevated without losing sight of the facts that rights do not raise children – loving family members do – and that much harm can result when reformers ignore the complex emotional and psychological reality of family relationships. Ideally, we would embrace an understanding of children's rights that encourages appreciation for the distinct personhood and moral standing of children but does not cause parents and other adults to overlook children's dependency and need for care, nurturance, discipline, and love. As is true with the law governing marriage, the law governing parent–child relationships should aim for some middle ground between fostering abject subordination and encouraging atomistic detachment and conflict. Many parents do find that middle ground, demonstrating that it is possible to do so.

Last, and crucially, the legal issues to which the analysis of this book is addressed are not directly about rights within family relationships – that is, rights that family members would assert against each other. Rather, they are about according children rights against the state, rights that would constrain the state in its structuring of children's family life. This would include, perhaps most importantly, the state's initial decision about who a child's parents will be, a decision that ideally would be over and done with before caretakers begin to bond with a child. Interactions between individuals and the state are a natural locus of rights as we understand them. We do not ordinarily expect caring and intimate connectedness to characterize the state's relationship to individuals. Thus, even if one believed it inappropriate to speak of children having rights as against their parents or other family members, one could embrace the idea that children should have rights against injurious actions by state actors, including legislators when they are crafting statutory rules for establishing, regulating, and terminating legal family relationships and judges and administrators when they are applying those rules. One would then simply need to recognize how extensively the state is already involved in children's relational lives now, as demonstrated in Chapter 2, to perceive the broad scope for potential enlargement of children's rights against the state.

It is true that some rights of children against the state can be viewed as indirectly specifying rights of children as against their parents. For example, if the law (e.g., by judicial interpretation of constitutional rights provisions) conferred on children a right that the legislature not bestow on parents a legal power or privilege to interfere with the child's positive relationships with third parties, such as grandparents, this would, in practice, mean that the child has a right against the parent's acting in such a way as to obstruct that relationship, just as children generally have a right against persons who are not their parents that they not interfere in the children's relationships with others. Likewise, if the law ascribed to children a right that the state suspend or sever their relationship with their legal parents if and when that came to be in the children's best interests, that would require the state to establish some standards by which to judge the value of the parent–child relationship for any particular child, and those standards might be viewed as specifying rights of children against certain forms of treatment by parents.

As noted above, however, the effect of this perceived, indirect establishment of children's rights against parents on parental attitudes might be entirely salutary. In addition, it is important to recognize that some rights of children against the state would presuppose and rest on children's need for intimacy with parents and would require the state to *refrain* from interfering in parent–child relationships when doing so would disrupt unjustifiably the bond between parent and child. For example, if a child had a right against the state that it suspend or sever a parent–child relationship if *and only if* that is in the best interests of the child, that would mean the state should not remove a child from the home if doing so would not produce benefits for the child that outweigh any negative effects of separation from parents. In that case, *removal* would violate a child's rights. Likewise, a child's right that the state order parents to comply with a schedule of visitation with grandparents if and only if that is, on the whole and all things considered, in the child's best interests, would properly be effectuated by taking fully into account the possible deleterious effects on the parent–child bond of upsetting the parents and diminishing their control over the child's life.

The point can be stated more generally: Legislatures and courts, in fashioning legal rules to govern the issues I address, should themselves be thinking in terms of children's rights against them, as state actors, and in fulfilling their own duties toward children they should be mindful of the effects that the rules they fashion can have in practice on the attitudes of children's caregivers and on the bonds between children and parents once parent–child relationships are established. Schoeman himself appears to accept this position when he writes: "As against society, we might yet think of infants and parents as having rights to conditions which permit or encourage, or at least do not discourage, the social and material conditions conducive to parent–child intimacy."[9]

II. Children's Rights vs. Limited Government

I consider at several points in this book the concern that attributing new rights to children would lead to a dangerous expansion of government power. The concern comes in several forms, and here I respond to the one that arises from an assumption that legal rights in western society are or should be limited to negative rights – that is, rights to be left alone – and should not encompass positive rights – that is, rights to assistance. Liberalism properly understood, and western governments founded on it, some say, recognize only negative rights of citizens against the state. The notion of individuals having rights against the state arose in a context of resistance to excessive governmental interference in people's lives. Modern western governments have been formed on the basis of an understanding that individual rights limit the state's authority over the lives of its citizens, confining the state's activities to ensuring that other private parties or other nations do not harm the state's citizens. Rights are not supposed to expand the state's involvement in private life or require the state positively to assist private individuals.

In light of this understanding, talk of children's rights in relation to the state might be thought inapposite, a category error, because what children need is assistance, not to be left alone. The rights that advocates for children typically demand in the context of state decision making about children's relationships are not rights against state intrusion into children's lives but rather rights to state action of a particular kind, which could be provision of special benefits or regulation of their family life in some way. Such rights appear to some inconsistent with a proper understanding of the role of government.[10] In fact, adherents to this view might say that recognizing such rights would amount to violations of taxpayers' negative rights, because any state action entails government expenditures from general tax revenues and therefore coerced redistribution of wealth. Children's needs should instead be met by private citizens voluntarily undertaking to provide for them.

A more modest expression of this view holds simply that negative legal rights stand on firmer footing than do positive legal rights in modern western democracies. There is a presumption in favor of individual freedom and therefore negative rights against the state, but there is a presumption against individual entitlements to government assistance. To justify creating a positive legal right for any individuals, then, one must argue not merely that there is inadequate justification for not conferring the right but also that there are compelling reasons *for* conferring the right.

Neither version of this view, though, should cause us any hesitation before postulating rights of children against the state in connection with the determination of their family relationships. In the first place, insofar as both versions appeal to historical understandings, they are liable to attack on the grounds that political theorizing historically has been unjustifiably centered on competent adults and has not given the interests and circumstances of children and incompetent adults the attention they are morally due. Any of the prevailing principles and platitudes in our political tradition that operate to the particular detriment of persons of lesser competence are inherently suspect for this reason. Unless and until proponents of such views construct a political theory on the basis of equal moral respect for all persons, including children and incompetent adults, and show that such a theory yields the same conclusions with respect to positive rights, their positions amount to little more than self-serving assertion.

In any event, prevailing understandings of the role of government have changed considerably over the centuries. Although libertarians might lament the arrival of the welfare state, it is here and most people accept that even adult citizens are morally entitled to assistance from the state (i.e., from the rest of society) in certain circumstances – for example, when they suffer great loss as a result of natural disaster or terrorist attack, when they lose their jobs through no fault of their own, or when they become incapacitated by disease, old age, or accident and family members cannot care for them. It truly does not stretch popular understanding or contemporary liberal theory to argue for according positive rights to the most vulnerable members of our society. In fact, constitution-like documents emanating from the unionization of Europe, a very modern experience of federalization, express numerous positive rights, especially for vulnerable persons. In particular, the Charter of Fundamental Rights of the European Union pronounces a right of children "to such protection and care as is necessary for their well-being" (Article 24) and a right of all persons to an education (Article 14), rights also announced, along with numerous other positive rights (and negative rights as well), in the United Nations Convention on the Rights of the Child (Articles 3 and 28). Indeed, the European Court of Human Rights has stated on numerous occasions that Article 8 of the European Convention on Human Rights, guaranteeing a right to family life and to private life, imposes on state parties not just a negative duty to refrain from interfering in family and other private life but also positive duties to implement measures to facilitate family relationships and to ensure that private parties respect the private life of others.[11]

Furthermore, the libertarian view is vulnerable to the criticism, familiar now to most legal scholars, that the positive rights/negative rights distinction they posit is illusory. Libertarians have tended to overlook the fact that the great complex of supposedly negative legal rights to property, freedom of contract, and bodily integrity that operate against private citizens, and the legal system that enforces those rights, are actually valuable benefits that the state confers on those who hold the rights. A state that truly avoided involvement in civic life would be a nonexistent state or perhaps a state that limited itself to protection against foreign invasion. But the state in western society has always involved itself in the interactions of its private citizens. Every legal rule governing social existence reflects a policy choice, one that favors some and disfavors others. For example, when the state creates legal rules that make providers of capital rather than providers of labor the "owners" of factories, decides precisely what powers and rights "ownership" will entail, and stands ready to enforce those rights on behalf of the owners, it makes a policy decision, one that generates great benefits for the providers of capital and effectively allocates the value generated by production as between laborers and capitalists. So too with other rules of property.

This critique of the negative rights/positive rights distinction can be extended to many sorts of claims made on behalf of children. Claims for financial subsidies arise only because the existing regime of property rights and taxation leaves some children in a situation in which their basic needs are not met. If instead the fundamental background legal rules assigned to children and other vulnerable persons a property right to a disproportionate share of the gross national product, based on a principle that need rather than transferred title or labor gives rise to property rights, children's claims on resources would appear to be negative rights, rights against having the wealth initially assigned to them taken away.

One need not go that far in rejecting the positive rights/negative rights distinction, however, to see that the libertarian objection has no purchase in the legal context this book addresses. I am concerned here with an aspect of social existence in which the state is already clearly intervening in profound ways in the lives of private individuals and in which it really cannot avoid doing so. The rights at issue are ones that would constrain the state in carrying out that intervention, requiring that the state do it in one particular way rather than any other – that is, in a way that replicates, as far as possible, what children would choose themselves, as a matter of self-determination, if they were able, rather than in a way that serves the interests or preferences of adults to the detriment of children. A child's claim in this arena might say, in essence: "If you, the state, are going to meddle in my life, by placing me into intimate relationships with particular adults, and at the same time thereby effectively preventing me from having intimate relationships with certain others, you may not do so arbitrarily and you may not do so for the purpose of serving the interests of any other persons but rather are strictly limited to doing it in a manner consistent with my welfare. You may interject yourself into my private life only on those terms." This is no more an assertion of positive rights than is a criminal defendant's demand for due process – for example, a jury trial or appointed counsel.

Objections based on a principle of limited government, then, are simply inapposite to the question whether children should have the sort of rights at issue in this book. This is clearest with respect to the state's creation and maintenance or destruction of legal parent–child relationships, where the state is choosing to exert direct control over private life. It will be less clear to some in connection with state decisions about children's relationships with persons other than parents, where what is at issue is whether established legal parents can dictate a child's relationships with nonparents, because one might think abstaining is an option for the state there and that that is what the state should do. But really abstention is not conceptually possible in that context. If the state decides that no one may invoke the power of the legal system to force legal parents to facilitate a relationship between a child and third parties, which might look like state abstention, it is actually thereby conferring on parents an additional increment of power over children's lives. That conferral of power on parents is a form of state action impinging on the interests of children, and even a libertarian could acknowledge that private citizens should have rights with respect to how the state carries out this intrusion into private life, this conferral on one private party of a power to control the relational life of another person.

Importantly, true state abstention from involvement in children's relational lives is not an option anyone would find desirable. True abstention would not mean giving biological parents strong legal rights over children but rather would mean giving no one any legal rights over children's lives. It would mean having no laws whatsoever about, for example, who may take custody of a newborn child. Thus, the approach the state now takes in many respects confers positive rights on certain adults – namely biological parents – yet libertarians do not argue against those, because they fail to recognize them as such. The state now does not simply refrain from interfering with the efforts of biological parents to associate with their offspring; it also bestows on them a legal status that entitles them to the state's assistance in excluding others from association with the children and to numerous other forms of assistance and recognition. The European Court of Human Rights has explicitly recognized this in many contexts, such as those in which noncustodial parents demand state action to ensure them contact with their children when custodial parents have obstructed such contact. For example, in *Glaser v. United Kingdom*, the Court interpreted Article 8 of the European Convention on Human rights thusly:

> The essential object of Article 8 is to protect the individual against arbitrary interference by public authorities. There may however be positive obligations inherent in an effective "respect" for family life. These obligations may involve the adoption of measures designed to secure respect for family life even in the sphere of relations between individuals, including both the provision of a regulatory framework of adjudicatory and enforcement machinery protecting individuals' rights and the implementation, where appropriate, of specific steps . . . . The Court's case law has consistently held that Article 8 includes a right for a parent to have measures taken with a view to his or her being reunited with the child, and an obligation for the national authorities to take such measures.[12]

Likewise, in the context of child protection, the Court has imputed to the European states a "positive duty to take measures to facilitate family reunification as soon as reasonably feasible" after removal of a child from the custody of abusive or neglectful parents, measures that should include assistance to the parents to improve their parenting.[13]

In a world in which the state did not confer parental legal status on anyone, and did not create legal rights to custody and control of children, chaos and violence would reign, as any and all adults who wanted to raise children would need to try to seize them and retain possession of them by force. No one really wants such a lawless state of affairs, such a regime devoid of positive rights to legal recognition and protection as a parent. Yet establishing any legal rules to dictate custody of and access to a child amounts to state action, state involvement in children's lives. So the pertinent question is never *whether* the state should structure children's relational lives but rather *how* – that is, on what normative basis it should do so. That is the ultimate question this book addresses.

III. How Do We Know a Right When We See One?

We can now proceed to consider what legal rights children currently possess against the state in connection with the state's decision making about their relational lives and then what legal rights they should possess. In describing existing rights and in fleshing out an ideal set of rights, though, we need to bear in mind that the law can embody rights in many forms. Although the law does speak explicitly in some contexts of children possessing rights, the law governing children's relationships in some countries generally does not. In the United States, for example, legal references to children's rights per se appear principally in contexts such as education and inheritance and rarely in the context of their family life.[14] Yet it is incorrect to infer from the fact that the law does not speak explicitly of children having rights in any particular context that they have none. Many code provisions in which the term *right* does not appear nevertheless, in their design and in their effect, protect individuals' interests and/or choices by imposing duties on others, just the same as they would if they said explicitly that the individuals have a right to protection of their interests or effectuation of their choices.

We should say that individuals have rights in those instances so long as it is sufficiently clear that the duties benefiting them are owed to those individuals rather than only to others. An explicit statement of rights is one means of showing to whom duties are owed, but there are others. One other way is that the explicit content of the duty is to protect or promote the interests of those individuals for their own sake – for example, language along the lines "take the action that is in the best interests of X, without regard to the interests or preferences of other parties." Another way would be that the benefited individuals have standing in court, on the basis of their own interests, to present a demand for enforcement of the duties, by themselves or through an agent acting in their behalf.[15] This last example might pertain even where a legal rule dictates a particular outcome given certain facts rather than announcing rights or requiring a discretionary judgment aimed as serving someone's best interests. For example, maternity rules stating simply that the woman who gives birth to a child shall be the legal mother appear generally to benefit children, and if newborn children had standing to enforce the rule, such that a guardian *ad litem* could initiate a suit in their name should state agencies fail to apply the law when it would in fact benefit them, then we might say that the rules confer a right on children.[16]

A complete account of children's relationship rights against the state, therefore, requires identifying not only those legal rules that explicitly confer such rights but also legal rules that, though not speaking in terms of rights, implicitly confer rights on children by imposing on state officials a duty owed to children to respect their wishes, to make and act on an individualized assessment of their best interests, or to take particular actions assumed to be generally conducive to their welfare. That a rule is generally conducive to children's welfare will, of course, be the most difficult to establish, because doing so would require a great deal of empirical information. Even if all the necessary information were available, it would be beyond the scope of this book to try to amass and present it. My focus is on theoretical questions, and so in some places I merely suggest reasons why particular rules might serve or disserve children's well-being.

2 The Existing Relationship Rights of Children

What is the current status of children in the various legal conflicts that arise over their relationships? No simple characterization would accurately capture the current state of the law in any single country, let alone in any collection of countries. It is certainly not true that the law relating to children universally reflects a "best interests of the child" principle, but neither is it true that the law in any western nation entirely disregards the welfare of children. Rather, in every jurisdiction, the law governing decisions about children's relationships on the whole reflects a mix of concerns for interests of children and adults. This chapter provides an overview of the complex reality of children's relationship rights in the West, with a particular focus on the United States and other English-speaking countries.[1] It is fairly comprehensive in terms of topics covered, but does not purport to provide the sort of contextual, in-depth study that comparative legal scholars perform and that might reveal nuances I gloss over.[2] This descriptive chapter is intended just to give some idea of how any normative conclusions might require a reformation of the law in certain jurisdictions.

Some overall assessment might be hazarded. On the whole, the United States appears, among western nations, one of the least protective of children's welfare, in terms of the legal rules it applies to state decision making about children's relationships. There is a strong sentiment in favor of parental rights in the United States, and parental rights often operate contrary to the welfare of children. Many other countries, such as England in its Children Act of 1989, have omnibus legislation providing that in all matters concerning children, the children's welfare shall be the paramount legal consideration.[3] The United States has no such legal pronouncement at either the federal or the state level. The European Court of Human

Rights (hereafter ECHR) has interpreted the European Convention on Human Rights as conferring on children a fundamental right to protection of their interests in all aspects of family life. The U.S. Supreme Court, in contrast, has studiously avoided attributing to children a constitutional right in any family context. Significantly, every other government in the world has signed on to the United Nations Convention on the Rights of the Child, whereas the United States stands alone in refusing to endorse this recognition of children's moral status and basic rights.

Conversely, family law scholars in England and elsewhere have suggested that certain provisions protecting "family life" in human rights conventions, including the European Convention on Human Rights, and in domestic legislation implementing those conventions, require some reformation of domestic law away from the principle that children's welfare should be the sole or even paramount consideration in decision making about family life and toward an approach of balancing children's welfare against the interests of adults in matters such as adoption and child custody, because those provisions naturally also apply to adults. John Eekelaar contends that "it should be legitimate to give independent weight to other interests, and weigh them against those of the children," so that in any given case "other factors might properly lead to a less than optimal result for children," so long as such balancing does not produce "actual harms" for children.[4] The ECHR has in fact interpreted the Convention as dictating such a balancing of interests in many types of cases where the interests of parents and the interests of children are in conflict, suggesting that the interests of children at stake in state decision making about their relationships might properly be sacrificed in some circumstances to satisfy the interests of parents.[5] The normative analysis of this book speaks directly to the question whether such a balancing of interests is appropriate.

The various laws governing children's relational lives can be categorized into those by which the state structures children's family lives directly and those by which it does so indirectly. Direct structuring of children's relationships arises from state decisions to create, maintain, or sever legal relationships and state decisions to guarantee persons who are in a legal relationship with a child an opportunity to carry on a social relationship with the child. Indirect structuring of children's relational lives arises from state decisions as to what power legal parents will have to control children's associations with third parties. Of course, children often form relationships independently of any decision by the state or their parents about those relationships. For example, children might form friendships with peers in school or spend time with extended family members without parents or state actors knowing about it. But there is no guarantee that a child will ever have an opportunity to form such relationships in the first instance or to maintain relationships once formed if the state confers on parents the power to deny children such opportunity. So whether children have any right in respect to relationships with people other than their parents does depend on state action.

I. Direct Decisions by the State

The state directly determines who a child's legal parents will be at the time of birth and then at every moment of a person's childhood. The state also determines whether a given legal parent will have custody of, or visitation with, a child. These determinations often go unseen, because the initial conferral of parenthood and custody most often occurs not by individualized review of each child's situation but rather by automatic operation of self-executing statutory rules, and decisions to continue existing arrangements are in essence decisions not to act overtly – that is, not to remove children from their parents' custody and not to suspend or terminate parental rights.

A) Assignment of Children to Legal Parents

The state creates legal parent–child relationships through rules for maternity, paternity, and adoption. Perhaps the closest thing to a uniform rule in family law throughout the western world is the rule that the woman who gives birth to a child automatically becomes the child's first legal mother, with a presumptive right to custody of the child.[6] No further action on her part or inquiry by the state is prerequisite to the state's conferring legal parenthood upon her. In a small number of continental European countries, women have the option of declining initial legal motherhood,[7] but the law in the western world, with rare exception (in the surrogacy context), does not deny legal motherhood to a birth mother who wants to have it. This is in large part because there is a strong cultural bias in favor of biological parents, especially biological parents who have provided care to and formed a relationship with the child, and giving birth is assumed to be indicative of biological connection, past care, and an already formed relationship.[8] This automatic conferral of legal parent status is thus explainable in part as reflecting an empirical assumption that a biological and gestational mother is likely to be a good caretaker of a child, an assumption that everyday experience suggests is true in most cases.

However, that there is no legal mechanism in western nations for denying legal parenthood to any birth mothers who want to have it suggests that this rule cannot be fully explained on the basis of an aim to maximize the welfare of children, because clearly in a significant percentage of cases the rule does not serve that aim. The legal system currently confers the momentous rights and responsibilities of legal motherhood even on women who are drug addicts and incapable of minimally adequate parenting, on women who have previously abused and neglected other children, on women who are incarcerated, and on thirteen-year-old girls. In many cases, the state confers legal parenthood on such birth mothers yet immediately after birth places the child in foster care, where the child lingers for years before the state finally attempts to place him or her in a parent–child relationship with adults who are able to be good parents. The great number of exceptions to any assumption about the value for children of the state's assigning them to their birth mothers suggests that maternity rules must also reflect either an assumption of adult entitlement, grounded in a proprietary view of biological offspring and/or a belief that women deserve a reward for their gestational labor, or else disregard on the part of legislators for the interests of those babies who are born in communities where drug addiction, crime, teen pregnancy, and so on, are most prevalent. If legislators instead fashioned maternity rules with only the welfare of children in mind, and had equal concern for the life prospects of all newborn children, they would certainly be more circumspect about which birth mothers they place in the role of legal parent.

From the perspective of children's rights, then, maternity rules clearly do not confer on newborn children an absolute right in connection with formation of a mother–child relationship. They certainly do not aim to ensure that each newborn child is placed in the care of the best available maternal caregiver – for example, if a woman who is clearly much better equipped for parenting than the birth mother, taking into account the biological tie of the birth mother but also the predictors of good parenting on which adoption agencies routinely rely, wished to adopt a child. Maternity rules can at best be said to confer a much lesser right, what might be called an imperfectly tailored right to a minimally adequate legal parent, imperfect in its tailoring because it applies even in cases where what it commands does not in fact ensure even minimally adequate caretaking. In any case, it is not clear that a child would have standing to enforce a maternity rule where applying it would be in a child's best interests but the state fails to do so; statutes generally do not speak to the issue and courts have not had much occasion to decide the matter.

In at least one nonwestern nation, Japan, the law does allow for denial of legal parenthood to birth mothers in some cases, to serve the welfare of children. The rules for parental status and rights dictate that they may not be conferred upon a "minor, incompetent, or quasi-incompetent" unless a court finds that this would be in the best interests of the child.[9] In other nonwestern nations, however, the law might deny women legal status with respect to their children on patriarchal grounds – that is, to afford men exclusive dominion over their offspring – and so children in those societies can be denied a relationship with their birth mother even where such a relationship *is* in their best interests.[10]

Importantly, the description above of maternity rules in the West is not the whole story of children's relationship to their birth mothers. There are situations in which a woman who is the first legal mother of a child loses that status soon after birth and loses physical custody of the child even sooner. First, women generally can relinquish their newborn children for adoption (surrogacy contracts, in most jurisdictions where they are enforceable, are essentially precommitments to do this). In addition, as noted above, in limited circumstances the state can remove a child from the mother's custody at or soon after birth. In even more limited circumstances, the state can petition immediately after birth for termination of a birth mother's parental rights, but this almost never occurs; instead states enter babies into the already overburdened and often inhospitable foster care system. I discuss adoption and termination of parental status below. Simply by giving birth, however, women acquire a presumptive right of possession, which they can choose not to waive and which can be overridden only in cases of gross unfitness and typically only after protracted legal proceedings.

Many who are involved in the child protective system bemoan the practical results of this legal regime. One family court judge in Rochester, New York, made national headlines in 2004 by ordering a drug-addicted, homeless woman who worked as a prostitute to stop having children, as a condition for return of the children she had already borne. The judge was exasperated with the situation created by this rule for bestowing legal parenthood, having previously been forced to remove four children from the woman's custody, all subjected to cocaine ingestion during pregnancy, and to place them in foster care. The judge noted that she had "seen as many as nine children from one family surrendered to foster care" and went on to vent her frustration with these all-too-common cases:

> All babies deserve more than to be born to parents who have proven they cannot possibly raise or parent a child. This neglected existence is an immense burden to place on a child and on society. The cycle of neglect often created by such births needs to stop. Our society has reached the breaking point with respect to raising neglected children, often born with extraordinary needs. One need only look at our schools, our jails, our Division of Human and Health Services budgets, and our Family Courts to see that a serious change of direction is necessary in the interests of children, the taxpayers, and the community as a whole. [11]

Yet this judge still ruled that the permanency goal for all the children of this woman, who was still consistently using cocaine and who had shown no interest in the children after they were removed, was to be returned to her custody! That is what the judge believed the law compelled her to do. Unsurprisingly, the mother was pregnant again soon after this ruling.[12] Later in 2004, the same judge issued a similar order against another drug-addicted, disengaged mother in proceedings concerning her seventh child, after the other six, conceived with six different fathers, had been removed from her custody.[13] Yet once again, although noting "the horrific record of the [mother] with respect to her prior six children" and finding that the mother "has demonstrated repeatedly that she has no capacity to exercise her responsibilities toward her children," the court agreed with the child protective agency's decision that "the permanency goal is reunification with parent(s), as is typical and preferred," citing a state law provision declaring that "parents are entitled to bring up their own children."[14]

If there had been appeals, appellate courts would likely have overturned this family court judge's orders that, as a condition for regaining custody of the children to whom they have already given birth, women must not conceive any more children, on the grounds that the orders violate the women's constitutional rights. Civil liberties groups and feminist organizations rushed to demand a reversal of the orders,[15] and such groups would likely oppose any legislative effort to deny such women legal parenthood status when they do give birth. Some legal scholars have been critical of court decisions and public policies that they view as in any way "punishing" women for using drugs during pregnancy, on the grounds that such action violates the liberty or privacy of women and/or the equal protection rights of minority-race women, because of a disparate impact on them, or is simply unfair to women who have suffered many misfortunes in life, concerns implicitly treated as more important than the welfare of children. Dorothy Roberts, for example, complains: "Like abuse and neglect laws generally, statutes making prenatal substance abuse proof of child abuse or parental unfitness have a disparate impact on Black mothers and their children. . . . Child protection agencies' removals of infants who test positive for drugs has [sic] therefore been grossly racially imbalanced."[16] Roberts does not consider that the "impact" of intervention at birth that she decries, although it might be negative for mothers, could be positive, even life saving, for children.

In contrast to the child's lack of a right to avoid a family relationship with a birth mother who is a very bad candidate for parenthood, birth mothers have an absolute right to avoid a family relationship with the children they produce. As noted above, mothers can hand over their children to adoptive parents they select or to a state or private adoption agency. In recent years, it has become even easier – in terms of the practical steps a woman must take, though not necessarily in terms of the emotional obstacles she must overcome – to accomplish this. In the United States, nearly every state has passed a "safe haven law," immunizing from legal repercussions parents who anonymously drop off their newborn children at a designated facility, such as a hospital. The principal aim of such laws is to prevent grievous harm to children before or after birth, as the opportunity for an anonymous transfer of a baby is assumed to make it somewhat less likely that a mother would have an abortion, commit infanticide, or abandon a baby in an unsafe manner. As a technical matter, this state-sanctioned form of abandonment might amount to terminating rights rather than preventing maternity from vesting in the first place, at least if the mother's name was originally entered on the birth certificate. The effect, though, is to enable genetic mothers, without legal proceedings and on no other basis than their own preference, to avoid ever having to associate with, or assume responsibility for, a child after the child is born or otherwise being prejudiced in any way by imposition of a legal relationship.

Several European jurisdictions take things a step further by facilitating anonymous births. France has for centuries allowed mothers anonymously to drop off their children at special facilities, and for the past century has allowed mothers to request nondisclosure of their identity at the hospital where they give birth, so that legal parent status never vests in them.[17] Today many women from countries neighboring France travel to France to give birth anonymously. In Italy and Luxembourg, birth mothers are under no legal obligation to register a newborn child or to state their identity if they do register a child. Several localities in Germany have recently established

Babyklappe, or "baby boxes," where mothers can deposit a child, ring a bell, and walk off. And in Hungary, hospitals have a special, unsupervised room where mothers can leave their children after delivery and then check out without their maternity ever being recorded.[18] Again, I do not mean to suggest that this is ever easy emotionally for a birth mother or that many women do this frivolously. The point here is simply that there is a clear trend throughout the West toward expanding the legal power of women to opt out of a parent–child relationship.

Legal rules for paternity are more complicated, more contested, and more variable across jurisdictions than are maternity rules, reflecting both the greater difficulty of identifying the biological father of a child and the absence of a presumption that biological fathers expend prebirth child-care labor or are as predisposed as biological mothers to be nurturing. As a general matter, though, paternity rules also predicate legal parenthood, and a set of rights entailed in that status, on biological parenthood, in most countries making it a necessary and sufficient condition for designation as a child's first legal father (though, as discussed below, certain indicators of likely biological paternity can serve as proxies).

Throughout the West, paternity laws distinguish between children born to married women and children born to unmarried women. In most western jurisdictions, the spouse of a birth mother is presumed the father of a child and receives parental status automatically, without needing to take action or simply by having his name recorded on the birth certificate. As a historical matter, this rule reflected in part an empirical assumption that the husband of a birth mother must be the biological father of the child; it was an evidentiary rule and admitted of rebuttal on the basis of evidence that the husband could not have had intercourse with his wife around the time of conception. It also reflected, though, concern for the reputations of the husband and wife, concern that a child deemed illegitimate could end up as a public ward, and concern for the welfare of the child, given that illegitimate children were disadvantaged in many ways.[19] All of these rationales for the rule are less compelling today; the fact of biological fatherhood can now be established easily through genetic testing, and there is now much less stigma or disadvantage arising from illegitimate births. Yet the rule persists. The main rationale today might be that a marital presumption avoids the substantial cost of doing genetic testing in the case of every birth.

That biological parenthood remains the predominant focus even with marital births is evidenced by the fact that throughout the West, a husband's presumption of paternity remains rebuttable on the basis of – and

only on the basis of – genetic tests showing that he is not in fact the biological father. In some continental European countries and in some U.S.
states, the opportunity for rebuttal is limited; only a mother, a child, or the
husband himself has standing to challenge the husband's paternity.[20] The
prevailing rule in common law countries generally goes further, however,
empowering men (other than donors to a licensed sperm bank) who are
not the mother's husband and who believe that they are the biological
father to demand a genetic test to disprove the paternity of the husband
and to establish their own, regardless of whether they have previously
manifested any inclination or ability to assume the responsibilities of parenthood, regardless of the wishes of the mother and her husband, and
regardless of the interests of the child.[21]

This is typically a legislative policy choice, not compelled by authoritative interpretations of biological fathers' constitutional rights. In fact,
in a few common-law jurisdictions there has been legislative movement
recently toward restricting the power of biological fathers to insert themselves into intact families, with statutes authorizing courts to refuse to hear
a paternity petition if they deem it improper in the circumstances of the
case.[22] In the United States, the Supreme Court has upheld against constitutional challenge a California statute denying "putative fathers" any
opportunity to challenge the paternity of a birth mother's husband, even
where they had an established relationship with a child.[23] Nevertheless,
most U.S. states do now give putative fathers such an opportunity, without regard for how that will affect the child. Needless to say, this power of
unwed fathers to interject themselves into the lives of children born to a
married woman can have quite adverse consequences for such children,
tearing apart a family that might otherwise have remained intact or simply
causing much turmoil in the child's life.

The law's treatment of children born to unmarried women is more
varied. In most western jurisdictions, men believing themselves to be the
biological father of a nonmarital child can petition for a declaration of
paternity and compel the mother to submit the child for genetic testing.[24]
In many jurisdictions, such as the United States and Ireland, men who
show biological paternity thereby become vested with full legal parent
status, with a right to visitation and to consideration for custody, again
without any showing that they are prepared to care for a child and to cooperate with the mother in raising the child.[25] Some western nations, though,
are less solicitous of unwed fathers' desires to claim a child. In Denmark,
for example, biological fatherhood is a sufficient basis for imposing a support obligation on a man, but unwed fathers do not acquire any parental

rights unless the mother agrees to it.[26] In Germany, an unwed father has only a limited right to visitation and cannot seek custody unless the mother consents to it or is unable to have custody herself, but is subject to a support obligation in any case.[27] Notably, forty years ago the law throughout much of the western world, including the United States, gave even less consideration to unwed fathers than Denmark does today; unwed fathers had no legal rights with respect to their children, regardless of the mother's preferences, yet still had a legal obligation of financial support (albeit one that was rarely enforced). So the status of unwed fathers today is in many places dramatically different from what it was a couple of generations ago.

In addition to giving unwed fathers the opportunity to come forward and demand parental status, the state in many countries today thrusts that status on many men who do not want it. The state routinely compels men suspected of being the biological father of a child to undergo genetic testing and, when the results are affirmative, imposes legal parenthood on them.[28] The state's aim in doing so is solely to extract financial support for the child's care, so that the child does not become a public welfare burden. Yet the law in the United States and many other countries is such that the state will not impose that obligation without also conferring full legal parent status, with all the rights that come with it, including a right to spend time with the child, to participate in decision making about the child's life, and to prevent any other man from becoming a legal parent to the child. Even in countries where no parental rights follow automatically from a declaration of paternity, imposing a financial support obligation leads most men to insist, at least initially, on an order of contact with the child, and in many such countries courts generally comply even if this is not best for the child. At the same time, the state does not compel the men upon whom it thrusts legal parent status to spend time with their children; custody and visitation are legal rights, not legal obligations. As such, the state's action can result in a child having no social relationship with any father.

As with mothers, a state's decision to make the biological connection determinative where a man seeks paternity might be based in part on an empirical assumption that a biological connection predisposes an adult to care for a child. But that decision also clearly rests in part on beliefs about the natural entitlement of adults to possess their genetic offspring, a property stake in "the fruit of their loins." Any assumed predisposition would, in a true assessment of what is best for the child, play only a partial role.[29] There is much more to being a good parent than simply having a desire to be a parent, although that is certainly one prerequisite. And in many men the biological connection does not produce the supposed disposition.

Perhaps more often than in the case of maternity, paternity rules operate to the detriment of children, as anyone who has witnessed paternity proceedings or abuse and neglect cases can attest. A large percentage of paternity cases in courts involve immature and irresponsible men or boys who had only a fleeting or superficial relationship with the mother and who have little or no genuine interest in caring for a child, but who are nevertheless pushed or welcomed into the position of bearing the immensely important and quite difficult responsibility of coparenting a child with the child's mother.[30] Many men who seek paternity do so solely or primarily in an effort to maintain a tie to the mother against her wishes, a tie that some attempt to use constructively but many others use vindictively. Of course, there are also many unwed fathers who genuinely care about their biological offspring and who seek parental status primarily because they want to provide for the child. My point is just that in a substantial percentage of paternity cases, the biological father is unwilling and/or unprepared to be a responsible parent. Moreover, most unwed mothers will go on to form long-term intimate relationships with someone other than the biological father of the child whose paternity is now in question, but a paternity declaration in favor of the biological father today typically has the effect of preventing a later partner or husband from becoming a legal parent to the child, even if the partner or husband assumes a supportive, caregiving role and forms an emotional bond with the child. It also has the effect of forcing the mother and her present family to deal with the biological father, in and out of court, for almost two decades.

A decision of the ECHR is illustrative. In *Nuutinen v. Finland*,[31] the Court reviewed decisions of Finnish courts restricting and ultimately terminating the visitation of a father with his daughter. Before the child's birth, the biological father had been convicted of causing danger to others, of attempted manslaughter, and of threatening, coercing, and assaulting the woman who later became the mother of the child in question. The biological father was released from prison eight months after the girl was born and then demanded recognition as a legal parent. A city court initially refused to declare his paternity, but over two years later, when the child was two and a half and the mother had married another man, with whom she had another child, a Finnish district court established the biological father's paternity and ordered visitation. The family then battled in and out of court with the biological father for the next five and a half years, until the ECHR ruled, upholding the most recent decision of the Finnish courts, which was to sever all contact between the child and the father! So rather than prescribe that, when this child was born, her imprisoned, violent father would never be a legal parent to her, Finnish law caused this girl to be subjected to eight years of legal battles and all the uncertainty and stress that accompany them. Moreover, her relationship with the man who is coparenting her with her mother might never be legally recognized.

Trial-level judges in the United States are well aware of the dim prospects for a good parent–child relationship with many of the biological fathers who seek a declaration of paternity, yet they are generally powerless to protect children from assignment to bad fathers. Discontent with the law is evident in a recent decision of the California Supreme Court, awarding paternity of a child to the birth mother's spouse rather than to the child's biological father, who was in jail for raping the mother, a decision that has drawn national attention for its perceived flaunting of biology-based paternal rights.[32] Some judges have also imposed on men no-procreation orders of the sort described above in connection with mothers who have multiple children they cannot care for, in cases where fathers have sired numerous children but provided no financial support or other care for them.[33]

In sum, the rules for initial assignment of children to legal mothers and fathers in most jurisdictions confer only very limited rights, if any, on newborn children. Children do not have even the right against the state thrusting them into a legal parent–child relationship with a biological parent who is presumptively unfit to parent, with a drug addict or a prison inmate or a high school student or someone who has abused other children. The rules appear driven more by assumptions about the proprietary rights of biological parents, by a societal unwillingness to impose financial responsibility for creating a child without also conferring rights over the child, or simply by a lack of concern for the welfare of certain groups of children.

A final way in which the state creates legal parent–child relationships, though, is the adoption process, whereby the state changes the assignment of children to parents, and the contrast between adoption laws and parentage laws is striking. Adoption law makes an adult the legal parent of a child to the same extent as a biological parent who becomes a legal parent and so is functionally equivalent to maternity and paternity rules. Yet in this context, where adults seeking a relationship with a child come with no "natural rights" to the "products of procreative labor," the law approximates a model of absolute rights for children.[34] It does so not by speaking explicitly of children having rights, but rather by applying a best-interests standard to individualized decision making – that is, by requiring that a court approve each adoption and by making it a necessary condition for court approval that the applicants' becoming legal parents to a child is in the child's best interests.[35] In most cases, the law requires that adoptive parents demonstrate through a detailed examination that they are prepared to provide a good home for and loving attention to a child.[36] With older children – in most U.S. jurisdictions, those fourteen or older, but elsewhere generally younger – the child must, as a matter of law or customary practice, consent to the adoption.[37] Adoption law is therefore worth examining in some detail, because it might provide a model for parentage laws that would confer on children rights in connection with family formation roughly equivalent to those possessed by adults. Significantly, adopted children do better on average on a number of measures of welfare than do children raised by biological parents.[38]

Adoption laws typically set forth a list of criteria in terms of which agencies and courts are to judge the worthiness of the applicants for parenthood. Some of the more common factors are as follows: the physical environment of the home; the applicants' parenting skills or ability and inclination to meet the needs of a child; the applicants' mental and physical condition, moral fitness, financial condition, and marital status; any affection or attachment already developed between the child and the applicants (e.g., if the adult applicants are members of the child's extended family or have served as foster parents); and the applicants' ability to comprehend and appreciate the child's cultural heritage, their motivation to adopt, and their philosophy of child rearing. Significantly, some characteristics reasonably assumed to make one unprepared to parent adequately, such as being too young, operate in this context categorically to exclude persons from adoption. In England and Ireland, for example, persons who are not stepparents must be at least twenty-one years old to adopt,[39] whereas in France applicants for adoption other than stepparents must be twenty-eight years old unless they have been married for more than two years.[40]

Apart from the substantive standard for finalizing the adoption, the prevailing rules governing adoption vary significantly, depending on whether an adoption creates an entirely new set of parents for the child or instead is by the spouse of an existing legal parent. With respect to "new family adoptions," the law in western countries typically requires a home study of potential adoptive parents, entailing visits to the home, interviews, and written submissions, before courts can make them legal parents.[41] Typically potential adoptive parents must provide character references, and the adoption agency must do a criminal background check. The law in most U.S. states and in England also requires that adoptive parents successfully complete a probationary period – for example, six months after initially receiving the child into their home, with additional visits by adoption agency workers during that period – before the court can finally vest parental status in them.[42] Agency regulations typically go beyond such statutory requirements, dictating investigation of applicants' attributes in substantial detail and in some jurisdictions requiring that applicants receive instruction in parenting. This qualification and probation process for new family adoptions is, in its design, remarkably different from the state's approach to conferring initial legal parent status on biological parents, which entails no prequalification process or postplacement scrutiny, but rather accepts all comers and sends new parents off on their own without monitoring.

The reality of adoption practice, however, does not perfectly match the ideal of a rigorous and comparative selection process. First, a significant percentage of new family adoptions are parental placement adoptions, meaning that the biological mother chooses and deals directly with the adoptive parents, and the state's role is in practice limited to ensuring that the chosen substitutes are minimally qualified rather than the best available adoptive parents, even though "best interests" remains the standard for ultimate approval.[43] Adoption law therefore confers on some children – those whose biological parents are unprepared to raise them but who want to decide who does raise them – only the limited right against placement with a substitute parent who falls below whatever minimum standard the agency performing the home study, or the court that ultimately approves the adoption, applies in such cases. In addition, in many jurisdictions the biological parent can change his or her mind at any time before a court finalizes the adoption, or at least until an adoption petition is filed, and take back the child regardless of whether that is best for the child; lawmakers are generally quite solicitous of the interests and feelings of birth mothers.[44]

Second, private and public adoption agencies have generally operated on the basis of certain substantive criteria that arguably compromise the child-centered nature of the adoption process. For example, the law in most U.S. jurisdictions and in most of Europe altogether precludes homosexual couples from adopting as a couple, either explicitly or by allowing only married persons to petition jointly.[45] One member of the couple might be able to adopt alone,[46] but then there is no legal recognition of the child's relationship with the other caregiver. In some places, such as Florida and France, homosexuals may not adopt at all, singly or as members of a committed couple.[47] Thus, even if, on the facts of a particular case, such persons would be better caretakers for children than any available alternative caretakers, the child could not enter into a legal parent–child relationship with those persons.

In addition, nonreligious people, whether single or married, might find it difficult to adopt. Although no law explicitly precludes nonreligious people, or people who belong to a particular faith, from adopting, the law in a number of jurisdictions directs adoption agencies to take into account the religious faith or background of applicants for adoption in their investigation of the applicants, and the language in some statutes and agency regulations could be read to exclude nonreligious persons from adoption.[48] Moreover, the largest private adoption network in the United States, Catholic Charities, in some locations has a religious faith requirement. Indeed, some Catholic Charities agencies require specifically that applicants for adoption be Christian. And in some sparsely populated areas of the Unites States, the Catholic Charities agency is the only private adoption agency available and therefore is the agency that potential adoptive parents must go through to adopt a child who has not been in the custody of the state child protective agency.

Other substantive considerations in adoption placement do not categorically exclude applicants from adoption but rather exclude them from consideration for particular children or simply disfavor them in placement of particular children. One such consideration that has been the subject of long-standing controversy is race. Federal law in the United States now proscribes the sort of categorical race-matching policies that were once common, and courts in England have held that race may not be the paramount consideration in adoptions.[49] English law directs adoption agencies merely to "give due consideration to the child's . . . racial origin."[50] Observers in the Unites States and England, however, believe many public and private adoption agencies today nevertheless follow an unofficial policy of categorical race matching – that is, applying a very strong, perhaps irrebuttable, presumption against transracial placement, because beliefs about community ownership of children or about the unnaturalness of mixed-race family relationships are deeply entrenched.[51] Such a policy might not present a great problem for children if the number of minority children needing homes matched the number of qualified minority applicants wanting to adopt children, but the reality is that there are many more minority-race children awaiting adoption than there are adults of the same race who apply for adoption and who meet the official qualification standards of adoption agencies. An unofficial race-matching policy results in some minority children living in institutional or foster care rather than being adopted by people of another race who are good parents.[52] Opponents of transracial adoption elevate the collective interests of the "Black community," the suffering of minority-race adults, and their own sensibilities above the welfare of individual children.[53]

Thus, the ostensibly child-centered nature of the law governing new family adoptions is compromised in various ways by certain subsidiary rules and entrenched practices. The law governing stepparent adoptions likewise falls short of a model of strong children's rights. It contains the same ultimate standard; courts may approve them only if they are in the child's best interests or are conducive to the child's welfare. But state review of the petitioner is generally slight or nonexistent. Statutes in many U.S. states exempt stepparent adoptions from the home study process and or the probationary period, at least when there is no objection by a biological parent whose rights would be terminated by the adoption. This likely reflects in part an assumption that an existing parent would not choose as a second parent for his or her child (or as a spouse) someone who would not make at least a minimally adequate parent. It might also reflect recognition that, absent a report that the spouse has abused the child, the child will live in the household with that spouse anyway. But it would be unrealistic to assume that parents always make the best, or even good, choices in selecting a new partner for themselves and a new parent for their children. The highest rates of child abuse are in fact among mothers' partners who are not a child's legal father.[54] Yet the transformation of a stepparent from merely a cohabitant to a legal parent has significant consequences for a child – in particular, in terms of custody of and visitation with the child should the initial parent and new parent divorce or if the initial parent dies.

Conversely, in one type of situation – namely that involving gay or lesbian couples – many jurisdictions deny adoption by a legal parent's partner for reasons other than the welfare of the child. Many same-sex couples plan to have a child together, with the idea that one will be the biological parent of the child and the other will adopt the child after birth. Other such couples form after one member of the couple already is the legal parent of a child, and the parent's partner assumes a coparenting role. The law governing these situations is now in flux but was originally written with new "spouses" in mind.[55] Many U.S. courts that have addressed the issue have read the law narrowly to categorically exclude unmarried partners from stepparent adoption. As a result, children in those jurisdictions have no right to form a legal parent–child relationship with a person who is serving on a daily and long-term basis as a social parent, and this often has traumatic results when the same-sex partners end their relationship or the legal parent dies. English law, in contrast, uses the term "partner of a parent" rather than "spouse of a parent" in its stepparent adoption provisions, thus facilitating adoption within same-sex couples.[56] California broke new ground in the realm of same-sex partners' parental rights in 2005, when its Supreme Court held, in three companion cases, that lesbian partners could both become the initial and only parents of a child when they jointly undertake to bring a child into their family. This approach marks a shift in thinking about parenting away from biology and toward intent and caring, and it would obviate the need for such couples to pursue a "stepparent" adoption in many situations.[57]

In sum, adoption laws approximate a children's rights model of assignment to parents much more closely than do maternity and paternity laws but do not do so completely. That an adoption would be in a child's best interests is always ostensibly a necessary condition for its occurring but generally is not a sufficient condition. In particular, as discussed below, termination of the rights of biological parents is generally also a necessary condition, and the best-interests standard does not control that state action.

B) Creating and Maintaining Social Parent–Child Relationships

None of the just-discussed laws creating legal parent status necessarily determines what social relationship a child will have with the persons chosen to be legal parents. They confer a legal status that entails a presumptive right to associate with a child, but the state sometimes limits the effect of, or overrides, that right. When two legal parents are married to each other, the state typically gives them both full custodial rights. But when legal parents are not partners, the state typically divides custody between them on an individualized basis, in judicial paternity or divorce proceedings, and dictates how much time each parent is entitled to spend with the child. Rarely does the state grant custody to a private party other than a legal parent, even if that other person has been the primary caretaker for the child for a long time, so long as a legal parent wishes to have custody and does not pose a serious threat to the child's welfare.

1) Custody disputes between legal parents
Custody of a child has two components – physical (having the child in one's care) and legal (having decision-making power concerning larger aspects of a child's life, such as education). In a substantial majority of

U.S. jurisdictions, in Canada, and in some other western countries, the basic standard of decision for courts' determination of postdivorce or post-paternity-action parenting time and decision-making power, or for courts' approval of custody agreements between the parents, is simply "the best interests of the child."[58] Courts interpret and apply that basic standard by reference to a statutory list of factors, which throughout the West includes consideration of the views of older children.[59] On the surface, then, this rule, like that for adoption, confers on children in disrupted families an absolute right in connection with state arrangement of their relationships with caregivers. This emphasis on the welfare, and to some extent preferences, of children is in this context explainable as a reaction to the otherwise unresolvable conflict of rights between two adults; where the rights of parents cancel each other, the law looks to the welfare of children as a tiebreaker. In a minority of American jurisdictions, though, and in the equivalent laws in numerous other countries, the governing rule is slightly different: the custody statute declares that the interests of children are to be a "primary" or "paramount" consideration, rather than the sole consideration,[60] or even more modestly that the child's interests are to be taken into account, along with other considerations such as "the welfare of the family" or "the welfare of the community." These statutory rules suggest ambivalence on the part of legislatures, as if they were reluctant to make children's well-being the sole focus, and they might in practice cause judges' attention to stray from the welfare of children to the interests of parents.[61] That this articulation of the rule is different from, and less protective of children than, a straightforward best-interests rule is confirmed by a statement of the Canadian Supreme Court concerning the 1986 revisions to Canada's custody rule: "The amendments to the Divorce Act in 1986 . . . elevated the best interests of the child from a 'paramount' consideration, to the 'only' relevant issue."[62]

Moreover, even where "the best interests of the child" is the sole standard for custody decision making, the child's welfare might nevertheless have to compete with the interests of adults, because of certain statutory or judicial presumptions in favor of particular structural arrangements of custody or because of specific substantive considerations included or excluded by statutes and courts. Several subsidiary rules have crept into legislative and judicial elaborations of child custody provisions, at various times and in various jurisdictions, principally at the urging of women's rights groups or of fathers' rights groups.

Perhaps the most hotly debated of these in recent years has been the "primary caretaker" consideration found in most common-law jurisdictions in one form or another. The predominant approach today is ostensibly to treat this consideration as simply one factor in a best-interests analysis, but even in jurisdictions that ostensibly treat merely as a relevant factor who has been the primary caretaker, family law practitioners report that in practice it tends to predominate. Some family law scholars defend an outright presumption in favor of the primary caretaker. They do so in part on child-centered grounds – namely that the parent who has in the past provided the most care is likely to be the best custodian for the child in the future and that awarding custody to the past primary caretaker affords children the greatest possible stability or continuity during and after their parents' divorce. But some defend a presumption in favor of the primary caretaker as an entitlement of – in the nature of compensation for – the parent who has sacrificed the most time in the past for direct care of the child,[63] and some judges appear to use the primary caretaker factor as a means of rewarding a parent for past behavior rather than as a means of determining what will be best for the child in the future.[64] David Chambers has contended that primary caretakers should be favored in custody decision making for a different, but also adult-centered, reason – namely because they are "substantially more distressed by the loss of custody" than are secondary caretakers.[65]

In Chapter 7, I discuss in more detail the reasons why such a backward-looking approach to custody decision making can produce outcomes that are not best for children. The principal reason is that parents' lives often change dramatically after divorce, and this is especially true for home-maker wives. Courts that do not take this into account invite further court proceedings to modify their orders. The problem becomes compounded, from a child welfare perspective, because many judges are reluctant to consider as a basis for shifting some parenting time from mothers to fathers, at the time of divorce or when modification is sought down the road, any career-related changes in mothers' lives following divorce – both time commitments to an academic program or to a new job and major relocations that will take children far from their current home and far from their father. Judges express sympathy for such mothers or concern for the social equality of women in general. Many also cite adults' constitutional right to travel, a right generally understood to include a right to change one's residence. As a result, courts in some jurisdictions apply a strong presumption in favor of relocation, balancing the interests of mothers against the interests of children. For example, in the Ontario Court of Appeals 1995 decision in *MacGyver v. Richards*, holding that a custodial mother must be allowed to move her child from North Bay, Ontario, to Tacoma,

Washington, for the sake of her new husband's career, Justice Abella wrote the following:

> [T]he custodial parent must be understood as bearing a disproportionate amount of responsibility.... When, therefore, ... a choice must be made between the responsible wishes and needs of the parent with custody and the parent with access, it seems to me manifestly unfair to treat these wishes and needs as being on an equal footing .... This argues, it seems to me, for particular sensitivity and a presumptive deference to the needs of the responsible custodial parent .... To conclude otherwise may render custody a unilaterally punitive order.[66]

The Canadian Supreme Court, in a different case, rejected this manner of reasoning in relocation cases, stating the following:

> The wording of the Divorce Act belies the need to defer to the custodial parent; rather, the Act has expressly stipulated that the judge hearing the application should be concerned only with the best interests of the child. The rights and interests of the parents, except as they impact on the best interests of the child, are irrelevant. Material change established, the question is not whether the rights of custodial parents can be restricted; the only question is the best interests of the child. Nor does the great burden borne by custodial parents justify a presumption in their favour. Custodial responsibilities curb the personal freedom of parents in many ways. The Act is clear. Once a material change is established, the judge must review the matter anew to determine the best interests of the child.[67]

On the other side of the gender divide, fathers' rights groups have, with some success, been pushing a legislative agenda of establishing strong presumptions in favor of joint physical custody or substantial visitation for noncustodial parents.[68] These presumptions, too, can operate to the detriment of children, either because they lead courts to prescribe custody arrangements that entail excessive moving between houses or because they make it difficult for courts to protect children from irresponsible or abusive parents.

Another, quite different context in which courts have excluded consideration of a fact relevant to children's welfare, because doing so might conflict with adults' perceived rights or with progressive societal aims, is where parents' new relationships following divorce could create difficulties for a child in socializing with peers. One might hope this is a moot issue today, when interracial relationships and same-sex relationships have become very common and the stigma attached to them has lessened dramatically, but in all likelihood it is still a significant concern in many locations and, in any event, the principle established in this area could be applied in other contexts. In a 1984 decision, *Palmore v. Sidoti*, the U.S. Supreme Court ruled that courts deciding custody may not take into account in any fashion the fact that a parent is now in an interracial relationship. A state trial court in that case had awarded custody of a child in a postdivorce dispute to the child's father, in part because the mother, who was white, had remarried, to an African-American man. The trial court anticipated, quite realistically, that at that time in Virginia the child would suffer considerably from the stigmatization attached to interracial marriages. Peers would likely ridicule and ostracize the child, and adults might also act with hostility toward the child out of disgust at his mother's intimate relationship. The Supreme Court did not find that the state court had overestimated the importance of that consideration for the child as an empirical matter. Indeed, in numerous other contexts, including some involving the welfare of adults, the Court has treated stigmatization as a serious harm.[69] Rather, the Court held that the constitutional rights of the mother required that it be entirely excluded from the custody calculus, reasoning that allowing state courts to take into account such effects from bigotry in the local community in making custody decisions would involve the state in giving effect to the bigotry. The liberty interests of parents and the societal aim of eradicating racial prejudice thus trumped the welfare of children. A few lower courts in the United States have extended this holding and reasoning to same-sex relationships.

In contrast, in the somewhat different context of deciding the custody of a biracial child, as between an African-American father and a Caucasian mother, the Canadian Supreme Court approved of trial courts' considering "evidence of race relations in the relevant communities" to "define the context in which the child and his parents will function" and in fact faulted the attorneys in the case for not presenting evidence about race relations in the respective cities of the parents.[70] The Court thus implied that a trial court could permissibly award custody to the father based in part on a finding that racial bigotry in the mother's community would negatively impact the child.

Another consideration that is factually relevant to children's welfare yet is sometimes excluded to some degree from custody determinations is conduct of parents that is ordinarily constitutionally protected but that might be directly harmful to a child. With respect to religious practices – for example, excessive dietary restrictions or teaching that nonbelievers (who could include the other parent) are destined for an eternity in hell – the prevailing rule in the United States today is that courts may take them into account if and to the extent they are proven already to have harmed the child or present a substantial threat of future harm to the child. Thus, courts will not assume a likelihood of harm, will not consider a possibility of harm if it does not rise to the "substantial threat" level, and will not consider adverse effects that do not amount to "harm," which courts generally interpret to mean a significant worsening of the child's condition or situation.

This treats religious practice and religiously motivated decisions somewhat differently from parental behaviors and decisions that are not tied to religious exercise or to some other fundamental liberty. In other contexts, courts freely make assessments of all the costs and benefits likely to flow from each parent's behavior or approach to parenting. For example, courts might take into account that a parent is an alcoholic or that a parent smokes tobacco without requiring the other parent to prove that the child has been or is very likely to be harmed by the drinking or smoking. In fact, courts in some jurisdictions will count *non*religiosity against a parent on the assumption that lack of religion in a child's life is detrimental. In a recent case in Mississippi, *Davidson v. Coit*, an appellate court upheld a change of custody to a father that was based in part on the mother's failure to take her child to church and thus to advance what the court supposed to be the child's spiritual interests.[71] So American courts, at least, appear to be balancing parents' interests in religious expression and exercise against the welfare of children. In Europe, the ECHR has approved of domestic laws and judicial practices treating as relevant any potential adverse affect on a child from religious practice or expression,[72] but it has also, as noted above, repeatedly prescribed a balancing of adults' and children's interests where they conflict in family law matters.

Treatment of parents' sexual activity and lifestyle has evolved to a point where it is, in theory, similar to treatment of religious practice, though perhaps not quite as protective of parental freedom. In the past, courts would use the custody decision to punish parents for conduct or ways of life of which the judges disapproved, even in the absence of a showing that the conduct or way of life harmed the child. For example, many applied a per se rule that homosexuality rendered a parent unfit to have custody of a child or at least less fit than a heterosexual parent. It also was common to take adultery by either parent into account in making a custody award at divorce. Today, though, the prevailing rule applies a "nexus test," under which a parent's homosexuality or partnership with a person of the same sex and related behavior, or a parent's extramarital affair or postdivorce heterosexual intimate relationship, are relevant to a custody decision if – but only insofar as – they have already adversely affected the child's well-being or likely will adversely affect the child in the future.[73] Under this rule, presumably, an otherwise superior parent could not be denied custody because of his or her homosexuality per se, but a court could count against awarding custody to that parent any social stigmatization or other adverse consequence of the parent's sexual orientation.

In a minority of jurisdictions, however, the ascribed immorality of a "homosexual lifestyle" in and of itself counts against awarding custody to a parent.[74] And in practice, some judges too readily perceive harm by assuming that merely being exposed to a homosexual lifestyle adversely affects a child simply because it is, in the judges' view, immoral. The Alabama Supreme Court recently upheld a custody award in favor of a father and against a lesbian mother, with this explanation: "Homosexual behavior is a ground for divorce, an act of sexual misconduct punishable as a crime in Alabama, a crime against nature, an inherent evil, and an act so heinous that it defies one's ability to describe it. That is enough under the law to allow a court to consider such activity harmful to a child."[75] The ECHR, however, appears to have departed from a child-centered approach in the other direction, proscribing consideration of any difficulties for a child, such as ostracism or stigmatization, that might arise from their being in the care of gay parents and doing so on antidiscrimination grounds of the sort underwriting the *Palmore* decision in the United States, elevating the interests and rights of adults above those of children.[76]

In sum, basic custody rules today, like adoption rules, do come close to conferring an absolute right to children in connection with structuring of family relationships, but there are a few subsidiary rules, motivated by adult-centered concerns, that tend to weaken that right in certain respects. The basic, written custody laws, though, might also serve as a model of rules that embody rights for children equivalent to those that adults enjoy in structuring their relationships with other adults, which are discussed in the next chapter.

2) Contact with a noncustodial legal parent

When courts in paternity or divorce cases order that one legal parent will have primary physical custody of the child, the other parent typically asks the court to order visiting time with the child. In both types of cases, the prevailing rule in the United States and Canada requires that courts order at least some contact with a noncustodial parent, however restricted, absent a showing that any contact would seriously endanger the child's welfare.[77] Washington State statutes provide, for example, that "[a] parent not granted custody of the child is entitled to reasonable visitation," although allowing that visitation may be "limited" where the noncustodial parent has engaged in the following:

> (i) Willful abandonment that continues for an extended period of time or substantial refusal to perform parenting functions; (ii) physical, sexual, or a pattern of emotional abuse of a child; (iii) a history of acts of domestic violence . . . or an assault or sexual assault which causes grievous bodily harm or the fear of such harm; or (iv) the parent has been convicted as an adult of a sex offense . . . .

Many legislators and judges believe parents have a fundamental right to spend time with a child after a divorce decree or paternity decision, regardless of whether this is on the whole good for the child. In some European countries, this is true at least in the case of marital children following divorce.[78] ECHR pronouncements that domestic institutions should balance the interests of noncustodial parents in having access to their children against the interests of children where there is a potential conflict between them, such as where contact with a parent present some danger, suggest that Article 8 of the Convention on Human Rights does not, in the Court's view, require states to apply a best interests of the child standard in deciding whether to order any access, though it might allow states to do so if they choose.[79]

Thus, in many jurisdictions, for a child to avoid a social relationship with a noncustodial legal parent, it is not sufficient for the custodial parent or the child's guardian *ad litem* to show that it would be better for the child not to spend time with the noncustodial parent. Such might be the case, for example, when the child has no established relationship with the noncustodial parent (as is generally the case when the child was just born and the father has not been in the same household as the mother) and the noncustodial parent, though he cannot be proven to present a serious danger, is unlikely to contribute much positive to the child's life and is likely to undermine the custodial parent's ability to care for the child. A 1990 Iowa appellate court decision, *In re Marriage of Hopkins*, addressed such a situation. A trial court had imposed paternity on a mother's ex-husband – over his objection that he was not the biological father and did not want to be the legal father – and granted the ex-husband a right to twice-yearly visits with the child, who was born six months after the mother had left the man and moved to Hawaii from Iowa, where the man still lived. The appellate court upheld this order.

Visitation might be contrary to a child's interests also when some psychological relationship exists between parent and child but it is not a very healthy one, because the parent is unloving and/or abusive, even if the parent's neglect or abuse of the child is not a sufficient basis for terminating parental status altogether. Consider a 1992 decision of a Maryland court, in *Hanke v. Hanke*. Parents of a four-year-old girl had separated before she was born, after the mother learned of the father's physical abuse and sexual molestation of the mother's daughter from a prior marriage, which the father admitted doing as a way of punishing the mother. There also was evidence that the father had physically and sexually abused the mother. In the first three years of the girl's life, the father had only a few visits with his daughter, supervised by child protective workers. The father then sought more visitation, and the trial court ordered weekly four-hour unsupervised visits. Soon there was evidence that the father had sexually abused his daughter, though apparently not enough evidence for a child protective agency to act. Remarkably, the trial court soon thereafter increased the father's visitation to unsupervised overnights, seemingly because the judge wanted to punish the mother for moving out of state without court permission and for resisting ordered visitation. The judge appears to have been entirely focused on the deservingness or undeservingness of the parents rather than on what would be good for the child. On appeal, the mother succeeded in getting the order of unsupervised visitation overturned, but the appellate court indicated that the father should still have supervised visitation with the child. The appellate court did not consider the possibility that the father should not have any visitation or, in other words, that the child might have a right to avoid any further connection with her biological father.

In this context, therefore, even the basic, nominal standard of decision making in the United States and some other countries confers on children only a weak, limited right to avoid an association that presents a serious danger. Elsewhere, however, one finds jurisdictions where the law appears to give less deference to the desires of noncustodial parents, particularly in the case of nonmarital children. In England and Ireland, for example, the rule for granting a contact order to a nonresident parent has long been ostensibly quite child centered, treating contact as a right of the child when it is in the child's interests and the parent wants contact and not as a right of the parent that operates independently of the contact's being good for the child. Courts might assume as a factual matter that contact is beneficial, but demonstration that that is not the case should suffice to deny it.[80] Similarly, in Germany and Finland, visitation with a noncustodial parent is viewed as a right of the child (again, so long as the noncustodial parent wants it) and so courts may deny a noncustodial parent's petition for access simply upon finding this necessary to protect a child's best interests.[81] The ECHR recently upheld that standard, against a claim by an unwed father in Germany that a local court's denial of his petition for visitation violated his rights to protection of family life under Article 8 of the Convention on Human Rights.[82]

The best-interests standard does play some role in visitation decisions even in the United States and other jurisdictions where noncustodial parents have a strong right of access. If and when noncustodial parents seek visitation and get past the threshold determination that they will get some visitation, then the best-interests standard comes into play. At that point, the court must determine the amount and particular form of visitation, and in most jurisdictions, courts ostensibly make that determination based on the best interests of the child.[83] To guard against a perceived possibility of abuse or neglect, a court might order only occasional, brief, and/or supervised visits. However, in most U.S. jurisdictions, there is a presumption that noncustodial parents will receive at least "standard visitation" absent a showing that this is likely to result in significant harm. Standard visitation generally means weekend-long stays every other week, one or two overnights every week, and a couple of weeks in the summer.[84]

In addition, as with custody decisions, certain extraneous, adult-centered considerations and biases creep into visitation decisions and further shrink the implicit right of the child. As evidenced in a number of published opinions, a noncustodial parent who is gay might receive less visitation time than he or she otherwise would because of a judge's condemnation of his or her sexual orientation. Conversely, courts are reluctant to restrict visitation on the basis of parental behaviors, even when they are potentially dangerous to children, if those behaviors are motivated by religious belief. Some apply a "substantial harm" threshold for considering religious activities, based on an explicit balancing of children's well-being against the perceived constitutional rights of parents.

Finally, it bears repeating that the law does not force any adult to take custody of or visit with a child. A parent in a divorce or paternity action who does not want custody or visitation can simply decline.[85] Even where children are said to have a right with respect to visitation, it is only a right against visitation that it is best for them to avoid, not a right to compel a parent to visit. Thus, unlike children, adults have an absolute right to avoid a parent–child relationship. Legal parents can be compelled to provide financial support for a child regardless of whether they want a social relationship with the child, but the state does not force any parent to have a social relationship with a child if the parent does not want one, even if such a relationship would be good for the child. Thus, in a 1995 Ohio case, *Hamilton v. Hamilton*, when a custodial mother of a girl with multiple disabilities petitioned to increase the noncustodial father's visitation time with the girl, so that the mother could have more than a few free hours a week for herself, the court held that it had no power to increase the father's visitation time against his will or even to force him to take advantage of the visitation time already granted him. The court stated: "Because it is a right, not a duty, a court cannot force a nonresidential parent to visit his or her child."

3) Custody disputes between a legal parent and a nonparent

The divergence between custody rules and a children's rights model, and the privileging of legal parents' entitlement over children's welfare, becomes even clearer where an adult who is not a legal parent has acted in a parentlike role in relation to a child and a conflict arises between that person and a legal parent. Legal parenthood, which our legal system will confer on only one or two adults, is still largely an exclusive status – that is, a status that excludes others from receiving legal recognition and protection of their role in a child's life, even when that role has been a primary one.[86] This is so despite the multiplicity of family forms that exist and despite research demonstrating that many simultaneous emotional bonds can and typically do constitute a healthy relational life for children. The law in the United States generally does not afford persons other than legal parents even standing to seek custody of a child, where a legal parent wants custody and the state has not adjudicated that parent unfit.

In a significant minority of U.S. states and in many other western nations,[87] statutes do authorize persons who are not legal parents to petition in some circumstances for custody of a child, even exclusive custody, as against legal parents. And in several U.S. states, in Canada, and in Australia, the welfare of the child is ostensibly the controlling consideration in deciding such a petition, just as it is in deciding custody between two legal parents.[88] Legislators in these jurisdictions appear to recognize that a social relationship with a caregiver can be more important to a child or to a child's welfare than a biological link or legal status.[89] In practice, though, some observers have noted, courts in those U.S. states will not award custody to a nonlegal parent absent a showing that the legal parents are unwilling or unfit to have custody. Ireland has an explicit fitness standard, though it places the burden of proof on the legal parent to prove fitness where he or she has left the child in the care of a nonparent for an extended period.[90]

A quite common situation involves children whose parents have left them in the care of their grandparents or other relatives for an extended period but then reenter the picture after being off pursuing other interests or wallowing in addiction. In most U.S. jurisdictions, the state gives the legal parents in such a situation the legal right to take the child away immediately and become the primary custodians of the child, absent grounds for terminating their legal status as parents. Thus, for example, in *Locklin v. Duka*, the Nevada Supreme Court in 1996 upheld a lower court decision returning a child to the custody of her mother after the mother had left the child in the custody of a grandmother for nine years, during which time the mother had only sporadic contact with the child, was addicted to drugs, and lived in an abusive relationship. Because the mother, after drug rehabilitation, now satisfied the state's standard of minimal fitness to parent and had, according to the law, not manifested a sufficiently clear intent to abandon the child, she was deemed entitled to have the child back. Jonathan Herring describes a similar case in England, *Re K*, in which biological parents with a criminal and drug history had given their child to a stable, financially secure older couple when the child was six weeks old and then returned much later, after the other couple had bonded with the child, and succeeded in getting a court to order return of the child. An appellate court ruled that the couple who had been caring for the child could not prevent return to the biological parents simply by showing that remaining with them would be best for the child.[91]

Children's relationships with substitute, de facto parents are even less likely to receive protection where those caregivers were selected by the state – that is, when they are foster parents. This can occur after legal parents voluntarily place the children in state custody or after the state removes the children from parental custody upon finding abuse or neglect. Even though foster parents go through a formal screening process (albeit one that varies considerably in rigor from one locale to another), and even though children might remain in the care of foster parents for years and develop strong bonds with them, generally neither foster parents nor children have any basis for objecting to the state's removing the children to place them in a different foster home or to return them to the legal parents.[92] And the substantive standard for returning children from foster care to their legal parents after an involuntary removal is typically not that it is in their best interests but rather that parental custody no longer poses an imminent danger of serious harm to a child.[93]

Virginia statutes, for example, authorize state custody only upon a finding that the child "would be subjected to an imminent threat to life or health to the extent that severe or irremediable injury would be likely to result if the child were ... left in the custody of his parents."[94] American courts and the ECHR have explained that the high threshold for denying legal parents custody reflects a balancing of the parents' interests against those of children.[95] Moreover, in most jurisdictions, there is no legal mechanism for attempting to maintain the relationship between children and foster parents through visitation after the state removes children from their foster home and places them again in the custody of the legal parents. Though foster parents might be the only parents a child has ever known, the state will permanently and completely sever the relationship out of deference to the legal rights of the legal parents.

In this context as well, though, we find outside the United States instances of states' being more open to recognizing a multiplicity of family relationships and focusing to a greater extent on the welfare of children. In Ontario, statutes authorize the government child welfare agency to change a child's foster care placement only where that is in the child's best interests.[96] The ECHR has recognized a right of children, under Article 8 of the European Human Rights Convention, to respect for the family life they have created with foster parents, even against the claims of parents to have a child returned to them.[97] And German law now authorizes an access order in favor of former foster parents with whom a child lived for a substantial amount of time.[98]

A somewhat different, but also very common, situation involves step-parents or nonmarital partners of a legal parent who have resided and coparented with a legal parent. A spouse or partner might for several years participate equally with the legal parent in raising a child and develop a strong emotional and psychological bond with the child. Yet in most U.S. jurisdictions the spouse or partner would not even have standing to seek custody, sole or shared, when the relationship between the adults ends. Many same-sex couples go through the procreation process together, intentionally and cooperatively enlisting the assistance of a third party, fully intending that both will be equal parents to the child, and then jointly raise the child for years, yet the law does not recognize both as parents for purposes of ordering custodial relationships after dissolution of the adult relationship. In some states, even if the legal parent exits the picture, because of rights termination, abandonment, or death, the partner who has helped raise the child might be pushed aside by grandparents or other relatives who are given preference in assigning guardianship. In any of these scenarios, the de facto parent would in most U.S. jurisdictions also be unable to petition even for visitation with the child.[99]

Children thus have no right under prevailing rules in the United States to maintain a relationship with a long-term caregiver if the caregiver has not had legal parent status conferred upon her or him under the laws governing maternity, paternity, or adoption. The wishes of legal parents trump the interests of children in such situations where they conflict. A state appellate court in Michigan recently stated explicitly that requiring the legal parent in such a situation to show that it would be in the child's best interests to return to her custody would violate "the fundamental constitutional right of parents to raise their children."[100] As noted above, some other western nations are, ostensibly at least, much more protective of children's interests in maintaining relationships with "psychological parents."

C) Ending Legal Parent–Child Relationships

When people think about termination of parental rights, they think of the state forcing a parent out of a child's life. What few realize is that parents themselves can terminate a social relationship with a child unilaterally, just as they can avoid such a relationship in the first place. The state does not force any adult who does not wish to do so to continue an association with a child, even if that adult has been a custodial parent. Parents may not abandon a child in a way that endangers the child – for example, by leaving a baby in a dumpster. But if they do so, the remedy is not to force them to continue the relationship, which would be nonsensical. Rather, the law's reaction is likely to be to terminate the parents' legal rights whether they want that or not and perhaps to prosecute them criminally. And there are no adverse repercussions for ending one's relationship with a child in a manner that does not endanger the child. As noted above, parents can voluntarily relinquish their parental rights with respect to a newborn child by placing the child for adoption by other adults, and in some circumstances they can just place a child of any age in state custody without ending their legal status as parents. When there are no willing adoptive parents and the state refuses to take custody, parents can leave a child with relatives or friends and then disappear, without penalty. They might be precluded from reclaiming the child later on, and awareness of that possibility might deter some parents from abandoning their children, but they are still free to do so.

Conversely, when indifferent, incompetent, or malevolent parents take no action themselves to end their parenthood, a child's interest in ending the parent–child relationship receives little protection. Children have no comparable right to exit a parent–child relationship. Termination does not occur simply because it is in a child's best interests that it occur – that is, in a situation where it might reasonably be said that the child would, if able, choose to end the relationship. Legislatures generally have not made a best-interests finding a sufficient condition for termination, and some courts have expressed the view that it would violate parents' constitutional rights to terminate their legal parental status solely on the grounds that it is best for the child.[101] Many legal scholars would oppose easing standards or expediting the process for removing children from parental custody and terminating parental rights, out of sympathy for parents and out of concern for the disparate impact termination rules tend to have on poor and minority parents.[102]

Consistent with this perception of legal parents' strong entitlement to maintain their parental status, statutes set a much higher threshold. Termination provisions typically authorize courts to end an adult's role as legal parent of a child, against the parent's wishes, on any of several separate grounds – abuse, neglect, abandonment, nonsupport, and incarceration being the most common. Termination can occur by one of two procedural routes. The state can petition for termination under child protection provisions in state codes. In addition, private parties seeking to adopt a child can, in connection with their petition to adopt, seek termination of an existing legal parent's rights. Importantly, in most jurisdictions, neither children themselves nor their representatives can initiate proceedings to end a parent–child relationship.[103]

With respect to state petitions for termination under child protection laws, state statutes typically admonish courts to consider in some fashion what is best for the child involved. This requirement usually appears in precatory language separate from the actual rules that the courts must apply. In many places, the best-interests standard is also stated as a necessary, but not sufficient, condition for terminating parental rights in one or more of the substantive grounds. In other words, state laws might prohibit courts from terminating parental rights when that would be worse for the child than the status quo but do not require that courts do terminate when that would be better for the child, and in fact preclude courts from terminating solely on the grounds that that would be better for the child. In almost all cases, courts must also find either that the parent manifested an intent to waive his or her claim to the child or that the parent is in some way culpable – egregiously so and for a protracted period of time.

Abandonment, nonsupport, and noncontact predicates for termination of parental rights effectively base termination on a decision by the parent that he or she does not wish to have a parent–child relationship with the child. The concept of abandonment entails an intention on the part of the parent to exit the parent–child relationship, and statutory provisions in the United States regarding failure to support or contact the child typically state explicitly a requirement of willfulness. Simply having been absent and uninvolved is not sufficient; a court must find that the parent's absence and lack of involvement reflected an intention not to have a relationship. Thus, when a mother has prevented a biological father from becoming aware of, locating, or having contact with her child, courts do not find abandonment. And courts often find that the most meager of efforts to maintain a relationship require denial of a petition to terminate on abandonment grounds. A parent might leave a child for years in the care of another person, but occasionally drop in for a visit, and such occasional contact is sufficient to prevent termination.

These termination provisions therefore really effectuate a right of the parents – namely a right to end the relationship at their election. The parent is often absent in those cases from the proceedings, not objecting to termination but simply not having formally relinquished his or her rights. When the parent does object, a decision to terminate effectively holds the parent to the choice he or she implicitly made in exercising the right adults have to avoid or end a relationship with a child. The child might be said to possess, at most, a reliance interest that receives protection, at the state's discretion.

Provisions for termination based on criminal conviction and incarceration are sometimes justified as reflecting the same sort of judgment about a parent – namely that he or she has effectively chosen to end the parent–child relationship. Some courts have stated that parents who choose to engage in conduct they know could result in being incarcerated, while also knowing that they have a child and parental responsibilities, effectively choose to abandon the child. In addition, in most jurisdictions, the mere fact of incarceration, no matter how long the sentence, is not sufficient basis for terminating; a court must also find an additional reason for thinking the convict is unfit to parent – for example, if the crime for which he or she was sentenced was a physical attack on a child.

When termination is based on abandonment, nonsupport, or incarceration, the best interests of the child might not be relevant at all; it is generally neither a necessary nor a sufficient condition that termination be best for the child. This means that a parent–child relationship can continue even when that is not best for the child – for example, because it prevents the child from entering into other relationships, even though the existing legal parent is incapable of acting as a parent. Children thus have no right to end a legal relationship with a parent who has abandoned them. In contrast, an adult could readily secure a divorce from a spouse who abandoned him or her.

Abuse and neglect predicates for termination of parental rights are generally the most complicated. In many jurisdictions, one of the findings a court must make to terminate on the basis of abuse or neglect is that termination would be in the best interests of the child. In addition to finding that termination would be best for the child, however, a court typically must also find, by clear and convincing evidence, that the abuse or neglect was severe, that state agencies have made "reasonable efforts" to rehabilitate the parents, and that the parents have failed to respond appropriately to the state's efforts. Thus, termination does not occur even when that would be best for the child, if (a) the abuse or neglect was not so egregious as to trigger the judge's sense of moral outrage; (b) the state agencies have not yet supported the parent in efforts to become rehabilitated, even if the likelihood of rehabilitation is slight; or (c) the parent has tried to reform himself or herself and has had some modest success. This has caused many children to remain in foster care, or to bounce back and forth between their legal parents and foster parents, for years, waiting for a court finally to decide that the parents have been given sufficient opportunity to become minimally adequate caretakers. Abuse and neglect predicates for termination reflect a balancing of the rights of parents against the welfare of children, with parents' rights coming out the winner except in extreme cases. In any event, as noted above, children and their representative generally have no authority to initiate termination proceedings on this basis. As with abandonment, nonsupport, and incarceration, then, children have little right to end their relationship with parents on the grounds that they are abusive and/or neglectful per se.

In 1997, the U.S. Congress endeavored to end the chronic problems of long-term foster care, and of state agencies undertaking exercises in futility, by passing the Adoption and Safe Families Act (ASFA). The most salient features of ASFA are provisions requiring that states, as a condition for receiving certain federal funds, direct their child protective agencies to (1) develop a plan for permanent placement of a child after the child has been in foster care for twelve months; (2) petition for termination on the grounds simply that a child has been in foster care for fifteen of the prior twenty-two months (the "15–22 rule"); and (3) forego the reasonable efforts requirement in instances where the parent in question has previously had parental rights terminated as to another child, has subjected a child to "aggravated circumstances" such as torture or severe and chronic physical abuse, or has engaged in one of a number of specific, heinous crimes such as having killed another family member or having created the child in question by raping the mother. State agencies and courts may avoid application of the rule in any individual case by showing that it would operate contrary to the best interests of the child. ASFA also requires that whenever states begin the termination process and there is not another existing legal parent available to care for the child, they must concurrently begin the process of making the child available for adoption or otherwise finding a suitable permanent custodial arrangement.

These are positive steps toward securing permanent loving parent–child relationships with other adults. And it might be that ASFA, by mandating termination proceedings in certain circumstances, gives children and their representatives a basis for triggering a termination action when the state fails to initiate one. It does not confer on children standing per se to petition for termination, but it provides a clear basis for a "show cause" order against the state child protective agency, compelling the agency to justify in court its noncompliance, which a guardian *ad litem* might be able to request in a foster care review hearing or in an initial adjudication of abuse or neglect. This could be one respect, then, in which children can be said to have a right to end a parent–child relationship, albeit a limited one. ASFA inspired efforts in England and Australia to pass similar adoption-facilitating legislation. England's Adoption of Children Act 2002 requires local agencies to pursue adoption in more cases but does not go as far in establishing concrete triggers for mandatory termination proceedings or in waiving rehabilitation requirements. Legislation in New South Wales modeled after ASFA failed to pass.[104]

ASFA contains significant gaps, however. Even if a petition for termination is filed within twenty-two months of a child being placed in foster care, given the length of typical termination proceedings, the child is likely to be in foster care for three years before being available for adoption, a very long period in a child's life. In addition, when a child has been in and out of foster care, rather than in it continuously, and has been out for periods sufficient for the 15–22 rule not to be triggered, the child might linger in the system for much longer than three years, even though he or she might be a viable candidate for adoption. When a child has not been in foster care at all – for example, when the child has been in the custody of another parent, he or she might permanently remain legally tethered to a terrible parent. Moreover, ASFA leaves the "reasonable efforts" requirement in place even for cases in which there is no real likelihood of transforming a legal parent into a good caretaker but where that parent has not engaged in conduct so extreme as to trigger the aggravated circumstances exception. Whether termination is best for a child in any of these situations depends, of course, on what the alternative is, but the availability of a better home is something that courts can and routinely do now consider in assessing whether termination is in a child's best interests.

Adding further complexity to the law of termination of parental rights, there are, in addition to the provisions for state petitions to terminate in child protection statutes, provisions in adoption laws for involuntary termination of parental rights. These provisions identify special circumstances in which a legal parent's consent to the adoption is not required and stipulate that adoption terminates the rights of any parent who is not a spouse of the petitioner. The circumstances in which parental consent is not required generally include the sort of "implicit relinquishment" predicates found in child protective statutes – that is, abandonment and noncontact/nonsupport. Otherwise, the biological parents must be proven unfit on the basis of misconduct or must voluntarily relinquish their claim on the child. It is not enough to show that it would be in the child's best interests for the persons petitioning for adoption to be his or her legal parents.[105] Courts in England and the United States have expressed the view that the substantive standard must be more protective of the parental interests than a best-interests rule would be.

This has been so even in the notorious "botched adoption" cases, such as those in the United States involving "Baby Richard," "Baby Jessica," and "Baby Emily," and such as the *Keegan v. Ireland* decision of the ECHR,[106] where an adoption has been formally approved and adoptive parents have proceeded to care for a child for a significant period, but then the biological father surfaces and claims that his consent was required for the adoption but not secured. Courts in the United States have held in those cases that they may not even consider the interests of the child, and as a result state agency workers have been compelled to wrench children from their psychological parents to hand them over to men who are strangers in every way other than biological. Courts consistently have rejected claims by adoptive parents that they and their children have a right to maintain the relationship they have formed, rejecting even requests for visitation after the child is transferred to the biological father. As a result, children are completely and suddenly cut off from the adults they view as their parents, an outcome likely to inflict long-term psychological harm as well as short-term trauma. Barbara Bennett Woodhouse writes as follows:

> While blood tests proving or disproving biological relationship may mean a great deal to adults, they have little relevance to a three year old child who has formed a deep attachment to a caring adult. For that child, the crucial fact is whether bonds of trust have formed between the child and the adult she perceives as Mommy or Daddy. Shattering such bonds, child psychologists tell us, can inflict serious damage to the young child's sense of self and permanently affect her ability to trust.[107]

These outcomes were so troubling that a few state legislatures in the United States responded by passing legislation requiring that the best interests of the child control in those situations. Perhaps because the claim of the non-biological-parent caregivers seems so strong in these situations, the law is beginning to treat them as on the same footing as biological parents and so to resolve the disputes on the basis of a rule similar to that applied in custody disputes between biological parents in divorce and paternity proceedings. But the prevailing rule is still that the child's interests are irrelevant in these situations and that everything turns on the possessory rights of biological parents.

In sum, children have at best a very weak right to end a relationship with bad parents. Their interests are generally subordinated to the conflicting desires and claims of parents, and, with very limited exception, even when the rules would serve their welfare they have no standing to insist on their enforcement. However, children do have an absolute right in some situations in most jurisdictions against the state severing their relationship with their parents when that would *not* be good for the child. A finding that termination of parental rights would be in the child's best interests is a necessary condition for severing the parent–child relationship on the basis of abuse or neglect and perhaps on other bases as well. But then their right is superfluous, because their parents' rights are sufficient basis for preventing termination.

D) Children's Relationships with Siblings

In addition to creating parent–child relationships, the state creates legal sibling relationships – in other words, determines whom the law will treat as a sibling and therefore afford some protection for siblinglike social relationships. These relationships are the most important relationships in the lives of some children and central to the lives of most, typically entailing emotional ties stronger than those with any other nonparent relatives, such as grandparents, aunts, uncles, and cousins.[108]

The state generally creates a legally recognized sibling relationship by creating parent–child relationships between an adult and more than one child. There is no distinct legal proceeding for creating a sibling relationship. Yet the rules governing creation of parent–child relationships for the most part require no consideration of whether it would be in a child's best interests for a legal sibling relationship to arise. If the law required individualized consideration of children's welfare in creating parent–child relationships, courts could consider whether the adult in question is a parent of other children and what effect the presence of those other children might have on the child in question (and vice versa). But maternity and paternity rules do not call for an individualized determination of a child's best interests. Only in the context of adoption might the law command consideration of sibling relationships, and then, in most jurisdictions, only in terms of the interests of the child to be adopted, not as to children already in the family. Germany is an exception again here; current law requires children in the adopting family to consent to the adoption.[109] In the vast majority of situations, therefore, children have no right in connection with the initial formation of their legal or social sibling relationships.

The law takes greater direct interest in sibling relationships once they are formed, and the law in recent years has become increasingly protective of these relationships. Courts in the United States have generally rejected claims that siblings have a constitutional right against state action separating them, but there has been substantial legislative action in the past decade toward protecting these important relationships, as awareness has grown of the great importance that sibling bonds can have for children, particularly in the midst of family disruption.[110] Direct state decisions affecting the continuation of sibling relationships take place in the context of custody decision making in divorce and paternity proceedings and in the context of foster care and termination of parental rights decisions.

Custody decisions in divorce and paternity proceedings often entail explicit consideration of whether siblings will continue to be part of the same household. When parents have more than one child, courts have the option of awarding "split custody," which means giving each parent primary custody of one or more children. Statutes governing custody generally do not prohibit splitting up siblings, but increasingly courts apply a strong presumption against it. Ultimately the decision whether to split siblings is governed by the same standard governing the award of custody of a single child to one parent or another – that is, in most jurisdictions, the best-interests standard. Many states' custody statutes today include, among the factors courts are to consider, each child's relationship or inter- actions with siblings, and some legislatures and courts have gone so far as to establish an explicit presumption against split custody,[111] The prevail- ing rule thus affords children an absolute right as to their remaining in the same household as siblings following divorce; if it is in the best interests of all siblings, in light of their total circumstances, to remain together, then that should be the result.

When siblings are placed in different households, courts typically arrange visitation time between each child and the parent who is not the custodial parent of the child so that the visiting child also spends time with his or her siblings. Thus, there is rarely an issue of sibling visitation postdivorce. If a court failed to do so, however, and the parents did not independently arrange for siblings to spend time together, the question would arise whether children have a right to maintain contact with each other, a right that limits the decision-making authority states confer on parents as a component of custody. I discuss that issue in the next and final section of the chapter.

Sibling relationships also are disrupted by child protective proceedings and receive significantly less protection in this arena. Often, only one child in a family is removed, cutting that child off from any siblings, even though the siblings might have been a source of emotional support and stability. Other times, more than one child is removed, and the question is whether the removed children will be placed together. State agencies have great discretion in placing children in foster care, and though the law in some U.S. states requires such agencies to attempt to keep siblings together in the same residence, in most the law does not require them to keep siblings together even if that would be best for them. Other considerations, such as resource constraints or administrative convenience, might therefore result in separate placements.[112]

Likewise, if the state terminates the rights of parents as to siblings, the law generally requires state adoption agencies to attempt to place siblings together with the same adoptive parents, but does not require them to do so. Ultimately, as discussed above, an order of adoption must be in the best interests of a child, so a court would in principle order adoption of one child without his or her sibling only if this were in the child's best inter- ests all things considered, in light of the available alternatives. Arguably, then, children do have a strong right in connection with maintaining their relationships with siblings when it comes to adoption, though one con- strained as a practical matter by the availability of adoptive parents willing to adopt more than one child. If siblings are placed in different adoptive homes, the opportunity for visitation with each other generally depends on the rules governing parental authority over children's interactions with nonparents, discussed below, though some jurisdictions now have special statutory provisions authorizing courts to order postadoption visitation between siblings.

* * *

That concludes our overview of the many direct decisions the state makes concerning children's family relationships. Among them, only two are even nominally governed under prevailing rules by a standard tied to the welfare of the child – namely approval of petitions for adoption and allocation of custody between legal parents in divorce and postpaternity custody proceedings. Yet even in those situations, subsidiary rules inject considerations tied to the interests of individual adults or of society as a whole that result in compromising the welfare of children. Other decisions give little or no weight to children's welfare. In determining whether particular adults will become a child's first legal parents, the interests of the child are of no direct relevance. The state entitles legal parents to associate with their children even when that is not in the child's best interests and will divest long-term caregivers of custody in favor of a legal parent so long as the parent is not unfit. And in determining whether an established legal parent will be involuntarily removed from that role and his or her relationship with a child terminated, the child's best interests are sometimes a necessary, but never a sufficient, condition for action.

II. State Delegation of Decision Making to Custodians

Once the state has established a child's nuclear family – that is, who the child's legal parents will be – those legal parents directly determine the remainder of a child's associations. Generally, a child's legal parents decide what friends the child has, which relatives – including grandparents, uncles and aunts, cousins, and even siblings – the child visits or welcomes at home, and which other adults act in a caretaking role. This is clearly a desirable state of affairs from a child welfare perspective. It would not be good for children for the state routinely to make decisions directly about, for example, with whom a child will play. Nor would if be good for children if the state delegated to private citizens other than parents (again, assuming the child is in the parents' custody and the parents are competent) the power to make these decisions on a daily basis. Parents otherwise are orchestrating children's daily activities and presumptively are motivated to make choices concerning children's interactions with third parties that are in their children's best interests. State micromanaging of all children's daily lives would be overly intrusive and less likely to result in sound decisions. The state's decision to confer substantial legal decision-making authority on parents is therefore justifiable on the basis of children's welfare. Children might be said to have a right to that conferral.[113]

Beyond the assignment of principal legal decision-making power, however, there is the question of how extensive an authority the state grants parents or, from another perspective, what restrictions or standards, if any, the state imposes on parents' exercise of that authority. Does the state confer complete power and then exit the scene, leaving parents to act however they choose, perhaps using their authority arbitrarily and contrary to children's well-being? Or does the state require that parents make decisions in a certain way – for example, subject to a mandatory minimum level of contact with peers or relatives or in accordance with a best-interests standard – and override parental decisions when they fail to comply? States must, and do, determine the extent of parental power over children's relational lives to resolve the disagreements that arise between parents and other persons, including their children, about whether third parties can have some relationship with the children. In other aspects of children's lives, such as education and medical care, the state throughout the West does impose some restrictions on parental freedom, requiring that parents secure some form of schooling for children at particular ages and that parents secure medical care when children are injured or sick. Does the state similarly impose a requirement that parents secure some modicum of social life for a child? Do children have any right to maintain relationships with particular persons outside their immediate family?

Limits on state-conferred parental power to dictate children's association with third parties might be discerned both in child protection laws and in third-party visitation laws. First, as with most other decisions parents make within the family setting, parental decisions about children's relationships are in theory constrained by the general prohibitions on abuse and neglect. In at least one common-law jurisdiction, Ontario, the law more affirmatively mandates that parents exercise all of their child-rearing rights and responsibilities in accordance with the best interests of their children.[114] Statutory definitions of abuse and neglect in the United States and in most other countries do not mention relationships specifically, however, and it is unlikely that legislators drafting abuse and neglect laws think at all about the quantity or quality of children's relationships with persons other than parents. One apparent exception is Sweden, where the law explicitly announces a parental obligation to facilitate contact between children and other adults with whom they have a close relationship.[115]

Despite this silence as to children's socialization or relationships, abuse and neglect definitions could be read to encompass gross misuse of power over children's relationships. A typical definition of "abuse" includes infliction of serious psychological or emotional injury by nonaccidental means, which might include severing a child's relationships with certain people if that would be traumatic for the child. And a typical definition of "neglect" includes failing or refusing to provide care necessary for a child's health, which could include a failure to facilitate or encourage a sufficient number or depth of relationships with persons other than the parents, such as extended family members and peers, if that results in stunted psychological or emotional development, depression, or a "failure to thrive."

General child protection laws thus arguably impose on parents an affirmative obligation to ensure substantial socializing for a child outside the parent–child relationships and an opportunity to form deep and lasting relationships with extended family members and persons outside the family. It is unlikely that parents' failure to nurture a relationship with a particular person – even a grandparent – in and of itself would be harmful to a child. But abruptly cutting off any one existing, strong relationship could be harmful to a child, and a failure to nurture any significant relationships with persons outside the nuclear family could be quite detrimental in the long run and constitute emotional and psychological neglect. Sensationalized incidents of militant recluses or religious cults staring down FBI SWAT teams usually signify an underlying family environment that is potentially quite damaging to children, because of the profound effects it must have on children not only to be cut off from all outsiders but also to be indoctrinated with paranoid beliefs about the danger of contact with outsiders. Even in less dramatic cases, cutting off all or nearly all of a child's contact with the outside world is a kind of deprivation that carries the potential for serious harm, a severe thwarting of a child's emotional and psychological development, and a truncating of a child's life prospects.

The reality, however, is that state child protective workers do not charge parents with abuse or neglect based on the parents' severing or preventing relationships with third parties. They do not treat as unlawful even a complete withdrawal of a child from the world outside the family. Implicitly, parents are deemed entitled to establish whatever social circumstances they wish for their children. In most parts of the western world, if there is any protection of a child's interest in relationships with persons who are not parents or siblings, it comes from rules granting those other persons standing to petition a court for an order of visitation with the child.

Throughout the West, special statutory provisions authorize some non-parent individuals to petition a court for an order of visitation in some circumstances if parents refuse to allow them contact with the child.[116] The substantive rules governing these requests in the United States are now in flux, because of the Supreme Court's 2000 plurality decision in *Troxel v. Granville*. Building on a line of precedents extending back to the 1920s, establishing parental constitutional rights to freedom in child rearing, the Court ruled in *Troxel* that one state's law authorizing courts to order visitation with any nonparent whenever that would be in a child's best interests was, as applied by the state's courts, an unconstitutional infringement of parents' rights.[117] In their analysis, the Justices who found a constitutional violation principally emphasized that the state courts had given no deference to the parents' decision and that there had been no finding that the children had been affected adversely by the absence of visitation. There was, however, no holding of the Court that a best-interests standard inherently violates parents' constitutional rights.

After *Troxel*, many state courts have held that judges considering third-party visitation petitions simply must apply a presumption that the parents are acting in the child's best interests and must impose a burden on the petitioners to demonstrate otherwise. This rule, which is also found in many non-U.S. jurisdictions, also seems consistent with an absolute children's rights model; it simply injects an evidentiary rule based on a seemingly accurate empirical assumption about the presumptive good faith and good judgment of parents. Indeed, one might challenge on child-centered grounds the rule in France, which effectively creates a presumption against the parents.[118] Such a rule might reflect greater solicitude for the interests of grandparents than for the welfare of children. Some state courts in the United States, however, have interpreted *Troxel* as requiring third-party petitioners to show that a child will suffer harm absent visitation with them, and harm is generally understood to mean a more severe consequence than just the children's being somewhat worse off than they would be if visitation were ordered. Those courts have thereby diminished children's implicit rights somewhat. In addition, in most jurisdictions, the circumstances in which grandparents are permitted to seek an order of visitation are quite limited, typically divorce proceedings and a parent's death. In contrast, the European Court of Human Rights has held that Article 8 of the Human Rights Convention imposes a duty on states to promote development of relationships between children and their grandparents.[119]

Even before *Troxel*, though, the rights of children in the United States in connection with third-party relationships were quite narrow, limited in most states to relationships with grandparents. Yet grandparents are not the only nonparents who seek visitation with a child and whose association might be valuable to a child. Others whose association might be important to a child include other relatives who have served as caretakers, same-sex partners of a parent, former stepparents wishing to see their stepchild after a divorce, biological relatives seeking visitation when a child has been adopted or parental rights have been terminated, foster parents seeking visitation when a child has been removed from their care, and siblings who live on their own or who for some reason are in the custody of other adults. Yet most U.S. states, and some other western nations, including England,[120] have long limited the category of petitioners to grandparents. Several other countries authorize third parties other than grandparents to seek visitation but typically only persons who have shared a household with the child, such as stepparents, and only in limited circumstances, such as divorce or death of a parent.[121]

In sum, the state imposes some limitation on parental power over children's relationships with third parties, but it is rather slight. There is no effective general standard of minimum socialization and no state-initiated protection for a child's important relationships with people other than legal parents. The only protection comes from recognition of standing for a narrow range of persons, in limited circumstances, to petition for a court order of visitation. Children thus have no right in many jurisdictions to maintain relationships with adults who are not parents or grandparents, even if those other adults have previously served as de facto parents for the children, and in the case of grandparents, children's right is limited to certain special circumstances. Most likely this legal regime is, for most children most of the time, not a problem. Most parents likely are motivated to do what is best for their children and, at least with respect to relationships with third parties, sufficiently competent to do so adequately. But it would be foolish and irresponsible to deny that some parents are sometimes motivated by things other than what is best for their children. There are numerous examples of parents acting out of deep-seated but unwarranted resentment toward other family members, especially toward those who have had to serve as primary caretakers for the children because of the parents' dereliction of duty. One example of how petty some parents can be is reflected in a Missouri court's decision in *Barker v. Barker*, where the court had to step in to order visitation between grandparents and a child, where the child's father had refused the grandparents contact with the child because the grandparents had sided against the father in a dispute over a neighborhood basketball game. Such incidents are suggestive of how the law has encouraged parents to view their dominion over their children.

The state's decision to confer extensive power on parents thus inevitably results in some loss of well-being for some children. This is not to say that the loss is easily avoidable or that a legal regime more protective of children's interests is possible and feasible. It is simply to acknowledge that state decisions indirectly determining children's relationships with persons other than their legal parents also cause some children to suffer.

Conclusion

The foregoing survey of the legal landscape makes plain that the state is deeply involved, in a complex way, in ordering children's relational lives. Idyllic views of the family occupying a private sphere untouched by the coarse hands of the state, absent serious dysfunction, are simply fiction. It also makes clear that, contrary to widespread belief, many important decisions the state makes about children's relationships are not based on a "best interests of the child" standard or on any other standard or rule that is clearly intended to, or does in fact, serve as a means of effectuating rights of children. On the contrary, most of the governing rules serve interests of individual adults and/or society as a whole in addition to, or instead of, the welfare of children. And in every context, these other interests that are given protection clearly can conflict with those of the children affected by the decisions, so the failure to confer absolute rights on children is morally significant in every context.

Advocates for children have lamented the law's failure to accord children greater protection for their interests in forming, avoiding, maintaining, or exiting personal relationships. Some assert that children should be deemed morally and even constitutionally entitled to greater protection of their welfare. But to date there has been little more than assertion. Much more would need to be said about why children ought to have legal rights in these situations, to convince those for whom it is not self-evident that there is something morally amiss about the current state of the law. The remainder of the book considers whether there is more that can be said.

3 Paradigmatic Relationship Rights

How should one go about analyzing what legal rights children should have in situations where the state is creating, structuring, or severing their family relationships? One way would be to address each type of situation one at a time – for example, first paternity, then custody, and so forth – and to reason about children's normative position within the one type of situation under review. It seems inevitable, though, that any good theoretical account of children's rights in any relationship context will appeal to very general principles – principles concerning rights, concerning the respect owed to persons, and concerning the extent, if any, to which decisions about fundamental aspects of one person's life should be influenced by the interests of other persons. The bedrock premises on which any argument for or against particular rights for children is constructed are likely to be quite broad, not limited to particular types of decisions about children's relationships. And there appears to be a great deal of commonality in the normative questions raised by each type of situation. They are all at base about the state making for children kinds of decisions – with whom to form close relationships, how much time to devote to each relationship, and when to end relationships – that competent adults ordinarily make for themselves, and there are well-established, general moral and legal principles concerning the rights of competent adults in making all such decisions. So there is reason to believe that addressing all decisions about children's relationships at once, and constructing a general theory of their relationship rights, is a promising approach.

Several strategies are possible for constructing a comprehensive theory of children's rights in personal relationships. The one I take here is a "coherentist" analysis, by which I mean that it looks to widely agreed on general principles governing the "standard" case of individual rights in our society, which historically has meant the case of individual competent adults, and then examines whether and how these principles can be extended to the "nonstandard" case of less competent persons, and of children in particular. A coherentist approach presupposes that rational consistency in moral beliefs and practices is an aim of moral agents and examines whether such consistency now prevails across different areas of life, and if not, whether and how consistency can be achieved.[1] In the context of children's relationship rights, this approach takes a simple, three-step form: In this chapter, I explore what legal rights competent adults have in connection with forming, maintaining, avoiding, and ending personal relationships and examine the extent to which the legal system has extended the same or similar rights to incompetent adults. Then, in Chapter 4, I consider what the prevailing moral justifications are for the legal rights that adults currently enjoy. Finally, in the remaining chapters, I analyze whether and how those principles could be applied to children's situation.

It is a truism among political and legal theorists today that our received views on matters of justice and rights were developed by persons operating from perspectives that considered only a subset of all human beings as proper subjects of normative reasoning. The great Anglo-American political traditions treated certain persons (the standard description is "property-owning autonomous white adult males") as the norm and, in developing their core theories, reasoned as if there was only that one class of persons who mattered. That these traditions did not develop with proper recognition of the potentially different situation or experience of women, persons of minority race, incompetent adults, or children provides some reason for questioning whether they have any value for us today, when our moral compass is wider and we grapple with issues that present potential conflicts of interest between groups of persons marked by such characteristics as race, gender, and competence. We might wonder whether the received traditions are fundamentally flawed because formed within such a narrow perspective on the human world or, less radically, whether they can speak to only a narrow category of human problems, ones that do not appear to present such conflicts of interests. Such questions are certainly worth pursuing. It can also be very fruitful, however, to look to the rules and normative principles that the historically most privileged and empowered group developed for itself, based on an assumption of equal moral respect for all persons who were thought to matter, and to ask whether those principles can and should now be extended, to some degree or in some fashion, to the groups of persons who historically were excluded, who historically were treated as not counting but now must be treated as counting. This is the strategy I pursue.

This chapter reviews the law governing adults' relationships among themselves. It reveals that competent adults have adopted for themselves a legal regime in which they enjoy plenary rights in connection with their personal relationships. As discussed in Part A, competent adults collectively give themselves a nearly absolute entitlement to enter into and maintain relationships with each other on a mutually voluntary basis and to refuse for any reason to have a relationship with any other person, regardless of the other person's wishes. Part B shows that the legal system in modern times has extended this model of relationship rights to incompetent adults, conferring on them some of the same rights as, and otherwise rights equivalent to, those possessed by competent adults.

I. The Relationship Rights of Competent Adults

What rights do we competent adults have with respect to forming, maintaining, avoiding, and ending personal relationships? I speak here principally of having some relationship with others, interacting with and forming connections with others in some way, rather than about rights to engage in particular behaviors in the context of relationships. What limitations, if any, are there on our liberty to enter into, carry on, avoid, or terminate relationships with particular other persons? Competent adults' legal rights in connection with their relationships with other competent adults have two significant formal characteristics, relating to their strength and their scope.

A) The Strength of the Right

Our right to have relationships of our choosing is contingent on mutuality. This is the only significant limitation on the strength of adult relationship rights, essentially making them what might be called "conditional absolute rights" – that is, rights that become more or less absolute upon the satisfaction of one simple condition, that of reciprocal choosing. Our right to establish and maintain legal and/or social relationships with other adults we choose is entirely dependent on the other adults with whom we want the relationship also wanting that relationship, also choosing to enter into and carry on a relationship with us.

Thus, I cannot force anyone even to have a conversation with me, let alone to socialize with me on a regular basis or to form a family relationship with me. My wanting to have a relationship with a particular other competent adult has no legal significance whatsoever if that other person does not wish to have such a relationship with me. I have no right against an unwilling adult individual. I have a negative right, as against the state, that it not interfere with my respectful efforts to pursue personal relationships, a right to be available for other private individuals to choose, even prior to others agreeing to enter into a relationship with me. But in the absence of another person's choice to associate with me, I have no right as against anyone to actually have a relationship with that person, not even to be in his or her presence and interact with that person, let alone to enter into a legally recognized intimate partnership. Only after a person with whom I wish to have a relationship has chosen to enter into a relationship with me can I be said to have a right to be in a relationship with that person, a right that would impose duties on the state and other private parties not to interfere with my nonharmful, mutually voluntary interactions with that person. The various international conventions and domestic constitutional and legislative provisions pronouncing a right to form a family or a right to protection of family life must be read as consistent with this broadly accepted limitation on adults' relationship rights.[2] Such pronouncements do not entitle anyone to a family life *no matter what* – in particular, to a family life even if no one wants to be in a family with a particular person. No one argues that such provisions authorize private or state coercion of *any adult* into a relationship with another person. In fact, many human rights charters contain a prohibition against compelling any person to enter into a marital relationship.[3]

Some legal relationships, it should be noted, do exist between adult individuals without their having chosen them, even in modern western societies. The law deems certain persons to be one's siblings, cousins, and so on, by virtue of connections through one's legal parents. However, in western nations at least, these legal relationships are of very limited significance. In the United States, their significance is limited to rights of inheritance in cases of intestacy and to presumptive priority in receiving decision-making authority for persons who become unable to make medical and/or financial decisions for themselves. In other words, they create a benefit or opportunity for one member of the relationship, which that person is free to decline, on the assumption that the other person in the relationship would want them to have that benefit or opportunity, an assumption that that other person can freely eviscerate by manifesting a contrary intent. In contrast to the situation in some nonwestern societies, these unchosen legal relationships between adults do not, in the western world, give rise to any burdens; they entail no obligation of financial support. They certainly do not bestow on anyone the power to compel association with the other member of such a relationship against that person's will. In fact, even the principal form of chosen legal personal relationship between competent adults in the United States – marriage – does not entail a power to compel association. If one member of a legal marriage absents himself or herself, the only recourse the other member has is to terminate the legal relationship; he or she cannot, by physical force or by invocation of state power, compel the absent spouse to return or even converse.

A corollary of the mutuality condition of adults' relationship rights among themselves is that every competent adult possesses an absolute right to avoid personal relationships with particular other persons. Each of us has a right against the state or any private person forcing us to enter into a personal relationship with someone else.[4] No one can legally compel us to socialize with another person, or live with another person, or have an intimate relationship with another person. This right we possess extends also to impersonal associations; we can never be legally required even to speak to someone else.[5]

Of course, with both personal and impersonal associations, there can be practical impediments to avoiding an undesired relationship. If someone I prefer to avoid happens to have a close relationship with a third person to whom I am close, I might have to interact with that someone to preserve my relationship with the third person. In-laws are perhaps the best example of this practical constraint. And if a person one would prefer not to interact with happens to be one's teacher in a required course, one's boss or co-worker, or a member of a social organization of which one is also a member, one might be unable to avoid the interaction without incurring a substantial cost – quitting school or one's job or the organization. But in each context, we adults possess the right to avoid the undesired association if we so desire. A married person has no legal power to force her spouse to visit her family, professors have no legal power to stop students from dropping out of school, neither the state nor any private person may compel any competent adult to work in a particular workplace, and private organizations cannot force people to become or remain members.[6]

In fact, each of us adults is legally free to go off and live an entirely solitary existence if we wish and never associate with anyone. Our right not to associate is absolute in the context of intimate associations. This is true even in the context of one's own family. Neither the state nor private persons may force me to visit my parents or my siblings, no matter how much they desire my company. There are informal social sanctions for refusing certain associations, but the law accords each of us the right to dissociate ourselves from anyone we choose, a right operating against both other private parties and the state. The legal relationship between myself and my parents and siblings might be inextinguishable, but I can ensure that it has no practical consequences whatsoever. For example, I can renounce any legal powers or financial claims I might have by virtue of my familial relationship, and I can execute legal documents to ensure that my parents and siblings derive no benefits or powers by virtue of the legal relationship between us – for example, executing a will that excludes them and designating a nonrelative as a proxy decision maker in the event of my incapacitation. As noted above, the legal relationship does not entail any power on the part of other family members to compel a social relationship.

What about adults' rights in connection with ending relationships? Those, too, are absolute. Today we take it for granted that our unilateral desire to get out of a relationship entitles us to do so, even out of the most intimate of relationships. The state does throw up some legal obstacles in the way of ending one kind of relationship between competent adults – namely marriage. But those obstacles have become quite minimal following the advent and spread of no-fault divorce throughout the western world.[7] Jonathan Herring notes that in England and Wales, divorce generally occurs quite rapidly and with only perfunctory judicial review of the parties' reasons for requesting a divorce.[8] The same is true in the United States; judges rarely demand demonstration that a marriage is unsalvageable. Only a few U.S. states' statutes authorize judges hearing divorce petitions to require that the couple attend counseling before they can proceed with a divorce. Canadian law and English law require simply that lawyers advise their divorce clients of the availability of reconciliation services.[9] The greatest legally imposed obstacle in most cases is a waiting period, something between six and twenty-four months in most common-law jurisdictions, which is essentially a paternalistically imposed cooling off time, forcing people who are likely to be under the sway of intense emotions to engage in more rational reflection about their situation before taking this major step. Marriage has thus become "functionally a contract terminable at will by either party";[10] "either spouse can terminate the relationship at any time for any reason (or no reason) upon notice to the other."[11] The law governing even this most important of adult relationships is "grounded in norms of short-term, rational self-interest."[12] This is so even though the other party to the relationship might suffer terribly as a result of the severance and even though intended third-party beneficiaries to the contract – that is, children – might be seriously harmed by termination of the contract.[13]

For the most part, the rights we competent adults demand for ourselves are negative rights; they are rights against state or private interference or compulsion and powers restricting the authority of the state to create or dissolve legal relationships against our will. However, in many contexts we can also call on the assistance of the state, and we have settled expectations that the state will assist us, even if such assistance is not a matter of fundamental or constitutional right. For example, if we want to avoid or end a social relationship with a particular person and that person will not leave us alone, we can secure police protection. We can do so without showing that they have seriously harmed us in the past; it is enough that they will not desist in their efforts to associate with us even after we have expressed our desire that they leave us alone. In addition, legal recognition of and state financial support for the marital relationship has come to be viewed as a right, as is evident when one contemplates the uproar that would ensue were a state legislator seriously to propose that marriage no longer be recognized anywhere in the law for any purpose. The Supreme Court of Massachusetts recognized this in its decision requiring extension of marriage to same-sex couples:

> Civil marriage enjoys a dual and in some sense paradoxical status as both a State-conferred benefit (with its attendant obligations) and a multi-faceted personal interest of "fundamental importance." As a practical matter, the State could not abolish civil marriage without chaotic consequences. The "right to marry," is different from rights deemed "fundamental" for equal protection and due process purposes because the State could, in theory, abolish all civil marriage while it cannot, for example, abolish all private property rights.[14]

Thus, the state does not merely leave us unfettered with respect to our relationship choices; it also provides positive assistance to us in forming particular types of relationships of our choosing and in avoiding others.

B) The Scope of the Right

The second significant formal feature of our rights in having relationships is that our right to have relationships with others is virtually unlimited in scope. There are almost no legal limitations on with whom one may choose to have a mutually voluntary social relationship. Apart from certain narrow restrictions imposed by the criminal law and, in some jurisdictions, by civil domestic violence law,[15] there are no competent adults with whom one is prohibited from associating. I can choose to pursue a mutually voluntary personal relationship with just about any adult in the world, and if the other adult also wishes to have a relationship, then we each have a right against the state's or other private parties' interfering with our carrying on an association.

That is quite impressive when one thinks about it. But of course we never do, because this right we adults have to form relationships with whomever we choose is so well established and so plenary, limited only by the requirement of mutuality, that we take it for granted, like breathing. For this reason, one will not find litigated cases on the right to form relationships with other willing, competent adults any more than one will find litigated cases on the right to breathe.

There are legal restrictions on what conduct one may engage in, in the context of a relationship. In theory, a restriction on conduct could amount to a limitation on the type of relationship one may have with others. However, increasingly such restrictions are limited to conduct so harmful to someone in the relationship that it suggests a lack of genuine consent or conduct believed to harm third parties. In particular, all western jurisdictions prohibit physical violence within relationships, and state authorities today are more willing than in the past to enforce this prohibition regardless of the wishes of the victim of the violence. Significantly, legislation prohibiting nonharmful interpersonal conduct on the grounds that it is offensive or immoral is gradually being erased from the law books. This has happened more belatedly in the United States than in other western nations, but the Supreme Court's 2003 decision in *Lawrence v. Texas*, holding antisodomy laws unconstitutional, was a momentous declaration of personal liberty within adults' intimate relationships. In *Lawrence v. Texas*, the Court noted that such laws "purport to do no more than prohibit a particular sexual act" and so purport not to infringe the well-established right of intimate association. However, affirming the great force of the right to freedom in choosing with whom one will have an intimate relationship, the Court continued: "Their penalties and purposes, though, have more far-reaching consequences, touching upon the most private human conduct, sexual behavior, and in the most private of places, the home. The statutes do seek to control a personal relationship that, whether or not entitled to formal recognition in the law, is within the liberty of persons to choose without being punished as criminals." The ECHR, significantly, had held twenty-two years earlier that prohibitions on homosexual conduct violate Europe's Human Rights Convention.[16]

In addition to prohibitions of harmful conduct, there are limitations on state recognition of relationships between competent adults – marriage being the principal example. Most western nations deny legal marital status to couples whose members are close blood relatives, with the boundary of permissible consanguinity varying to some degree from one jurisdiction to another. This denial of recognition is justified by the perceived potential for harm to third parties – namely the children such a couple might conceive – in light of an empirical assumption that legal recognition of a relationship encourages the parties to procreate (in fact, in some jurisdictions, only married persons can legally have intercourse). So this restriction is an outgrowth of a prohibition on conduct. Significantly, western nations generally also refuse to confer legal marital status on persons below a certain age – eighteen in most western European countries and sixteen in most U.S. states[17] – in contrast to rules for conferring legal parent status on biological parents, which contain no minimum age requirement.

Conversely, exclusion of same-sex couples from marital status, though widespread now, might cease within the next few decades, as did exclusion of interracial couples. Massachusetts recently began to confer the legal status of marriage per se on same-sex couples, moving a step beyond the "civil union"-type status that Vermont and some local governments had earlier created for same-sex couples. The 2004 presidential election revealed that most Americans are not yet ready to accept same-sex marriage, but most do now accept conferral of civil union status, demonstrating that the country is much more tolerant of homosexuality today than it was a generation ago. And the world around the United States is moving more steadily toward acceptance of same-sex marriage. As of this writing, four nations – Canada, Spain, Belgium, and the Netherlands – confer this legal status on same-sex couples, whereas others provide a civil-union-type status.[18]

In any event, neither legal prohibitions on particular interpersonal behaviors nor exclusionary marriage laws prevent anyone from carrying on a social relationship or from having their relationships recognized within their churches or other private communities. Denial of legal marital status itself works no necessary change in the social relationship between persons; it does not prevent the individuals from having whatever sort of relationship in a practical sense they wish to have. It affects only certain legal consequences of the relationship, such as public benefits and default rules for property and decision-making powers, the latter of which can be effected by private contract anyway. Neither type of law in any way diminishes the freedom of any two consenting adults simply to associate with each other, to enjoy each other's company, to express feelings to each other, and to form an emotional bond between them.

In sum, our rights to form and continue relationships with other competent adults depend crucially on mutuality, our rights to maintain mutually voluntary relationships are plenary in scope, our rights to avoid relationships in the first instance are absolute, and the state assists us in various ways in effectuating our relationship choices, in addition to simply staying out of the way most of the time. These are characteristics that do pertain to competent adults' rights to establish, maintain, and avoid relationships. Also worth emphasizing are what characteristics our rights to establish, maintain, and avoid relationships do not have.

C) What Adults' Rights in Relationships among Themselves Do Not Include

One characteristic that does not pertain to competent adults' relationship rights was implicit in the reference above to the rights being contingent. The mere fact that I want to form a relationship with a particular someone is never enough to give rise to a right to have such a relationship. Persons suffering from unrequited love know this all too well. This is true regardless of any prior connections, social or otherwise, between us. Nor does such a desire generate a right to be given an opportunity to become attractive to the other person, to have the door kept open while one makes efforts to eradicate or mitigate one's faults. This state of affairs stands in sharp contrast to the legal right that biological parents currently possess to form a relationship with children, which does not depend on anything more than the biological parents' desire to establish a relationship.

So, too, with termination of relationships; one person's desire to continue the relationship does not generate a right to do so in the face of the other person's wish to end it. Significantly, neither in the case of marriage nor any other relationship does the law require that the other person be given an opportunity to "rehabilitate" himself or herself before the relationship is terminated. As noted above, in a small minority of U.S. states, a judge can order a divorcing couple to seek counseling,[19] but this is not viewed as compulsory rehabilitation efforts for an at-fault spouse. It is viewed, rather, as a compulsory joint effort to reconcile differences and is not supposed to be ordered where a spouse has been abusive. In some of those states, either spouse can avoid compulsory counseling simply by waiting a longer time for a divorce decree.[20] And of course there is no compulsory counseling before terminating a friendship or acquaintanceship or even a nonmarital family social relationship (e.g., a relationship with a sibling).

In any of these kinds of relationships, I might voluntarily give the other person an opportunity to reform before I cut off the association. But that is my call, which I am free to make exclusively on the basis of what I think is best for me. The other person's wanting to maintain the relationship is not sufficient to compel me to give him or her another chance. Nor is any disadvantage or disability under which the other person labors; I am not required to sacrifice my welfare for the sake of redressing societal inequities or natural misfortunes. Once I destroy the mutuality in any relationship, for whatever reason, I may walk, and the law respects, and if need be enforces, my decision. The other person's rights do not include any claim that would override my decision as to what is best for me, regardless of how sympathetic a figure he or she might cut. The contrast with legal parents' rights with respect to their children is again sharp; those rights entitle a parent to state-provided services and a significant period of time to mitigate his or her faults, while the child lives in the limbo of foster care, before the state may terminate a parent–child relationship, regardless of whether this makes sense in terms of the child's interests. And even after the rehabilitation efforts have been made, it is not sufficient that termination would be best for the child; the rights that the law now gives to parents require more.

Another characteristic our rights do not have is that our right to form a relationship with another competent adult who wishes to do so is not dependent on the approval of any other persons with whom either of us has a personal relationship, not even those with whom we are most intimate. No private individual has the legal power to override my choices as to with whom I will associate. My friends and family members certainly cannot thwart my decision to form a relationship with another person on the grounds that I am displeasing them, no matter how upset they are by my choice. I am entitled to associate with people whom my spouse, my parents, or my friends dislike. Nor is it relevant that my forming or maintaining a relationship with one person is inconvenient for another person with whom I have an established relationship, perhaps because I am less available to the other person or because the other person must rearrange his or her schedule to spend time with me.

Of course, those with whom one already has a close relationship have practical means of deterring one from forming certain new relationships. For example, a spouse might have means of nipping a new friendship in the bud. But calling the police is not one of them, nor is physical restraint. The most that spouses or other intimates can legally do is to threaten to terminate one's relationship with them, if one does not stop associating with the other person – something they are free to do at any time anyway, independently of one's making decisions that displease them. Contrast this state of affairs with the legal power of parents to complete control over a child's associations with third parties, a power parents are, for the most part, legally free to exercise arbitrarily and to serve their own interests and aims.

In sum, some of the characteristics that our rights in relationships with other competent adults do not have are that they do not include the power to force oneself on others who have not chosen to be in a relationship with one, that they are not limited by any right of others to an opportunity to make themselves more attractive, and that their exercise and effectiveness are not dependent on any third party's approval. Coupled with the findings above regarding the characteristics that our rights do have, these findings demonstrate that competent adults possess an exceedingly strong and extensive right to create the relational life that they deem best for themselves, a right legally limited only by the equal right of other adults. Apart from the mutuality requirement, our choices about our relationships – to form, to maintain, to avoid, and to end them – are absolutely effective and inviolable. Whatever we decide we want for ourselves, in terms of whether we will have a relationship with a willing other person or will not, we are entitled to. The state may not force us to do otherwise, and the state will assist us in preventing other persons from forcing their association on us.

D) Contrasting Adults' Rights with Children's Rights

This state of the law governing relationships between adults, as explained above, stands in sharp contrast to the state of the law governing children's relationships with adults. Of course, actual mutuality of choice is not possible with respect to very young children, so we should not expect the rules to be identical in the two situations. But as described in Chapter 2, the law governing most state decisions about children's relationships bears very little resemblance to the law governing adults' relationships among themselves, with little effort made to approximate the mutuality requirement or to maintain the broadest feasible scope for children's associations. In many contexts, certain adults are legally empowered to force their association on children, without actual consent by the children and without a finding of circumstances such that it is reasonable to assume the children would consent if they were able or, what might amount to the same thing, that it is in the children's best interests. Moreover, persons who stand in one particular kind of legal relationship to children – that is, custodial parents – are empowered to restrict children's associations with third persons even to extreme degrees and for the most part without being required to make decisions on the basis of what is best for a child. They can use this power to sever a child's connections with particular other persons even when those connections are valuable for the child, and they can use this power to reduce a child's relational world to an association with only themselves – that is, to monopolize a child's relational life, with the narrow exception of the potential for grandparents to insist on having contact with the child. Children have quite weak rights in connection with forming, maintaining, avoiding, and ending relationships relative to those enjoyed by competent adults.

Could it, practically, be otherwise? Is it feasible for the state to confer on children relationship rights equivalent, if not identical, to those enjoyed by adults? There would appear to be a strong presumption against believing so, because family law scholars and state child protective workers appear generally content with most existing legal rules, troubled more by problems of implementation than of design in the family law system. And the undeniable fact of children's lesser preparedness to make choices about their personal relationships provides, in the minds of many people, a ready explanation for any disjunction, however large, between the law pertaining to adults' rights in relationships among themselves and the law structuring children's relational lives.

However, the reality that some adults also have substandard competence creates the possibility for empirical testing of the implicit assumption that diminished capacity in one party to a relationship requires as a practical matter, or permits as a normative matter, a dramatically different legal approach to, and set of rules for, the relationship. In Part II, therefore, I examine the law governing the relational lives of incompetent adults.

II. The Relationship Rights of Incompetent Adults

The law governing the social lives of incompetent adults is illuminating for our purposes in two ways: First, it provides some sense of what is practically feasible with respect to according relationship rights to incompetent persons. Second, it suggests what the prevailing moral attitudes are as to what incompetent persons are owed as a matter of justice in intimate aspects of their lives. In both regards, it bears mention that law and attitudes relating to the mentally ill or disabled have undergone substantial change in the past several decades.[21] Thus, the description of current law and policy below should not be assumed reflective of the way western society has always treated such persons.

The category "incompetent adults" actually encompasses adults in a variety of circumstances. It includes those who have been mentally disabled their entire lives, those who have lost competence as a result of the mental degeneracy that often accompanies aging, those who have become incapacitated by trauma or drug abuse, those with serious mental illness, and others. However, the rules governing guardianship for these different groups, which are the rules of greatest relevance here, are largely the same for all. For guardianship purposes, the law defines incompetence in terms of adults' capacity to care for themselves and to make significant decisions about their lives. A common formulation in the United States, set forth in the Uniform Probate Code, defines incompetence as lacking "sufficient understanding or capacity to make or communicate responsible decisions,"[22] a definition that equally well captures the common understanding of what makes children incompetent.

Many of the decisions state institutions make about care for incompetent adults are analogous to decisions described in Chapter 2 in relation to children's lives. Appointment of a guardian for an incompetent adult is somewhat analogous to creation of a legal parent–child relationship; in both circumstances, the state selects someone to serve in a caretaking role with respect to an incompetent person and imbues the appointed caretaker with decision-making authority over certain aspects of the incompetent person's life.[23] The principal difference is that a guardian is not legally obligated to provide financial support for the ward, the person under the guardianship.[24] The guardian's role does entail substantial responsibilities, however, including ensuring that the ward has the resources and services necessary to meet his or her needs, which might entail an obligation to secure public assistance or to bring legal action to assert the rights of the ward.[25] And many guardians do voluntarily provide financial support for their wards.

A court's determination of the specific scope of a guardian's powers, including whether the guardian may assume physical custody over the incompetent adult and how much discretion the guardian has in directing the incompetent adult's daily life, is roughly analogous to a decision as to a child's custody and as to the extent of parental power over a child's associations with other persons. Decisions as to institutionalization of an incompetent adult are analogous to decisions to remove a child from the home into state custody for "dependency" reasons. And proceedings to terminate a guardianship resemble proceedings to terminate a parent–child relationship. Notably, with respect to most of the decisions for mentally incompetent adults, the state is viewed as acting principally or exclusively in a *parens patriae* role, as agent or ultimate caretaker for the incompetent individual.

The law is well established as to some of these decisions regarding incompetent adults, less so as to others. The associational rights of incompetent adults in particular have not received much attention from legislators and are rarely the subject of litigation.[26] The description below is therefore sketchy and tentative in parts. It should also be borne in mind that it is a description of the formal rules and not of actual practice and, as is true with many areas of law that undergo substantial transformation, actual practice might not yet have caught up with legal reform.

A) Creation of Guardian–Ward Relationships

Perhaps the most frequently disputed aspect of guardianship is when it should exist – that is, when an adult is incompetent – rather than who should occupy the role of guardian. Many petitions for guardianship are advanced against the wishes of the person who is to become a ward. The law affords such persons substantial due process rights and, as a substantive matter, generally requires a strong evidentiary showing that a person is not able to care for himself or herself adequately, such that appointment of a guardian is necessary and the least restrictive means to providing for the person's basic needs.[27] As one court explained, "whatever the extent of a guardianship, it inevitably entails a deprivation of liberty and is therefore a legal proceeding of constitutional dimensions which entitles any prospective incapacitated person to constitutional due process protections . . . and should not be commenced lightly or without substantial cause and basis."[28] It is not sufficient that a person is above a particular age, even if most people above that age are incompetent, nor is it sufficient that the person is relatively lacking in physical ability. The petitioner for appointment of a guardian must show that the particular person is incapable of rationally exercising the specific powers sought to be assigned to a guardian. In contrast, the legal system and society as a whole are comfortable with across-the-board legal dependency for persons below a certain age.

Once an adult is declared incompetent, the state must appoint a caretaker. Disputes as to who will serve as guardian are much less frequent than disputes over who will be a child's legal parents. This might be because the rewards of serving as a guardian for an incompetent adult are typically much less than those which parents typically derive from raising a child, and the burdens can be more onerous. In many families, when one member steps forward to care for an elderly parent or an incapacitated sibling, the others are quite happy to let that member shoulder the primary burden by becoming guardian. Disputes do occasionally arise, though, and legislatures have fashioned statutory rules for selecting a guardian among willing candidates.

Where persons, although competent, have properly executed a document specifying whom they would like to serve as guardian in the event of their incapacitation, the law respects that choice unless it presently appears that the specified person is unfit to serve as guardian.[29] The underlying assumption is that a now incompetent person was, at the time of prospectively designating a guardian, in the best position to determine who would be the best guardian for him or her. In most states, courts will also give some weight to preferences expressed by a person after becoming in need of a guardian, unless they find that the incompetent person has little or no understanding of what appointment of a guardian would mean.[30] In the absence of a determinative choice by the person to be placed under guardianship, however, courts must select a guardian themselves from among available persons, and then the decision is more comparable to the standard case of establishing a parent–child relationship.

Most jurisdictions authorize any person, any "interested" person, or any "proper" person to petition for guardianship of an incompetent adult.[31] Statutes commonly set forth a list of priority among potential guardians, typically putting spouses and parents at the top and other family members below in an order consistent with the closeness of typical family relationships.[32] Even in jurisdictions without such a list in their statutes, courts generally follow the same practice.[33] Notably, the family relationship the law recognizes is a legal relationship rather than a biological one; the parents and siblings given priority are the incompetent adult's legal parents and siblings, who are likely to be biological parents and siblings as well but might not be, if the incompetent person was adopted.[34] They are likely also to have a close pre-existing social relationship with the incompetent adult. The priority list reflects an assumption that close family relationship correlates with commitment to the welfare of the incompetent adult and an inclination to promote his or her rehabilitation or comfort.[35]

More importantly, guardianship statutes typically contain a threshold requirement that any potential guardian be "suitable" or a "qualified person."[36] In many jurisdictions, that standard goes unexplained, but New York statutes contain a list of considerations, including the existing social relationship between the potential guardian and the ward; the potential guardian's educational, professional, and business experience; and whether there is any conflict of interest between the potential guardian and the incompetent adult.[37] New York law characterizes this qualification threshold as a right of incompetent adults: "Each incompetent person is entitled to a guardian whom the court finds to be sufficiently capable of performing the duties and exercising the powers of a guardian necessary to protect the incapacitated person."[38] It also directs courts to appoint a "court evaluator" to investigate the proposed guardian, assessing that person's ability to meet the needs of the incompetent adult and the potential for a conflict of interest.[39] As among persons at the same level of priority, for example, two offspring of the incompetent adult, courts are to select the one "who is best able to manage the incompetent's estate and further his personal happiness."[40] In some jurisdictions, guardians must go through a special training program before they can assume the role.[41]

Most importantly, all appointments are subject to an ultimate best-interests standard, meaning that a court is supposed to disregard a statutory priority list if it would be in the incompetent adult's best interests to do so.[42] Ohio statutory law states, for example: "Notwithstanding any law as to priority of persons entitled to appointment . . . the court may appoint some other individual . . . if the court determines it is for the best interest of the ward."[43] Thus, in *In re Zdeb*, a New York court, applying a similar statutory provision in that state, rejected a woman's petition to serve as guardian for her father. The court found that the woman was not suitable to act as a guardian, based on her failure to develop an habilitation plan for him and her failure to cooperate with his health care providers.[44] In many other cases, courts have rejected requests that particular persons be appointed guardian upon finding a conflict of interest between the nominated persons and the incompetent adult.[45]

Thus, statutory priority lists are designed to serve merely as a guide to what is likely best for the incompetent adult or what the incompetent adult would most likely choose if able to do so. They create only a presumption, one that is overcome by a preponderance of evidence that another person would be a better caregiver. The ultimate and exclusive aim of the law is to place an incompetent adult in a relationship with the best available caregiver or with the caregiver it is assumed the incompetent adult would choose if able. It suggests a model of absolute rights for incompetent adults. It might be that in practice courts do not truly examine whether the presumptive guardian is better than all willing alternative candidates and instead conclude that appointment of the presumptive guardian is in the incompetent adult's "best interests" so long as there is no substantial problem posed by having that person as guardian. But ostensibly the rule requires selection of the best available person to serve in this role, and an appellate court should overturn the decision of a trial court if the evidence strongly suggested in a particular case that someone else would be better than the person preferred on the basis of statutory priorities or designation.

B) Determining Living Arrangements

The issue of where and with whom an incompetent adult will live breaks down into two questions: (1) Who has the legal power to decide where and with whom an incompetent adult shall live? (2) Are there any substantive restrictions on the exercise of that power?

With respect to the first question, the possible holders of decision-making power are the state, the guardian, and the incompetent adult himself or herself. A court establishing a guardianship would generally be required to limit the guardianship to those aspects of the ward's life as to which it is necessary, to protect the welfare of the ward or of other persons, to deny the ward autonomy and instead confer authority on a guardian.[46] Statutes generally require that guardianship be structured so as to constitute the "least restrictive form of intervention," meaning "that the guardianship imposed on the ward must compensate for only those limitations necessary to provide the needed care and services, and that the ward must enjoy the greatest amount of personal freedom and civil liberties consistent with the ward's mental and physical limitations."[47] This is true whether the ward was once fully competent and autonomous or instead has always been dependent.

Courts must therefore presume any adult, even one who has had a lifelong mental disability, competent with respect to each aspect of life, including place of residence, and require sufficient evidence of incompetence as to overcome the presumption with respect to any aspect of the person's life over which the court will extend the guardianship.[48] On that basis, the New Jersey Supreme Court held that an adult with mental retardation had a right to decide with which of her parents she would live, absent a showing by clear and convincing evidence that she was not competent to make that particular decision.[49]

Thus, if a guardianship were limited to control over financial affairs, the ward would retain the right to decide where and with whom he or she lives. Such a situation would resemble somewhat that of an adolescent, whose preferences for primary residence as between the homes of parents not living together is usually determinative, even though the adolescent does not have the rights and powers of an adult in other aspects of life, such as finances. There is some difference, though, in that the law in most western jurisdictions does not give adolescents an absolute right to make that decision but rather authorizes courts to override any minor's preferences as to custody based on judges' views of the minor's best interests. Minors acquire an absolute right to make that decision only upon emancipation, in which case their situation would be like that of a competent adult rather than like that of an adult under a limited guardianship or conservatorship.

If an adult is deemed incompetent to make decisions as to living arrangements specifically, or if the court establishes an unlimited guardianship of the person, the guardian will typically have all the same powers over the ward as a legal, custodial parent has over a minor child, including the authority to decide where and with whom the incompetent adult will live. New Jersey law provides, for example, that "[a]mong other powers and duties, the guardian is allowed to have custody of the mental incompetent's person, including establishing the incompetent's living space."[50] A guardian might choose not to have the ward live with him or her, but would have the power to decide among other available alternatives. In some cases, a court might make the decision as to residence itself and would typically do so using either a "substituted judgment" approach, under which it reasons about what the incompetent person likely would choose if competent to do so, relying on any known preferences or values of the ward while incompetent, or an objective determination of the ward's best interests.[51]

With respect to the second question, whether there are any constraints on a guardian's power to choose with whom a ward lives, the appointing court retains ultimate authority over the person of the incompetent adult and could override a guardian's choice of living arrangements for the ward if the court found the choice to be contrary to the best interests of the ward.[52] Guardians are typically required to file a periodic report with the court describing the ward's situation, including the suitability of the living arrangements.[53] On the basis of that report, a court might order a different living arrangement. Or a court might, after reviewing a report and finding the current living arrangement beneficial for the ward, prohibit a guardian from changing the ward's residence.[54]

In some states, there is more specific direction in guardianship laws as to residence. New York law authorizes guardians to choose a ward's place of abode but requires that any choice be made in light of "the existence of an availability of family, friends and social services in the community, the care, comfort and maintenance, and where appropriate, rehabilitation of the incapacitated person, [and] the needs of those with whom the incapacitated person resides."[55] It further provides that a guardian may not place a ward in a nursing home unless the ward consents or unless it is unreasonable under the circumstances for the ward to remain in a private residence.

C) Taking into State Custody

A state would assume physical custody of an incompetent person only when it is not feasible for that person to remain in the custody of any private party, which could eventuate either because the person's needs are too great for noninstitutional care or because there is no private party willing and able to care for the person. Included in the former category would be involuntary commitment of adults to mental health facilities, which has been the subject of great controversy in courts and legislatures. The principles that have emerged from activity in both categories are instructive.

In the United States, the Supreme Court has identified rights of incompetent adults against institutional commitments in federal constitutional and statutory law. In 1975, the court established that a "wholly sane and innocent person has a constitutional right not to be confined by the state when his freedom will pose a danger neither to himself nor to others."[56] More recently, the Court ruled that the federal Americans with Disabilities Act confers on mentally disabled persons a limited right to community-based treatment and the greatest possible integration with nondisabled persons.[57] When persons must be committed to an institution, they are entitled to "reasonably nonrestrictive confinement conditions," commensurate with the purposes of the confinement.[58] And a person involuntarily committed has a right to be released when the standard for involuntary commitment is no longer satisfied.[59]

As a result of such decisions of the Supreme Court and of lower federal and state courts,[60] and as a result of legislative initiative, the law in the United States has, after a long history of easy and unwarranted institutionalization of mentally disabled or mentally ill adults, come around to recognizing that respecting the dignity of such persons requires ensuring them the least restrictive living environment consistent with their welfare and with the safety of others and respecting their interest in remaining in their home once it is established.[61] There is today a strong presumption in favor of individuals remaining in a home setting and maintaining established relationships, and there are strong procedural protections for

persons who are the subjects of institutionalization petitions.[62] As the
Pennsylvania Supreme Court has stated, the law today commands that
incompetent adults "have the right to live a life as close as possible to that
which is typical for the general population."[63] The same principle applies
throughout the common-law world today, as other nations have gone
through a similar historical progression from the state largely disregard-
ing the needs of the mentally ill and disabled to mass institutionalization
to community care.[64]

Of greatest relevance to the comparison with the situation of children
are situations where state "adult protective services" workers remove an
incompetent adult from the custody of a guardian because of perceived
abuse or neglect by the guardian. When the state does seek to remove
an incompetent person from the custody of a private party and assume
custody itself over that person, it must comply with legal standards both
for limiting the powers of the guardian and for assuming custody itself.
Significantly, when a petition for involuntary removal is brought, there is
no question of rehabilitating an abusive or neglectful guardian; as discussed
below, if the fact of malfeasance is shown, the guardianship is terminated.
And where it is possible for the incompetent adult to remain safely in
a private residence, which might be true only after the state imposes a
protective order on the abusive guardian, there is no question of the state
assuming custody of the incompetent adult.

D) Termination of Guardianship

A person appointed guardian for an incompetent adult might be removed
from that role for several reasons. First, the adult might regain competence.
He or she would have the right to petition for removal of the guardian.[65]
The proceeding would be somewhat analogous to emancipation of a
minor, except that emancipation does not terminate a legal parent–child
relationship but rather only removes a minor's legal disabilities.

Second, the guardian might wish to be relieved of the guardianship
responsibility. This is analogous to voluntary termination of parental
rights, and the rules for the two cases are similar. As shown in Chapter 2, parents can generally exit the parent–child relationship at will and
with impunity. Analogously, guardians for incompetent adults may resign
from that role at any time.[66]

Third, and most pertinently, a court can remove a guardian involuntarily where the guardian has not adequately fulfilled the duties of the
guardianship. This would be analogous to involuntary termination of

parental rights. This rarely occurs, but the law of every U.S. jurisdiction provides for it.[67] New York law states: "Upon motion, the court appointing a guardian may remove such guardian when the guardian fails to comply with an order, is guilty of misconduct, or for any other cause which to the court shall appear just." Statutes typically authorize a designated public official or any person acting in behalf of an incompetent adult's welfare to petition for removal of a guardian.[68] Significantly, most direct courts to apply simply a best-interests standard in adjudicating a petition for removal.[69] Abusive or neglectful guardians are not entitled to rehabilitative services before being removed.

E) The Guardian's Power over Other Associations

Last, there is the question of what rights incompetent adults have to develop or continue associations with family members, friends, and acquaintances who are not their guardians. As noted in Section IIB, the law generally requires that the authority of a guardian be strictly limited to those aspects of an incompetent adult's life as to which that adult is incapable of making rational decisions and the incapacity would likely result in harm to the adult or others if the adult retained control. As a New York court explained, modern mental health laws are based on "the concept of the least restrictive alternative – one that authorizes the appointment of a guardian whose authority is appropriate to satisfy the needs of an incapacitated person, either personal or financial, while at the same time tailored and limited to only those activities for which a person needs assistance."[70] Absent such need, there is no moral justification for giving someone else power over a particular aspect of a person's life. Institutions in which incompetent adults are residents are likewise required to limit their restrictions on patients' self-determination to only those necessary to the habilitation plan for the patient and to the safety of others.[71] Thus, there is a legal presumption that adults under a guardianship will make their own decisions as to with whom they will associate in addition to their guardians.

To overcome the presumption in favor of self-determination, someone seeking control over any aspect of an allegedly incompetent adult person's life must show that that person is likely to make decisions harmful to himself; it would not be sufficient to show that the person was simply impulsive or irrational.[72] Thus, if an adult becomes unable to manage complex financial matters but is still able to express reasonable preferences about with whom she socializes, the law requires that the adult retain power over her social life and that the guardian's or institution's powers not include the authority to restrict the ward's social interactions with persons of her choosing. This is so even though the choices of the person under a guardianship might be viewed as unwise by the guardian or might create some inconvenience for the guardian or institution, in terms of having to allow others access to the ward or arranging time to meet with the ward.

When a guardianship does extend to control over all of an incompetent adult's daily activities, including social interactions, does the law empower guardians to cut off a ward's relationships with particular other persons or with all persons? This, too, is an issue as to which the law is undeveloped, suggesting that it is not nearly as controversial as is the issue of third-party visitation with children. As noted above, many state statutes declare that a person serving in an unlimited guardianship has all the same powers as the parent of a minor child, which would suggest that guardians have the same plenary power to restrict their wards' social life. If nothing else, the power to determine where one's ward lives can certainly have a great effect on the ward's relationships with others. In addition, some states' laws explicitly empower guardians of the person to make decisions regarding a ward's "social environment."[73]

Conversely, guardianship law also generally requires that any guardianship operate pursuant to a plan of habilitation, the overriding aim of which is to assist the ward in regaining or developing for the first time the ability to manage each aspect of his or her life – in other words, to promote and preserve the ward's autonomy to the greatest extent possible.[74] Oregon law, for example, states that a "guardianship for an adult person must be designed to encourage the development of maximum self-reliance and independence of the protected person."[75] New York law more directly commands guardians to "afford the incapacitated person the greatest amount of independence and self-determination," restricted only to the extent necessitated by the ward's functional limitations.[76] These are more explicit statements than one finds in the parent–child context of a caretaker's legal responsibility to facilitate advancement toward independence, which would certainly entail giving the person under care opportunities for deciding such matters as with whom they interact.

Moreover, guardians are understood to operate in a fiduciary role, with a legal obligation to act in the best interests of the ward, and not to use the powers of the guardianship in a self-serving way.[77] New York law states that "a Guardian shall exercise the utmost care and diligence when acting on behalf of the incapacitated person" and "shall exhibit the utmost degree of trust, loyalty, and fidelity in relation to the incapacitated person."[78] Guardians operate under the ultimate authority of, and subject to the direction of, the appointing court.[79] A court could therefore override a guardian's decision concerning social interactions if the decision were brought to its attention and found to be contrary to the ward's best interest. As noted above, guardians are required to make periodic reports to a court of their activities and of their wards' welfare. These reports typically must include a description of the ward's social needs and whether and how they are being met.[80]

Though this is not an issue that has been the subject of much litigation, relevant court decisions can be found if one looks back far enough. For example, in 1949, the Michigan Supreme Court held, in *Holland v. Miller*,[81] that a guardian could not prevent his ninety-year-old ward's great grandson and the grandson's wife from coming into the ward's home to share meals with her. The court found that the elderly woman felt kindly toward these visitors and enjoyed their company and that was sufficient to override the objections of the guardian.

Further, most states have enacted "patients' rights" statutes that limit the restrictions institutions may impose on the activities of incompetent adults.[82] At the most general level, they entitle patients to the least restrictive environment consistent with their treatment.[83] They also guarantee institutionalized persons a right of "privacy,"[84] which could be interpreted to include a right to spend time alone with family members and friends of the patients' choosing. Minnesota statutes, for example, provide: "Patients and residents shall have the right to every consideration of their privacy, individuality, and cultural identity as related to their social, religious, and psychological well-being."[85]

More specifically, laws in most jurisdictions bestow on institutionalized incompetent adults a right of association, visitation, and communication with whomever they choose.[86] Michigan law, for example, requires all licensed health facilities and agencies to adopt and inform patients of a policy of patients' rights that includes the statement:

> A patient or resident is entitled to associate and have private communications and consultations with his or her physician, attorney, or any other person of his or her choice and to send and receive personal mail unopened on the same day it is received at the health facility or agency, unless medically contraindicated as documented by the attending physician in the medical record. A patient's or resident's civil and religious liberties, including the right to independent personal decision and the right to know of available choices, shall not be infringed and the facility shall encourage and assist in the fullest possible exercise of these rights. A patient or resident may meet with, and participate in, the activities of social, religious, and community groups at his or her discretion, unless medically contraindicated.[87]

Several lower courts in the United States have held that such a right is constitutionally mandated.[88] In holding that the Americans with Disabilities Act confers on mentally disabled persons a right to community-based treatment to the extent possible and the greatest possible integration with nondisabled persons, the United States Supreme Court cited the importance of family and social life for all persons. "Unjustified isolation," the Court concluded, "is properly regarded as discrimination based on disability."[89] In a handful of states, the established rights of institutionalized adults include a right to interact with members of the opposite sex.[90] The administrators of a facility can suspend these more specific rights for short periods, but only where necessary for safety or medical reasons, and guardians have no power to restrict their wards' social life in institutions.[91] Statutes in a few states also make explicit that the right to control one's own social interactions includes a right to refuse visitation with particular persons.[92]

A clinical issue relevant to social interaction is use of seclusion with a patient in a psychiatric facility. Whereas it was once common for staff to use these very freely, for their own convenience or to punish a patient for misbehavior as well as for supposed therapeutic or safety purposes, the law today prohibits use of seclusion except where necessary to ensure the physical safety of patients or staff.[93] Thus, a mentally incompetent person who wishes to interact with other patients cannot be prevented from doing so simply because a staff member, guardian, or family member wants to restrict the person's interactions.

Less commonly, states have statutory provisions conferring rights of visitation and communication upon incompetent adults who are not in institutions and who might be living with their guardians.[94] In some states, the class of persons who may petition for an order of visitation under one of these statutory provisions might be very limited – for example, to parents only.[95] In others, it is broader, including any family members[96] or anyone of the ward's choosing. Courts are to resolve such requests for a visitation order on the basis of the best interests of the incompetent adult.[97] These laws are much like the third-party visitation laws for children in the United States, at least prior to the Supreme Court's *Troxel* decision. In addition, some courts have held that noninstitutionalized persons have a right to refuse visitation with particular other persons, including family members, for any reason, [98] a right that children do not have. More generally, there is the limitation on private guardians' power precluding them from restricting the activities or interfering with the choices of adult wards except to the extent necessary to ensure that the wards' basic needs are satisfied.[99]

One aspect of the law relating to incompetent adults that is without parallel in the law governing children's relationships involves termination of an incompetent adult's marriage. As a general rule, if guardianship only covers financial matters and does not extend to power over personal life, the ward would have the same power as a fully competent adult to petition in his or her own behalf for divorce.[100] Where a guardianship is plenary, a guardian generally has the power to acquiesce to a divorce petition by the ward's spouse.[101] States are divided, however, over the question whether a guardian of the person has the power to initiate divorce proceedings on behalf of the ward. Until recently, the majority position was that guardians do not have that power. Courts holding to that effect reason that a divorce action "is so personal and volitional that only a party to the marriage may bring such an action."[102] They also recognize the danger of guardians who are members of the ward's original family seeking divorce to enhance the inheritance of family members.[103] The current trend, though, is in favor of holding that the guardian does have the power.[104] Courts holding to that effect reason that a contrary rule would create an inequity as between spouses with respect to power over continuation of the marriage, creating a potential for abuse.[105] They generally require evidence that the ward currently wishes to seek a divorce and/or that before becoming incompetent the ward indicated a desire to exit the marriage, though some have indicated that it would be sufficient, and perhaps necessary as well, to demonstrate that divorce would be in the best interests of the ward – for example, where a spouse had become abusive toward the incompetent person.[106]

Conclusion

Reference to legal rules pertaining to incompetent adults here is only suggestive of an alternative way of treating children. There might well be significant factual distinctions between the situation of incompetent adults and the situation of children that justifies treating the two groups differently. For example, it might be that the nature of incompetence in adults is such that the law should embody a presumption of their being competent, whereas the nature of children's incompetence is such that the law should operate on the basis of a presumption of incompetence, and the different presumptions might warrant different legal rules. Or it might be that differences in the responsibilities of parents relative to those of guardians justify a difference in the rights and powers each holds. The analysis of subsequent chapters will address these possibilities.

If the rules governing incompetent adults do present a model for treatment of persons of lesser competence, though, they suggest that an appropriate set of laws would be much more protective of the desires and interests of dependent persons in connection with their intimate associations than is the law governing children's relationships today. Under such laws, caretakers for children would be assigned on the basis of certain presumptions favoring those with a "natural" connection to a child, but those presumptions would be rebuttable on the basis of a showing that the child's welfare requires that another person care for him or her. The state would examine potential caregivers to ensure at least minimal preparedness to provide good care and might require some training for the role before appointment. Caregivers would have presumptive authority to determine the child's residence, but would be legally required to choose a suitable residence with adequate opportunity for socializing. Where courts needed to make a decision as to residence, their decisions would be focused only the child – his or her preferences and/or interests. If a caregiver were abusive or delinquent in caring for a child, he or she could be removed based simply on a court's finding that it is in the child's best interests, and the child would have a right to remain in a private home and not be taken into state custody, if this is feasible and best for the child.

Finally, the child would have a presumptive right to choose with which third parties he or she would associate, a right that a guardian could overcome only by showing that the child's choice would likely result in harm. In situations where the child had not made a choice, perhaps because unable to do so, at least some specified third parties would be able to petition for an order of visitation, and courts would grant or deny those petitions based on a determination of the child's best interests. In all contexts, the parent would not be viewed as a right-holder, as someone entitled to control the child's life, but rather as someone who holds some degree of authority – the least amount necessary to serve the child's welfare – as a matter of legal privilege, because and only because this is conducive to the child's well-being.

4 Why Adults Have the Relationship Rights They Do

W hy do we competent adults have the powerful legal relationship rights described in Chapter 3? Why does the state not limit to a greater extent our freedom to enter into and get out of personal relationships – whether friendships, association with our parents or siblings, or intimate partnerships? Why are other people not permitted to force their association upon us? Why do we not have state-arranged marriages and state-arranged relationships of every other sort? Or why are other private citizens not empowered to decide with whom we may or must have relationships?

Answering these questions leads us into the moral justifications for rights to freedom in general as well as into special justifications for the particular right to freedom of intimate association. To some degree, a right against interference with our chosen personal associations is a derivative right, one specific extension of the core general right against interference with pursuit of our chosen aims. But there are also reasons for according a right of freedom of intimate association that are particular to that aspect of human life. The more prominent traditions in modern political philosophy have had much to say about freedom in general, but not so much about freedom of intimate association in particular, so developing a solid understanding of the normative foundation of that particular freedom requires some extension of existing arguments into a new realm.

In this chapter, I identify and examine two prominent strains in modern political thought – those reposing ultimate moral value, respectively, in welfare or in autonomy – to uncover what might be the most widely endorsed normative bases for the rights we adults enjoy in connection with our personal relationships. There are many ways one could divide up the universe of moral beliefs and political theories. I have chosen to do it on the basis of ultimate values in this way because this approach fits well with the basic tenet of modern liberalism that the legitimacy of political principles and practices depends on their being justifiable in terms of shared values. As John Tomasi explains:

> The ambition underlying all versions of liberalism has long been to define the common good of political association in terms of a minimal moral conception – that is, a basic value or set of values that most citizens share despite even their many important differences. Political principles are neutral – and thus satisfy the liberal principle of legitimacy – insofar as they can be justified by reference to such shared values .... [1]

Legitimacy does not require that political principles rest on a single value that all share, but rather can rest on a convergence of views among people who hold different values most dear – an "overlapping consensus" of sorts. The aim of this chapter and the next is to determine whether there ought to be a convergence around some conception of the rights of children in connection with state decision making about their relationships among people who assign highest value to human welfare or autonomy as a political value or aim of the state. To do that, I look to what political theorists have found to be the implications of those values or aims for the association rights of adults, and then reason about whether those implications can be extended in some way to children.

Invoking the values of welfare and autonomy is consistent with the sort of explanations most people in western society might be expected to give for why competent adults have the liberties they do. Most would likely state that these liberties are instrumental to our pursuit of happiness and/or that we have these liberties because our lives are our own to live by our own lights. And many of the political theories that have been most influential in the modern era can usefully be viewed as elaborations of these basic ideas, taking one of these ultimate moral values as their starting points.[2] To be clear, I do not assert to be true in an absolute or foundational sense that happiness or autonomy is or should be viewed as the ultimate moral or political value; my ambition is just to determine whether, from an outlook that does give primacy to one of these values, one should also ascribe certain rights to children. My project is an exercise in coherence theory, one that begins only with certain widely shared political values and some not-particularly-controversial accounts of how those values translate into individual rights, and aims only to show what implications those values so understood might have for the rights of children, so it is not necessary for my purposes to enter into debates between rival foundational theories.

I. A Welfare-Based Account of Freedom of Intimate Association

Among the most influential philosophical arguments for freedom in general have been consequentialist ones – that is, arguments of the sort that individual liberty produces good consequences. And the most important of these have been utilitarian arguments of the sort that John Stuart Mill presented in his 1859 work *On Liberty*, which later philosophers have refined and expanded. These arguments will be already familiar to some readers, but I draw out some generally overlooked assumptions in them, and many other readers will not be familiar with the arguments, so it is worth rehearsing them.

As a political morality, utilitarianism directs the state to produce the greatest possible welfare for the members of a society, subject to the constraint that every person is of equal moral worth and, therefore, that the state must have equal solicitude for every person's interests.[3] This is consistent with expression in many nations' foundational documents of the essential aim of the state, to promote the well-being of all its citizens. For political theorists operating within this tradition, then, the ultimate political value is the welfare of human beings, which is usually understood to mean their happiness, maximizing their pleasures and minimizing their pains, or satisfying their desires. From the fundamental aim of advancing this value, Mill derived the principle that the state should interfere with the self-determining freedom of individuals only to prevent them from harming others, where "harm" is understood as unjustified injury. The state should not deny individuals freedom to prevent them from merely offending others, injuring themselves, or doing things that are not harmful to others but that some view as nevertheless immoral. "Over himself, over his own body and mind," Mill wrote, "the individual is sovereign. . . . The sole end for which mankind are warranted, individually or collectively, in interfering with the liberty of action of any of their number is self-protection."[4] The U.S. Supreme Court's decision in *Lawrence v. Texas*, holding antisodomy laws unconstitutional, can be read as adopting the Millian "harm principle" as a basic principle of constitutional rights jurisprudence.

Utilitarian arguments for this principle of liberty have focused principally on freedom of thought, expression, and religious practice, though sexual activity has also received much attention in recent decades. Certainly no utilitarian today would deny, however, that "private" social life is a principal site for humans' pursuit of happiness. Mill himself included in the list of liberties that an enlightened society should guarantee its members freedom of association – "the liberty . . . of combination among individuals; freedom to unite for any purpose not involving harm to others"[5] – and he referred in several places to freedom in social, and specifically family, life, including a right to refuse association with any person of whom one has an unfavorable opinion, a right of women to self-determination within marriage, and a right to greater freedom to exit marriage than existed at the time.[6]

Among the arguments utilitarians have advanced to show that this principle of liberty is most conducive to human welfare are some that focus on benefits specific to the liberty-possessing individual and some that go to more diffuse benefits that individual liberty generates for society as a whole. The primary and most compelling welfare-based justification for self-determining freedom is simply that persons are generally in the best position to make decisions about their own lives that are most likely to advance their welfare.[7] This is true because each is most strongly concerned for his or her own interests, each has more immediate access to his or her own experience and therefore presumptively better information about his or her interests, and each has unique tastes and dispositions. This contention does not presuppose that any people are perfect decision makers in matters central to their lives, but simply that competent adults are usually more accurate judges of their own interests than anyone else would be and that there is no practicable means of advancing human welfare superior to a universal right of self-determination.[8]

Importantly, implicit in this first utilitarian justification for liberty must also be two further assumptions: first, that people are generally disposed to make decisions about their lives so as to maximize their own welfare,[9] and second, that in matters essentially concerning one's own life, one's own interests are generally weightier than the interests of other persons, so weighty in most cases that they outweigh the interests that all other persons have in connection with how one's life goes. Without these assumptions, the case for individual liberty collapses. Mill and other utilitarians take for granted that the greatest interests at stake in connection with most questions relating to freedom of thought and expression – to freedom of religion, to freedom in use of one's own property, and to freedom in interacting socially with others – are those of the individual who is thinking, expressing, practicing a religion, using his own property, or choosing to associate with others. (With respect to the last of these, of course, there is at least one other person whose self-determination is at issue and whose interests are therefore of equal importance.) Absent conduct that inflicts injury on others, others' interests in one's self-determining activities are presumptively weaker than one's own interests. And utilitarians take for granted that people generally aim, above all else, to advance what they believe to be their own best interests.

Neither of these things is always the case. People sometimes act with the primary conscious intention of aiding others. And sometimes our exercise of our liberties is of trivial importance to us but of great concern to others. For instance, with respect to the right to freedom of speech, whether we make a particular statement at a particular time – for example, a compliment or a word of gratitude – might be a matter of no consequence to us but of great subjective importance to someone else. However, even in acting altruistically we experience some gratification, and most people do not sacrifice their self-regarding interests to a great degree for the sake of others. And it is presumed to be usually the case that one's self-expression and one's career, religion, lifestyle, and so on, impact one's own interests more than anyone else's interests, and it would be too costly administratively to try to limit our self-determining liberties to those situations in which our own interests are in fact the weightiest. If it were not the case that one's own interests in relation to direction of one's own life are generally weightier than the interests of others, then self-determination would be unlikely or much less likely to maximize aggregate welfare. A utilitarian approach, insofar as it commands policies that advance collective human welfare, therefore supports a moral focus on the interests of the individual whose person, property, and associations are at issue and attribution of choice-protecting rights to that person.

Of course, in many human interactions more than one person's self-determination is at issue, so with respect to any individual there might in fact be others whose interests at stake are of equal importance. For example, when two persons enter into a business partnership, both might have their entire livelihood at stake. Any number of people might want to use for speaking to the public a forum that can only accommodate a limited number of speakers. In such situations, a utilitarian outlook, based in part on an assumption of equal moral standing, leads to attribution of rights to more than one person and requires simply that the rights of each be diminished to whatever extent is necessary to allow for all to have equal rights. Thus, a business contract equally binds all parties to the terms on which they agreed, as well as protecting their interests. In access to limited resources for furtherance of life plans, such as a public forum, the law should either give all an equal share or give all an equal chance in a lottery for a share.

Applying this reasoning to the case of relationships, we would say that the best justification for our having plenary rights to choose our relationships is that a rule conferring those rights leads to more welfare-promoting decisions than would any alternative rule. Each of us competent adults is presumed to be in the best position to know which relationships are most conducive to our own well-being. And in fact, we typically make an assessment, consciously or unconsciously, before forming a relationship with someone, of whether the relationship would be worthwhile for us, taking into account the potential benefits and costs, including the opportunity costs if we would have to forego a relationship with a different person as a result. Likewise, when deciding whether to end a personal relationship, we take stock of whether the relationship is sufficiently rewarding to us and often of whether some alternative relationship would make us happier or be more beneficial to us in some other sense.[10] Another way to express this is to say that in each case, we determine whether a relationship is in our best interests. Again, this is not to say that we are always fully rational and well-informed in making these decisions. And it is also not to say that our interests are limited to selfish or pecuniary ones; our interests sometimes include satisfaction of altruistic desires. The assumption is simply that most of the time we make decisions about our personal relationships with the aim of advancing our own happiness and well-being on the whole, that no one else could do so across the board as well as we ourselves can, and that it would not serve individual or collective welfare for the state to attempt to determine when we are the best judges of our own welfare and when we are not.

There is here, as in other realms of life, the problem of conflicting choices. Person A might want a relationship with Person B, whereas Person B wants nothing to do with Person A. Such a conflict requires some limitation of the right of each, so that each has an equal but less than complete right of choice in relationships. The accommodation the law has reached, as described in Chapter 3, is to limit every adult's right to have a relationship with another adult to those situations where the desire to have the relationship is mutual or, in other words, to exclude from everyone's rights a right to a relationship with a person who wishes not to have the relationship. This makes sense on utilitarian grounds for at least two reasons. First, where one person opposes the relationship, it is unlikely to be rewarding for either person. We might even say that a person who still desires a relationship after being rejected is presumptively being irrational; this sort of situation might mark a common exception to the assumption that each person is the best judge of his or her own interests. Most of the time, though, people whose initial interest in forming a relationship with another goes unreciprocated cease to desire such a relationship. Second, being forced into an unwanted association would, in most situations, constitute a greater threat to a person's welfare than does an inability to form or maintain a relationship with someone who does not want the relationship. In other words, the cost to the unwilling person would outweigh the gain for the willing person. This might be so principally because the former experience limits one's other opportunities more so than does the latter experience. A person forced into an association loses whatever time must be spent with the other person, whereas a person refused an association remains as free as he or she was before to pursue other relationships or other interests.

A second welfare-based justification for individual liberty is that being in control of one's own life is valuable to human welfare independently of the wisdom of particular choices made. People who experience self-determination typically value it highly. They derive important gratification from feeling master and author of their lives and from seeing themselves as unique individuals about whom particularized decisions must be made. They also derive pleasure from exercising their higher faculties, their moral and rational capacities, in making decisions about and shaping their lives.[11] It is also important to our self-esteem, to our sense of our value and competence, that we be deemed worthy and capable of directing our own lives.[12] Thus, there are several connections between a welfare-based political morality and the value of autonomy. Within a utilitarian outlook, autonomy is of instrumental value, subsidiary to the aim of increasing human happiness, pleasure, or satisfaction.

Possession and exercise of liberty is also personally valuable, even when one is not the best judge of one's own interests, because persons learn and develop as human beings, and therefore become better at advancing their interests, from making free choices and dealing with the consequences.[13] We become more capable of making choices conducive to our welfare by applying whatever wisdom and rationality we have at a particular moment in time to choices that confront us and then seeing what happens, whether we are happier or better off as a result. Through trial and error we advance in self-understanding, in our understanding of the world, and in the strength of our powers of reasoning and of anticipating consequences.

Notably, this aspect of the argument, based on the personal development that liberty allows, also implicitly depends on the assumption, discussed above, that in matters fundamentally affecting one's own life, one's own interests are of greatest importance. It is valuable for us to become autonomous, from a utilitarian perspective, principally because we will then have superior competence in directing our lives so as to maximize our welfare, and that in turn is important principally because our own interests are weightier than those of anyone else in connection with the course of our own lives. Thus, the value of developing our capacities for rational decision making is in utilitarian thinking primarily instrumental or indirect, though there is also what might be termed inherent or direct value as well – namely the gratification we experience from awareness that we are growing as persons and becoming more mature and capable.

These arguments for the welfare value of liberty independent of the wisdom of particular choices assume that the benefits of experiencing autonomy and developing one's rational capacities outweigh any loss of welfare arising from making particular decisions less well than some other decision maker would. Applying this justification to relationship rights, we can explain why we have rights to choose even in those cases when we do not act rationally. It is better for each of us, and to that extent also for the collective welfare of our society, that we have the right to make those choices, because we will experience the satisfaction of being the author of our own life stories and because we will learn about ourselves and develop our capacity for choosing good relationships in the process. We feel more comfortable in pursuing relationships knowing that they will develop and continue only so long as they "work" for us, and after some false starts we experience the satisfaction of greater maturity and greater insight into ourselves and others.

One might add that we also usually derive satisfaction from being freely chosen for relationships. Others' freedom of intimate association thus generates benefits for us as well. Indeed, it might be prerequisite to a healthy sense of self-respect that we believe others regard us positively and want us to be part of their lives, and that might not be possible if others were compelled to associate with us. (Others' freedom can also generate costs for us, of course, when it results in rejection or when we are chosen even though we would prefer not to be.) The most important aim, though, is having good relationships with other human beings, relationships in which individuals mutually satisfy human needs for love, concern, respect, support, self-expression, physical affection, and other things.

These welfarist arguments for liberty based on the benefits to persons individually thus suggest that the state should aim to create social conditions in which decisions about individuals' lives are made by those most competent to determine the individuals' best interests, and in which individuals can achieve a "good life," in the sense of becoming, through exercise of freedom and by learning from trial and error, respected masters and authors of their own lives with well-developed higher faculties. In addition to these individually focused arguments, there are welfare-based arguments that go to more diffuse benefits, for society as a whole.

One such argument is that individual liberty is conducive to experiments in living and therefore to social progress.[14] Freedom produces novelty and diversity, thus enhancing the ability of individuals to formulate and pursue life plans that best advance their unique interests and give them the most satisfaction, by presenting them with more models and opportunities. Another is that substantial dangers inhere in the state's directing people's lives – namely that the state will thereby become too powerful and private citizens will become too dependent and enfeebled.[15] Individual liberty in choosing personal associations can again be seen as one type of liberty that serves these aims for the welfare of individuals and of society as a whole. The freedom we adults have to associate freely with one another creates varied opportunities for creative, productive, and rewarding inter-actions. The alternative of the state choosing our personal relationships for us is frightening for a number of reasons, including the likelihood that less diversity of arrangements would exist, the likelihood that state actors would abuse their power to serve their own ends or the ends of other private individuals, and the likelihood that our individual decision-making capacities would atrophy. Here, too, though, the ultimate aim is to promote individuals' ability to make choices for themselves, on the assumption that in connection with basic aspects of any individual's life, such as personal associations, the individual himself or herself has the most at stake.

In addition to resting on these justifications for liberty in general, freedom of intimate association is generally regarded as having special importance among personal liberties in humans' pursuit of happiness. There is universal agreement that interpersonal relationships are central to human well-being. Mill referred to "the case of the family relations" as "a case, in its direct influence on human happiness, more important than all others taken together."[16] Empirical accounts of the value of family life for individuals and society bolster this view and help to fill out the utilitarian account of liberty in its application specifically to intimate association.

Kenneth Karst identifies four categories of goods that intimate association provides: enjoying the society of other persons, giving and receiving caring and commitment, enjoying closeness, and forming one's identity. Colin Macleod presents a similar list. The family is a source of value, Macleod explains, insofar as it presents the opportunity for "close, loving relationships characterized by both mutual concern and participation in shared activities and projects," as well as by affection; "allows for efficient recognition and response to the particular needs of particular individuals," including but not limited to basic welfare needs such as food, shelter, clothing, and education; and provides "a tangible sense of identity," by "locating [family members] in a distinct family history and ongoing participation in practices identified as valuable by the family," which identity and source of value in turn supply "a context of choice from which individuals can deliberate about the merits of different conceptions of the good." Macleod additionally notes the developmental benefits that families provide to children and the role of family life in "the maintenance and social reproduction of distinctive and valuable cultures and their traditions."[17]

The U.S. Supreme Court has noted similar instrumental and intrinsic forms of value arising from intimate associations. In explaining the different levels of constitutional protection given to different forms of association, the Court stated in *Roberts v. United States Jaycees*:

> [B]ecause the Bill of Rights is designed to secure individual liberty, it must afford the formation and preservation of certain kinds of highly personal relationships a substantial measure of sanctuary from unjustified interference by the State. Without precisely identifying every consideration that may underlie this type of constitutional protection, we have noted that certain kinds of personal bonds have played a critical role in the culture and traditions of the Nation by cultivating and transmitting shared ideals and beliefs; they thereby foster diversity and act as critical buffers between the individual and the power of the State. Moreover, the constitutional shelter afforded such relationships reflects the realization that individuals draw much of their emotional enrichment from close ties with others. Protecting these relationships from unwarranted state interference therefore safeguards the ability independently to define one's identity that is central to any concept of liberty. . . . Family relationships, by their nature, involve deep attachments and commitments to the necessarily few other individuals with whom one shares not only a special community of thoughts, experiences, and beliefs but also distinctively personal aspects of one's life. Among other things, therefore, they are distinguished by such attributes as relative smallness, a high degree of selectivity in decisions to begin and maintain the affiliation, and seclusion from others in critical aspects of the relationship. As a general matter, only relationships with these sorts of qualities are likely to reflect the considerations that have led to an understanding of freedom of association as an intrinsic element of personal liberty. Conversely, an association lacking these qualities – such as a large business enterprise – seems remote from the concerns giving rise to this constitutional protection. Accordingly, the Constitution undoubtedly imposes constraints on the State's power to control the selection of one's spouse that would not apply to regulations affecting the choice of one's fellow employees.[18]

Research psychologist Paul Wright likewise emphasizes the ways in which personal relationships differ from impersonal ones. He writes that "a personal relationship is one in which the participants express a personalized interest in and concern for one another," rather than seeing each other "as replaceable by other persons." Thus, "each participant responds to the other as a person-qua-person – that is, as a unique individual rather than a mere role occupant."[19] This type of recognition of ourselves by others in personal relationships makes us feel special and important, gives us a sense of self-worth and individuality. It is self-affirming, provides ego support, allowing us to see ourselves as competent and worthwhile. Research subjects reported that their personal relationships "made them feel important, wanted, needed, accepted, connected, part of something bigger than themselves, more than just anonymous cogs."[20] In addition, the experience of loving and ascribing special value to another person generates utility for the loving person, because love is an inherently pleasurable emotion, because loving another is a form of self-expression, and because it enhances our sense of self-worth to see ourselves as loving persons.[21] Last, personal relationships typically provide some kinds of benefits that impersonal relationships also provide, such as stimulation, opportunities for play, intellectual challenge, and material assistance.[22]

These accounts make clear that intimate associations are particularly vital to our emotional and psychological well-being. Legislative bodies and courts throughout the western world have recognized this in affording constitutional protection to family relationships.[23] There is no ready substitute for the family in provision of essential affective goods; where private sources are lacking, a state agency can provide food, shelter, clothing, and some forms of education, but not loving concern, values, and identity. Macleod notes that the affective goods depend on the partiality that characterizes family relationships and that this "helps to explain why the family can merit its status as a specially protected sphere of interaction."[24] Without a solid foundation of interconnectedness with persons who love and value us in a special way, we cannot feel secure and valuable, pursue our life projects effectively, achieve a sense of fulfillment, or enjoy material, intellectual, and artistic goods as fully.

Significantly, though, these benefits do not derive exclusively from core family relationships; those are simply the personal relationships on which most theorists and most researchers focus. Barry McCarthy emphasizes that less intimate relationships, such as friendships, also provide important benefits to individuals, including many of the benefits that family relationships provide, such as a sense of individuality and self-worth, emotional security, ego support, stimulation, opportunity for self-expression, affection, and resources.[25] They might simply do so in a less intense, or just different, way. And when core relationships fail, these more peripheral relationships serve as a backup and partial substitute for the core relationships, coming to assume a more central role in persons' lives.

This empirical account best connects with the first two welfare-based justifications for liberty, supporting the implicit premise that in connection with central aspects of one's own life, including consensual intimate relationships, one's interests are extremely weighty and presumably weightier than the interests of any other persons, except those who are also involved in these relationships. The interests of one's neighbors in connection with one's choice of an intimate partner or friend are generally trivial in comparison with one's own interests. Coupling this premise as to the relative importance of interests with the further assumption that each competent adult is the best judge of her own interests, one arrives at the conclusion that human well-being is likely to be greater on the whole if intimate associations among competent adults are the product of voluntary choosing by the participants in the associations – that is, if we are free to enter into them only when we choose to and if we are able to exit them when we wish to, based on our assessment of the degree to which the relationships can provide these various benefits for us. At the same time, personal relationships can generate certain benefits for society as a whole, including the diversity and check on state power that utilitarians have cited as reasons for ensuring individual liberty.

A right of self-determination in this area of life thus commands great utilitarian support. The principal, necessary limitation on this right arises from the fact that other persons' interests in connection with *their* personal relationships are equally as weighty as our own, and we cannot justifiably expect our interests to trump theirs. We therefore also cannot justifiably expect to have a right to a relationship with others regardless of their wishes, and so our rights as to relationships with other adults must be limited by a mutuality requirement.

II. An Autonomy-Based Account of Freedom of Intimate Association

An alternative strand of popular moral thought and of moral and political philosophy reposes ultimate value, at least in discussing the moral basis for guaranteed freedoms, not in happiness or welfare per se, but in a particular form of human flourishing or self-realization characterized by the achievement and exercise of autonomy.[26] What are seen by many as the highest or truest aspects of human nature – rationality, morality, independence of will, defining one's own ends and conception of the good, becoming a fully participatory member of a political community – become the focus of political principles and proposals. A central aim of the state is to facilitate, or at least to avoid hindering, its citizens' living of an autonomous life, meaning "one in which a person charts his own course through life, fashioning his character by self-consciously choosing projects and assuming commitments from a wide range of eligible alternatives, and making something out of his life according to his own understanding of what is valuable and worth doing."[27]

Isaiah Berlin expresses the longing of the human individual to be autonomous:

> I wish my life and decisions to depend on myself, not on external forces of whatever kind. I wish to be the instrument of my own, not of other men's, acts of will. I wish to be a subject, not an object; to be moved by reasons, by conscious purposes, which are my own, not by causes which affect me, as it were from outside. I wish to be somebody, not nobody; a doer – deciding, not being decided for, self-directed and not acted upon by external nature or by other men as if I were a thing, or an animal, or a slave incapable of playing a human role, that is, of conceiving goals and policies of my own and realizing them. This is at least part of what I mean when I say that I am rational, and that it is my reason that distinguishes me as a human being from the rest of the world. I wish, above all, to be conscious of myself as a thinking, willing, active being, bearing responsibility for my choices and able to explain them by reference to my own ideas and purposes. I feel free to the degree that I believe this to be true, and enslaved to the degree that I am made to realize that it is not.[28]

Eighteenth-century German philosopher Immanuel Kant, with whom the modern conception of autonomy originated and whose work continues to inform much of the philosophical writing about autonomy, presented an argument for the supreme moral worth of this autonomy for which we strive.[29] Kant contended that because humans and nonhuman animals are passive recipients of feelings and inclinations, those aspects of experience cannot be bases for according respect. They arise simply from the workings of the natural world, for which we are not responsible. Only the decision of a free will to use certain mental powers to exert control over those feelings and inclinations and to regulate our conduct and make decisions about our lives on the basis of reasons – in particular, on the basis of morality – is potentially worthy of respect.[30] That activity is our own doing, something for which we can claim credit and be held accountable. So if there is anything in human life that can be said to be morally good, Kant maintained, it is just the proper exercise of those capacities encapsulated in the concept of autonomy.

The connection between valuing autonomy and conferring freedom-protecting legal rights is more straightforward than the connection between welfare and freedom-protecting rights. A person fails to be autonomous or to exercise autonomy to the degree he or she is subject to external compulsion. By ensuring the opportunity for free expression of ideas, for pursuit of self-chosen aims, and for control over various aspects of one's daily life, laws imposing on others duties not to interfere in our lives make possible the exercise of free will and therefore the realization of our true humanity. We collectively create political and legal institutions to make that possible. To most people this connection is self-evident, and so there is much receptivity to natural rights-type reasoning that from man's capacity for moral discernment and for choosing ends and means there follows directly, without need for further explanation, a "natural liberty" entailing "a power of acting as he think fit, without any restraint or control."[31]

In addition to this perfectionist aspect of autonomy-based reasoning about rights – that is, the idea that rights principally or exclusively protect the opportunity for achievement of full humanity, the concept of autonomy includes a sense of the self-ownership, sovereignty, and inviolability of the individual. I am entitled to make my own choices about my medical care, my intellectual and recreational pursuits, and my personal relationships because my life and person are my own, and no one else may properly seek to take command of my life or body to serve their own purposes.[32] A human life, at least one led by an autonomous person, is not to be treated instrumentally by others, but rather must be treated as an "end in itself." Thus, laws protecting freedom of association also embody the respect for personal sovereignty and integrity that we believe is owed to human beings, or at least to those manifesting the transcendent, morally significant property of autonomy, the capacity for rational self-mastery.

These arguments for the value of autonomy and for legal guarantees of freedom do not, however, establish what scope rights of self-determination should have. Does reposing ultimate, or even exclusive, value in autonomy entail ascribing to every autonomous person an absolute, unlimited right to do whatever he or she wants? Of course not, for obviously different persons' self-determining choices can conflict. My pursuit of a particular job might conflict with another person's aspirations. I might wish to develop a relationship with another person but that person might wish to avoid associating with me. In his moral theorizing, Kant maintained that autonomy in a true sense means comporting one's decisions and actions to universal laws; true freedom, for Kant, lay not in acting out of self-interest but rather on the basis of the moral law, of maxims that are impersonal and apply equally to all. In other words, the moral value lies not simply in acting free of external constraint, but also in acting free of selfish impulses and self-serving motivations.[33] On that view, we would have no reason to ascribe rights beyond what is needed to ensure the ability of individuals to act on the basis of universal moral principles, and we might suppose that no action that comports with universal moral principles could conflict with the aims of other autonomous persons, which would also be in accordance with those universal principles. Prevailing moral beliefs today, however, are not so demanding; we have a less grandiose conception of autonomy, one that encompasses making decisions for oneself with the principal aim of making oneself happy. And so we believe autonomous persons are entitled to freedom to pursue some ends that they have chosen for themselves solely for the sake of giving themselves a richer, more grati-fying life.[34] And certainly different persons' pursuit of their own happiness can lead to interpersonal conflicts, so some limitation on rights of self-determination would seem necessary to avoid or resolve such conflicts. Moreover, we are also less sanguine about the ability of humans to dis-cern and reach agreement on moral principles, and so political theorizing about the rights of autonomous persons must take account of the ineradi-cable diversity of "conceptions of the good"; conflicts can arise even when people are motivated only by moral beliefs rather than by self-interest.

How, then, would an autonomy-based moral outlook address this potential for conflicts among autonomous persons? The principal strat-egy has been to accept that there is an equality or impartiality constraint on autonomous persons' rights of self-determination, a constraint uni-versally accepted in western culture today. A Kantian might argue for this constraint by reasoning that insofar as we ascribe objective value to our own autonomy – which we arguably cannot help but do – and on the basis of that assertedly objective value demand that others respect us and refrain from interfering with our pursuit of our aims, we must acknowledge that autonomy also has value when others possess it and that others' auton-omy is deserving of the same respect and deference that we demand for our own.[35] In other words, when I elevate from mere assertion of pref-erence to a moral claim my demand that others respect my sovereignty over my own life and grant me freedom to pursue my aims, then I am rationally committed to accepting that other autonomous persons have an equal claim to respect and freedom, and so that, to the extent different persons' actions can conflict, we all must accept some limitations on our freedom and our legal rights so that all have an equal share. To say "you must grant me freedom because I am autonomous" presupposes that being autonomous, as a general matter, has a certain moral significance, and so I must acknowledge that same moral significance when others possess autonomy and assert claims on the basis of it. Any moral reasoning at base entails such impartiality, such a recognition that one's own aims and desires do not have special weight in a moral community simply because they are one's own, but rather only insofar as they partake of qualities collectively recognized as having moral significance for all.[36] Thus, contemporary public discussions of individual liberty generally presuppose this equality constraint, though at times it becomes necessary to point out to some people that they cannot expect to have more extensive rights than they are willing to concede to other, similarly situated persons. As a political matter, we understand our basic legal liberties to be the product of an implicit agreement or social compact to afford reciprocal and equal respect to the sovereignty and strivings of others.

The fullest and most influential elaboration of this idea has been the social contract theory that late-twentieth-century political philosopher John Rawls constructed on the foundation of Kantian moral principles.[37] A moral outlook that accords greatest significance to autonomy fits well with a social contract approach to political theory insofar as that outlook demands that autonomous persons be subject to rule by a state and its laws only if they consent to be so ruled. Milton Regan explains: "Respect for the equal value of each person requires that each decide on her own what obligations she will accept in return for the benefits of participation in social life."[38] Thus, Thomas Hobbes and John Locke, earlier proponents of social contract theories, advanced the idea of civil society as a social compact based on what was then a rather new conception of the human person, articulated by Sir William Blackstone, as "a free agent, endowed with discernment to know good from evil, and with power of choosing those measures which appear to him to be the most desirable."[39]

Early social contract theories, however, encountered an obstacle to justifying existing or possible political systems, in the difficulty of showing that there ever had been or ever could be actual free consent by all members of a society.[40] This difficulty arises from many facts about the real world, including the infeasibility for most people of exiting the society of their birth and the unequal bargaining situations of different people arising from preexisting disparities in wealth and other resources. David Hume's observation of three centuries ago remains true today: "Can we seriously say that a poor peasant or artisan has a free choice to leave his country, when he knows no foreign language or manners, and lives, from day to day, by the small wages which he acquires?"[41] These realities undermine the freedom of persons to withhold consent to a proposed social arrangement, and so any resulting political society could not be said fully to respect the autonomy of persons.[42] These realities also have produced actual systems of law that did not accord equal rights to all autonomous persons but rather gave some greater freedom and power than others.

Rawls's innovation was explicitly to change the focus from actual social compacts to an idealized hypothetical contract, one that all reasonable and rational persons should agree to, and would agree to if the content and justifications of the contract were explained to them, even if they were truly free to take it or leave it. All reasonable and rational persons should endorse a social compact that they can see to embody a fair system of cooperation among free and equal persons who live in circumstances where individuals' interests, projects, and values inevitably come into conflict.[43] An insistence that such a hypothetical contract be defensible in principle to all reasonable persons as just respects the equal moral standing of all autonomous persons: "On the contract interpretation, treating men as ends in themselves implies at the very least treating them in accordance with the principles to which they would consent in an original position of equality."[44] In other words, to get a clear idea of what is a just solution to the problem of conflicting aims and interests among members of a society, Rawls does not look to the constitution or legislation that any society has actually adopted, because those always reflect preexisting power inequities, but rather to a hypothetical, idealized contracting situation in which the interests of all persons are, in a sense, fairly represented and given equal weight.

This move to hypothetical consent – that is, to what persons would agree to if certain impediments to free and informed decision making were removed, which has been widely embraced among contemporary political theorists, is quite significant for theorizing about children's rights, and I return to it in the next chapter. It suggests acceptance of the idea that we can respect the moral status and sovereignty of persons by means other than just heeding actual, autonomous choices. Where certain conditions pose an obstacle to such choices, we can reason meaningfully about what persons would choose if that obstacle did not exist, and giving our conclusions on that score moral bindingness amounts to treating those persons with the respect they are due as "ends in themselves." This, I will suggest, we can do with nonautonomous persons as well as with autonomous persons.

Rawls further reasoned that a fair system of social cooperation would be one that resulted from a decision-making process according equal respect to all, meaning that no persons' interests received greater or lesser consideration or protection in the process because of facts about themselves that are widely regarded as morally arbitrary – that is, that are not a proper basis for saying that one is entitled to less consideration or benefits than another.[45] In other words, a constitutional framework and legal system should be justifiable in principle to every autonomous person if it is the outcome of rational deliberations in which no group of persons has an advantage over others or greater bargaining power simply by virtue of having certain characteristics that, from an objective standpoint, do not make them more deserving. Such morally arbitrary facts would include not only preexisting alliances or accumulations of power and wealth of the sort that have skewed the results of actual state formation throughout history but also some personal attributes that might in actual social life cause one to be favored or disfavored by others because of illicit prejudices – for example, one's race.[46] No one in a just society would be worse off because they belong to a class of persons, defined by such morally arbitrary facts, whose interests were simply discounted or ignored in the deliberations that led to the formation of the basic structure of an actual society and its governing principles. Thus, the basic principles governing such a society should be defensible to every reasonable person; all should see that the principles contribute to their good as much as possible consistent with the equal, legitimate demands of other persons to protection of their good.[47]

Rawls's conceptualization of this decision-making process he termed the "original position," a hypothetical bargaining situation in which persons who would become members of a just society consider alternative basic principles for the drafting of the laws that will govern their collective existence. Operating behind a "veil of ignorance" that shields from them much information about their individual characteristics, parties in the original position must deliberate about what sort of society would best protect their various interests.[48] Lacking knowledge about themselves as unique individuals, they must rely on knowledge of widely shared human needs and aims, with particular concern to secure for themselves certain "primary goods" – that is, those things that "are generally necessary as social conditions and all-purpose means to enable human beings to realize and exercise their moral powers and to pursue their final ends."[49] A less stylized thought experiment along these lines might ask us to imagine that we are going to be reincarnated tomorrow and that we know nothing about our next life except that we will be human and a member of a society characterized by material circumstances much like those in the one we now inhabit, and then to think about what basic rules we would want to govern that society, given our uncertainty about our place in it.

In giving content to the idea of primary goods, of the basic things we would be most concerned to guarantee ourselves, Rawls's reasoning again displays a Kantian emphasis on autonomy. Rawls assumed that parties in the original position would assign priority to ensuring for themselves the ability to realize their essential human nature as reasonable and rational agents – that is, as autonomous persons.[50] From this assumption, Rawls concluded that the very first principle of government established in the original position would be a guarantee of basic liberties for all, because personal liberties are fundamental prerequisites to developing and exercising autonomy, to formulating and pursuing a conception of the good. Thus, in a just society, "[e]ach person has the same indefeasible claim to a fully adequate scheme of equal basic liberties, which scheme is compatible with the same scheme of liberties for all."[51] The specific liberties included within this category of guaranteed basic liberties are determined by considering "what liberties provide the political and social conditions essential for the adequate development and full exercise of the two moral powers of free and equal persons."[52] Rawls describes the two moral powers as "the capacity to understand, to apply, and to act from (and not merely in accordance with) the principles of political justice" and "the capacity to have, to revise, and rationally to pursue a conception of the good."[53] The full exercise of these moral powers includes "judging the justice of basic institutions and social policies" and "pursuing our conception of the good."[54] Exercising these moral powers in these ways, Rawls writes, "is essential to us as free and equal citizens."[55]

In fact, Rawls concluded that the parties to the original position would assign "lexical priority" to this principle of equal basic liberty, meaning that they would not allow sacrifice of freedoms for the sake of other things that people might want, such as career opportunities or material goods.[56] They would do so because such liberties are absolutely prerequisite to the preservation and exercise of autonomy,[57] to developing one's own conception of the good and carrying out a plan of life based on that conception of the good.[58] Underlying Rawls's reasoning about what the parties in the original position would choose is an ideal of the person, or an assumption as to what most people regard as the essence of a person's human nature, as "a rational chooser of his own ends and plans," and as the overriding aim of human life – namely autonomous self-realization.[59] Such a view provides an explanation different from that of the utilitarian as to why, in the context of relationship decisions, the state does not limit adults' freedom to choose to advance what state decision makers believe to be conducive to their happiness or to collective prosperity. Being the agent of one's own course in life is, from a Kantian standpoint, simply more important than being happy or materially more comfortable.

The requirement that liberties be enjoyed equally arises from the assumption of impartiality built into the original position. From that standpoint, ignorant of our actual characteristics or position in society, Rawls supposes (at least when he is thinking only about competent adults as the objects of political theory), we would have no reason to distribute liberties unequally. We would adopt a principle that would ensure for ourselves as full a measure of liberties as possible, whoever we should turn out to be.[60] Doing so entails imposing some restrictions on liberties, equally for all (competent adult) persons, given the potential for conflict between persons in the exercise of their liberties.[61] The mutuality requirement in existing law governing adult relationship rights is just such a necessary restriction, designed to ensure an equal freedom of association for all. Entitling, or even merely permitting, some persons to force their association on others would significantly diminish the liberty of those others and therefore interfere with their self-determination, while adding little to the favored persons' opportunity for self-realization. The current regime of relationship rights ensures for adults the fullest measure of liberty compatible with equal liberty for all.

Reposing ultimate value in autonomy thus connects with arguments for personal liberty in general in at least two ways. First, it makes appealing an approach to reasoning about just political principles that emphasizes the consent – actual or hypothetical – of all who are subject to political principles. Second, it suggests what content political principles would need to have to garner the consent of reasonable persons, and this includes a guarantee of the conditions for development and exercise of autonomy, which in turn includes a robust set of liberties.

All of this is quite familiar to political theorists. However, political theory has devoted little attention to the place of intimate association within theories of justice and rights. Rawls's work is typical in its substantive focus. In identifying particular liberties encompassed by his first principle of justice, he listed freedom of thought and expression, freedom of religion, and rights of property and contract. He also included "freedom of the person," which he came to define as "the rights and liberties specified by the liberty and integrity (physical and psychological) of the person,"[62] but appears to have been thinking primarily of rights of bodily integrity and free movement. At times he mentioned freedom of association, but appears to have had in mind a political right of assembly and/or a right to participate in community organizations.[63] In fact, commentators have criticized Rawls and contemporary political theory in general for ignoring important political and legal issues pertaining to relationships within families.[64]

Moral philosophers and political theorists writing within the autonomy-focused tradition have never, however, taken the position that freedom of intimate of association should *not* be among the basic liberties that a liberal society and its members should respect. As noted earlier, this freedom is one that tends to be taken for granted in the West and rarely requires public reaffirmation. But it is important to a theoretical analysis of any persons' rights of intimate association to articulate how those rights fit into a broad scheme of justice. They can, in fact, easily and sensibly be incorporated into any discussion of personal liberties, such as Rawls's first principle of justice as fairness, under the heading of freedom of the person or freedom of association or standing on its own. An autonomy-focused outlook could justify including freedom of intimate association among guaranteed basic liberties on at least two grounds.

First, personal relationships are an important site for exercise of the moral powers. Put simply, creating a life for one's self includes determining one's close associations. In fact, personal associations are so central to the story of most persons' lives that they are an especially important site of autonomous choosing. Constitutional law in the United States and elsewhere reflects this, granting greater protection to intimate associations against state interference than it gives to more impersonal associations. And in an early interpretation of Rawls's theory, T. M. Scanlon inferred that freedom of the person in a Rawlsian scheme would include "freedom of choice in aspects of one's personal life" on the grounds that "the interventions these liberties are intended to preclude constitute particularly deep intrusions into a person's life which anyone has strong reasons to want to avoid."[65] New family relationships, in particular, form an important part of the life plans of most persons upon reaching adulthood, and making choices about such associations is one common way by which persons exercise their capacities for reasonableness and rationality. Our choices in friendships and intimate partnerships are as much an expression of who we are and as much a test of our maturity and powers of discernment as are our choices in careers and lifestyles and religion. And the broader the scope for choosing – that is, the fewer the limitations on with whom we may choose to associate – the greater is the challenge to our moral powers and the greater is our opportunity to mature as self-determining and self-aware individuals.[66]

Second, personal relationships are part of the material circumstances necessary for developing and sustaining autonomy. Robert Taylor explains freedom of the person generally as a right that is "necessary to create a stable and safe personal space for purposes of reflection and communication," suggesting both a privacy right of the individual and a right to unimpeded relationships in communion with others.[67] Without this right, Taylor asserts, "rationality would be compromised if not crippled."[68] More directly, Thaddeus Metz argues that a Rawlsian liberal "can view close relationships as themselves being primary goods," principally because of their instrumental value in securing other primary goods, including the capacity for self-determination:

> Close relationships are ones of mutual beneficence or generalized assistance. Parting from friends and family means losing people who are significantly willing and able to help one pursue any number of one's goals. [In addition,] bonds with people and place facilitate the realization of a distinct primary good, namely, self-esteem. Supportive relationships with other people typically enhance the degree to which one finds one's goals worthy and deems oneself able to achieve them. Leaving friends and family usually results in a weaker self, viz., anxiety and depression, which reduces one's effectiveness as an autonomous chooser. It would take a lot of other primary goods to equal the cost of depression and isolation. Self-esteem and friendship might even be prior to other social primary goods in that the latter's effectiveness is arguably contingent upon one's having enough of the former.[69]

Although Metz's comments are directed principally at harm from severance of existing bonds, the basic idea applies equally to the ability to form new relationships. A person who is involuntarily isolated from other humans generally, or who is excluded from particular types of relationships, such as an intimate long-term partnership or sibling relationships, because he or she was never able to form such relationships in the first place, might as a result suffer depression and lowered self-esteem and thus a diminished capacity to formulate and pursue higher aims in life. A right to freedom of intimate association is thus especially important among all our liberties, because our personal relationships are foundational to our lives as autonomous persons and central to our plans of life.[70]

Paul Wright makes the somewhat different but related point that personal relationships have "self-affirmation value," by which he means that they help a person to see him- or herself as a unique individual: "[I]ndividuals in such relationships see their partners as treating them in ways that facilitate the recognition and expression of their more important and highly valued self-attributes."[71] This is particularly true of relationships characterized by love, as love is a particularly intense form of recognition of the value and goodness of another. The experience of feeling and expressing love also enhances one's self-estimation, because it manifests a capacity or faculty generally deemed to elevate humans above other creatures and some humans above others; people and lives are often characterized as good or bad in terms of the degree to which they manifest loving.[72]

Finally, in addition to generating a general sense of well-being, security, and self-worth, our relationships help us give specific content to our identities, to our vision of the kind of person we are or want to become. Katharine Baker explains:

> Families help individuals traverse that vast intermediate space between the self and everyone else by providing a core of others to whom one belongs and whom one can claim as one's own. Without that sense of belonging, we cannot develop . . . autonomy because we form our personalities, thoughts, and passions only through interaction with the communities of which we are a part. . . .[73]

Communitarian writers, in particular, have emphasized the fact that we form our identities in and through communion with particular others, not in isolation from personal attachments. The relational web in which we are embedded supplies default values, meanings, and aims that constitute a starting point or foundation for pursuing self-chosen projects, based on some conception of who we are as a member of a community and as a person valued within that community because of our unique individual characteristics. Ultimately, this sense of one's individuality and importance that arises from positive interpersonal experiences gives rise to the motivation to act autonomously, to the perception that it is worthwhile and morally requisite to engage in self-authorship.

Implicit in these accounts of the connection between intimate associations and the preconditions for possessing and exercising autonomy must be an assumption that being free to choose whether and when to enter into or to remain in a particular relationship is essential, because not every relationship turns out to be mutually beneficent, supportive, and generative of a sense of belonging and self-worth. In fact, abusive relationships can substantially undermine our sense of self-worth and our ability to feel that we are in control of our lives and so diminish our autonomy. We are more likely to realize the positive goods that relationships can provide when we are free to pursue and maintain those relationships that do appear to us to offer them and to avoid or end relationships that we believe will not or are not producing them.

Milton Regan notes a tension between the two ways in which family life is tied to autonomy. He agrees with communitarians who have emphasized that the intimate relationships forming the foundation for enjoyment of autonomy are necessarily characterized by a certain givenness, the quality of being taken for granted and constitutive of who we are, rather than always being viewed from a critical distance as an object of rational choice. Otherwise they cannot provide certain of the goods inherent to intimate relationships, such as mutual trust and a sense of shared values. Yet at some point or at some level autonomous persons must hold those relationships up to objective scrutiny and freely embrace or reject them. Otherwise they fail to be the authors of their own lives and so to realize fulfillment of their true human nature.

Regan explains this tension in terms of the possibility of taking an external stance or an internal stance to relationships, his own focus being on marital relationships. When persons take an external stance to a relationship, they stand back cognitively from the commitment and "independently evaluate the moral demands made by the relationships in which [they are] involved." They consider "the contribution of that relationship to the ends of the individuals who participate in it" and the consistency of the relationship with the kind of person they are or want to be. They engage in cost–benefit reasoning from an individualistic perspective. And they stand prepared to exit a relationship if, on balance, it provides insufficient satisfaction for them relative to available alternatives.[74] In contrast, when persons in a relationship take an internal stance to the relationship, "the relationship is taken as a given without reference to individual costs and benefits." They operate "out of a sense of shared purpose that emphasizes collective rather than distinct individual benefits." And they feel an ongoing sense of obligation that arises not from continual consent or from application of principles of justice to their interactions but rather from their prior commitment to each other and from "the accretion of experience in a relationship of interdependence." Thus, although the external stance emphasizes the distinctness of persons, "the internal stance tends to blur the boundary between self and other."

Regan notes that the internal stance is important in its own right, because it gives rise to occasions for moral decision making of a kind different from that in which one engages when operating from an external stance toward relationships or other commitments, and he echoes the view of many other theorists, especially communitarians, that a life devoid of the experience of taking an internal stance toward relationships and other commitments, and of the kind of moral decision making that the internal stance entails, would be an impoverished human life.[75] In addition, and by way of resolving the tension between the two stances toward personal relationships, Regan explains that the experience of being in relationships in which participants take an internal stance is prerequisite to developing and maintaining the capacity to adopt the external stance – that is, to operate as an autonomous individual – and that a well-functioning person will go back and forth over time between the two stances:

> [W]e are always embedded in a network of relationships with others that is the very basis for our sense of our individuality and our capacity for meaningful choice. Individuals' core attachments "are not merely externally related to their self-conceptions. They are constituents of their identities and as such function, so to speak as premises of their agency."[76]

> Furthermore, the sense that any given choice has meaning depends upon a "pre-existing horizon of significance, whereby some things are worthwhile and others less so, and still others not at all, quite anterior to choice." Such a horizon is the product not of the individual but the culture in which she finds herself, which generates particular understandings of what is valuable in life. Attention to these ways in which individual reflection depends on a social matrix leads us to appreciate that attachments are a predicate for meaningful personal freedom, rather than merely an impediment to it.[77]

Regan goes on to explain that autonomous persons will, at any particular point in time, evaluate only a subset of all their commitments, while holding onto without questioning, and in fact relying on to make judgments about that subset, all other commitments. We do not question all our beliefs, values, and relationships at once, but each one is open to question at some time. Thus, a focus on autonomy and objective decision making in relation to intimate associations is not incompatible with a recognition that healthy personal relationships are not characterized by a constant questioning of their costs and benefits for us, but rather most of the time by an internal stance that entails taking the relationship as given and viewing one's self as intertwined with and devoted to another.

It is clearly valuable for any given autonomous person, then, to be able to choose with whom they associate. More needs to be said, though, to explain why the state does not compel any intimate relationships, for it might be autonomy-maximizing across society as a whole to allow some competent adults to choose their relationships while denying others that freedom. Some actual societies or subcultures do that even today – for example, by giving men the freedom to choose a wife from among all available women but not giving women any say in the matter. Why does the law in the West give every adult an absolute right to refuse any association?

At least two explanations can be given, and they resemble the utilitarian explanations for the reciprocity requirement set forth in the prior section. First, a regime in which some have a right to choose and other do not, and in which those who have the right can force their association upon those who do not have that right, in reality would not be "autonomy maximizing." The marginal gain by the first group in the efficacy of their choosing would do less to support the autonomy of the members of that group than the great loss of control for the latter group would do to undermine the autonomy of the members of that group. The scope of choice would be broadened somewhat for the first group, but severely curtailed for the second group. In addition, the relationships would not provide for the first group the affirmation that comes from being chosen, and although they would provide some affirmation to the members of the second group, because they are the ones chosen, the relationships would also reflect a tremendous insult to their personhood – namely their subordination to the will of others, which would further undermine their autonomy. Second, the sovereignty aspect of autonomy as a moral value – that is, the recognition of the individual as a site of independent moral worth and as ultimate master and judge of her own life – suggests both that there is less positive value in exerting control over things external to oneself and over other persons than there is in control over one's own mind and body and that there is a profound negative moral dimension to treating competent adults in so instrumental a fashion as to force them into intimate associations without regard to their wishes.

In sum, the relationship rights competent adults have in our society today are justified on the grounds that they are entailed by a basic principle of social cooperation that all reasonable persons should accept as fair, in light of the great importance to all persons of becoming and remaining autonomous and of having ample scope for exercising autonomy in important aspects of our lives, and therefore should agree to include in a new social contract if we were to draw one up today. We all recognize that freedom of choice in connection with personal relationships is of fundamental importance to our lives, both because a happy relational life is a prerequisite to effectuating our individual life plans and to developing our full humanity as autonomous persons and because the process of choosing relationships is an exercise of our essential human nature as rational and reasonable persons. In addition, we would consent to political arrangements that guaranteed an equal measure of this freedom for all autonomous persons, even though this means having less than a right to everything we want, because we recognize that respect for persons requires that political arrangements be defensible in principle to all members of society, which would not be the case if liberties were distributed unequally on morally arbitrary grounds, and because an equal but limited liberty for all is "autonomy maximizing" across society as a whole.

Conclusion

Both of the predominant strands in popular moral attitudes and in political philosophy – that which assigns ultimate political value to human happiness and that which assigns ultimate value to autonomy – offer robust support for the plenary rights we adults enjoy in connection with our personal relationships. A welfare-focused justification for freedom of intimate association includes both the basic welfarist support for liberty in general and an empirical claim that freedom of association has certain unique benefits vital to human well-being. We adults have plenary rights to enter into and maintain mutually voluntary relationships of our choosing because our intimate connections with other human beings are so central to our health, happiness, and self-conceptions; because each of us is generally in the best position to know which relationships are best for us; because the strongest interests at stake in connection with our personal relationships are our own; because when we are wrong about what relationships are good for us we nevertheless benefit from the experience of choosing and dealing with the consequences; because our society progresses as we experiment with different arrangements; and because reposing the power of choice in the government would be worse along a number of dimensions.

An autonomy-focused outlook more straightforwardly insists that autonomous persons be treated as sovereign over their own lives, including their participation in relationships with others. Our relationships constitute one area of our lives in which we can exercise our higher faculties and engage in self-authorship, and in fact it is an area central to our lives and self-conceptions. At the same time, one who places ultimate value on autonomy should view nurturing intimate relationships, which are more likely to arise when people are able to select with whom they associate, as instrumentally valuable to enjoyment of autonomy generally. The relational fabric of our lives clothes us with an identity and a sense of self-respect and provides psychological, emotional, and material support, thus enabling us to formulate a plan of life for ourselves and to go out into the larger world and make decisions on the basis of some understanding of who we are and what we value. Thus, we adults are entitled to choose with whom we have relationships both because our status as free and equal moral beings entails dominion over our own persons and destinies and because such dominion can only be meaningfully or successfully exercised when we have in place the emotional, psychological, and material foundation that self-chosen intimate associations provide.

5 Extending the Theoretical Underpinnings of Relationship Rights to Children

On the whole, the history of liberalism reflects a tendency to expand both the definition of the public sphere and the requirements of equal treatment.... [T]hese recent developments . . . reflect something fundamental about the inner logic of liberalism.[1]

C an the justifications for adult relationship rights elaborated in Chapter 4 be extended to the case of children's relationships, such that something approaching equal treatment of children might be warranted? Political theory to date, in addition to devoting little attention to intimate associations in general, has been almost entirely silent about family formation and dissolution for children in particular. From the outset, political philosophers have focused principally, if not exclusively, on issues of pressing concern to adults in the public sphere outside the home.[2] On the occasions when political philosophers have made mention of children, it has typically been with reference to children's formal education, because that was the one aspect of children's lives they deemed relevant to the public sphere and of interest to the state.[3] Education was the means by which children became future citizens, so both private individuals and the state had interests at stake. And discussion of education has principally been adult centered, focused on the desires of parents to control their children's upbringing and state interests in producing a certain kind of citizen.

There has been more discussion of child rearing among political theorists in recent decades than ever before, but it has remained largely confined to schooling, and the perspectives most prevalent are still adult-centered ones, focused either on the rights of parents or on statist aims such as producing tolerant future citizens.[4] There has, in fact, been a pronounced preoccupation with the instruction children receive about religion, because it is an important site of conflict between the liberal state and illiberal minority communities, and that type of conflict became a primary topic of attention for political philosophers in the 1980s and 1990s. Pressing legal issues relating to the state's creation of legal parent–child relationships, the state's termination of such relationships, children's relationships with non-parents, and other aspects of children's relational lives, which are foremost in the minds of family law scholars, social workers, family therapists, and others concerned about the development of our society's youngest members, have received comparatively little attention from political theorists. Yet children's family relationships are by all accounts more determinative of the quality of their upbringing, and therefore of the health of our society in the future, than is their formal education, so the societal importance of philosophers' addressing these legal issues would seem greater.

Because the philosophy of childhood is relatively undeveloped, I must make some assumptions without providing or citing to the sort of philosophical analysis that would demonstrate their reasonableness, and my aim is simply to show the implications of those assumptions for those who accept them. One such assumption underlying the inquiry of this chapter is that children are equal persons, in the limited sense that they are entitled to as much moral respect from state decision makers as adults receive. I take this to mean that their interests should count as much in state decision making as like interests of adults.[5] This is a sufficiently widely held assumption that the theoretical inquiry should be able to proceed without first undertaking a lengthy defense of it.[6]

Perhaps more controversially, I assume that the equal moral respect owed to children also gives rise to a presumption that children possess the same basic moral rights that adults do, even if some of those rights must be effectuated in a different manner for children than for adults – that is, must be embodied in legal rights that differ in content and method of implementation from the legal rights that apply in interactions between competent adults. That presumption is subject to rebuttal upon a showing that it is inappropriate, on conceptual or normative grounds, to attribute to children a particular moral right that is attributed to adults. The presumption simply puts the burden of persuasion on those who would deny children a particular right rather than requiring the converse – that is, that no moral right ascribed to adults be ascribed to children absent proof that it is fitting to do so. Thus, it only rules out assertions that children should not have certain rights where the assertion is not backed by good reasons, but rather appears to rest simply or primarily on a prejudice regarding the position of children in society. Although American law and public debate do not much reflect a presumption of this sort, contemporary

European law and ways of thinking appear to do so to a large extent, as reflected, for example, in the prohibition against age-based discrimination and the strong statement of children's rights in the Charter of Fundamental Rights of the European Union and in recent public debates in several European countries concerning the permissibility of corporal punishment. As shown in Chapter 3, the law in the West today does generally reflect such a presumption with respect to all adults, including those who have become or have always been less mentally competent than the normal adult, and it would be difficult to justify treating children less favorably in this respect than, for example, adults with a severe congenital mental disability.

My strategy in this chapter, then, is to assess whether the underlying rationales for adults' plenary relationship rights within the welfare-focused and autonomy-focused moral frameworks discussed in the preceding chapter necessarily distinguish adults from children, such that they show it to be appropriate to grant certain rights to adults in connection with their intimate associations but no rights or lesser rights to children in connection with their intimate associations, and whether instead those moral frameworks might actually support attribution of equal or equivalent rights to children. The first two parts of the chapter address in turn what each of the two moral views described in Chapter 4 might have to say about children's moral rights in connection with their personal relationships. In a third part of the chapter, I consider what the two views might have to say about the perennial question of when minors should come to enjoy choice-protecting rights rather than having only interest-protecting rights. In Chapter 6, I respond to likely objections to the conclusions I reach in this chapter.

I. Extending the Welfare-Based Justifications

On the surface, it might seem that the utilitarian justifications for liberty would offer no support to an argument for children's rights of any sort and that they in fact have negative implications for children's having choice-protecting rights. When Mill asserted that private individuals are in the best position to determine their own interests, he had in mind competent adults, and the typical assumption regarding children is generally the opposite. Indeed this is to some degree a definitional matter; in part what it means to be a child is that one is presumptively not in the best position to determine one's own interests. When we account for the developing capacities of persons approaching the age of majority, we call them "adolescents" or "mature minors" or something else to denote their relatively advanced but still less-developed-relative-to-adults powers of decision making. We do not call people "adults" until they reach the age at which it is assumed the average person comes into possession of more or less fully formed rational capacities. Moreover, a primary target of Mill's argument for liberty was paternalistic decision making for others, suggesting that his theory offers no support for attributing interest-protecting, as opposed to choice-protecting, rights to anyone. In justifying restrictions on freedom of thought, expression, or action, Mill insisted that a person's "own good, either physical or moral, is not a sufficient warrant. He cannot rightfully be compelled to do or forbear because it will be better for him to do so, because it will make him happier, because in the opinions of others, to do so would be wise or even right."[7]

In fact, Mill explicitly excluded children from his theory of liberty (though thereby also from his argument against paternalism). The harm principle, he said, under which the state may interfere with the liberty of the individual only to prevent the individual from harming others

> is meant to apply only to human beings in the maturity of their faculties. We are not speaking of children or of young persons below the age which the law may fix as that of manhood or womanhood. Those who are still in a state to require being taken care of by others must be protected against their own actions as well as against external injury.[8]

Therefore, the first justification for liberty, which might be understood as a defense of choice-protecting rights, resting on the superior ability of each individual to judge his or her own interests, would appear not to support attribution of any rights for children and would appear to provide a justification for treating adults more favorably than children.

Furthermore, with respect to justifications for liberty that invoke the special utilitarian value of autonomy, whereas Mill was undoubtedly correct that people learn and develop as human beings and achieve special satisfactions from exercising autonomy, children are generally believed not to possess autonomy. Again, this might be definitional; the concept of "child" entails a lack of autonomy. With respect to the justifications based on broader societal interests, although individual liberty is conducive to experiments in living and therefore to social progress, most people might say that assigning choice-protecting rights to individual adults adequately serves that purpose in connection with family formation and children's upbringing. And although it might be just as true with respect to children as with adults that it would be bad for society if the state directed people's lives, for Mill that meant private individuals should be left to determine their own lives, yet many people believe that the private individuals who should determine children's lives, instead of the state, are not the children themselves, but their biological parents.

Nevertheless, a welfare-based approach clearly does support attribution of rights to children in connection with their relationships – not rights identical to those that adults enjoy but rather rights that are analogous and equally as strong. To a great extent such rights would have to be of a different sort than we adults enjoy – that is, they would be interest protecting rather than choice protecting. Yet they would rest on the same ultimate principles as adult rights of self-determination. This is in part because of the crucial assumption implicit in certain of the utilitarian arguments for self-determination, highlighted in Chapter 4, that in matters principally concerning the course of one's own life, one's own interests are weightier than the interests of any other persons. This might be so obvious that it generally goes unstated. But truly it is not sufficient in a utilitarian account of liberty to point out that each (adult) person is the best judge of his or her own interests. It is also necessary to assume that each person's own interests are of greatest value in connection with decisions to be made about the person's life. In the absence of that latter assumption, one might justify enslaving a certain group of adults even if it were clearly the case that they were the best judges of their own interests; one could simply say that their interests are irrelevant or unimportant.

Critically, then, each of us competent adults has rights of self-determination because it is generally assumed as a moral matter that our interests matter, and matter equally, regardless of our status in society, and because it is assumed as an empirical matter that in connection with decisions about central aspects of our lives our own interests are weightier than those of other persons. This empirical assumption certainly applies to children as well, and if we are to respect children as equal persons, we must extend the moral assumption to them also – that is, that their interests matter as much as do adults' interests in state decision making. And these underlying assumptions can do much justificatory work on their own in relation to children's rights. The ultimate aim of utilitarianism's under-writing of adult relationship rights is thus not intrinsically tied to competency, except in the limited way that the experience of self-determination is gratifying in and of itself. Children's relative incompetence certainly does not make them incapable of having well-being, of possessing many welfare interests, and does not diminish the importance of their intimate relationships to their fundamental well-being.

In fact, it increases the importance, because children's relative incapacity gives rise to an especially pronounced interest in being cared for physically, psychologically, and emotionally and in receiving nurturing that will enable them to develop toward adult competency and to experience happiness throughout their lives, and these things are best provided within good long-term intimate relationships. In describing the goods generated by family life, Colin Macleod places special emphasis on the essential goods that family life potentially provides to children. Families are more constitutive of identity for children than they typically are for adults and largely determine to what extent children enjoy a sense of self-worth and competence and approach with enthusiasm developmental challenges such as schooling. The family might be the only source of culture and values for most children, and family members assume the primary role in "nurturing and developing crucial cognitive, emotional, and moral capacities."[9] Children are especially dependent on their parents for recognition as unique and important individuals and for growth in a stimulating and safe environment. Children's need for others to give them affection, unconditional love, concern, and basic material goods is generally greater than adults' need for others to give them those things. Children are particularly dependent on others to know them well and to identify and respond to their individual needs. Significantly, children's developmental needs are so great that more peripheral personal relationships, such as those with extended family members, might also be more vital to their welfare than is true with adults, both because it is difficult, and perhaps impossible, for parents alone to satisfy all of children's needs and because a backup must be in place in the event that the core relationship malfunctions or is disrupted. In addition, Macleod admonishes that we think not only about goods for children that are conducive to their enjoying success and happiness as adults, but also about the quality of their lives during childhood.[10] Children's daily lives consist of interactions with close associates – immediate family members, extended family members, and friends – to a much greater degree than is true of the average adult today. It is therefore especially important to the quality of persons' childhood that their personal relationships are ones that they enjoy, that produce happiness for them, that allow them to experience joy and love.

Arguments for individual liberty based on the special utilitarian value of autonomy also support attribution of interest-protecting rights to children in connection with their relationships, once we take into account children's potential to become autonomous in the future and then to realize the satisfactions that autonomy entails. Children are more likely to become persons able to develop a healthy individuality, to fashion and be masters of their own lives, and to enjoy the exercise of higher faculties if they have better rather than worse parents and a richer rather than poorer interpersonal life beyond their relationships with parents.

In addition, children's early relationships largely determine their preparedness to enter into relationships later in life, and later relationships will be central to their well-being as adults. Attachment theory holds that healthy attachment to parents in childhood is prerequisite to developing the capacity for empathy, a capacity crucial to a positive relational life for adults. Early relationships create models of interaction that are often replicated by persons when they become adults, as evidenced by the tendency for abuse to be reproduced in succeeding generations within families.

Thus, the quality of children's particular relationships appears to impact their well-being more fundamentally than adults' relationships impact adults' well-being. Quite plausibly, then, children have *greater* welfare interests at stake in connection with decisions the state makes about their family lives than adults have in connection with decisions they make about their own relationships. Children should therefore be seen, on welfarist grounds, as having a moral claim to legal rights protecting their interests in connection with family relationships that is at least as strong as the moral claim adults are seen to have.

But what sort of rights? Presumably, whatever sort of legal rights best protect their interests. The first utilitarian rationale for individual liberty, and other rationales to some extent as well, simply assume as an empirical matter that, for competent adults, choice-protecting rights constitute the best mechanism for serving the ultimate aim of maximizing the happiness and well-being of individuals, and therefore the welfare of society as a whole, because competent adults are the best judge of their own well-being. That such an assumption does not hold in most situations for children does not mean that the laws governing their relational lives cannot or should not seek to maximize their happiness and well-being. Because it is equally the case with children that in matters principally affecting their own lives their own interests are generally of great weight and are presumptively weightier than the interests of any other persons, the moral focus must remain on their well-being. It simply becomes necessary in many contexts to adopt a different mechanism for furthering their well-being. The obvious alternative is interest-protecting rather than choice-protecting legal rights.

Children's lesser competence just means, therefore, that it is necessary, for some aspects of children's lives and for children at certain stages of development, that some alternative mechanism be used to protect and advance their well-being. Mill assumed that for competent adults there was no superior alternative to choice-protecting rights, but with respect to incompetent persons, according them some other sort of rights and establishing some other decision-making mechanism for them could constitute a superior approach to maximizing welfare. In connection with momentous decisions about a child's relationships, utilitarian morality requires that we attempt to identify the best possible substitute for self-determining choices when the children in question are not the best decision makers, an alternative rule and process most likely to generate outcomes most conducive to the well-being of the child, the person who has the greatest interests at stake.

This is, in fact, the most common way (though not the only common way) of justifying the authority of legal parents to make decisions about children's education and health care.[11] With respect to decisions about who a child's legal parents will be, and about other components of children's relational lives, we should similarly seek to identify the decision maker, decision-making process, and substantive standard of decision making that are best for children. The end should still be the welfare of the child, with some means other than full self-determination used to serve that end. Some proxy must substitute, at least partially, for the choices of the individual.

Thus, unless and until it is shown that there is no feasible alternative way of advancing children's welfare in matters fundamentally affecting their lives when they are not themselves the best decision makers, or no alternative that does not generate incidental costs so great as to outweigh the utility gains of endeavoring to advance children's welfare, we should assume that, on utilitarian grounds, the morally correct thing for the state to do in these cases is to deploy a proxy mechanism for maximizing the welfare of the children involved. The correct thing to do is not to abandon the idea of affording rights to children and to instead make children's relational lives determined by the rights of other people. Nor is the correct thing to do to disregard or assign lesser weight to children's welfare. The correct thing to do is to stay focused on the child and to determine what legal rules create the best feasible analogue to the plenary choice-protecting rights that we adults enjoy.

The best proxy for self-determination, from a utilitarian perspective, could be articulated in an abstract way in terms of replicating what a child presumably would choose, on the basis of his or her individual characteristics and/or on the basis of generic interests, if fully competent to determine his or her own interests and if disposed rationally to advance those interests. More concretely, this might mean that when a child is deemed (by a legislature, based on presumptions tied to age, or by a court, based on an individualized assessment) incompetent to make a decision independently, certain other persons – who could be legislators, judges, parents, or someone else – should make final decisions in behalf of a child but do so solely as agent or proxy or fiduciary for the child. They should, ideally, put themselves in the place of the child, identify with the child, and put out of mind all interests other than those of the child. I discuss at greater length in later chapters what this might mean at the level of specific legal rules, but it might be useful here to convey some sense of what such proxy decision making might look like in practice.

Such decision making for children would largely mirror the existing approach to decision making about the relationships of incompetent adults, as described in Chapter 3, which reflects a belief about what a proper moral respect for less autonomous persons requires. As is generally done with incompetent adults, agents for children could make surrogate decisions partly on the basis of information about the child's actual preferences, values, and disposition to the extent those exist. They would do this because children have some interest in having their lives conform to what they want and value and to how they are individually constituted and because children's preferences might correlate to some degree with their objective interests. Otherwise, and ultimately, the proxies would reason on the basis of information about children's interests from an objective standpoint. With newborn children, there will be no preferences or values, so decision making would rest on any relevant unique physical characteristics of the child (e.g., a physical disability or exposure to drugs) and on generic interests of children (e.g., need for a stable, loving environment, for good nutrition, and for health care). As children grow, greater attention would be paid to their subjectivity. This model of decision making is applied to children already in the medical context, when for some reason doctors cannot rely exclusively on parental choices regarding treatment.

As I discuss further in Chapter 7, that such proxy decision making is for various reasons imperfect – for example, because no agent can have complete access to the mind or personality of another, because maintaining a single-minded focus on the welfare of another is difficult, and because any proxy decision maker will have some personal biases – does not mean that it is not the best, most utility-maximizing strategy for making decisions about children's lives, all things considered and in light of the available alternatives. Again, it is the approach we take to surrogate decision making for incompetent adults. Indeed the legal system uses such a mechanism already for making some decisions about children's relational lives, such as custody disputes between legally recognized parents, in which the state makes decisions for children and is governed by the best-interests standard. In those cases, a court or other state decision maker ostensibly acts in a purely *parens patriae* role, charged with acting as agent for the child to pursue outcomes most conducive to the child's welfare. This suggests that there is no conceptual obstacle to performing such proxy decision making in all the types of cases enumerated in Chapter 2. The state could in theory make all these decisions about children's relationships from an exclusively *parens patriae* standpoint, with a single-minded focus on the welfare of the child. If the ultimate aim of the law with respect to family relationships is individual well-being, and if it is assumed that the individuals whose relationships are to be determined have the most important interests at stake, and if state decision making of this nature is the best available way to promote children's well-being in a particular instance, then it would seem to follow that this is the approach that should be taken to determine children's family relationships.

As a matter of rational moral consistency, therefore, we should conclude on utilitarian grounds that in all cases in which the state structures children's relational lives, and in which children are not themselves in the best position to judge where their interests lie, the state should act as proxy for the children, with the singular objective of promoting their welfare. The state owes a moral duty to children to act in this fashion, incident to its duty to treat all persons with equal moral respect. With competent adults, the state carries out the moral duty owed them by entitling them to choose for themselves, and with children and other persons of insufficient capacity for self-determination, it can carry out the moral duty owed them by empowering a fiduciary to choose in their behalf. Correspondingly, we might say that children possess a moral right against the state that it endeavor, when it establishes the procedures for decision making about children's relationships and the substantive rules to govern that decision making, and when it applies those procedures and substantive rules, always to maximize the welfare of the children whose relationships are at issue. Such a right would be equivalent to the right we adults possess to make choices ourselves about our relationships so as to maximize our welfare.

Do any of the other utilitarian justifications for adult liberty support attribution of some form of rights to children in connection with decisions about their personal relationships? On the surface, Mill's justifications resting on the educative effect of, and the gratifications arising from, making choices for oneself would not appear to support interest-protecting rights for children at all. Underlying these arguments were assumptions that people should be allowed to develop their capacities and learn from their mistakes and that the experience of authoring one's own life and feeling respected as sovereign over the domain of one's personal life generates an elevated form of satisfaction, and these assumptions would not appear to support a right of children to outcomes that other people decide are good for them. The proxies might hone their decision-making abilities, but children would not develop a capacity for self-determination. And for children below a stage of development where the benefits of learning through doing and from feeling a sense of self-determination and responsibility outweigh the costs of deciding poorly, these justifications for adults rights would appear not to support attribution of any sort of right to children.

However, an interest-protecting right effectuated in the manner suggested above, with attention to the values and preferences of children to the extent they exist, is more likely than some other possible decision making mechanisms to entail that children at an appropriate age become involved in the decision-making process in some way – for example, by conveying information and perhaps expressing preferences to the adult decision maker – that does have educative benefits for the child and that gives them the satisfaction of having some measure of self-determination and of feeling respected. Children learn that their well-being is a matter of importance, that to make good decisions about their relationships they need certain kinds of information, and that they must balance conflicting considerations against each other. As a result, they begin to develop the capacity to make such decisions themselves. In contrast, when decisions are based solely on the interests or wishes of adults, children learn, if anything, only that they are unimportant, which can cause them suffering and thwart their development toward autonomy. These justifications based on the benefits of choosing for oneself more clearly support, though, conferral of choice-protecting rights on children at some stage of their development, perhaps at an earlier age than what the first justification alone would suggest. I return to this idea in Section III of this chapter, where I also consider potential costs for children of involving them in decision making about their family life.

Arguments for liberty based on benefits to society as a whole, flowing from diversity and experimentation, also support a child-centered approach to decision making concerning children's relationships. Such an approach would likely further the aim of fostering experiments in living to a greater extent than does the current legal regime, which privileges and reinforces the traditional nuclear family.[12] Legal scholars who write in this area generally assume that doing what is best for children means recognizing and protecting a multiplicity of family forms – for example, more than two parentlike individuals in the family, extended family members playing a bigger role in children's lives, and overlapping first and second families when parents divorce and remarry.[13] Children in western society today live in a great variety of de facto living arrangements, many of which are consistent with their developmental and other welfare interests, and disturbing established arrangements can be deleterious for a child. Thus, a focus on children's welfare might lead to as much protection for nontraditional families as would increased deference to adults' choices.

Finally, there is the concern about the state ordering people's lives. The first reaction many people would have to a proposal to increase state efforts to advance children's welfare through decision making about family relationships is to object that this would repose excessive power in the state to meddle in the private life of citizens. They are wont to label as totalitarian any suggestion that the state be more circumspect about how children are raised. For example, in the context of establishing legal parent–child relationships, John Harris argues against a policy of screening potential parents, requiring them to "demonstrate their adequacy as parents," in part on the basis of

> our reluctance to place so much power in the hands of any government: a power not only to regulate the population, but an immense one of general interference. This power would enable governments not only to interfere with what is acknowledged as one of the most important human freedoms, but also would give them the ability to use that power selectively and arbitrarily to intimidate or punish individuals or sections of the population for other and ulterior reasons unconnected with the desirability of protecting children. The power would have to be quite extraordinarily comprehensive, for it is difficult to imagine what areas of life would not be relevant to forming a view about an individual's suitability for parenthood. There would be no limit to the ambit of those officials charged with screening potential parents, and so no limit to a government's power to delve into the private affairs of citizens.[14]

In the context of child protection law, Martin Guggenheim writes, with respect to removal of children from abusive or neglectful homes and placement for adoption, as follows:

> The power of government to permit the formation or continuation of a family is totalitarianism at its most basic level. American constitutional law rightly insists that any government attempt to regulate the intimate details of family life be subject to the strictest scrutiny and justified only by a compelling state interest.[15]

Such views are simply oblivious to the fact that the state is already and inevitably ordering children's lives in the most fundamental way, dictating the very composition of families by making rules and decisions in all the contexts discussed in Chapter 2. As explained there, the state is today deciding who every child's legal parents will be and how much freedom and power parents will have in the way they treat a child and direct a child's life. Moreover, there is no reasonable alternative to the state's doing this; there is no private decision maker with whom we would entrust the responsibility of deciding to whom children will initially be assigned at birth for child-rearing purposes, who will become parents when the adults initially given that role abandon or forfeit it, and which parent will have custody of a child after divorce. In any event, it would have to be the state that decided to which private parties to give what sorts of power, and so the state would still be involved. This is a basic fact about nonautonomous persons; the state must determine, directly or indirectly, basic aspects of their lives. The numerous decisions the state is already making about children's relational lives, regardless of which way they go, constitute a dramatic "interference" in the most vital and intimate aspects of children's lives. These authors fail to realize that the pertinent question is never *whether* the state should determine who can be parents but rather *how* – that is, based on what criteria – the state should decide who it will place in the role of legal parents for any given child.

Often we just do not see the state's involvement, because the status quo seems natural rather than state created. For example, in situations of child maltreatment, a state decision not to remove a child from home looks like state inaction, but it really amounts to a state decision, despite evidence of abuse or neglect, to continue its – that is, the state's – placement of the child in the custody of particular adults. To the extent state decision making in this realm should be closely scrutinized, it should be so scrutinized whether the decision is to remove children or to leave them in their current situation. No matter what the standard for removal, the state is continuously determining the structure of children's families, thereby exercising an awesome power over children's private lives. If removing a child when that is in the child's best interests were totalitarian, then it would be more clearly so for the state to continue the placement of a child with certain adults even though that is *not* best for the child all things considered. In fact, the latter sort of decision is much more clearly totalitarian and should need stronger justification, because it cannot plausibly be characterized as a proxy decision in behalf of a nonautonomous private individual, constrained by rights of that individual, whereas the former can be. Likewise with parentage laws: nothing is more clearly totalitarian than the state's effectively saying to a newborn child "We are going to assign you to an intimate and dependent relationship with this adult, with no regard for the way that adult is likely to treat you." We should ask what gives the state the authority to make any decision about who a child's parents will be, and it would be much less troubling from a liberal perspective for the state to say "Someone other than the child must make the decision because the child cannot make it for him- or herself, there is no feasible alternative to the state's assuming the role of substitute decision maker, and in doing so we aim solely to replicate what we believe the child would choose for him- or herself if able, based on the best available information about the best interests of children in general and of this child in particular, because we respect the personhood of the child." Much more troubling is for the state to say "We are protecting the traditional right of adults to possess the children they produce, which by the way is usually not horrible for the children." This becomes clearer if one imagines similar responses to the question why the state makes any decision about who an incompetent adult's guardian will be.

Even in those cases where what is at issue is not who will be a child's legal parents, but rather whether a child's established parents can cut off third parties from association with the child, as in the grandparent or "de facto parent" visitation cases, the state ultimately must make some determinative decision. It must either empower parents to do with the child whatever they want or it must repose some decision-making power elsewhere (in its own agents or in other private parties), where it might be exercised contrary to the parents' wishes. This is true of child-rearing power more generally. When the state places children in the custody of certain adults, it must make a decision as to how much legal power to give them over children's lives, including power to exclude other influences – educational, social, and so on – from the children's lives and to alter or abrogate any rights the state confers on children generally (e.g., to a public school education or to medical care). The various court decisions and statutes that parents today invoke to support their demands for freedom and power in child rearing amount to state action just as much as do state efforts to constrain parental conduct. Parents possess legally enforced power over children's lives today because the state gives it to them.

In short, it is simply unavoidable that the state will play a decisive role in the lives of nonautonomous persons, and it does so quite clearly today. Moreover, many of the decisions the state now makes about children's relational lives it routinely makes on the basis of "ulterior reasons unconnected with the desirability of protecting children" – namely the supposed entitlement of biological parents, liberal societal aims such as the social equality of women and the elimination of racial prejudice, and a desire to punish certain adults for conduct of which it disapproves (e.g., homosexuality). It is difficult to see how changing the rules for such decision making, so that they command an exclusive focus on the welfare of children, could result in the state's acting on the basis of interests other than those of children more often than it does now. It stands to reason that such a change in the law would result in the state's acting that way much less often.

The pertinent question, it bears repeating, is not *whether* the state should "interfere" in family life by making crucial decisions as to children's relationships but rather on what substantive basis it should make those decisions, as it inevitably must. The real question is whether the state ought to be required to focus exclusively on the welfare of the children when it does, inevitably, interfere in their family lives in ways that will largely determine their well-being throughout life, and should operate as a fiduciary for children, or may instead continue to interfere in a way that either balances children's welfare against the welfare of adults or ignores children's interests altogether and treats them purely instrumentally. Establishing basic rights for children in connection with such decisions would actually have the effect of adding a constraint on state power, just as the individual constitutional rights of adults amount to a constraint on state power. The constraint created by children's rights might substitute for an existing constraint in some contexts – for example, if attributing such rights entails eliminating certain rights of adults, such as a right to parenthood founded upon biology. But in any area where the state is currently more or less unconstrained by adult rights, such as adoption, attributing rights to children results in a net *diminution* of state power, not an increase. In any context, adults could guard against state violation of children's rights by petitioning for judicial intervention on the basis of the children's rights; indeed, in many circumstances legal proceedings to challenge state action would look very much the same as under current law, with the same persons appearing before a judge, only the adults involved would be asserting rights of children instead of rights of their own.

It might be, though, that this particular constraint on state power – that is, interest-protecting rights of children – would require more individualized decision making and therefore more investigation of individuals' lives than existing constraints do, at least in some areas of the law. But that is not necessarily the case. First, as discussed further in Chapter 7 and as illustrated in Chapter 8, the moral right of children that state decisions about their relationships aim to maximize their welfare might be effectuated through statutes establishing a strong presumption in favor of certain outcomes in certain types of cases, based on particular readily demonstrable facts. Strong presumptions can dramatically reduce the number of contested cases. For example, the legal rule for maternity might be changed only modestly so that there is a rebuttable presumption that a woman who gives birth to a child will be the child's first legal mother but not automatic conferral of legal parenthood on such women without exception. The presumption might be rebuttable only by clear and convincing evidence that a particular birth mother is not the best available caretaker for the child to whom she gave birth, all things considered. There could also be presumptions as to what constitutes such clear and convincing evidence – for example, proof that the mother has a serious drug addiction that prevents her from caring for a child or that the birth mother is serving a lengthy prison sentence. The presumption in favor of the birth mother would be justified not by a supposed moral right of birth mothers but by empirical assumptions concerning the benefits for a child of having his or her birth mother as a caretaker. And the bases for rebutting the presumption would be justified not by any collective impulse to condemn women who engage in certain behaviors but by empirical assumptions concerning the threats to a child's welfare posed by being in the care of someone having certain characteristics or circumstances.

Second, in several contexts, such as paternity, termination of parental rights, and custody, the state is already routinely conducting individualized hearings that involve extensive fact-finding about people's private lives and therefore impinge on the privacy of individuals. In some respects, shifting to a child-centered approach to decision making might actually lessen the degree of impingement or might simply change the nature of it. For example, in paternity cases, there is often inquiry into the mother's sexual activities and contraceptive practices before genetic tests are ordered. If the rule for paternity placed greater emphasis on a man's qualifications for fatherhood and less on biological connection, the resulting inquiry might be less intrusive for mothers or might not occur at all if some biological fathers elect not to petition for legal parenthood because they recognize that they are unprepared to care for a child. In addition, and crucially, being more discriminating in assigning children initially to parents would reduce the need for state child protection agencies to disrupt families' lives down the road. The state is currently heavily involved in the private lives of some adults – for example, coercing them to attend parenting and anger management classes, receive services, take certain jobs, clean their homes or move, submit to tests and searches, and so on – only because the state made them legal parents in the first place when, from a child-welfare perspective, it should never have done so. Anyone troubled by state micromanagement of family life who also recognizes that the state may not simply leave children unprotected against parental violence ought to embrace the idea of at least minimal screening of potential parents, to exclude the very worst candidates for parenthood from the outset. Adoption practices go far beyond this in screening potential parents, yet there is no outcry against this as unduly intrusive or totalitarian.

Furthermore, it is not obvious that increased examination of potential parents' private lives would be a worse state of affairs for children or for society generally. As a general matter, it would likely make adults think more about preparing themselves for parenthood, make them more aware of the importance of parenting, and give them a greater sense of accountability for their conduct as parents. It would deflate current notions of adult entitlement and ownership as to children. And it should spare some children from placement with people who are truly unprepared to be adequate parents and so from various serious harms and so in turn spare society from much dysfunction and antisocial behavior. Analogously, the great "intrusion" into families represented by the advent of domestic violence laws – once condemned as totalitarian interference in private life – is believed to have positively altered the attitudes of many men, to have spared many women from much suffering, and to have reduced costs of domestic violence borne by the public, such as state expenditures on medical care and reduced worker productivity.

Last, the concern about state power is much less compelling in a society in which all adults are guaranteed substantial liberty and in which state control over intimate relationships is largely confined to children and incompetent adults. The danger Mill perceived was true totalitarianism, where all or nearly all citizens lacked the power to check the will of a sovereign who was not subject to the rule of law. That is not a danger presented by child-centered state decision making about children's relationships in a society where all citizens are free to complain about government misuse of power and where parents and other individuals interested in the lives of children are entitled to present their views to legislators, vote against particular legislators and (in many jurisdictions) judges, and bring lawsuits against state officials who violate established legal rules. (As noted above, some adults should be empowered to bring such suits even in a regime of children's rights, as agents for the children.) Given the great political power adult private citizens have, relative to children, rights of children are more likely to serve as a check against misuse of government power by agency employees and judges than they are to foster such misuse.

In sum, Mill's welfare-focused arguments for liberty do not show that adults alone should have rights in connection with forming, structuring, and dissolving personal relationships but in fact support attribution of moral relationship rights to children, and arguably even stronger rights than adults have, in light of the relatively greater importance of family relationships to children's well-being. At the most general level, they support attribution of a right that state decision making occur within an exclusively *parens patriae* framework, with any state actor aiming only to advance the welfare of children, so that children's right is equivalent to the right of adults to make relationship choices solely on the basis of their own interests. In some contexts, doing this at the legislative level might mean conferring on children legal rights to choose for themselves, whereas in other contexts it would mean establishing legal rules designed to protect what some other decision maker determines is best for children. Subsequent chapters bring the analysis down to the more detailed level of specific legal rules and standards.

II. Extending the Autonomy-Based Justifications

A moral focus on autonomy as the basis for moral respect and rights would appear especially unpromising as a basis for extending rights to children. This moral outlook attributes rights to competent adults in connection with their intimate relationships out of respect for their status as competent moral agents, as reasonable and rational beings, rather than simply as living creatures with welfare interests. Children are presumed not to be rational moral agents, at least not to such a degree that we would characterize them as autonomous; their powers of rationality have not developed sufficiently to enable them to reflect at a distance on their motivations and on the views of others and so to arrive at their own independent conclusions about right action, and they are not sufficiently in control of their will consistently to comport their actions to the dictates of reason. Marina Oshana elaborates on the ways in which children – and incompetent adults – fall short of the ideal of the autonomous human individual as follows:

> [A] small child, an individual afflicted with Alzheimer's disease, and an insane person lack the rudimentary ability to be self-governing. Absent from all three is the characteristic of being a good "local sociologist," of apprehending the complexities of one's external environment, of

consistently distinguishing malevolence from benevolence, and of comprehending the normative expectations of other persons and adapting one's behavior accordingly. Absent from all three is the power of self-appraisal and the ability to plan, to fix on preferences, and to function in a farseeing, deliberative, and self-protective manner.[16]

Children and never-competent adults might also be said to be nonautonomous in that they have not reflectively and independently formulated for themselves a set of values by which to direct their lives – that is, they do not have a sufficiently well-formed sense of self.[17] Given these deficiencies of children, there might appear no reason, within a moral framework that assigns ultimate value to autonomy, to attribute rights to children that would constrain state decision making about their lives.

There are several responses one can make to this conclusion. One is to deny that autonomy is the only basis for attributing rights to persons. One could say that the autonomy-focused moral outlook is incomplete; other characteristics of beings, such as just being alive, or being sentient, or being human, are also proper bases for attributing rights.[18] That response would lead us back to the welfare-based account of rights in connection with intimate association, and we could say simply that that account is an adequate independent justification for attributing to children rights against the state when it makes decisions about their relational lives.

Another response would be to assert that autonomy develops earlier than many suppose and that a substantial portion of persons legally treated as "children" – perhaps those fourteen and older – are as autonomous as the average adult or are sufficiently autonomous that the arguments for giving adults rights apply to them as well. With that amendment to the starting empirical assumptions, an autonomy-based account of the right to freedom of intimate association can straightforwardly support attribution of that right to some "children." But that still leaves younger children, those who are more clearly not autonomous, without rights in connection with their personal relationships, and it is generally younger children for whom the state establishes or changes family relationships and for whom such actions have the most profound consequences.

Can the autonomy-focused account itself generate duties that public or private actors owe even to those who are truly "children," in the sense of being clearly nonautonomous, and correspondingly generate rights possessed by those children? What response might we expect from any contemporary philosophers disposed to acknowledge right claims only insofar as they serve the value of autonomy, upon having pointed out to them that a great portion of humans are not autonomous and therefore would not be holders of any rights under their basic moral theory? They might reply by boldly denying that currently nonautonomous beings have any moral claim on the state or on autonomous members of society. They might grant that adults may not treat small children in just any way that the adults wish but contend that any constraint on adults' treatment of children arises from duties owed to other autonomous persons, such as parents. Few would be comfortable with that position, however. That all moral agents owe some duties directly to nonautonomous persons, even to newborns (for example, a duty not to assault them), is a nearly universally held assumption today. Philosophers operating from an autonomy-focused outlook who contemplate the political situation of children must therefore modify or supplement their basic theory in some way to generate duties owed to children, and correspondingly rights held by children, if they hope to retain plausibility for that theory. In short, there is a conflict of intuitions – autonomy is the ultimate and exclusive moral value, but nonautonomous persons have moral standing and claims on the rest of us – and something must be done to eliminate or mitigate the conflict.

An amendment many Kantians have made to accomplish this is a stipulation that not only current possession of autonomy commands respect and generates rights but so too does the potential for becoming an autonomous being. Rawls made this move, writing in *A Theory of Justice* that "moral personality is . . . a potentiality that is ordinarily realized in due course . . . [and] the capacity for moral personality is a sufficient condition for being entitled to equal justice."[19] He recognized that a contrary conclusion would be at odds with contemporary popular moral beliefs and social practices as follows:

> I have said that the minimal requirements defining moral personality refer to a capacity and not to the realization of it. A being that has this capacity, whether or not it is yet developed, is to receive the full protection of the principles of justice. Since infants and children are thought to have basic rights . . . , this interpretation of the requisite conditions seems necessary to match our considered judgments.[20]

The language in these passages is somewhat confusing, but the idea is that children have a moral claim of some kind on the state and on society's current autonomous members insofar as children can be expected to become autonomous.[21] That claim is not necessarily identical to that which adults have – that is, children might not be entitled to be treated in precisely the same way, but they are entitled to whatever treatment amounts to affording them "equal justice," or protection for their autonomy-related interests equivalent to the protection adults receive.

This amendment might not be a logically necessary feature of a moral outlook founded on respect for autonomy. One operating from this outlook might consistently say that autonomy merits respect and generates rights where it exists but that there is no moral obligation to respect the potential for it or to seek to produce more of it. From that standpoint, one might view a child as in the same position as an unfertilized human egg. Rawls and others have simply stipulated this extension of rights-generating moral value from actual autonomy to the potential for autonomy. Yet many people do believe that placing ultimate value on autonomy does entail attempting to develop it wherever the potential for it exists. This is so even with respect to adults. We believe adults who are able to do so have an obligation to nurture their own autonomy, and so we are critical of adults who allow their parents, bosses, or spouses to control their lives excessively; we expect persons addicted to drugs or alcohol to take steps to free themselves from that impediment to autonomy; and even those who are free of such extraordinary forms of external or internal compulsion feel a responsibility to continue improving their powers of self-control and their moral faculties.[22] And we believe we owe a collective obligation to some other adults to provide them the assistance they need to be as autonomous as they are capable of being – for example, to make public spaces accessible to persons with physical disabilities, to give financial assistance to those unable to earn an income, to provide rehabilitation services to those with a mental illness, and to train mentally disabled adults to work and to fulfill their own basic needs at home.[23]

This sense of duty is most clearly and keenly felt in relation to children, however. Most adults believe we have a collective obligation to all children to provide them the means to develop their innate potential for becoming autonomous, and so we support policies of taxing and spending for the purpose of educational and other developmental services even for children other than our own, or at least for those children whose parents cannot afford entirely to absorb the cost of such services for their children. In addition, parents generally believe they have an individual moral obligation affirmatively to advance their children's cognitive capacities and moral powers, and our law ostensibly treats as neglect an abject failure to nurture children toward autonomous adulthood – for example, by failing to secure any schooling for them. This is likely so not because we adhere to some abstract maximizing principle by which whatever we deem of highest moral value should be made to proliferate as much as possible but rather because of a basic intuition that each child is morally important and deserving of a life that includes the highest forms of human fulfillment and the respect that comes from achieving autonomy. Assuming that we do perceive ourselves to owe such a duty to children, either collectively to all children or individually to specific children with whom we stand in a special relation, then it follows that every child who has the potential to become autonomous has a right – against society as a whole and/or against specific persons – to receive the care necessary to their successful development toward autonomy.[24]

Once this move to respect for the potential for autonomy is made, an argument can easily be constructed for conferring on children some rights in connection with state decision making about their relationships, as a corollary to the widely perceived societal obligation to children to foster their development into autonomous persons. Although political theorists have devoted great attention to children's schooling as a means to the end of fully autonomous personhood, family relationships are at least as important to children's cognitive development and more important to their psychological and emotional development. Onora O'Neil suggests this when she writes as follows: "On Kantian views it will be important to devise institutions and practices that secure and sustain basic capacities for agency and autonomy for all .... A Kantian starting point may show that some specific forms of dependence and interdependence are morally valuable, even a source or precondition of developing strong abilities to act and to act autonomously."[25]

At a minimum, those who repose ultimate value in autonomy would seem committed to guaranteeing that the state not act so as to *destroy* or *undermine* children's potential for becoming autonomous beings, which it now does when it places children in relationships likely to interfere substantially with their development toward autonomy. Children would appear to have, at the very least, a negative moral right, arising from their potential for autonomy, against the state's assigning them at birth to parents likely to harm them cognitively or deny them self-respect, such as by physical violence, malnutrition, or persistent degradation. There is no obvious reason, though, why the state's duty, when it makes life-determining decisions for a child, would entail so limited a set of protections for children's interest in becoming autonomous rather than entailing an obligation to endeavor to place children in family relationships most likely to optimize their development toward autonomy. If "equal justice" means conferring on children autonomy-promoting rights equivalent to the autonomy-promoting and autonomy-protecting rights that adults enjoy, then children should be deemed entitled to have decisions made for them in a manner that approximates the way in which adults are assumed to decide. Adults generally choose relationships in part for consistency with their existing values and already-formed life plans but also in part for their perceived potential to supply the goods that are foundational to the maintenance and advancement of autonomy. As discussed in Chapter 4, these goods include self-esteem, which depends on being consistently affirmed as uniquely valuable; a positive value context from which to draw a sense of identity; emotional health and security, which depends on being loved and receiving consistent attention and support when needed rather than being psychologically abused or neglected; and physical well-being, which depends on having adequate shelter, clothing, nourishment, and medical care and avoiding violations of one's bodily integrity. In choosing life partners, we adults generally aim, consciously or unconsciously, to find a person, among those available, who is more likely than others to supply these goods for us insofar as we need them. Our right to freedom of association entitles us to choose on that basis, and in fact part of the reason that we have that right, rather than living in a regime of arranged marriages and other forced associations, is that we are presumably more likely than some other decision maker to make a correct choice for ourselves – that is, to select the person, among those who might reciprocate, most likely to provide those goods for us to the greatest degree. So, again, if we think of the state as an agent for a newborn child, as simply stepping in to make a choice in behalf of someone unable to do so for herself, we would expect the state, ideally, to choose the best available candidate for a family relationship and not just someone who is not horrible. We might even characterize as a negative right of the child that the state not place the child in a family relationship with anyone other than the very best applicants – that is, not divert them from the family they would choose to belong to if they were able to choose.

There must be some limit, of course, to what may be done to regulate the decisions and actions of parents once parent–child relationships are established, because of parents' own rights of self-determination and because parenthood must not be made so burdensome that too many people would choose not to undertake it. Imposing on parents an obligation to act on a daily basis in every possible way to maximize their children's development could so interfere with parents' pursuit of ends other than parenting, such as career advancement, as to constitute an unjustifiably great interference with the parents' own autonomy. Of course, knowing in advance what the law requires, adults who choose to become parents would thereby voluntarily accept this limitation on their freedom to pursue other ends, and so strictly speaking, embodying such an obligation in the law of parenting would not actually infringe the autonomy of adults who choose to become parents thereafter. But for a variety of reasons, it would not make sense from a child-welfare perspective to make adults' willingness to sacrifice their independent aims in life to such a degree a precondition for their becoming legal parents. It would also simply expect more than any human can do. However, making decisions as to which adults are to stand in a parent–child relationship with a child in the first place does not directly constrain any adult's self-determining freedom any more than my right to refuse association with another adult constitutes an interference with that other adult's autonomy. An adult denied the role of parent with respect to a particular child remains entirely free to pursue an infinite number of other projects, including relationships with persons other than that child. In addition, making some effort to place children in the care of adults who are, among all who are willing and available, most likely to nurture the children toward autonomy does not in itself entail imposing any particular legal requirements on those adults once they are selected to serve as a parent.

Thus, children's fundamental interest in becoming autonomous, for those who place highest moral value on autonomy and who would extend this valuing to the potential for becoming autonomous, appears to generate a moral duty owed to children that any decisions the state makes about the formation and continuation of their family relationships be such as to provide them the best opportunity for healthy development toward autonomy, within the limits of reasonably available alternative family arrangements. This conclusion finds support in several aspects of Rawls's theory, which, again, many find a compelling account of justice and rights in modern liberal society.

First, we might consider what conclusions we would reach about the rights of children when reasoning from the original position, the hypothetical situation in which we think through what rules we would wish to govern our society if we did not know our own individual characteristics. Rawls did not adequately account for children in his description of the original position, but it is a simple matter to amend his description so that children are represented; one need only take into account that when the veil of ignorance is lifted, it might turn out that one is a newborn child.[26] I suggested in Chapter 4 that one could also think in terms of reincarnation; imagine that you will die tonight and be born again tomorrow and that you have no idea who your biological parents will be or into which of the many possible social circumstances in modern society you will be born. Incorporating children into this process for thinking through what justice requires and for deciding on basic principles for one society – drafting a new constitution, one might say – recognizes them as ends in themselves, as persons who own themselves rather than being owned by others, as distinct sites of moral importance, and as autonomous-persons-in-the-making.

Assuming still, as Rawls and other Kantians would do, that from this perspective we accord preeminent value to the achievement and exercise of autonomy, we would aim still to secure robust personal liberties for adults, because we would take into account that we might be adults when the veil is lifted or that if we are children we will become adults. But taking seriously also the possibility that we will turn out to be in our infancy, we will want to guarantee to children whatever rights are conducive to their optimal development toward autonomy. Then the analysis becomes much like that in the previous section of this chapter for resolving the perceived conflict between the aims of adults and the interests of children, only now with an emphasis on autonomy rather than happiness. As adults, we might want a basic right to raise our biological offspring, and indeed we might want to have a right to raise some child regardless of whether we ourselves procreate, but such a right can conflict with children's interest in optimal development toward autonomy, if there are other adults who would provide a superior upbringing in that regard. We would then ask which is worse, in terms of negative impact on autonomy – being denied an opportunity to parent or being raised by bad parents.[27] As explained in Chapter 4, an assumption underlying adult relationship rights is that being denied one particular relationship, however much one might want that relationship, does not seem a great threat to anyone's autonomy, because one remains free to pursue an infinite number of other projects and relationships, whereas being thrust into one intimate relationship has the potential for tremendous damage to one's autonomy-related interests. For a biological parent to be denied a relationship with a child might generate a great sense of loss for some period of time, just as being rejected by another adult might do so, and it might also lessen a biological parent's self-esteem for a time, and this psychological impact might weaken that adult's autonomy to some degree, but from an objective standpoint being forced to spend one's childhood in the care of a person ill-equipped to provide consistent nurturance, security, and instruction is a greater threat to autonomy. I delve more deeply into this question in the next chapter, but assuming for the moment that a child has greater autonomy-related interests at stake in connection with creation of parent-child relationships and assuming, as Rawls did, that in the original position we would aim above all to avoid the worst case scenario for ourselves and so would be most solicitous of the interests of persons in the least advantaged situation, then we should decide to grant children relationship rights at least equivalent to those which adults enjoy. That is, we would guarantee for children a right to be placed in a parent–child relationship with a willing adult whom a suitable surrogate decision maker concludes is, among all those available to a child, most likely to promote autonomy-related interests. We would also guarantee children a right to avoid any relationship that a surrogate decision maker deems undesirable. Correspondingly, we would decide in the original position to grant to adults no greater right regarding relationships with children than they have regarding relationships with other adults – in other words, a right to be considered for a relationship but not a right to be in a relationship regardless of whether there is a reciprocal choice.

Rawls in fact offered some observations specifically about treatment of less competent individuals in modern society that are consistent with this extrapolation from the basic theory – that is, with a view that children are entitled to the conditions necessary for optimal development toward autonomy, including relationship rights equivalent to those of adults. Rawls referred to children, as well as to permanently nonautonomous persons and to adults who have lost their rational capacities, in the context of discussing justifications for and limitations on paternalistic denial of liberty. He wrote that parties in the original position would recognize that sometimes or for some people "their capacity to act rationally for their own good may fail, or be lacking altogether" and that in response to this recognition they would "adopt principles stipulating when others are authorized to act in their behalf and to override their present wishes if necessary."[28] Rawls conceptualized this paternalistic decision making for all incompetent persons as a substituted judgment procedure of the sort the law now requires with respect to incompetent adults as follows:

> Others are authorized and sometimes required to act on our behalf and to do what we would do for ourselves if we were rational, this authorization coming into effect only when we cannot look after our own good. Paternalistic decisions are to be guided by the individual's own preferences and interests insofar as they are not irrational, or failing a knowledge of these, by the theory of primary goods. As we know less and less about a person, we act for him as we would act for ourselves from the standpoint of the original position. We try to get for him the things he presumably wants

whatever else he wants. We must be able to argue that with the development or recovery of his rational powers the individual in question will accept our decision on his behalf and agree with us that we did the best thing for him.[29]

In another passage, addressed specifically to the moral claims of children, Rawls asserted: "We must choose for others as we have reason to believe they would choose for themselves if they were at the age of reason and deciding rationally."[30]

This view of how to deal with incompetence finds support in an autonomy-focused moral outlook in at least two ways. First, it presupposes that the surrogate decision maker will aim to secure for the incompetent person the goods necessary for development toward autonomy, so that paternalistic decision making is only a temporary situation. Second, it reflects a respect for the self-ownership and moral standing of the person for whom paternalistic decisions are to be made. Rawls's reasoning about incompetent persons operates against a background assumption or framework that he termed the "General Conception of Justice as Fairness," an over-arching ideal of equality toward which a society should always strive.[31] This conception assumes, as I have throughout the analysis, that equal treatment of all persons is the default position. It further assumes that departures from that baseline must be justifiable in principle to any persons denied some good, such as liberty, that others receive as actually being to their advantage, and it assumes that the state must always endeavor to eliminate the need for inequality. Current treatment of incompetent adults, with its "least restrictive means" constraint on denial of equal rights and its requirement to promote self-determination for such persons, is consistent with these assumptions. This conception reflects a further assumption that parties in the original position, forced to imagine themselves in every possible social position, would take the conservative approach of first and foremost protecting themselves against very bad fortune should they turn out to be among the least advantaged in society in terms of natural abilities or personal resources.[32] In this way, the original position device captures a moral intuition each of us might have if we seriously contemplated the situation of persons who are in dire condition through no fault of their own – namely that the rest of society ought to be willing to make some sacrifices to ensure, as far as possible, that no one ever falls into that situation. So in the original position we would be particularly solicitous of the interests of children, and we would place substantial restrictions on others' exercise of control over children's lives, including both state actors and private parties, requiring that any such control be to the children's benefit, and we would in fact establish rules aimed at ensuring the best possible situation for children, in light of children's relative inability to protect and further their own interests.

The last sentence of the indented passage above sets forth a retrospective assent requirement or standard; we must act in such a way that we believe a person who is now a child will, upon reaching maturity, see as having been best for him or her. Gerald Dworkin and Isaiah Berlin advance similar views in discussing justifications for paternalistic restrictions on liberty, contending that such restrictions must be ones we have good reason to believe the persons treated paternalistically would consent to if currently fully autonomous and rational or will later, upon becoming autonomous, acknowledge to have been proper.[33] In Dworkin's view, such hypothetical or predicted future consent is, with respect to restrictions on the liberty of adults or children, "the only acceptable way of trying to delimit an area of justified paternalism."[34]

This way of thinking about proper treatment of currently incompetent persons is consistent with a Kantian endorsement of the sovereignty of the individual, with a view that each person should be treated as the ultimate judge of how his or her life should go and that action by others impacting fundamental aspects of a person's life ought to be ultimately approved by, and therefore justifiable to, that person. John Tomasi characterizes this view as the core of liberalism generally: "For liberals, . . . individual citizens must be recognized as the ultimate arbiters of what gives value to their own lives. Political power must be justifiable in principle to each of them."[35] This requires that the action be good for the less competent person and not just for the others who are acting upon him or her. It respects the self-ownership of every individual by thinking of each person as a choosing rational agent even when they are not now so and by insisting that our actions be likely to receive the person's free and informed endorsement after the fact. It treats each individual as a person whose life, standpoint, interests, and, ultimately, independent thinking about the matter in question are important, more important than that of any other individual. It does so in a way no more indirect or attenuated than does the notion of hypothetical consent that is central to Rawlsian contractualism, which is applied to competent adults as well as to nonautonomous persons. For both autonomous and nonautonomous persons, including children, Rawls recommends thinking in terms of imputed choices, of what they would choose if certain impediments were removed to free and informed decision making about basic principles, constitutional rules, and legislation, and in the case of incompetent persons Rawls extends this also to the level of individualized decisions about the course of their lives, as a necessary substitute for actual choices.

Admittedly, the notion of imputed choice or hypothetical consent is conceptually untidy, and some philosophers have raised objections. Peter King notes that Thomas Hobbes, writing in the early seventeenth century, advanced the idea that parents hold dominion over children only by virtue of children's hypothetical consent to the arrangement, which children presumably would agree to as the better alternative to the parents' killing them, and King goes on to criticize this view as incoherent as follows:

> We encounter serious difficulties with personal identity in trying to spell out the hypothesis under which the infant consents, and these difficulties are not readily resolved and perhaps not capable of resolution. For no matter what we try to put into the hypothesis, we will have recourse to (non-existent) cognitive capacities. Do we claim that the infant would have made such a promise were it to have adult cognitive capacities as an infant? That once grown it would have wished to have made such a promise were that the only way to survive infancy? That were the infant a helpless adult it would enter into such a promise? But such a helpless adult, grown infant, or infant with adult intelligence is clearly not the person the infant in the here-and-now is, and pointing out that it could be or become such a person is to beg the question.[36]

In response to this objection, I would point out that there are several ways to conceptualize the notion of hypothetical consent, some more appealing than others, that all are intended as heuristic devices for respecting the distinct personhood and self-ownership of a child rather than as attempts to model an actual choice by infants, and that the legal systems of all western nations comfortably rely in several areas of practice – decision making for incompetent adults being just one example, rules for intestate succession of decedents' property being another – on the assumption that thinking in terms of what a person now unable to choose would have chosen helps decision makers keep their focus on the moral and legal claims of that person, whatever disjunction there might be between that actual person and the posited, hypothetical person imagined to be choosing. This is deemed preferable to transferring focus to the preferences and self-regarding aims of other persons. The more appealing ways of conceptualizing hypothetical consent build in as much of the actual person into the hypothetical person as possible. With once-competent adults, we take into account individual values and personal traits as well as objective interests. With infants we can take into account some individualized characteristics, such as special medical conditions, as well as more universal interests. The retrospective assent approach invites consideration of probabilities – that is, of what the infant of today is likely later in life to perceive as the best decision for him or her, based on information about what most people upon reaching adulthood approve of or disapprove of with respect to decisions made about their lives as infants (e.g., how many children adopted soon after birth later conclude that they would have been better off staying with their birth parent(s), how many children seriously abused by their natural parents or housed in a series of foster homes later conclude that they would have been better off having been adopted at birth, etc.).

As Rawls recognized, such retrospective assent is not a proper guide if people are "brainwashed" into approving what has happened to them, and so he cautioned that we must imagine and aim to create persons who are able later in life to make a free and independent assessment of their past treatment. It bears repeating that many legal rules, from those governing trespass on property to medical care to products liability, are based in some respects on assumptions about what people would after-the-fact view as the best decision for them, in circumstances where they are unable for whatever reason to make a decision themselves. And that much of contemporary political theory consists of reasoning about what people would agree to if entirely reasonable and rational, even though most actual people are often not such.[37] It is therefore incumbent on anyone disposed to reject an imputed choice approach to decision making for children to demonstrate either that it is less appropriate in the case of children than it is in the case of adults or deceased persons or that all these other areas of law and political theorizing should be overhauled.

To put the point about respecting personhood somewhat differently, and consistent with the discussion of totalitarianism in the prior section, we might distinguish three different ways in which the state might treat individuals in connection with decisions about central aspects of their lives. One way is to give them choice-protecting rights when they are capable of choosing autonomously. Another is to give them interest-protecting rights when they are not capable of choosing autonomously, including especially a right to protection of and nurturance of any potential they have to become in the future a person for whom choice-protecting rights are suitable. And a third is for the state to give them no rights but instead to give rights to other persons to make decisions about their lives on whatever basis they wish or for the state itself to make the decisions arbitrarily or on the basis of corporate interests. Clearly the first two of these options respect the personhood, self-ownership, and ultimate sovereignty of the individuals whose lives are at issue in a way that the third option does not. Thus, those who believe that the state must, above all, respect its citizens' "autonomy," including the self-ownership and "ends in themselves" aspects of that concept, which can pertain to children and incompetent adults as well as to competent adults, should embrace the second option for children and reject the third.

We should conclude, therefore, that parties in Rawls's original position, motivated by a sense of the inviolateness and inherent value of each person as an actual or potential autonomous moral agent, would choose to guarantee for themselves, during their childhood, treatment that is respectful in the sense of doing for them what they would likely do for themselves if able. They would reject any principles or laws that entailed or facilitated instrumental treatment of any human being (at least any who are now, or possess the potential to become, autonomous). They would therefore reject any laws that placed children in relationships for the purpose of gratifying certain adults or advancing diffuse societal aims rather than requiring the placement that best serves the children's developmental needs. And, if operating on the basis of Kantian assumptions about the ultimate good for humans, they would be particularly concerned to ensure each child the circumstances most conducive to healthy intellectual and moral growth from among available alternatives. [38]

Finally, we might look more closely at the content of the basic liberal principles that Rawls derived from the original position, and in particular at the Second Principle of justice, for support of a robust set of rights for children in connection with their relationships. This second principle requires that social and economic inequalities "be to the greatest benefit of the least-advantaged members of society" and "be attached to offices and positions open to all under conditions of fair equality of opportunity."[39] This second principle can be seen as arising out of Kantian suppositions in two ways. First, the strongly egalitarian principle of economic distribution reflects in part Rawls's recognition of the importance of the "worth" of liberties. He was aware that formal legal rights are insufficient to ensure all persons the opportunity to maintain and exercise autonomy and so concluded that parties in the original position would also ensure for everyone some measure of resources necessary for meaningful exercise of liberties.[40] Second, the fair equality of opportunity principle embodies a sense that all persons should have a fair chance at the personal fulfillment that comes from fully effectuating their talents and abilities, from operating in their work lives at the highest level of which they are capable, and from exercising their reason to the greatest extent possible. Formal equality of opportunity is not sufficient; "those who have the same level of talent and ability and the same willingness to use these gifts should have the same prospects of success regardless of their social class of origin, the class into which they are born and develop until the age of reason."[41]

These two aspects of Rawls's Second Principle, relating to the worth of liberty and to equal opportunity, have implications for all aspects of children's upbringing. Not only wealth but also mental and physical health and a substantial measure of self-respect are prerequisite to meaningful exercise of liberties once bestowed.[42] Rawls places particular emphasis on self-respect, suggesting that it might be the most important of primary goods, because "[w]ithout it nothing may seem worth doing, or if some things have value for us, we lack the will to strive for them. All desire and activity becomes empty and vain, and we sink into apathy and cynicism." Rawls concluded from this premise that "the parties in the original position would wish to avoid at almost any cost the social conditions that undermine self-respect."[43]

Persons' health and self-esteem can certainly be seriously impaired by early family relationships that are unloving, nonnurturing, inconstant, neglectful, or abusive and by decision making about their lives that disregards their welfare and any personal preferences warranting respect. As with discussions of autonomy, political theorists generally dwell on formal education in discussing fair equality of opportunity, but it is also tremendously important to persons' long-term prospects, in their civic, work, and personal lives, that as children they have close, loving, stable relationships and see themselves as having inherent worth. Depriving children of such relationships and of a sense of self-worth can seriously undermine their ability to develop and carry out a life plan that realizes their potential, one that fully develops and exercises their native talents and abilities and moral powers. In fact, it can lead to mental and physical problems and social pathologies later in life that compel the state severely to restrict their freedom or their pursuit of careers and other projects (including parenting!). Rawls noted that a necessary condition for enjoying self-respect is "finding our person and deeds appreciated and confirmed by others," and this has clear implications for the sort of parenting children need. Childhood is the most critical portion of life for establishing the physical, psychological, and emotional foundation necessary to successful pursuit of a fulfilling life plan, and those who truly embrace the ideal of equal opportunity ought to take a strong interest in all important aspects of children's development, not just their schooling.

This conclusion finds further support in the previous chapter's empirical accounts of connections between personal relationships and autonomy. Recall Regan's description of the interplay between the internal stance toward commitments, including relationships and values, and the external stance that is constitutive of autonomy. To engage in self-authorship requires evaluating some beliefs, projects, and associations from an objective, external perspective, but to engage in such evaluation requires having other beliefs and values that are, at that point in time, taken for granted on the basis of which to judge. And the initial set of beliefs and values that persons deploy, when they first come to possess the ability and opportunity to choose among commitments, must be derived from early personal relationships – principally from parents, though to some extent also from participating in an extended family and in a community. For a person to acquire a set of beliefs and values that can give content to a self-conception, Regan explains, relationships must involve trust, because trust is necessary for persons to take an internal stance toward a relationship, to treat it as taken for granted rather than being doubtful of its value. In addition, for persons to be motivated to make free and informed choices for themselves at some point about what to believe, what projects to pursue, and what relationships to form, they must come to understand that their choices have meaning, which in turn depends on their having a sense of self-worth and believing that they can find meaning in life.[44]

This account of the tie between personal relationships and autonomy can be further developed to generate several conclusions concerning state decision making about children's relationships. First, the account needs to be supplemented with a recognition that the quality of relationships matters; not just any relationships will provide the prerequisites for development toward autonomy. Perhaps most importantly, not all family relationships provide children with a sense of self-worth. Some parents make children feel worthless, and we see the result in the self-destructive behaviors of the adults that the children later become. Threat to self-respect can also come simply from having an upbringing much worse than others have enjoyed, unless that disparity can be justified on the basis of neutral principles that respect one's equal personhood, which is not the case where the reason for it was simply an aim of furthering the interests of others, such as one's biological parents. As Rawls notes, "it is natural to experience a loss of self-esteem, a weakening of our sense of the value of accomplishing our aims, when we must accept a lesser prospect of life for the sake of others."[45] For this reason, too, liberals should condemn family law rules that effectively use children as means to satisfy the desires of adults, with little or no regard for the disparate consequences for different children. Being raised by very bad parents in horrible circumstances, as many children are today, and suffering in comparison to peers who were raised by good parents can make one feel, at some point in life, inferior and less worthy, and this can undermine one's ability to form and pursue fulfilling life plans. Studies of child abuse victims reveal that a high percentage feel shame as well as anger and confusion. A threat to self-esteem would seem particularly likely if the explanation a person receives for her bad fortune is that she was deemed to have no rights in connection with the state's deciding to place her with those parents and that those adults were deemed to have a kind of property claim over her.

In addition, not all family relationships provide children with a sense that life has positive value and meaning, as seen in the resulting aimlessness and criminality among many adults and juveniles. In communities where addiction and violence are pervasive, children become deeply cynical very early in life. Many conclude that they are not likely to live to adulthood and that they have little reason to want to. Further, not all relationships provide a coherent set of beliefs or values. As a result, we see adolescents and adults easily manipulated by stronger personalities and lacking the inclination or even capacity to consider whether their choices and actions are morally correct. Moreover, not just any values and beliefs will do. For example, children who learn from their parents only self-centeredness and hedonism might not develop the moral power of reasonableness, the ability and inclination to see others as having an equal claim to protection of their interests and to reason morally about a fair resolution of conflicts between interests of different persons, which is an important component of autonomy. One need not blame parents for having such attitudes, or overlook the unjust social circumstances in which some parents themselves grew up that fostered those attitudes in them, to conclude that a child born today has a right to avoid being raised in such circumstances him- or herself and to reject the idea that sympathy for the parents should influence decision making for the child.

Further, children might fail even to have any taken-for-granted core relationships. Such relationships, Regan notes, depend on trust, and some parents behave in ways that prevent a child from trusting them – for example, by acting erratically as a result of drug addiction or committing crimes that land them in jail. Parents can also act in ways that are inconsistent with the child's sense of what parents should be like, a sense that might be intuitive – for example, a feeling of violation and betrayal when parents beat or sexually abuse them – or that might arise from seeing other children's parents or hearing teachers or social workers say parents should do certain things for their children. This can create doubts in a child's mind about the appropriateness or goodness of this relationship at the center of their lives. In addition, some parents act in ways that require the state to remove a child from their custody for long periods of time, with the result that children are placed in the care of people whose role in their lives is legally tenuous, subject to disruption at any moment. In all these situations, children might fail to form the kind of inner self that would enable them to become autonomous. They might also fail to develop a capacity for intimacy and so have no intimate relationships as adults, thus depriving them of an important site of autonomous decision making and of an ongoing source of the emotional and psychological goods that underwrite autonomy.

Some contemporary political theorists have recognized the importance of family circumstances to equal opportunity, but they have failed to recognize the implications of this fact for children's rights. For example, Rawls wrote that "the principle of fair opportunity can be only imperfectly carried out, at least as long as the institution of the family exists. The extent to which natural capacities develop and reach fruition is affected by all kinds of social conditions and class attitudes. Even the willingness to make an effort, to try, and so to be deserving in the ordinary sense is itself dependent upon happy family and social circumstances."[46] This passage suggests a fatalistic view on Rawls's part that the institution of the family presents an insuperable obstacle to equal opportunity. But he and others who make a similar observation[47] appear simply to assume that family arrangements will arise in the first place independently of any concern for the life prospects of children, that assignment of children to particular parents and families is preordained and must simply be dealt with as well as can be done. They fail to consider that the state's creation of families should itself be constrained by the principles of justice, including those aspects of it that are designed to protect every person's fundamental interests in developing autonomy and enjoying equal opportunity for a fulfilling life.

Yet in other respects, liberal theorists generally assume that the state must make reasonable efforts to prevent or compensate for natural disadvantages – for example, physical disabilities.[48] Why is that not also true with respect to disparities in the quality of home life? Indeed, unequal family circumstances should not be viewed as a natural disadvantage at all but rather as a state-created disadvantage. It is an action of the state – enactment of particular legal rules for conferring and continuing parenthood – that effectively places each child in a particular family. Viewed in that light, the state surely has an obligation to avoid placing any child in a legal relationship with or in the care of grossly inadequate parents. Family circumstances could never be made equally good for all children, of course, but the state could do much more than it currently does to ensure that it does not create extremely disadvantageous family circumstances for any children. Theories that aim at equalizing persons' ability to pursue a fulfilling life plan and at providing substantive and not merely formal equality support the conclusion that children are entitled to the state's best efforts.

An objection that might be raised to this conclusion as to the rights of children flowing from placing ultimate value on autonomy is that interfering with family life can itself be autonomy defeating for children. Many political theorists have responded to arguments for increased state regulation of children's education by asserting that overriding the wishes of parents and encouraging children to question the belief system of their parents can be counterproductive in terms of fostering autonomy in the children. This resonates with Regan's point that some taken-for-granted intimate relationships are necessary for persons to develop a sense of self on the basis of which to engage in autonomous choosing. Children's optimal intellectual and moral development would seem to require that they have a solid foundation of values and moral beliefs on which to build an identity and an understanding of the world. They also require that children have strong emotional and psychological connections with parents and other family members so that they can feel secure in exploring the world and in exercising their emerging rational capacities to make decisions in the world. These preconditions for progress toward autonomy are threatened by a state-mandated liberal education, some contend, for children whose parents strenuously oppose and feel threatened by their children receiving such an education.[49]

Whatever force this objection might have in connection with questions about certain aspects of public school curriculum or about state regulation of private schools, they have little or none with respect to the issues under discussion in this book. Here we are principally concerned not with the power of parents in established legal parent–child relationships to control their children's intellectual formation free of constraint but rather with which adults will be in such legal parent–child relationships in the first place. And, in fact, any sound empirical observations about the preconditions for children's development toward autonomy, including the need for parents to provide children a solid, coherent set of values, could be used to formulate criteria for the state's selection of adults to fill the role of parent. These assertions about the importance of a secure family environment of a particular sort actually support the case for the state's being more selective in assigning children to parents, as explained above. They suggest that not any sort of family arrangement is conducive to children's proper moral development and that children will suffer insofar as they are assigned to parents who are not inclined or able to undertake moral education or to offer to, and model for, their children a coherent and positive set of values. And they support a set of legal rules aimed at avoiding occasions in which the state must step in to constrain parents or otherwise disrupt parent–child relationships, rules that place children from the start with parents who are able and willing to provide their children with an upbringing conducive to their healthy development toward autonomy.

We *are* also concerned here with established legal parents' control over one important aspect of children's lives – namely children's associations with nonparents. Conflicts over this aspect of children's lives would likely continue to arise even in a world where the least qualified parents were weeded out, though probably much less often, because most such conflicts arise in dysfunctional families. And with respect to these conflicts, this child-centered, autonomy-focused objection is pertinent. Litigation and court-ordered visitation with nonparents, if very disruptive of family life, could erode the foundation for children's development toward autonomy. This possibility counsels in favor of imposing some limitation on the power of nonparents to force parents into court and on the power of courts to force parents to cooperate with a schedule of visitation with nonparents.

At the same time, association with some persons other than parents is surely necessary to a child's healthy psychological, social, and moral development, and association with extended family members in particular might also be necessary for, or at least especially conducive to, healthy development. Extended family relationships foster in children a sense that they are part of a larger, cultural community and a normative tradition, which can strengthen the moral foundation from which a developing youth confronts the larger world.[50] Relationships with other children within and outside the family are an important site of moral development, because in them children work out their own rules of behavior and through that experience come to understand why they should accept generally applicable rules of behavior rather than insisting that they always get their way.[51] From a perspective concerned to optimize development toward autonomy, then, a balance is called for between protecting the core parent–child relationship once it is established and ensuring a wider association. In fact, the relative ability and inclination of different adults, acting as parents, to achieve a healthy balance for children could also be a relevant factor in selecting from among them for the role of parenthood in the first instance. Indeed, adoption agencies today commonly inquire of prospective adoptive parents as to their relationships with their own parents and their siblings and other extended family members for this very reason.

In sum, as others have shown in connection with children's education, placing ultimate value on autonomy commits one to attributing substantial moral rights to children in connection with this aspect of their upbringing – their relational lives, including the state's decisions to create or dissolve particular legal relationships and to protect or not protect particular social relationships. This would include attribution of some choice-protecting rights, insofar as any minors already are sufficiently autonomous or insofar as conferring such rights is appropriate to foster autonomy. But it would also include interest-protecting rights – that is, rights protective of children's interest in becoming autonomous.

III. Choice-Protecting vs. Interest-Protecting Moral Rights

Reasoning about what specific legal rules might best effectuate children's moral rights entails addressing the question of who the proxy decision maker should be in any particular context where proxy decision making is appropriate – whether a judge, social work professional, court-appointed guardian of the person, parent, or some other party. It also entails assessment of the best-interests standard as a substantive rule of individualized decision making, including consideration of the many criticisms leveled against it. I do these things in subsequent chapters. I consider here one other aspect of that larger question of what specific rules best realize children's moral rights, an aspect that can be addressed, to some degree at least, at a theoretical level. This is the perennial question of when minors should have choice-protecting legal rights in connection with their relationships, rather than having a proxy decide in their behalf. Both the welfare-based and the autonomy-based analyses generated the conclusion that children are morally entitled to both interest-protecting legal rights and, at some point, choice-protecting legal rights. Interest-protecting legal rights could include a right to have one's preferences taken into account, but would entail another party second-guessing one's preferences and having the power and obligation to override them if the other party deemed them contrary to one's welfare. Having choice-protecting legal rights, in contrast, would mean that children's choices would be entirely determinative, not subject to override on paternalistic grounds. Where might each of the moral views discussed above draw the line between choice-protecting rights and welfare-protecting rights?

The first welfare-based argument for children's relationship rights suggests an initial, tentative answer to this difficult question, one that will be modified below in light of other considerations. At no point, though, do I provide more than a general framework for answering the question, because a final answer to the question would entail extensive empirical analysis as well as incorporation of more considerations than I can usefully address in this book.[52] An easy first conclusion to draw is that, with respect to some family law issues, such as maternity and paternity, children's legal rights must be exclusively interest protecting, because these matters are generally determined at birth or during infancy, when children are utterly incapable of making a choice among potential parents. In fact, all of the legal issues discussed in Chapter 2 can arise with infants, and when they do, the conclusion would be the same. With respect to most of the kinds of decisions the state makes about children's relationships, however, the need to make them can arise with children of all ages. Parents of infants and parents of adolescents get divorced, commit abuse, and get into conflicts with grandparents. As to those situations, there must be rules or at least guides with respect to when, if ever, children's own preferences factor into decisions about their best interests and when, if ever, children should be empowered to decide for themselves without being subject to override on the basis of someone else's view of what is best for them.

The first welfare-based justification for liberty suggests that a surrogate decision maker should elicit information from any children capable of communicating meaningfully about their interests. It likely would not support eliciting statements of preference, however, except with children old enough or mature enough that their preferences are likely to be somewhat reliable guides of their overall well-being. And it would not support conferral of choice-protecting rights on children in general until they reach an age when they are presumptively better decision makers than anyone else involved as to the particular issue in question. Much of the disagreement among family law scholars over the years regarding whether children should have any choice-protecting rights and, if so, what sort of rights they should have rests on different assumptions as to this empirical issue of when children are presumptively the best decision makers. The age at which minors become the best judges of their own welfare in connection with personal relationships might be lower or higher than the minimum age for conferral of choice-protecting rights in other areas of life; it is widely recognized today that competence is specific to the type of decision to be made. The age could in fact vary by specific legal issue. For example, a welfare-maximizing set of rules might empower children to decide whether they will visit grandparents at a younger age than it empowers them to decide which parent will have primary custody in the event of divorce.

In addition, the first welfare-based argument for liberty might support creation of a mature minor judicial procedure in this area, conferring on minors at an age lower than that at which choice-protecting rights generally vest a procedural right to an individualized determination of whether they are the best decision maker. For example, if a thirteen-year-old wished to terminate his or her legal relationship with biological parents, perhaps to be adopted by foster parents, the law might entitle the minor to a determination of his or her competence to decide what is best for himself or herself, as the law generally does today with respect to abortions. Whether a welfare-maximizing approach would support such a procedure would depend in part on whether certain costs of providing it (e.g., administrative costs, psychological costs to the minor) outweigh the expected gain in decision-making accuracy. In some contexts, such as postdivorce custody decision making or third-party visitation cases, the process might be a quite simple, relatively low-cost one, such as having a guardian *ad litem* represent the child and render a judgment whether to advocate for the minor's best interests or for the minor's wishes, based on an assessment of the individual minor's maturity, as routinely occurs in some jurisdictions today.

In legislative determination of the age at which minors generally will enjoy choice-protecting rights, and of factors judges might consider in granting exceptions to the general rule, decision makers could rely on a number of objective criteria of competence. Willard Gaylin presented a useful matrix for making such decisions in his 1982 book, *Who Speaks for the Child?*[53] Gaylin suggested that persons' general competence be assessed in terms of degrees of consciousness, intelligence, rationality, knowledge, perceptiveness, and experience and that the level of competence required to make a particular kind of decision be established by reference to the risk of harm to the individual, the potential gain for the individual, and the potential costs and benefits for other members of society. Naturally, the complexity of a particular type of decision – that is, the number of variables involved and the relative comprehensibility of the information relevant to the decision – would also be an important factor. Other criteria are suggested by legislative rules and judicial doctrines that have developed in other contexts involving minors, including criminal proceedings and health care decisions, such as the landmark *Gillick* decision in England.[54] Admittedly, any such a schema would not dispel all disagreement, but it might help to narrow the range of reasonable positions.

The second welfarist rationale for adult liberty, emphasizing the educative effects of exercising liberties, counsels in favor of some modification to the conclusion just reached. Children develop primitive capacities to choose very early in their lives, and they become capable of learning from their mistakes and of using the guidance of others at an age well before they are sufficiently mature to be left entirely to their own devices. In fact, children must be given opportunities to make some decisions for themselves, with the risk of making mistakes, before they become truly the best judges of their own welfare, for them to develop properly as human beings. And although the law or adult caregivers might establish some bounds to the choices a child can make, to protect against grievous harm, for the educative effects to be realized children's choices must actually be effective within those bounds, not subject to override by any adults, and pertain to nontrivial matters. If they are truly to apply themselves to the task of making the best decisions they can, children must have the sense that the decision is actually theirs and that they will bear some costs as a result of a bad decision.

Thus, good parents gradually expand the range of their children's freedom, giving them increasing decision-making power over their daily lives, offering as much guidance as the children can usefully absorb, but ultimately letting the children stand on their own, with the real possibility of failing or incurring costs. At some point, this extends even to more momentous decisions such as which high school they will attend, which academic "track" they will follow (e.g., vocational vs. college preparatory), and whether and where they will work outside of school hours. Parents allow this freedom or power because they recognize that gradual assumption of control over their lives is as necessary to children's cognitive development and maturation as is the instruction they receive in school and at home. Parents also do it because children have an ever-increasing desire for freedom and independence and would simply be miserable if allowed no control over their own lives. Being empowered also becomes important to their sense of their own competence and therefore to their self-esteem. This second rationale for liberty therefore straightforwardly supports giving children choice-protecting rights to an increasing degree as they develop, and that would presumably include at some point a right to choose with whom they will have particular relationships. The current approach in some jurisdictions, which largely ignores children's views in most decisions about their relationships, is difficult to defend on child-centered grounds. As Jane Fortin notes, this approach "is difficult to justify ... to children who are being brought up in a society which constantly urges them to develop their powers of critical awareness and to act responsibly and independently."[55]

However, as Fortin recognizes, one important counteracting factor is the great potential downside to empowering a child in the context of choosing intimate relationships, or to a child's awareness of being empowered, because of the emotional fallout relationship decisions can have. Children can experience tremendous guilt when they see themselves as responsible for causing a parent or other family member to suffer intense frustration or disappointment, and that guilt can undermine a child's welfare and development. In addition, many children would experience great stress during the course of legal proceedings that called on them to make a decision. Research in the United Kingdom reveals that children involved in divorce, for example, want to be involved in the custody decision-making process and to have their views taken into account, but do not want to choose between parents or feel responsible for the postdivorce arrangements.[56] Consistent with this concern, guidelines for court-appointed guardians *ad litem* who represent children in custody or child-protective proceedings typically discourage the guardians from soliciting preferences from very young children, instructing the guardians instead either to attempt to discern preferences indirectly by asking the children questions about their daily lives, or not to look for or encourage formation of preferences at all, but rather just to get a sense of the children's environment and relationships with parents. Custody rules and practices in many countries make the child's views relevant to court decision making only if the child is above a certain age, typically twelve.[57]

It could be that, as a general matter, the most appropriate realm for children to practice making relationship decisions, and a fully adequate realm, is just their relationships with peers – that is, their friendships and associations formed around particular activities, such as sports. This realm is not one of those of principal concern to family law scholars or the legal system, and it is likely not one in which there is a widespread problem; bad parenting is more likely to entail a lack of interest in children's associations outside the family than unwarranted prohibitions of associations with certain others. It is, however, an aspect of children's relational lives currently governed by law – namely by laws conferring on legal parents plenary power to control children's residence, activities, and associations. It might be that the law should be changed so as to restrict this power somewhat, perhaps by amending definitions of neglect in child protective statutes so as to prohibit excessive restriction of children's association with nonfamily members or denial of choice in such matters, authorizing involvement of child protective workers in cases where children appear truly to be suffering from extremely isolating or tyrannical parenting practices. But it might be that the legal system cannot realistically be expected to protect children's interest in practicing decision making about relationships, because doing so would be too disruptive of daily family life or would stretch limited government resources excessively.

The sum total of these welfare considerations suggests that the age at which minors presumptively enjoy choice-protecting rights in connection with their family relationships should be an age at which they can be presumed to be either the best independent judges of their own overall welfare or amenable to guidance by others toward rational and reasonable judgments, but also at which they can be presumed emotionally and psychologically capable of handling responsibility for making a particular sort of decision. Again, this could vary from one type of decision to another. For example, it might be proper for children to have a choice-protecting right with respect to formation of new parent–child relationships (e.g., by adoption) at an age earlier than they have a choice-protecting right with respect to termination of existing legal parent–child relationships, because in the latter case there is likely to be a social relationship already in place that raises the psychological and emotional costs for children of frustrating or disappointing the adults involved. This is, in fact, what existing law does, only it does not give minors a choice-protecting right with respect to termination of a parent–child relationship at any age.

Variation among decisions might also be warranted because of the importance children are likely to attach to having control over one decision or another. For example, adoption of an older child by foster parents might produce much unhappiness for the child if he feels forced to accept the arrangement or not adequately consulted, even if he would not have been the best judge of where his interests lay in the matter. The concern about the burden of responsibility also suggests that any choice-protecting legal rights conferred on minors should be coupled with a legal power to waive the right to choose. That is, they should be given and have explained to them the option of not expressing a wish and instead having an adult representative make a judgment about their best interests and advocate on that basis. They should not have responsibility thrust upon them unwillingly.

An autonomy-focused moral outlook would yield more or less the same results. The respect for self-ownership it entails might suggest, however, that as in the case of adults of diminished capacity, a presumption of competence should apply and the burden should be on those who would restrict minors' freedom to make their own decisions about relationships to prove incompetence and to take the least restrictive means to protecting a minor from the adverse consequences of incompetence. This outlook would naturally support conferral of choice-protecting rights on persons when they become generally autonomous, which could for some be before the age of legal majority. It would counsel in favor of a default rule setting the age of majority at that age when the average person becomes generally autonomous, but it would also embrace the sort of emancipation rules that exist throughout the West and that allow persons under the age set by the default rule to demonstrate on an individual basis that they are autonomous. This outlook would also approve of issue-specific rules conferring choice-protecting rights on minors as to any decisions for which the capacity of autonomous choosing might develop earlier than it does for other decisions, and it would allow for a mature minor exception to decision-specific rules.

In addition, for the same reason suggested by Mill's second justification of liberty, those who attribute ultimate value to autonomy should also endorse the proposition that children have a moral right to make some effective choices at some point prior to attainment of autonomy. Assuming that they assign great importance to developing autonomy where the potential for it exists, they will be concerned to create the optimal conditions for children to realize their potential, and that must include opportunities for effective decision making prior to maturity as to a gradually expanding range of decisions about their lives. Decisions about relationships are ones that children must learn how to make to become autonomous within this important area of life, and they entail some considerations different from any encountered in other areas of life. They can also be very complex decisions, requiring some understanding of human psychology and social dynamics and appreciation of other persons' character and therefore provide an especially challenging test of young people's developing faculties, one perhaps best undertaken while they are still amenable to parental guidance.

Like those concerned with children's happiness, however, those aiming principally at optimal development toward autonomy will wish to guard against children suffering any consequences of decision making, such as a feeling of responsibility for the unhappiness of a parent or other family member, that so threaten a child's basic emotional or psychological well-being as to thwart their development.[58] A young child could, for example, be traumatized by being asked to pick a parent at divorce to such an extent that her self-respect is undermined and she becomes terrified of ever again making an independent decision about her relationships with others. A focus on autonomy rather than happiness might simply allow for a somewhat greater empowerment of children, encompassing some situations where a child might experience significant anxiety about how her decisions affect others but not so much as to undermine her development toward autonomy.

Again, though, it is not necessary to children's proper development that they be faced with such momentous decisions as whether to return home to abusive parents or instead sever legal ties to those parents, unless perhaps they affirmatively seek to make such decisions for themselves. It is principally necessary that they have a significant number of associations outside the family and have some say as to with whom those associations will be. Yet this is an area where it is difficult for child protective workers to identify and address parental shortcomings, at least without being so intrusive in families as to disrupt the relationships on which children primarily depend for their development. But the difficulty would not necessarily be greater than it is in other aspects of child rearing, such as emotional nurturance, as to which the law currently speaks, however vaguely. Like emotional injury, inadequate socialization might be the sort of harm that is typically uncovered only when the state investigates charges of other, more overt harms, such as physical abuse or malnutrition, but that it is worthwhile to include in whatever statement of parenting standards a state's laws contain.

Conclusion

The predominant theoretical justifications for adults' rights in personal relationships, relying on widely shared assumptions as to which values the state should aim to advance, turn out not to support the current disparity between the strong rights adults enjoy and the quite limited and weak rights that the law accords children. In fact, the welfare-focused and autonomy-focused moral outlooks both support the conclusion that children are morally entitled to legal rights equivalent or analogous to those enjoyed by adults, with equal force and effect. A welfare-focused moral outlook supports attributing to children a moral right to state decisions – legislative and judicial – that best promote their welfare. State decision makers should view their role as a fiduciary one, entailing an obligation to focus exclusively on the interests of the children whose family lives are at stake, taking into account anything known about a child's unique characteristics as well as knowledge of children's generic needs. An autonomy-focused moral outlook supports attributing to children a moral right to state decisions that respect any measure of autonomy they already possess and that optimize their development toward full autonomy. Both outlooks support a conclusion that, where it is appropriate for state decision makers to choose for children, rather than to give children choice-protecting rights, it should choose as the children would choose for themselves if able and in such a way most likely to gain the uncoerced approval of children when they reach maturity. The model of decision making suggested is one of "imputed choice," with the choice imputed to children having the same force in law as have competent adults' actual choices.

Given the widespread acceptance of welfare and/or autonomy as the ultimate aim, or at least a very high priority, of the state, there should therefore be a broad acceptance of these propositions: First, children possess a moral right to enter into and continue relationships with other, willing persons when, in appropriate circumstances, they choose or, in all other circumstances, when some other party determines that this is in their best interests or that it is reasonable to impute to them a choice to be in those relationships, taking into account what is known about them individually and the needs that children in general are presumed to have. Second, children possess a moral right to avoid or terminate relationships with other persons, regardless of the others' wishes and regardless of any broad societal aims, when they so choose, when this is in their best interests, or when it is reasonable to impute to them a choice to do so.

Of course, the flip side of children's moral right to avoid relationships that are not conducive to their welfare or to their development toward autonomy is that other persons have no right to enter into or continue a relationship with a child when mutuality is lacking – that is, when children do not wish to be in the relationship or it is not in their interests to be in the relationship, all things considered. Others' legal rights to be in a relationship with a child would be contingent, just as they are in connection with relationships between adults, on such mutuality. Others would have an equality-based right to be considered for a relationship with a child on the same basis as other, similarly situated persons, but no right to have a relationship, on the basis of which they could object to state or private action inhibiting a relationship, unless and until the child's right is exercised in their favor. This implication of children's rights will likely cause the most consternation, and so I address objections to it in Chapter 6, along with other concerns these conclusions might raise.

Finally, although this is not a matter of central concern in this book, it is worth mentioning that affording children rights equivalent to those enjoyed by adults would also entail that children have no right to a relationship with unwilling adults. Thus, it would not require change to existing law in that respect. The analysis above does not compel this result but is consistent with it. Absent a persuasive argument for giving children stronger or more extensive rights than adults enjoy, therefore, children would not possess a legal right to compel a biological parent to assume the role of day-to-day caregiver or "psychological" parent (though a sound argument for financial support might still be constructed), nor to prevent a legal parent from exiting that role and terminating any social relationship with the child, regardless of whether this would be best for the child. They also would not possess a right to compel unwilling grandparents or other third parties to spend time with them. There might be persuasive arguments to the contrary, but I do not pursue the matter further.

6 Rebutting Defenses of the Status Quo

The conclusion that children are morally entitled to legal relationship rights equivalent to those of adults, and therefore to state decision making that either respects their wishes or focuses exclusively on their welfare or on establishing the conditions for their healthy development toward autonomy, would entail a diminution of the legal rights adults currently enjoy. In particular, biological parents' right to occupy the role of legal parent would diminish, and legal parents' rights to custody or visitation and even to remain in a parental role at all would shrink. This conclusion would also run directly up against certain broad societal aims, including some, such as racial, gender, and religious equality, that are reflected in constitutional norms.

Of course, the legal rights we competent adults possess in connection with our intimate associations authorize us to make choices solely for our own benefit, without giving to the interests of others the sort of deference that the law governing children's relationships now gives to the interests of adults and without having to serve any broad societal aims. It should mute objections to some degree to point out that what is being claimed here for children is no more than what we adults have given ourselves and that resisting this conclusion would entail arguing that children should have less than equivalent rights. Nevertheless, the idea that the family law decisions addressed in this book ought to accommodate, to at least some degree, the interests of adults and the progressive aims of a liberal society has a strong hold on many people. It might qualify as "dead dogma," Mill's term for a belief that goes unquestioned to such a degree and for so long that people currently have little sense of why they do or ought to hold it. In this chapter, therefore, I look directly at these competing claims or impulses – parental rights and constitutionally embodied societal aims, to see how one might defend the view that decisions about children's lives must be constrained by them and to assess the strength of any such defense. If the defense is strong, it might require a rethinking of the positive theory developed in the previous chapters or might suggest some limits to its application.

I. Parents' Rights

The principal objection to the positive theory constructed in the preceding chapters is likely to be that imputing to children a moral right to state decision making that aims exclusively to respect their wishes or to advance their welfare and their interest in developing toward autonomy would result in an unjustifiable interference with the welfare or autonomy of others – in particular, those denied a relationship with a child as a result or of those prevented from exerting control over children's associations.

A) Rethinking the Welfare-Based Analysis

Undeniably, state decisions about children's relationships affect the welfare of adults as well as the welfare of children. Having and raising children is an important element of the life plan of most adults, and having that ambition thwarted to any degree can greatly diminish a person's happiness. John Robertson writes with respect to parentage that "[t]o deny someone who is capable of parenting the opportunity to rear a child is to deny him an experience that may be central to his personal identity and his concept of a meaningful life."[1] A proper application of utilitarian reasoning requires attention to all whose welfare is affected by a decision, so it might be that some balancing of interests is called for in making any decisions about children's relationships and that such a balancing would show the appropriateness of retaining some, perhaps all, of the rights adults now enjoy in these legal actions. As noted in Chapter 2, the European Court of Human Rights, courts in some other jurisdictions, and some family law scholars have explicitly endorsed such a balancing of adults' interests and children's interests both in crafting statutory rules to govern the various aspects of adult–child relationships and in adjudicating individual disputes relating to each aspect. Their reasoning seems to rest on the simplistic (and obviously incomplete) syllogism: "Adults have interests too, therefore adults' interests should also be taken into account."

In particular, many people think it self-evident that the suffering some biological parents would experience from being denied the opportunity to raise their children gives rise to an entitlement on their part to assume the role of legal parent and to retain it absent terribly blameworthy conduct. Mary Midgley argues with respect to birth mothers: "To bear children is . . . normally to be put in a situation where their removal will cause one great pain and lasting psychological trauma. If that does not ground a 'right,' it would be interesting to know what does."[2] But even when what is at stake for parents is something much less than whether they can be legal parents at all – for example, whether they can relocate after divorce without losing primary custody or whether they can have complete control over a child's associations with third parties, many scholars perceive an interest on the part of parents strong enough to give rise to a right, one that can override the interests of children. John Eekelaar asserts with respect to relocation, for example, that if a custodial parent would suffer more from not moving than the child would suffer from moving, then it is appropriate to protect the parent rather than the child and authorize the parent to move with the child.[3]

There are several reasons why this line of defense for the status quo will not succeed. First, the positive theory developed in the preceding chapters does not rule out adults' rights altogether. As noted in Chapter 5, the theory presupposes that adults would enjoy, in their relationships with children, the same sort of rights they possess in connection with their relationships with other adults – namely a right to make themselves available for a relationship and a right against third parties that they not interfere with any relationship that is the product of reciprocal "choosing." What it ultimately denies adults is a further right unlike any they enjoy in the context of adult relationships; it denies them a right to be in a legal or social relationship with another person and to determine the structure of that relationship regardless of any actual choice by that person or any proxy or imputed choice made by an agent in behalf of that person. It also denies them a right to a balancing of their interests against the interests of another person in the making of decisions as to what sort of relationship, if any, they will have with that other person or in the determination of where that other person will live. We have no such rights in connection with adult relationships, even though those relationships are central to most persons' personal identity and concept of a meaningful life and even though denial or severance of a relationship with a particular other adult can cause us "great pain and lasting psychological trauma." As a general matter, we do not have a right to everything that we really, really want nor to everything that would spare us from suffering.

Second, although it is true that a balancing of interests should, within a utilitarian analysis, take place at some level, the only level at which the state balances interests in the context of adults' relationships with each other is at the level of constitutional decision making, when the basic rights of all persons are established. The previous chapter did essentially the same thing in determining the basic rights of children and concluded that children's basic relationship rights should be at least as strong as those of adults. If that conclusion is correct, then no further balancing should be done at legislative or judicial stages of decision making. The paradigmatic relationship rights – that is, those we adults currently enjoy in our encounters with each other – do not call for any balancing in individual instances of conflicting preferences or interests. When I approach other adults about forming a relationship, or want friends or family members to continue or intensify a relationship, I have no right that they take my interests into account in reaching a decision. Their right is to do what is best for them, period. A legal claim by one adult against another on the grounds that the other has refused a friendship or marriage proposal would have no validity whatsoever, regardless of the relative impact on each in the given circumstances. And if one member of a married couple petitions for a divorce and shows that the other was abusive or that they have lived apart for the requisite period, a protest by the other spouse of the sort "but your honor, a divorce will be devastating to me" would not even make the judge glance up from the divorce decree he or she is signing; that is simply not a legally relevant consideration.

The state's decisions in the cases described in Chapter 2 should be viewed as the functional equivalent of adults' exercise of their rights, made as an agent for a child to effectuate the rights of the child, coming after the respective rights of adults and children have been established by a balancing at the constitutional level. At the point where those rights are being exercised – that is, when the state makes decisions about specific aspects of children's relational lives at the legislative or judicial level of state decision making, the state should act solely as surrogate for the child and no longer in the role of arbiter of competing interests among citizens. The state's role at that point should therefore be solely one of imputing a choice to the child or making a substituted judgment for the child – in other words, a purely *parens patriae* role. It need not have any regard for the welfare of others, at least not as a matter of others' rights.

An argument against the conclusion of the utilitarian analysis in Chapter 5 would therefore presumably need to challenge the empirical assumption regarding the relative weight of adults' interests and children's interests as a general matter in connection with decisions about children's relationships. It would have to show that, whereas the interests of adults in

connection with forming, maintaining, structuring, and ending relationships with each other are generally of equal weight for all, when it comes
to adult–child relationships, the interests at stake for adults and children
are of unequal weight and the weight is greater for adults than for children. Certainly much family law scholarship and much political theorizing
about child rearing appear to assume that adults' interests are more compelling than those of children in connection with children's upbringing.
But from an objective standpoint, that is patently implausible. The benefits
of parenthood can be profound, but they are transcendent, not essential
to basic well-being. Becoming a parent is an ulterior aim in our lives, like
getting married and pursuing a particular career. It might have great subjective significance for many of us, just as marrying a particular person
or securing a particular job is immensely important to many people, but
achieving it is not so essential to our basic well-being that failure to do so
would disable us from pursuing other aims in life. This is apparent from
the fact that many adults get along quite well without having children and
from the fact that many adults who do become legal parents are indifferent
to the role. Moreover, the adults most likely to be denied the status of legal
parent under an appropriate regime of children's rights are those who do
not place great subjective value on being a parent, because motivation is
certainly an important qualification for that role.

In this regard, it is significant that adults who are unable to conceive
children themselves are not deemed to have a fundamental interest in or
right to adopt a child. Thus, in a decision upholding France's exclusion of
homosexuals from adopting, the ECHR stated that "the Convention does
not guarantee the right to adopt," that "the right to respect for family life
presupposes the existence of a family and does not safeguard the mere
desire to found a family," and that the state's denial to the petitioner of
authorization to adopt "could not be considered to infringe his right to the
free expression and development of his personality or the manner in which
he led his life."[4] Signaling the greater importance of family formation
for children than for adults, the Court stated further: "Adoption means
'providing a child with a family, not a family with a child,' and the State
must see to it that the persons chosen to adopt are those who can offer the
child the most suitable home in every respect."[5] Also significant is the fact
that biological fathers' desire to become parents hardly registers in public
debate and legal analysis of abortion; a woman's interest in controlling her
body, even after her voluntary conduct produces a human life within her,
in the minds of pro-choice advocates and courts dwarfs the interest a man
might have in raising his biological offspring.[6]

In contrast, children's basic, fundamental well-being and developmental interests are clearly at stake in the determination of who their parents will be and what other relationships they will have. Children do not fare well in life and have great difficulty pursuing any higher aims if they do not receive nurturing from caring, competent parents. Parents who perform poorly, out of indifference, immaturity, inability, or dysfunction, can seriously undermine children's mental health, self-respect, and cognitive and emotional development. The plain fact is that children have weightier interests at stake than adults in connection with state decisions about children's family life, not vice versa.

This conclusion from comparing interests would apply also to the claims of parents already in established parent–child relationships with respect to custodial arrangements and control over children's associations with nonparents. Once adults do have their interest in being parents satisfied, the incremental benefit they receive from having somewhat more time with a child or from having absolute rather than somewhat limited control over the child's other associations is much less significant. Children, too, have less at stake in connection with these issues but still presumably have at least as much at stake as do the adults. For example, children's intellectual, psychological, and emotional development can be much affected by relationships with siblings and extended family members, and either relocation or parental choice can disrupt those relationships. Certainly children's interest in having some association with persons other than their parents is weightier than any parent's interest (if it can be said to be such) in satisfying a desire to deny the child all other associations, to have complete dominion over the child's life, and to create a family life entirely isolated from the outside world. Conferring on parents the power completely to isolate their children, as the state now does in most western nations with very limited exceptions, is clearly unjustifiable on theoretical grounds. And in many of the visitation disputes that make their way to court, the interest of children at stake is the substantial one of maintaining contact with a person who is not a legal parent yet who has played an important caretaking role in their lives, whereas the interest of the parent might be just one of avoiding the annoyance and inconvenience of occasional interactions with someone they resent and of retaining the ability to spite that third party.

As with adults, it is not true in every instance that decisions about a child's life have a greater impact on the welfare of the person for whom the decision is made than on the welfare of others. For example, with a newborn, decisions about which family members visit with the child might be of little or no (immediate) consequence for the child, who would have little awareness of such persons being in the room. Yet the decisions might have a significant effect on the happiness of some family members. But certainly decisions as to who will have custody of a child and who, in the long run, will have the opportunity to form a close relationship with a child have a substantial impact on the child's life and generally have a greater impact on the welfare of the child than they have on anyone else's interests. Again, treating children as equal moral persons entails presumptively affording them rights equal or equivalent to those enjoyed by adults. And the relationship rights we adults enjoy are not limited to situations where we can show our interests are in fact more important than the interests of other persons, including other persons whose efforts to form a relationship with us we rebuff. We have the right to refuse a relationship no matter how intense the other person's disappointment and no matter how insignificant the matter is to us. Significantly, this is true also when parents abandon their children; that visiting a child might only be an inconvenience for the parent, and that the child might be devastated by the parent's disregard, do not under current law diminish the right of the parent to avoid the relationship. Attributing to children a right in every context to whatever relationship outcomes are best for them, even if in some set of cases their interests are not particularly pronounced, would therefore give children no stronger right than we claim for ourselves. To insist that they should have weaker rights than we enjoy is to ask that the state accord children less than equal moral respect.

B) Rethinking the Autonomy-Based Analysis

Some might resist the conclusions reached in Chapter 5 about children's rights on the grounds that I have ignored the autonomy interests of adults, particularly parents. It is quite common among legal scholars and political theorists who write about the law relating to children's upbringing to speak of everything parents want as a matter of their autonomy.[7] Schoeman writes, for example, as follows:

> To set terms for emotional parenting more stringent than required for the protection of children from abuse and neglect constitutes an interference in a person's claim to establish intimate relations except on the society's terms.... Thus, as a way of transcending oneself and the boundaries of abstract others, as a way of finding meaning in life, and as a means of maintaining some kind of social and moral autonomy, the claim to free-dom from scrutiny and control in one's relations with others should be

thought of as a moral claim as important as any other that can be envisioned. It must not be up to society in general, without there being some special cause, to decide whom one can relate to and on what terms. Other things being equal, parents consequently are entitled to maintain their offspring and seek meaning with and through them.[8]

On this view, denying biological parents legal parent status is an infringement of an autonomy right, as is terminating legal parent status or ordering visitation with third parties over parental objection. Yet my elaboration and extension of the autonomy-focused strain of moral attitudes and political theory gave no consideration to adults' autonomy.

This objection, however, rests on a basic misunderstanding and misuse of the concept of autonomy. This sort of argument must presuppose a notion of autonomy that includes the power to dictate the life of another person, at least when the other is nonautonomous. Only on this basis could one say that frustrating some adult's desire to be the parent of a particular child or to control a child's other associations is a restriction on the adult's autonomy. But this notion is mistaken. Autonomy means "self-rule." Although discussion of the concept usually focuses on the aspect of autonomy that contrasts with being ruled in one's life by external forces, another essential component is its limiting the sphere of an autonomous agent's control to the agent's own life, in contrast to a power to control or liberty to impact the life of another. In other words, the *auto-* part of *autonomy* refers, in established usage, not only to the source of the nomos but also to the proper scope of application for the nomos that emanates from the self. Consider Mill's description of the realm in which individual liberty should prevail, often cited as paradigmatic of the liberal account of autonomy:

> The only part of the conduct of anyone for which he is amenable to society is that which concerns others. In the part which merely concerns himself, his independence is, of right, absolute. Over himself, over his own body and mind, the individual is sovereign. . . . [T]here is a sphere of action in which society, as distinguished from the individual, has, if any, only an indirect interest: comprehending all that portion of a person's life and conduct which affects only himself or, if it also affects others, only with their free, voluntary, and undeceived consent and participation. . . . This, then, is the appropriate region of human liberty.[9]

Actions impacting the lives of others and efforts to control the lives of others, Mill wrote, "require a totally different treatment."[10] Mill drew a definite distinction between "self-regarding" and "other-regarding" conduct and insisted that moral arguments for liberty support only the former category of action. In fact, he applied this view explicitly to child rearing as follows:

> A person should be free to do as he likes in his own concerns, but he ought not to be free to do as he likes in acting for another, under the pretext that the affairs of the other are his own affairs. The State, while it respects the liberty of each in what specially regards himself, is bound to maintain a vigilant control over his exercise of any power which it allows him to possess over others. . . . It is in the case of children that misapplied notions of liberty are a real obstacle to the fulfillment by the State of its duties. One would almost think that a man's children were supposed to be literally, and not metaphorically, a part of himself, so jealous is opinion of the smallest interference of law with his absolute and exclusive control over them, more jealous than of almost any interference with his own freedom of action: so much less do the generality of mankind value liberty than power.

Similarly, contemporary philosopher Thomas Hill writes that "autonomy is usually thought to be freedom to make one's own decisions about matters which most deeply affect one's own life, not to control others in matters which more seriously affect them." He cites as examples of decisions that lie within properly understood bounds of autonomy "choices about what jobs to take (among those for which one is qualified), what people to associate with (among those willing to reciprocate), what books to read, where to live, etc." And as examples of decisions that lie outside the properly understood boundaries of autonomy, he cites "my son's choice of college major, his hair style, and his dating partners," things in which a parent might take intense interest but that are, quite simply, not within the realm of the parent's autonomy, any more than one's spouse's decisions about his or her education or personal grooming are within the realm of one's autonomy.[11]

The concepts of autonomy and self-determining liberty thus contain a limiting principle as well as an affirmative claim to something; they exclude a power of "other-determination" or control over the life of another. This limit is created not by the equal claim of other autonomous agents to self-rule but by the inherent boundaries of the underlying moral rationale for valuing and protecting autonomy. Control over others bears no connection to the foundational moral assumptions of self-ownership and integrity of the moral agent's own self. And although one underlying assumption of Kantian moral theory, as to the uniqueness or metaphysical significance of humans' capacity for reasonableness and rationality, could be connected to a right to actualize any and all preferences a person might develop, it is certainly not the case that this capacity can be realized only if given unlimited scope and effect. In fact, it is inherent in the notion of reasonableness that one is prepared to accept limitations on one's desires and rational pursuit of preferred ends, especially limitations that reflect a recognition of the separateness and equal moral standing of other persons.

Thus, there is simply no moral purchase in autonomy-focused moral theory to a demand for power to control another person's life or to be in a relationship with another person who has not in any sense chosen to be in that relationship, regardless of whether that other person is autonomous. It is the sort of demand men once made to retain possession of and exclusive control over their wives, when wives were not treated in law as persons in their own right. We now view such a demand as entirely inconsistent with a proper treatment of women, because they are in fact distinct persons, whether married or not. Treatment of children as persons, distinct from any adults, likewise makes such a claim entirely inapt, even though children are presumed nonautonomous, simply because they are persons rather than property or appendages of their parents. In short, the normative gap between the fact of being autonomous and having a right to be the legal parent of a particular child, or having a right to control a child's associations with others, is infinitely large and unbridgeable.

This conclusion is consistent with the understanding of autonomy that prevails outside the realm of child rearing. In discussing both competent and incompetent adults, we do not regard as an infringement of autonomy frustration of a person's desire for a relationship with another when that other person has not independently chosen to be in such a relationship or frustration of a person's desire to dictate how another person's life should go. That is a denial of other-determining power, not of autonomy, and other-determining power is something to which we generally do not believe anyone is morally entitled.[12] Thus, it is not the case in connection with relationships among adults that individuals are entitled to associate with whomever they choose, regardless of any reciprocal choice. As emphasized in Chapter 3, we are entitled in the first instance only to be available for a relationship with others; we have a self-determining right to "put ourselves out there." The theory I have advanced grants adults no more nor less than this in connection with relationships with children; they are entitled to be available for a relationship with a child but have no right to be in a relationship nor to carry on a relationship in a particular way absent a reciprocal choice. The principle difference between the two contexts is that in the case of relationships with children a surrogate generally must do the choosing for a child. That children in the relevant legal contexts generally cannot choose for themselves conceptually need not, and morally should not, mean that adults thereby acquire more extensive rights in those contexts than they have in connection with relationships with other adults.

Alternatively, one might object that thwarting the aspect of some adults' life plans that entails having and raising children impinges not on the exercise of autonomy but on the preconditions for developing or maintaining autonomy. Being denied legal parenthood with respect to one's biological offspring, or being disqualified from adopting, can be emotionally devastating and humiliating, and so might undermine one's health and self-respect, which I have suggested are prerequisites to a person's realization of autonomy. This objection does put in question what trade-offs the state may make between the autonomy-underwriting interests of adults and the autonomy-underwriting interests of children when making the decisions under review here, which are, in reality, decisions not just about the relational lives of children but also about the relational lives of adults.

This objection can be answered in a number of ways. One would be to compare the relative autonomy-related effects on adults and children of having particular legal rules and to choose a rule that protects against the more severe effects. That approach would presumably favor child-protective rules, because, as discussed previously, children have more at stake in connection with decisions about the basic structure of their family lives. The early stages of personal formation are more critical to health, self-respect, intellectual growth, and the other preconditions for autonomy than are those traversed in adulthood. Children's needs with respect to family relationships are simply much greater than adults' needs. Adults can, and many do, carry on with few or no close personal relationships. In particular, a significant percentage of adults never become parents and yet have satisfying, fully autonomous lives. They can experience the benefits of intimacy in relationships with other adults.

Of course, most of us who are parents experience a unique and profound satisfaction, a sense of fulfillment and transcendent joy unlike that which we have with other adults. Those of us who have that experience of parenthood – and not all parents do – are willing to sacrifice a great deal to secure and maintain it. Ultimately, though, the benefits we receive from a parent–child relationship are simply not as vital to our basic emotional and psychological makeup as the benefits that our children receive are to their internal resources. As noted above, our experience is transcendent, something we do – ideally – after already having developed into mature human beings, with a solid cognitive, psychological, and emotional self in place. It is not formative of our basic selves in the way that a child's experience of being loved and nurtured is. It might complete us or change us, but it does not get us started in the way that family life does for children. Moreover, adults who are altogether denied the opportunity to parent by appropriately child-protective rules are likely to be ones whose basic well-being suffers already from other causes, such as addiction or imprisonment, and for those people being parents is not likely to bolster their health or self-esteem appreciably.

This comparison of the respective stakes for adults and children can, as suggested in the previous chapter, be subsumed within a hypothetical contract model of moral reasoning. I explained in Chapter 5 that Rawls's contractarian theory rested in significant part on assumptions about the implications of respecting other persons as free and equal beings who are also autonomous or have the potential to become autonomous. Thinking in terms of a contract presumes the need to fashion rules for social ordering that all rational persons should see as fair and therefore accept, and thinking in terms of a hypothetical rather than actual contract allows us to imagine children being among or having proxies among the contracting parties. Legal scholars Elizabeth Scott and Robert Scott have in fact proffered a hypothetical bargain model for reasoning about the appropriate balance of parents' and children's interests in fashioning legal rules for one area of family law – namely that concerning the authority that legal parents exercise over the lives of their children.[13] Their model can usefully be assimilated to a Rawlsian framework to aid the analysis of not just parental authority over third-party relationships but also rules for removal of children from legal parents and termination of parental rights, which are effectively limits on the child-rearing freedom of parents.

Scott and Scott suggest viewing parents as agents for children, charged with management of a child's life and subject to special duties because of the particular dependency and vulnerability of their principal, and then reason about what the terms of the agency relationship should be. They imagine a negotiation session between a child and a potential parent of the sort you might expect a person to engage in when seeking to retain a personal manager or other agent. They speculate about what terms parents would insist on including in the agency agreement, with the threat to walk away from the deal backing up their insistence on those terms. They then arrive at conclusions about the proper scope of parental freedom in ordering children's lives, and correspondingly about the proper extent of legal regulation of parental decision making, by considering the costs and benefits of serving in a parental role and the effects on a person's motivation to act as a parent of being subject to legal restrictions.

Scott and Scott conclude that parents should have extensive authority and that this authority should be deemed a matter of "right," because otherwise parents would feel too aggravated and disrespected to continue in the parental role.[14] They might also say this authority should be cloaked in the protective aura of "autonomy" terminology, however conceptually incoherent that might be. Looked at another way, their position is that extensive authority and rights must be afforded parents "as compensation for the satisfactory performance of voluntarily assumed responsibilities to provide for the child's interests."[15] Absent such compensation, or quid pro quo, adults would decline to enter into the agency arrangement. They did not do so, but Scott and Scott might have distinguished parents from guardians for incompetent adults, to whom "rights" of control are not attributed, on the grounds that parental responsibilities are typically more involved and prolonged than are the duties of a guardian. Scott and Scott conclude in a general way from application of their model that "in many respects, current law fits comfortably within the fiduciary paradigm."[16]

This conclusion, it should be noted, is not necessarily incompatible with the conclusions reached in Chapter 5. If Scott and Scott's empirical assumptions are correct, then the legal regime they recommend might be viewed as the best that the state can do for children at the legislative stage of decision making. If plenary control over their children's lives, characterized in the law as a "right," is what adults would need to be given for them to be sufficiently attracted to parenthood, then a legislature or court acting solely out of concern for the interests of children – in particular, children's need for at least some parental care if they are to advance toward autonomy – would seem justified in writing such a rule into statutory or doctrinal law. It is conceptually possible that effectuating the moral right of children established above would involve writing legal rules that on the surface appear designed instead to effectuate moral rights of parents (even if they are not).

Nevertheless, the conclusion should be rejected. It appears to be in part a product of circular reasoning. In speculating about what degree of regulation parents would be willing to accept in the hypothetical negotiations with the child, Scott and Scott rely in large part on existing expectations of parental freedom, which determine what "demoralization costs" regulation will have.[17] But those expectations are shaped by the current law in a particular place; they are neither eternal nor universal. Change the law and eventually people will not expect such freedom to be part of the deal. One illustration of this is attitudes toward the permissibility of parents' hitting their children for disciplinary purposes; American parents have a greater expectation of freedom in this regard than do parents in many other countries, and even within the United States the expectation has diminished significantly over time, with some forms of physical punishment once thought normal and acceptable now regarded as extreme and abusive. Attitudes toward physical chastisement of spouses have also changed, yet this does not seem to have discouraged men from marrying.

Their conclusion is also the product of an incomplete picture of the benefits that children bring to the bargaining table. At certain points in their article, Scott and Scott emphasize the great importance that parenting has in the emotional lives of most adults who choose to become parents, the tremendous happiness and fulfillment that can come from being able to care for a child.[18] Yet oddly, when they spell out their quid pro quo argument for limited regulation, the only benefit to parents that they acknowledge is enjoyment of authority over the child's life.[19] They reason at that point as if all that parents get out of parenting is gratification of a desire to be in control. This is clearly an inadequate account of the hypothetical bargaining situation. Like many defenders of parental entitlement, they want to have their cake and eat it too; to generate sympathy for adults who want to become parents, they portray parenting as vitally important to the happiness of those adults, satisfying a great need they have, but then to oppose legal limitations on parental authority they portray parenting as a great burden and a Herculean act of self-sacrifice. The reality is that parents generally derive profound fulfillment from that role, and that the role, although imposing demands that are often exhausting, also creates an opportunity for joy, love, affection, play, transcendence, greater self-awareness, and a sense of purpose unlike that created by any other role in life. The efforts many adults make, and the costs many are willing to incur, to become parents, reflect the immense payoff they can realize. And this, too, distinguishes parenthood from guardianship for an incompetent adult; parenthood is usually more work, but it is also typically much more rewarding, and so we do not see many people avidly seeking to become guardians for an elderly relative. Guardianship for an incompetent adult is likely experienced more often as a net burden than parenthood is, yet we still do not think it appropriate to treat such guardians as entitled to control their ward's life however they see fit.

A better strategy for determining what parents would agree to in a hypothetical bargain might be to ask how many adults would forego or give up on parenting at successive stages of increased regulation and whether the loss of those particular adults from the parenting profession would be bad for children. I am not aware of any empirical studies that would inform this inquiry, but my sense is that parental power over children in general could be lessened considerably relative to what it now is before any significant percentage of adults would throw up their hands and say it is not worth it to become parents. I cannot imagine many parents making that decision, for example, simply as a result of being compelled to allow visitation with third parties, for short periods and at the third parties' expense, when a court determines that this would be in the child's interests. It is inconceivable that a contrary decision of the U.S. Supreme Court in the *Troxel* case, one that applauded rather than derided the "breathtakingly broad" Washington State statute, as a commendable protection of children's interests in relationships with extended family members, would have caused the birth or adoption rate in the United States to drop. Changing the rules for termination of parental rights so that they serve only the welfare of children would also be unlikely to scare many adults away from becoming parents in the first place, and any who would be scared off presumably would not be good parents.

Thus, although the heuristic model Scott and Scott offer is a useful adaptation of the hypothetical contract strategy, feeding in more accurate and complete empirical assumptions leads to conclusions much different from theirs. Their model actually supports a conclusion that children should have a legal right to contact with third parties when they make competent choices to have such contact or when such contact is in their best interests and that courts should be authorized to order parents to allow such contact when the parents do not voluntarily accede to their children's right in this respect. I believe it also supports a conclusion that adults should enter parenthood subject to a rule that they will be removed from that role if and when that proves to be best for the child, all things considered. I elaborate in Chapter 8, but note here that among the things to be considered would, of course, be an existing bond between parent and child and the child's interest in stability.

Looking at the issue of third-party visitation from the somewhat different hypothetical contract perspective of Rawls's original position, we would anticipate that, should we turn out to be a child when the veil of ignorance is lifted, our relationships with persons other than our parents could be very important to our emotional well-being and psychological stability and therefore to our development toward autonomy. This would particularly be so if those third parties have participated in nurturing us and particularly if they constitute a psychological and emotional link to a deceased parent. And realistically, we would not assume that the potential for legal enforcement of a right to maintain such a relationship would deter any adults who would make good parents from choosing to become parents. Moreover, we would judge, from the original position, that if and when we become parents, any displeasure we might experience as a result of being ordered to allow third parties contact with our child simply would not impact our basic well-being or the preconditions for our maintaining and exercising our autonomy, and so this is not something we would insist on preventing. Undisturbed dominion over the life of another person, even one's offspring, is simply not a primary good. This judgment would be supported by the fact that the legal rules would be known to us as adults in the real world before we decided whether to become parents. Rules prescribing parental rights termination based on particular behaviors or incapacities could be analyzed similarly.

An additional way to answer the question about permissible trade-offs between the autonomy-related interests of adults and the interests of children is by appeal to the generally unstated assumption of autonomy-focused theorizing that it is categorically impermissible to use the lives of nonconsenting persons to shore up for others their capacity for autonomy. In discussing the liberties of adults, including rights to freedom of intimate association, it goes without saying that the state should not place certain nonconsenting adults into intimate relationships with certain other persons for the purpose of bolstering the health and self-respect of the other persons. Adults whose affections toward other adults are rebuffed also suffer a loss of self-esteem as a result and can be traumatized and debilitated by the experience, yet no one would suggest that an appropriate response of the liberal state would be to force some adults to accept undesired relationships. Again, this is not just because of a respect for the other adult's rational capacities but also because of a respect for the other adult's integrity and self-ownership and a well-settled understanding that it is wrong to use any person instrumentally in this way to advance the interests of others. We apply this understanding equally to children in other contexts – for example, in debating the legal rules for medical experimentation with children. There is no principled basis for failing to apply the same understanding to children in the context of state decisions about their family relationships.

In sum, adults receive all the protection they are due for their interest in developing, maintaining, and exercising their own autonomy when they are given the right to make themselves available for a relationship with other persons, including particular children, and when they are given the right to avoid or end a relationship with any other person at any time. In fact, having to work to deserve a relationship with a child should induce adults to improve themselves, including their moral powers, just as does the need to make oneself an attractive candidate for a friendship or intimate partnership with another adult. And, in a just legal regime, the adults of today would, in their own childhoods, have received protection for their interest in becoming autonomous in the first place, from the very rights I have argued children should receive. Enjoying from birth to death a set of relationship rights equivalent to those described as paradigmatic in Chapter 3 – no more and no less – should be enough for every person to develop toward autonomy as a child and to then maintain and exercise that autonomy in a fulfilling way as an adult.

C) Rethinking Parents' Interests

As a parting thought on the issue of parents' rights, I suggest that we rethink the basic assumption that parents are always better off when they win in the various legal disputes over child rearing described in Chapter 2. Scholars and legal actors typically presuppose that adults are injured when the state denies them a relationship, or a relationship of a particular sort, with their biological offspring or when the state frustrates the desires of legal parents to dictate particular things about their children's lives. But that presupposition is not always correct.

Parents usually do, of course, experience immediate disappointment and frustration when they lose in these cases, and the feelings can be pronounced. But people have interests other than avoiding disappointment and frustration. They also have an interest in avoiding being set up for failure in a major undertaking. The long-term suffering of a person who is initially placed in the role of parent and who proves incapable of fulfilling the role adequately can also be pronounced. This is certainly true if they must be removed from the role, with all the humiliation and emotional upset that can create, but it can also occur even if they remain in the role. They might at some point realize their own failing, or have their failing pointed out to them by others, and this can cause a substantial loss of self-esteem. And to the extent that they genuinely care about the welfare of their children, seeing the children's lives go poorly because of their bad parenting or seeing their children physically harmed and psychologically devastated as a result of their abusing the children can cause parents profound and lasting sorrow and remorse.

As a case in point, consider the U.S. Supreme Court's 1989 decision in *Deshaney v. Winnebago County Department of Social Services*. A mother sued a state child protection agency, charging a violation of her child's constitutional rights, on the basis of its repeatedly returning the child to the custody of a father whom the agency knew to be seriously physically abusive. As a proximate result of the state's creating and maintaining that particular parent–child relationship, rather than attempting early on to assign Joshua Deshaney to a better caregiver, Joshua was permanently and severely brain damaged. The Supreme Court held that the state agency violated no rights, because the Court (wrongly) interpreted the child's claim as asserting a positive right to state assistance rather than a negative right against the state's placing the child in a dangerous situation. The Court also explained itself by pointing out that if the state had done more to protect Joshua Deshaney, it would have had to worry about violating the rights of his father, Randy Deshaney.

Scholarly discussion of *Deshaney* treats it as an instance of the state, with the imprimatur of the Supreme Court, serving the interests of parents at the expense of children's welfare. But it is ludicrous to suppose that Randy Deshaney was a winner in the situation, that he was better off as a result of the state's actions. Having custody of his son apparently did not make him happy. And for the remainder of his life after the last incident of abuse, he would have to live with the knowledge that he bashed in the head of his own child and he would have to live without the love and companionship of his son. He became known to his family, friends, and community as a child beater, a vicious beast, and a horrible failure as a parent, which must have affected his self-image. The reality is that the state caused misery to everyone in the Deshaney family when it respected Randy Deshaney's "rights."

The same is true of a legal parent's power over a child's associations with others. When parents' reasons for cutting a child off from grandparents or former caregivers or siblings are selfish and petty rather than focused on their children's welfare, empowering them to decide can set them up for resentment from their children and ultimately remorse at having harmed their children. It can also reinforce in their minds a sense of ownership of their children that will lead them to act selfishly in directing other aspects of their children's lives. Yet self-aware parents are not likely to realize a sense of fulfillment from their parenting role if their carrying out of that role does not entail much of the other-regarding concern that is said to constitute its essence.

Those who champion parents' rights and parents' interests need to reflect on the goods and the virtues of the parental role. Assertions about the great societal and personal value of parenthood ring hollow if they presuppose a conception of parenthood as consisting of adult owners' doing whatever they want with their helpless human possessions. Those who take an interest in social policy and law concerning child rearing should aim to develop and effectuate a conception of parenthood that is actually worth valuing, that truly carries the sort of nobility and dignity that defenders of parents' rights attribute to it.[20] Effectuating such a conception would entail establishing qualifications for assuming the role, just as other noble professions have qualifications. It would entail making a serious effort to prepare individuals for the role and to ensure that they carry it out on the basis of its intrinsic virtues. And it would entail recognizing that occupying the role when one is unwilling to or incapable of carrying out the role in a manner consistent with its intrinsic virtues represents a loss of welfare for everyone involved.

II. Constitutional Constraints and Progressive Social Policies

Ordinarily, when the state acts, through any of its agencies or institutions, it is constrained by numerous constitutional commands. (As noted earlier, I use *constitution* to signify whatever basic rights document governs in a given jurisdiction.) These commands include not just ones specifying individual rights to freedom of intimate association of the sort that I have principally been analyzing, but also ones protecting other individual interests, such as religious freedom, and ones prohibiting state actors from supporting social evils, such as racial inequality and bigotry. In addition, there is a range of situations in which the state is permitted to take certain actions designed to advance the norms reflected in constitutional commands even though those commands do not require those particular actions and even though its actions entail some diminution of the rights or opportunities of some citizens. For instance, in the United States, the Supreme Court has held that universities may to some extent apply affirmative action policies in their admissions practice, treating minority-race applicants more favorably on the whole than white applicants. Even though this amounts to a prima facie infringement of the white applicants' equal protection right, it is permissible if the universities do so for a compelling reason, such as to rectify past discrimination against minority applicants and therefore to serve the fundamental aims of equal opportunity and social equality for persons of minority race that underlie the Fourteenth Amendment's Equal Protection Clause.[21]

Chapter 2 identified several contexts in which the interests of children can conflict not just with adults' interests in having a relationship with them or in controlling their third parties but also with other interests adults might have that ordinarily receive constitutional protection and with certain progressive societal aims, some of which are embodied in constitutional provisions. In some situations, courts and commentators have concluded that these constitutionally significant interests and aims preclude the state from taking certain actions for the sake of children's welfare. An example is the U.S. Supreme Court decision in *Palmore v. Sidoti*, holding that courts deciding custody of a child may not pay any heed to societal reactions against a parent's mixed-race marriage, because doing so would violate an equal-protection-type right of adults to marry someone of another race without penalty and would amount to the state giving effect to racial bigotry. Katharine Bartlett observes as follows:

> The Supreme Court took a hard line in this case, holding that it is impermissible for a court to give effect to private, racial prejudice in custody cases, at any time and under any circumstances.... In taking this position, the Court did not deny that children may suffer as a result of ignoring race. Rather, it concluded almost categorically that the harm of considering race in a custody case is greater than the possible gains. Race must be ignored to serve a greater good than the possible welfare of an individual child.[22]

Many legal scholars would extend the *Palmore* principle to the context of same-sex relationships, out of concern for the freedom and social advancement of persons who are homosexual. In fact, the American Law Institute's Principles of Family Dissolution (ALI Principles), the drafting of which Bartlett oversaw, contains a provision that would proscribe consideration of many parental characteristics and choices, including not just race or ethnicity but also sex, religion, and sexual orientation.[23] It does so because Bartlett and other of the ALI drafters embrace the normative outlook of the Court; they believe it appropriate for the legal system to sacrifice children's welfare for the "greater good." Bartlett writes, for example, that "if the child's interests do not justify race-based custody decision-making, arguably neither are they sufficient to trump society's interest in avoiding sex discrimination."[24] In the context of child maltreatment, scholars such as Dorothy Roberts complain that child protective practices have a disparate impact on minority-race families, as if to suggest – by a line of reasoning that could appear logical only to someone operating from a purely adult-centered perspective – that the norm of racial equality requires the state to refrain from protecting minority race children until it begins to take an equal interest in white children. A similar complaint arises about disparate impact on poor parents.

Another set of constitutional commands that sometimes conflicts with children's welfare is that guaranteeing freedom of religion and prohibiting the state from passing judgment on the validity of religious beliefs. As noted in Chapter 2, courts generally require a somewhat stronger showing of harm to a child from religiously grounded behaviors or teachings before they will base a custody or visitation order on it, relative to things parents do or say that are not motivated by religious belief. For example, courts are less likely to count against a parent that he teaches his child that the other parent is destined for hell because not "saved" than they are to order custody or impose a restriction on conduct during visitation on the basis of a parent simply telling a child that the other parent is a horrible person. This deference to religion reflects a widespread belief that the First Amendment presumptively precludes the state from action at any level, even when making individualized decisions about children's lives, that restricts religious practice or teaching or that influences religious belief.

In addition, there are many situations where children's welfare appears to conflict with social policies that are consistent with constitutional norms but might not be a matter of constitutional compulsion. In the adoption context, it is clearly not mandatory that agencies apply race-matching or religious-matching policies, but many have done so anyway, even though this can cause a delay in placement of a child or result in a placement with less qualified adoptive parents. Race-matching practices are in part a response to calls for protection of minority communities, and religious-matching rules in part reflect an impulse to show respect for the religious beliefs of biological parents who relinquish their children for adoption. In the divorce context, some courts have striven to advance the aim of social equality for women by insulating them from any decisions that could inhibit their pursuit of careers – for example, by refusing to count mothers' increased career commitments or relocation against them in custody decisions.

In all these contexts, there are at work certain considerations of constitutional significance that go beyond just the basic interest adults have in maintaining relationships with children. The question therefore arises whether these additional considerations require some amendment to the general conclusions yielded by the analysis in Chapters 3 through 5. That analysis assumed that adults' interests consisted just in realizing the benefits of being in a relationship with a child and that the only other relevant interests were those of children in having a happy life and in becoming autonomous. Does the presence of additional individual adult interests or of special societal interests – the latter of which are presumably shared by all citizens, including children – require a scaling back in some situations of children's right to have all decisions for them based only on what is best for them personally? Does it require a balancing of interests even at legislative or adjudicatory stages of decision making or even make children's welfare altogether irrelevant in some contexts, as the *Palmore* decision suggests? Are there some hard-and-fast limits on what the state can do to effectuate the moral rights of children, because of constitutional prohibitions against certain kinds of state action or against state action that has certain effects? Do constitutional norms such as social equality for racial minorities and women or state noninvolvement in religious matters at least *authorize* the state to compromise children's welfare in some situations, even if they do not compel that?

One response to these questions might be to answer yes in each case but to maintain that legislatures, courts, and legal scholars have in many of the contexts noted above simply overemphasized the special considerations and given insufficient weight to the interests of children and that as a result they have scaled back children's rights too much or balanced interests incorrectly. In other words, one might grant that it is proper for statutory rules and judicial application of them to reflect some special consideration for religious freedom and race and gender equality but still object to some of the decisions that have been made on the grounds that legislators or judges did not pay enough attention to the impact on the children. One could concede that adults' rights in relationships with children are enlarged by certain constitutionally recognized supplemental interests but insist that those rights cannot be absolute, that state decision makers must always assess whether their decisions will be especially detrimental to children, and that they have often not done this adequately. Even under the strict scrutiny courts apply to infringements of the strongest constitutional rights, including rights against racially or religiously discriminatory state action, courts will uphold such state action if it is necessary to serve a compelling state interest, and courts generally treat protecting children from harm as a compelling state interest.[25] Thus, one could criticize the Supreme Court's analysis in *Palmore*, for example, for not even considering whether the child's interest in not being ridiculed and ostracized constituted a compelling state interest that would justify awarding custody to the father despite the conflict with equal protection rights and values. A showing that a legislative or judicial decision is not optimal for children might not be sufficient to override the enlarged right of adults in these contexts, but a showing that a decision would cause significant harm to a child – for example, by causing psychological trauma or putting a child's health at substantial risk – might be. Last, one might acknowledge that constitutional norms create some hard-and-fast limits on state efforts to protect children's welfare but argue that legislatures and courts have exaggerated those limits – for example, by assuming that the state may not impose any cost on adults for entering into particular types of relationships with other adults or for having certain religious beliefs rather than viewing the constitutional proscription as only precluding the state from prohibiting certain relationships or religious practices altogether.

However, the positive theory developed in the preceding chapters actually supports the starker position that the state should not even recognize, let alone act on, rights of anyone other than the children in these cases and that the state should be viewed in these cases as stepping outside the bounds of the Constitution to a large extent – specifically, to the extent of being freed from the restrictions ordinarily generated by the constitutional rights of others or by public policies. The positive theory led to the conclusion that, in making decisions about children's relationships, the state should be viewed as acting as an agent for the child, in its *parens patriae* role as protector of dependent individuals whose interests would otherwise go unprotected – that is, as a fiduciary. Ordinarily, fiduciaries are charged with a strict duty of loyalty to their principals, which entails an absolute prohibition on self-dealing and on acting out of concern for the interests of third parties (absent direction to do so by the principal). The law makes this duty particularly demanding in the case of fiduciaries for incompetent persons, because of incompetent persons' relative inability to monitor their agents' conduct. Fiduciaries for incompetent adults, as shown in Chapter 3, must act and make decisions solely for the advancement of the ward's interests or presumed preferences. They are to put themselves in the place of the ward and choose as they think the ward would choose.

If the state is in these cases acting simply an agent for a private party, then presumptively it exercises on behalf of the principal rights as extensive as those ordinarily held by private individuals in comparable contexts. It is therefore instructive again to consider the relationship rights of adults among themselves and whether they are qualified in any way by others' interests in avoiding the effects of bigotry or in feeling unconstrained in practicing a religion or by progressive societal aims that presumably would benefit all, such as race and gender equality and economic justice. The reality is that they are not. Adults are entitled to choose not to associate with others for any reason, including a desire to avoid adverse societal reactions or an aversion to others' religious beliefs and practices or because another person's career commitments make her unable to devote sufficient time to the relationship. We competent adults are not legally required to compromise our own welfare to ensure that we do not in any way increase the effects on others of existing social injustices or inhibit others' freedom to pursue their aims or exercise their religion. If we do not want to deal with negative societal reactions or what we regard as idiosyncratic religious practices or others' preoccupation with their careers, we are completely free to avoid a relationship, even though these things would generally have less effect on our welfare as adults than they would have on that of a child. And we are clearly entitled to terminate or avoid in the first instance an intimate relationship with someone who is addicted to drugs or who has been abusive to us or to other persons or who is in prison, regardless of whether that person ever had a fair shake in life and regardless of whether a consequence of our action is to heap further suffering on someone who is poor and has had a miserable life. Although each of us would share in the collective benefits of eliminating bigotry, of social equality for women and for persons who are of minority race or who are homosexual, and of economic justice, neither law nor common moral beliefs dictate that we must act to advance those aims or sacrifice what we believe to be in our best interests in choosing with whom we form a family. There are many ways a society can pursue those aims, but dictating individuals' family arrangements is not among the legitimate ones.

If the state is acting simply as agent for private individuals – namely children – when it creates statutes to govern parentage or termination of parent–child relationships or when it determines who will have custody of a particular child after a divorce, is it not free to act on the same basis, with the same, solely "self"-regarding attitude? Is it not, in fact, required to do so? Surely if a private party were acting in a similar fiduciary role for a child, that private decision maker would not be constrained by interests of third parties in nondiscrimination or religious freedom or required to act so as to advance social equality for disadvantaged groups but would rather be expected to think only of the child's welfare. In fact, this is true of parents today when they make decisions about a child's associations with peers and relatives. Neither the legal system nor other citizens would fault a parent for declining an invitation for his child to play at the home of a classmate whose parents conduct snake-handling religious ceremonies at home or whose parent has been driven by poverty and discrimination to prostitution and drug addiction, even though such a choice by the parent could be viewed as imposing on others a cost for having certain religious beliefs or as exacerbating the suffering and isolation of members of a disadvantaged group. To the contrary, we might condemn the parent if he accepted the invitation, especially if his reason for doing so were that he elevated the ideals of complete religious freedom and social equality for all above the safety of his child.

One fact that gives us pause, however, is that we are *not* here talking about one private entity acting as agent for a private individual. We are talking about THE STATE, and our intuitions tell us that there is something different about the state as agent and that the state is always both bound by constitutional prohibitions and free to pursue its public policies unless doing so would violate someone's trumping constitutional rights. The reasoning of the Supreme Court in *Palmore* reflects and reinforces this intuition: "Private biases may be outside the reach of the law, but the law cannot, directly or indirectly, give them effect."[26] It is difficult to imagine the decision in *Palmore* coming out otherwise, with the Court holding that states may allow local racist attitudes to influence child custody decisions. Likewise, it would make anyone squeamish to see a state officer telling a mother who worked as a homemaker and primary caretaker of her children during many years of marriage that she must, at or after divorce, choose between continuing in a primary role in her children's life or pursuing a career ambition that she has put on hold for many years. To many people, it seems intuitively that she should be able to have both. And it seems cruel to take children away from their biological parents when those parents have been victims of racial discrimination, live in squalor with meager public assistance, and suffered severe deprivation themselves as children. Raising a child might be the only thing in their lives that they find makes life worth living.

These intuitions need to be closely examined and rethought, however. They are based in part on concern about any compromising of the under-lying social ideals, in light of the state's crucial role in promoting those ideals, in part on concern for the relatively great practical and expressive power of state action, and in part on sympathy for the adults involved. As to the last concern, it must be recognized that these are situations in which someone is going to suffer in some way, no matter what, and so the issue is whom the state should allow to suffer most – adult or child – or whether the state should aim to distribute the suffering evenly among parties, perhaps to achieve the least aggregate suffering. I addressed this issue in the previous section, in discussing the appropriateness of balanc-ing interests in individual cases. Here what is called for is some discussion of the special character of the state when it acts as a fiduciary for a private party, of the characteristics of the state that make it unlike any other fiduciary.

With respect to the concern about compromising social ideals, given the state's central role in pursuing these ideals, we need to ask whether the state may or must also act in what is commonly called a "police power" role in these situations, in addition to acting in its *parens patriae* role as agent of the child. In its police power role, the state represents society as a whole – its interests and its collective preferences. Certainly in that role, state actors are ordinarily bound by constitutional limitations and by established public policies. If the state is or should be wearing both hats in these cases, then perhaps it is so bound, and its commitments in the police power role constrain its carrying out of its *parens patriae* role.

Our beliefs about proper state action have been formed principally in contexts involving only competent adults, and in those cases the state is typically wearing only its police power hat, acting as an agent for society as a whole.[27] In the criminal context, the state is protecting the rest of society from an individual's harmful conduct. In the civil context, when resolving conflicts between competent private parties who can adequately assert their own interests, the state is enforcing the social rules of engagement its citizens have collectively chosen and not acting as agent for any private individual. It is because political theorists and legal scholars tend to focus on such contexts involving only competent adults when thinking about the proper conception of the state's function that the idea has become so firmly entrenched that the state is always constrained by all the norms and rights-based commands embedded in the constitution. We need to rethink this idea, in light of the fact that the state does purport to wear a different kind of hat in some contexts.

The question we must ask, therefore, is for whom the state is acting as agent in a given case. Is it all citizens? Is it all residents of the geographical area over which the state has jurisdiction? Or is it a single, vulnerable individual? In many of the situations discussed in Chapter 2, the state currently clearly does not act solely in a police power role or solely as arbiter of the claims of private individuals. It has also, or instead, explicitly assumed the role of protector of the children, the *parens patriae* role. In theory, it could do otherwise; the state could perhaps in these cases delegate to some private agent – for example, to a guardian *ad litem* (GAL) that is not treated as a state actor – the power to decide conclusively what is in a child's interests. However, although many courts do appoint a GAL in contested custody, visitation, and adoption cases and in child protective proceedings, the GAL typically does not have ultimate authority to decide what is best for a child. The GAL role varies somewhat from one jurisdiction to another, but generally the role entails bringing information to the court, for the court better to decide what is in a child's best interests, and/or urging the court to find that a particular outcome is best for the child.

There has not been public discussion about changing this situation so that GALs do have final say as to a child's best interests, which might be in part attributable to the fact that GALs typically receive little specialized training and so are generally not well prepared to make such judgments. Transitioning to a regime in which GALs had final say on children's best interests might be desirable, but it would require states to make a great commitment to specialized training. It might also simply shift the conundrum to a different location; some might then insist that the GAL is a state actor and bound in the same way as a court by constitutional commands. In fact, a GAL today is viewed as a special officer of the court, typically chosen by the judge and compensated by the state, and so arguably is already a state actor. In some large cities, the GALs are permanent employees of municipal agencies. The same problem might arise with appointment of any other conceivable sort of private decision maker; so long as they are selected, trained, and compensated by the state, they would be viewed as state actors, and then some might contend that these representatives for children may not decide for a child on the basis of concerns about stigmatization nor make decisions that interfere with women's social advancement.

Assuming that some kind of state actor will continue to hold and exercise ultimate authority to decide children's interests, and will therefore continue to occupy at least a *parens patriae* role in decision making about children's relationships, should it also assume a police power role in these cases? Can it comfortably wear two hats? I do not believe it can or should. Quite simply, an agent cannot serve two masters with conflicting interests. This is clearly recognized in the law of agency and in rules of ethical conduct for professional agents, such as attorneys. How can a judge serve adequately as an agent for a child while at the same time striving to further the state's conflicting policies and to adhere to the state's conflicting constitutional obligations? Acting as an agent requires avoiding conflicts of interest and acting with a single-minded focus on the wishes and interests of one's principal. If children's moral rights are to control legal decisions about their family relationships, and if children are therefore to have an agent in a real sense in these decisions, that agent must not have divided loyalties, must be prepared to act exclusively in the children's interests.

This is, in fact, the prevailing understanding of what the *parens patriae* role is supposed to entail:

> [W]hen the state acts as parens patriae, it should advance only the best interests of the incompetent individual and not attempt to further other objectives, deriving from its police power, that may conflict with the individual's welfare. ... [T]he state should seek, if possible, to make its decisions in the same way that the individual would were he fully competent.[28]

Thus, for the state to balance the interests of children against the constitutionally recognized interests of individual adults or of society as a whole in making decisions about children's relationships effectively amounts to abandoning its *parens patriae* role and function and slipping into a solely police power role, as arbiter among competing interests and representative of collective societal interests. In fact, given the severe undercounting of children's interests in current legal rules and decision making, the state is doing something even worse; it is abandoning its *parens patriae* obligation and it is carrying out its police power role very badly, in a way that fails to give children's welfare even equal weight relative to that of adults.

The state, it would seem, should be required to abandon one role or the other. It cannot coherently wear both hats. They are logically incompatible with each other. Courts have recognized this in certain decisions concerning the care of mentally incompetent adults. For example, when faced with requests for appointment of a public official as a guardian, courts have responded in a way that supports the view that when the state acts in behalf of an incompetent adult, it must do so with a single-minded allegiance to the welfare of the ward and cannot serve another master at the same time. In *In re Bessie C.*,[29] the Appellate Division of the New York Supreme Court held that the Commissioner of the local state Department of Social Services could not be appointed guardian of the property for an incapacitated woman, because the Department of Social Services is a preferred creditor with respect to persons receiving public assistance. The elderly woman was receiving care in a public nursing home when she inherited money from her deceased husband. If competent, she could have renounced the inheritance, allowing it to pass to her children rather than being taken by the county to recoup expenditures on her care. The county's interest in the inheritance therefore created a conflict of interest between the woman and the Commissioner, and the court ruled that this conflict disqualified him to serve as guardian. Likewise, when the state steps in to make medical decisions for incompetent adults, courts require that it do so with an exclusive focus on the welfare of the incompetent person.

In connection with petitions for sterilization of incompetent adults, the law prohibits judicial consideration of society's interest in avoiding "the genetic and financial burden of children produced by retarded persons."[30] And in connection with decisions about withdrawal of life support from a person in a persistent vegetative state, courts have held that no one has any rights in the matter other than that person and that state actors may not interject into their decisions for such a person either societal interests or interests of other individuals. Even though other persons might care profoundly about the outcome of such cases, state actors act in a purely *parens patriae* role to make in behalf of the incapacitated person the decision it believes she would have made if able.[31]

These decisions demonstrate that the state *can* put aside its police power hat in some cases, and they support the general principle that the state should do so when called on to act as protector of an incompetent private individual. It is not necessary that the state occupy a police power role every time it acts. Thus, no situations of conflicting obligations need arise. And consideration of the legal regime governing adult relationships suggests that the state has no business injecting itself, as agent for society as a whole, in these cases. The state does not today inject itself, as agent for society as a whole, into adults' decisions about with whom they will have relationships, with whom they will have visits, with whom they will live. That is understood to be, quite simply, not the business of the rest of society. It is, rather, a quintessentially private matter.

Should it be any different in the case of children's relationships? The only justification for the state injecting itself at all into children's relationships with others, it would seem, is that some entity must stand in the place of children to make choices in their stead in relation to other persons, to protect the children's rights and interests, because they are not autonomous, and that there simply is no private entity in place to do this adequately. If there were adequate private agents in place, these situations should never appear in court in the first place and there would be no question of any police power being exercised. In a regime where children had rights equivalent to those of adults in connection with their relationships and those rights were effectuated by private agents, their private agents' decisions would be controlling, and no one could mount even a prima facie case for invoking the power of the state to override those decisions on the basis of their own interests or the interests of society as a whole or constitutional norms. The only proper basis for objection would be that the private agent breached a fiduciary duty owed to the child. The mere fact that such private agents do not exist, that the state has chosen to assume that function itself, does not justify diminishing children's rights, attributing to adult individuals or to society as a whole a stake in the matter, and giving the state the power to compromise children's interests on that basis. Further justification would be required for the state to go beyond the *parens patriae* role by also or instead exercising the police power in connection with children's relationships, injecting social policies and competing interests into the mix, and neither legislatures nor courts have provided such justification.

One might still contend, however, that there is something different about the state as agent that justifies imposing on its decisions limitations we would not impose on private agents making the same kinds of decisions. That difference, it might be said, defeats the analogy to adults' rights and makes it simply unworkable to bestow equivalent rights on children. The difference is principally that the state is a very powerful entity. It possesses great resources, and occupies a commanding role in society, and so its decisions in any context have effects larger than those of decisions by private entities. One might reasonably be concerned that, for example, a state decision to award custody to a father in part because the mother has remarried to a man of another race would have a much greater negative impact on society than would a similar decision by a private agent. Members of society would receive a message of state endorsement of racism in the former case but not the latter. This is a realistic concern, and the objection must be taken seriously. There are other contexts – principally, that of church–state separation – in which courts have held that the state may not do certain things that private parties may do, simply because of the message the state sends when it acts, and those holdings seem correct. For example, although private citizens may erect elaborate religious displays on their property, liberal societies do not permit the state to erect sectarian displays on its property. This is not because religious displays are deemed inherently bad but rather because for the state to erect them on public property can have a more coercive impact on observers than private displays have.

There are several reasons, though, why this concern is insufficient to change the conclusion in this context. In the first place, it should be noted that holdings concerning religious displays on public property are distinguishable on the grounds that there is no necessity of the state involving itself in religious expression or celebrations. In contrast, there is a necessity – absent development of an adequate private alternative – for the state to involve itself in relationship decisions for children. The principle of equal concern for the welfare of all persons compels state action in the case of children's family life. That same principle operates *against* state construction of religious displays.

In addition, there are several reasons to think this concern is overstated in the context of state decision making about children's relationships. First, family court decisions are typically not as visible as are decisions about, for example, erecting a religious display on public property, and the bases of decision are typically not as clear. Child custody decisions, for example, are made by local trial-level courts, often by courts not of record (i.e., their decisions are not published). They are based on a long list of factors, so that concerns about community reaction to a parent's choice of partners are likely to be just one aspect of a complex analysis of a child's best interests. For this reason, the concern is somewhat less pronounced in this context.

Second, the public is capable of understanding that the state occupies different roles in different types of cases. The public is accustomed to seeing the state operate in a great variety of roles – for example, as operator of schools and universities, hospitals, parks, and transportation services; as defender of the nation; and as administrator of agencies that prosecute criminals, collect taxes, and conduct welfare programs – and to seeing that the state has different obligations in these various roles. Were the state to adopt the position I advocate, that it should occupy only a *parens patriae* role in cases involving children's relationships, it could readily communicate to the public that that is what it is doing, that it is acting solely as a surrogate for the child, because it must, and so is under a different set of duties than in other contexts.

Third, although there is always the danger that relieving state actors of constitutional restrictions in making decisions about children's lives will invite those with racist or other discriminatory views to manipulate decisions to satisfy their own preferences, there is also always the possibility of appellate judicial review, so that at least in the worst cases, a concerned parent or other party can have a second chance at securing a decision not infected with illicit prejudices. Although many parents cannot afford to bring an appeal on their own, there are civil liberties groups providing support for such appeals today. In addition, it might well be that judges are less likely to act on the basis of illicit prejudices than would be any private agents. There is a professional culture among judges fostering an aspiration for objectivity, and judges' decisions, although not as visible as religious displays in front of city hall, are more open to public gaze than the decisions of private agents would be likely to be. Legislators, too, are under close public scrutiny. As noted in discussing the danger of state power in Chapter 5, that danger is lessened where some adults are empowered to challenge any state action as contrary to the best interests of the child, and I have suggested that effectuating the rights of children would entail assigning such power to some adults, and in most cases that would include parents. Thus, the very same people who under current law would allege violation of their constitutional rights would be able to challenge state action under a children's rights regime, and can be expected to be just as vigilant, only they would have to state a claim in terms of the children's rights rather than their own. The concern about bias therefore does not seem so great as to warrant the sacrifice of children's welfare that imposing the constitutional limitations would seem to entail.

Fourth, to the extent that the state unintentionally sent a message to the public by making a particular decision for a child, the message should be that the child's welfare lies in a certain direction because of unignorable, if unfortunate, facts about the local community rather than a message of endorsement of local attitudes. Legislators have plenty of opportunity to explain their decisions to the public, and judges could be granted greater opportunity to articulate precisely, for anyone who is paying attention to their decisions, the basis for their decisions, to make clear that they do not condone prejudices but are compelled to do what is best for the individual child. They might be expected to make a special effort to communicate the legitimate, child-protective basis of their decisions in cases that could raise suspicions. Any decision might nevertheless be misperceived by some, either because they do not pay close attention or because they doubt the sincerity of a judge, but this ability of judges to clarify their decision making should mitigate the concern further.

Finally, whatever danger might remain, despite the state's best efforts to avoid it, that some will perceive state decisions as endorsing racism or antipathy toward gays, as hostile to certain religious faiths, or as disapproving of women working outside the home will in most cases be outweighed by the welfare interests of the children involved. Those interests are more directly and fundamentally affected than are the interests of anyone else. As I have emphasized, the harms to be avoided for children are ones relating to their fundamental well-being, their emotional, psychological, and physical health, their self-esteem, their cognitive development, and their striving to become autonomous and happy individuals. It is always possible to argue that any such anticipated harms to children are illusory, or that they are outweighed by compensating benefits to the child, such as learning to deal with adversity, but such an argument would simply be for a different empirical conclusion based on all relevant considerations about what is best for the child. In other words, such arguments can be made within an exclusively child-centered legislative or judicial analysis. Existing rules that inject concern for adult interests and social aims, however, present the real danger of a different kind of bias, an adult-centered bias, by encouraging legislators and judges to shift their attention entirely away from children to focus on the interests of adults.

That the state should be unconstrained by constitutional norms and social policies when deciding in behalf of children should become even clearer when one considers a comparable situation involving a once competent but now incompetent adult. Suppose a member of the KKK were to fall into a coma and become a ward of the state in a state hospital. And suppose that an African-American co-worker wished to spend several hours every day visiting the KKK member, holding his hand and praying over him. Would the state be precluded from deciding that the KKK member would choose, if able, not to allow the African-American person to do this and on that basis refuse the request to visit? Would the state be constrained by the Fourteenth Amendment to allow the African-American person to visit to the same extent that it would allow a white co-worker to visit? It might trouble us greatly, but I suspect most would say that the state, regrettably, owes a duty to the patient in its care to respect what would likely be his wishes in this regard, however condemnable. This would be even clearer if the KKK member had executed a living will making explicit a preference that no African-Americans be permitted to visit him if he became incapacitated.

If one believes, as I have argued, that children ought to have legal rights equally as strong as those of adults, in connection with their relationships, then the state's duties to the child, to act on the basis of what the child would choose if able, should also be just as strong. And fortunately, any preferences imputed to children would not be of such a condemnable sort. Even in those cases that give us the greatest unease, the imputed preference would be just to avoid some concrete harm, such as ridicule or separation from a noncustodial parent and extended family members or death from a curable disease, a preference that in and of itself would be entirely reasonable. The state would not be imputing racist or homophobic views or antipathy toward particular religious faiths to children and then acting on such views.

Last, one could also think about this troubling conflict of state aims in light of general moral principles as to what it means to accord persons the respect they are owed as persons, and in particular Kant's maxim that persons be treated as ends in themselves, not as mere means to the ends of others. This maxim would, I think, support the position that decisions about children's relationships should be based solely on what is best for them, rather than what will advance the self-fulfillment of other persons or what is best for society as a whole. Law and normative scholarship on use of children for organ transplants or medical experiments reflect this belief. The law governing their relationships ought to as well. Race and gender equality and religious freedom are important social aims, just as curing disease is. But it is no more appropriate in the relationship context than it is in the medical context to put children's basic welfare at risk to serve such societal aims.

Conclusion

The conclusions yielded by the positive theory of children's rights developed in Chapters 3 through 5 therefore withstand challenges based on parental rights and constitutional norms. Under a morally appropriate legal regime, children's rights alone would control state decision making about their relationships, both legislative decisions about what general rules shall apply and any judicial decisions in individual cases. The state, in making those decisions, would be acting solely in a *parens patriae* role and not also or instead in a police power role. The state would therefore experience no conflict of interests. It would be obligated to advance only the interests of the children and not to consider or act on the interests of any individual adults or the interests of society as a whole. Not only parental rights but also the societal aims of racial equality, gender equality, and equal religious freedom would be out of bounds.

This theoretical analysis stands on its own, independent of questions about how its conclusions regarding children's moral rights might be implemented in the legal system. In the next chapter, I discuss implementation and I address certain difficulties said to plague child welfare-directed state decision making. But that is not what the book is principally about. It is about demonstrating that child welfare ought to be the singular aim of state decision makers and of legal scholars when they reason about what the legal rules and outcomes should be in connection with children's relationships. This is important because many state actors and scholars do not take that to be their sole aim in analyzing issues such as paternity, custody and visitation, termination of parental rights, and third-party visitation. Sympathy for adults is apparent in much of the reasoning about those issues. In addition, family law scholars tend to focus on practical aspects of family legal matters, but we cannot know what practical questions are morally relevant or what should be concluded as a moral matter when practical obstacles to pursuing a particular child-oriented approach arise, unless we have a clear understanding of the moral claims of the various parties involved. It might be that sometimes we cannot by any means do for children what they are morally entitled to, but if and when that happens we should acknowledge that we have failed them. And unless and until we are sure there is no way to give children their due, we should keep searching for a way and should not allow difficulties with one attempted strategy so easily to lead us to focus on adults' wishes and interests and feelings.

7 Implementing Children's Moral Rights in Law

The normative theoretical analysis has generated the conclusion that children possess these moral rights against the state in connection with disputes about their family relationships: (1) that they enjoy the freedom to choose for themselves in a significant range of cases and (2) that for all remaining cases, if the state presumes to involve itself in the disputes, it may do so only as agent for the child involved and must act with the exclusive aim of securing for the child the outcome that the child would likely choose for herself or himself if able. The second of these moral rights is likely to play a larger role in decisions about children's family relationships than the first, and it could be incorporated into the law in a variety of ways. In Section I below, I consider whether any particular approach is superior to others. Because I conclude that an ideal set of legal rules would likely prescribe individualized best-interest decision making in a broader range of cases than now occurs, I address in Section II criticisms that have been leveled against best-interests decision making for children. Then in Section III, I raise some novel questions about making children's interests determinative of relationship decisions, and in particular about how expansive a view one should take of the interests children have – for example, whether they should be deemed to include "other-regarding" interests in the welfare of other individuals, such as their biological parents, or of society as a whole.

I. Effectuating Children's Interest-Protecting Rights

When children are not prepared to choose sufficiently well for themselves and the state assumes control over their relational lives, children have a moral right that the state act only in a fiduciary capacity in their behalf and with the exclusive aim of securing for them the outcomes that it can reasonably suppose they would have chosen for themselves if they were so prepared. How should we understand this idea of "what children would have decided for themselves"?

Fortunately, the practice of fiduciary decision making is a familiar one, and there are established legal models for the activity. Many competent adults have proxies act on their behalf on a regular basis. Financial managers of various kinds make some investment decisions without consulting their principals, lawyers exercise independent judgment in negotiating and advocating on behalf of clients, and corporate managers make decisions large and small with little oversight by the shareholders they represent. Even public officials are, in theory, fiduciaries – agents of the people they represent – yet often make legally effective decisions without a referendum to tell them what their constituents want. The rules governing these various fiduciaries command that they act with an exclusive focus on the interests of their principals and in accordance with any actual choices the principals (at least the autonomous ones) have made (collectively in the case of shareholders or citizens). And in acting to further the principals' interests, fiduciaries are guided by what they know about the individual values and aims of the principals (e.g., distaste for companies that mistreat employees or a conservative or risk-taking attitude toward investing or social initiatives) as well as by assumptions about general human interests (e.g., in having more wealth or living in peace).

In addition, incompetent adults generally have guardians making decisions in their behalf. As discussed in Chapter 3, the law imposes on these guardians a similar obligation to act with the exclusive aim of advancing their wards' interests, taking into account any settled preferences, values, and individual characteristics of the wards of which they are aware, as well as assumptions about more objective interests. The nature of guardians' decision making is often characterized as a *substituted judgment*, a term meant to capture the idea of standing in the shoes of the incompetent adult and deciding what he or she would choose if able.

At a basic or abstract level, this same approach seems entirely fitting for decision making in behalf of children. It is sometimes said that applying a substituted judgment approach with children is nonsensical, because children do not have settled, rational preferences about important aspects of their lives nor values sufficiently well formed that they should influence decisions. This objection, however, rests on an overly narrow preconception about what substituted judgment or proxy decision making entails, as well as on a shallow understanding of children's reality. The concept of a substituted judgment entails simply making in behalf of another person a decision that the other person ordinarily would make for himself or herself; one decision maker substitutes for the other. And the idea of standing in the shoes of a child makes perfect sense as long as there is something about the child that can be relied on, as opposed to the self-regarding interests of the decision maker, to make the decisions. This would be true even if the only thing that could be relied on is objective interests – that is, interests every child is presumed to have, such as interests in not being physically harmed.

But, in fact, children do have unique characteristics, from the time of birth (and even before). At any time in a child's life some of those unique characteristics could be relevant to a decision about their relationships. For example, a child might be born with a disability or unusual medical condition, and that might be relevant to selection of legal parents in the first instance or to a custody decision between legal parents not living together; one adult might be better prepared than another to help the child overcome or deal with the disability or medical condition. Many people believe a child's race is relevant to selection of parents. Further, children develop personalities and inclinations at a quite young age, and differences in personality could also be relevant to a decision about relationships. A given child might, because of his personality or abilities, connect well with one parent more so than the other or with certain extended family members, or might need greater socialization with peers than another child. At what age or developmental stage people can be said to have values that should be respected is a thorny issue, but certainly this ordinarily occurs before the age of majority. An adolescent might, for example, develop a strong interest in her family's cultural background and cultural community, and that might have implications for a custody decision or for her ability to maintain relationships with particular nonparents. Some adolescents have moral views that affect their attitude toward their parents, and those views might warrant respect.[1]

As long as some individual attributes of a child could be relevant to decision making, they stand in no different stead than competent or incompetent adults in terms of whether it makes sense to think of someone else acting in their place, choosing in their behalf. Of course, all such attributes of a child could be taken into account in a decision based on a "best interests" standard, along with more universal interests, and it is not crucial to the analysis here that the term *substituted judgment* be used instead of or in addition to the term *best interests*. But there are advantages to conceptualizing the decision as a substituted judgment. One is that substituted judgment might connote more strongly the proxy and fiduciary nature of the decision making, reinforcing in decision makers' minds that they are supposed to be putting themselves in the place of the person for whom they are deciding rather than furthering their own agenda. Another is that it folds children's situation to some extent into the broader phenomenon of incompetence, and assimilates treatment of children to some degree to treatment of incompetent adults, as to whom we have a better developed moral sense of the requirements for proper proxy decision making.

A third reason is that the idea of substituted judgment makes clearer that the child stands in a moral posture equivalent to that of a competent adult with whom some other person wants to have a relationship, a posture that entails having a choice to make and having that choice be decisive as to whether the relationship will exist. Correspondingly, substituted judgment might more clearly communicate to adults than best interests would that they have no greater right themselves with respect to developing or maintaining a relationship with a child than they do with respect to relationships with other competent adults. In every case, with every other human being, having a relationship depends on a mutuality of independent choices between the two parties. In the case of children and incompetent adults, the other party's choice will simply be made through an agent.

To say that the state should engage in a kind of substituted judgment exercise to make decisions for children is not to say that a particular type of legal rule or process should govern these relationship decisions. The most straightforward way of carrying out this responsibility might be to establish a legal rule that with respect to every aspect of every child's family relationships some state decision maker, such as a judge, is to determine on an individualized basis which outcome among the available options each child would likely choose for himself or herself if able to do so competently. Thus, for example, the law could in theory dictate that at the time of each child's birth some state official is to determine who, among all the adults wishing to serve as a child's legal parents, are the best candidates for the role of caregiver. Who the best candidates are might depend in part on unique characteristics of a given child, but otherwise would turn on what characteristics the adults have that are conducive to good parenting in general.

However, individualized best candidate or best outcome determinations by state actors are not the only way to carry out the state's fiduciary responsibility, and in some situations they might be undesirable. Another approach that might best effectuate children's moral right in connection with some decisions would be to establish legislatively a legal rule prescribing a particular outcome in all cases presenting a particular fact or set of facts, based on empirical assumptions about what is best for children generally in certain circumstances. For example, most people would deem well suited to serving children's welfare a rule for paternity that automatically confers legal parenthood on any man who is both the biological father of the child in question and the husband of the child's mother at the time of birth. To the extent that it is generally better for a child that a man who is in this position, rather than anyone else, be made the child's legal father, significant benefits to the child flow from having this established automatically and immediately at birth, without need for a legal hearing of any kind.

Yet another approach would be for the state to delegate individualized decision-making authority to some private party. In connection with children's relationships with nonparents, for example, some scholars argue on child-centered grounds for a general rule giving legal parents complete control over interactions with third parties, based on a premise that parents' choices in such matters are usually consistent with children's wishes and/or interests, and on a premise that direct state involvement in such matters entails great costs for families as a whole, including the children.[2] Still other approaches might combine one or more of the foregoing strategies. For example, the law might command individualized assessment of the best outcome for each child in all instances of a certain type of decision but also create a presumption that a particular outcome is the most desirable whenever certain facts are present. Conversely, a statute might dictate a particular result as a general matter in a certain type of case, but allow for an individualized assessment in specified exceptional circumstances. Or the law might delegate decision-making authority to parents but empower state actors to override parental decisions on substituted judgment grounds in a limited range of situations. There are many possible approaches.

Any of these approaches might be best suited to produce the optimal outcomes for children in particular legal contexts and therefore to fulfill the state's fiduciary obligation to children. Determining which approach is best for a particular type of decision – that is, for initial assignment to parents, termination of parental rights, grandparent visitation, or any other aspect of children's relational lives – would require extensive empirical analysis. In Chapter 8, I propose statutory rules for a few types of decisions, to lend greater concreteness to the conclusions of the theoretical analysis, but I cannot undertake in this book to do all the work that would be needed to establish definitively what sort of rule would in reality be optimal on child-centered grounds for each legal issue. My aim here is just to show the moral necessity of a purely child-centered set of legal rules and to clear away some theoretical objections to reforming the law on that basis.

I will undertake in this chapter, though, a defense of unadorned individualized best-outcome decision making, because it does seem, on the surface at least, that it would play a substantial role in family law, more so than it does today, if children's moral rights were fully effectuated. First, in a large percentage of cases, a rule attributing choice-protecting rights to children obviously would not be appropriate. For instance, the vast majority of decisions as to who a child's legal parents will be are now made, and should be made, at or immediately after birth, when children are incapable of making and communicating any decisions, let alone rational and well-informed ones. Other decisions, such as whether to terminate a legal parent–child relationship, are more likely to be made after children have reached an age at which they could make and articulate some sort of decision, but children might not be sufficiently competent at making such a decision, by any reasonable measure of competence, until some point in the later stages of their minority. My daughters, ages nine and seven, could both answer the question "Would you like to end your relationship with your father and find some other?," but their answer is not likely to be a reliable guide as to whether terminating their relationship with me would be good for them, regardless of whether they answer affirmatively or (as I would hope!) negatively. Moreover, asking children really to decide such things could be quite traumatic for them, and that provides independent reason not to confer choice-protecting rights on children with respect to some relationship decisions until at least the later stages of minority.

In addition, it is implausible that for many types of decisions a rule dictating the same outcome in all cases presenting a certain fact, without exception, would be the optimal rule for children – that is, would consistently secure for them the outcomes they would choose for themselves if able. Certainly presumptions would likely play an important role in an ideal set of rules, because there are substantial demonstrated correlations between certain facts and the appropriateness for children of particular legal outcomes and because presumptions can be (but are not always, as discussed below) conducive to predictability and therefore less family-disrupting litigation. For example, a presumption that it is best for any child to confer legal parenthood on his or her birth mother, even when the birth mother is not married to the biological father, might be well founded, and putting the burden on others to show it is not true in the case of any particular child should result in fewer contests than if every nonmarital child's mother–child relationship were entirely up for grabs at the outset. However, given the complexity and variability of the situations in which questions about children's relationships arise, it stands to reason that in an optimal set of rules – that is, the set of rules best suited to securing for children the outcomes they would choose if able to do so competently – there would need to be provision, with respect to most and perhaps all types of decisions, for rebutting any presumption in individual cases.

The basis for rebutting a presumption need not, of course, be an individualized substitute judgment. It, too, could be simply a demonstration of particular facts. For example, in the case of paternity or maternity, a presumption in favor of biological parents who are married to each other might be rebutted by a showing that one or both previously severely abused another child. But to fulfill each child's moral right that the state aim to secure the best outcome for him or her, there would likely need to be numerous such bases for rebutting many presumptions. And those bases for rebuttal might simply reverse the presumption, with a need to allow for rebuttal of the reverse presumption. A sufficiently fine-tuned, fact-specific rule might therefore be quite complex and require a decision maker to investigate the private lives of the parties pretty thoroughly and probably also to do some weighting and balancing of considerations. The authors of the American Law Institute's Principles of Family Dissolution (ALI Principles) note with respect to custody decisions that "it is difficult to imagine sound outcomes in custody cases unless the diverse range of circumstances in which family breakdown occurs are taken into account ... predictability is important, but so is the customization of a result to the individual, sometimes unique, facts of a case."[3] The same can be said of other contexts in which the state takes it upon itself to shape children's relational lives, including creation of legal parent–child relationships for children whose parents are not in a stable and committed relationship with each other, separation of parents from children on account of abuse or neglect, and protection of children's relationships with nonparents.

Thus, rules relying on specific factual triggers that are sufficiently nuanced to account for the myriad situations in which children live are, with respect to many types of decisions, not likely to generate the savings in administrative and human costs that such rules generally promise, relative to a broad standard. A more straightforward rule requiring a judge or other state actor to determine the outcome most desirable for the child in each case, with appropriate guidelines for making that determination, would likely not have significantly greater administrative or privacy costs and would on the surface appear more perfectly to effectuate the moral right of children in some range of cases. Past experience with the best-interests standard in custody decision making arguably bears this out. At various times different presumptions have been deployed to short-cut decision making, to reduce litigation and fact investigations. As to each presumption, there have been widespread complaints from legal practitioners and parents that the fit is not good and that many children are being disserved as a result of applying the presumption. Various presumptions have been scrapped over the years for that reason, so that today the prevailing rule commands for each case a judicial decision based on a best-interests standard, guided by a statutory list of nonexclusive relevant factors.

Of course, many of those who criticize the best-interests standard think this a mistake. They instead favor new presumptions they believe better fit an overriding aim of securing the best outcomes for children. Or they argue that one of the presumptions that has been tried should be used despite its imperfect fit, because they believe open-ended best-interests assessments in practice make for a worse fit. The persuasiveness of their arguments for alternative rules depends largely on the validity of their criticisms of the broad standard, and so the next section of this chapter examines those criticisms. Significantly, though, many who support presumptions are not opposed to making them subordinate to an ultimate best-interests standard; they would simply require relatively strong evidence to support a best-interests rebuttal of the presumption, so as to minimize the number of cases in which custody has to be litigated.

In sum, thinking about how best to implement children's moral relationship rights in the law, in a manner abstracted from the practicalities of implementing a particular legal rule, leads to the conclusions that an ideal set of legal rules for decision making about children's family relationships would rely heavily on individualized determinations of the most desirable outcome for the children whose lives are in dispute and that this presumably would entail applying something like the "best interests of the child" standard. It therefore seems reasonable to conclude, preliminarily, that children are morally entitled to have state decisions about their personal relationships, in cases where it is not appropriate to attribute choice-protecting rights to them nor to assume that single facts correlate sufficiently well with the best outcomes for them, governed ultimately by a substituted judgment or best-interests standard, with any subsidiary rules, such as presumptions, subordinate and in service to that ultimate aim. The burden should then be on critics of a best-interests standard to show that this is not in practice the best means of implementing children's moral right or cannot feasibly be made into the best means by effecting certain changes in practices. The next section assesses whether they meet their burden.

Before proceeding to that assessment, one more preliminary point: The particular term the legal system and academy have adopted for the prevailing approach to child-centered decision making – *best interests* – is admittedly somewhat incoherent and/or misleading. We do not generally think of interests as being good or bad, better or worse, best or worst.[4] Rather, we think of interests as being more or less weighty or important. In addition, in most actual situations presented to the legal system, the best of all possible worlds is not realistic for a child. Some have recommended, on the basis of this reality, less ambitious sounding terms such as *least detrimental alternative*.[5] It would not be so difficult, however, to craft a term that is at once consistent with common usage, reflective of the imperfection of alternatives in legal disputes over children's relationships, and aspirational – that is, encouraging judges to look for positive things in the available alternative outcomes and to focus on what children need to thrive and not just to avoid misery. *Best feasible outcome* and *best available option* are possibilities. Given how entrenched *best interests* is, though, and how readily intelligible it is to people who have been using it for many years, I will use it at times, often alternating or juxtaposing it with other terms, in the discussion below of the relative merits of individualized, child-centered decision making and the alternatives that have been proposed. When I do, I mean by it the best outcome for a child in light of what is reasonably available or possible, taking into account the reasonably foreseeable costs and benefits of different potential dispositions.

II. Problems in Applying the Best-Interests Standard

The best-interests test has been around for centuries. Though the test has really been the primary basis for resolving disputes over children's relationships only in custody contests between legal parents, those contests make up a large component of the family court docket in this country, so we have a great deal of experience with it. Despite the test's endurance, it has come under substantial criticism, and that criticism warrants serious consideration.

Nearly all criticisms of the best-interests standard have focused just on postdivorce custody decisions, precisely because that is the one area of family law in which a substantial number of disputes are today decided on the basis of this standard. Some aspects of the criticisms therefore rest on assumptions about the realities of marriage and of shared parenting between former spouses and to that extent might not have much bearing on use of the best-interests standard for other types of decisions, such as termination of parental rights. However, many aspects of the criticisms advanced in the custody realm would carry over to other contexts, and in presenting the challenge to best-interests analysis below, I supplement existing arguments with special concerns that might arise outside the custody context.

Significantly, criticisms of best-interests decision making for children are usually not ostensibly normative ones challenging the privileging of children's interests over those of adults. Most purport to recommend some other rule of decision making – for example, a primary caretaker presumption, deference to maternal preference, or a joint custody presumption – at least in part on the basis of its supposed superiority in serving the needs of children. But solicitude for adults' interests is nonetheless often apparent, and in fact one prominent family law scholar, in an article dominated by concern for the pain mothers experience as a result of having less time with their children after divorce, has pronounced: "Scholars also tend to agree that parents' needs should be given some consideration in awarding custody, and the [best-interests] standard ignores these considerations."[6] The criticisms of the best-interests test can usefully be divided into those that are process-related, those focused on the vagueness of the standard, and those based on epistemological obstacles to meaningful application of the standard.

A) Process-Related Criticisms

One common complaint about deciding child custody based on the best-interests standard has to do with the process through which it typically occurs. The prevailing approach is to put the ultimate decision in the hands of judges. What is often underemphasized is that parents can submit to the court an agreement as to custody, that it is extremely rare for a judge to reject an agreement, and that in close to ninety percent of divorces involving children parents in fact reach an agreement and custody is not litigated. In only the ten percent or so of cases in which the parents do not reach an agreement do judges truly decide the matter. Conversely, couples usually negotiate agreements in light of what their attorneys tell them the local judge would be likely to decide if custody were litigated, or in light of the very unpredictability that concerns some critics of best-interests decision making, so any flaws in judicial application of the best-interests standard might infect the settlement process as well.

In recent decades, some legal scholars and psychiatric and social work professionals have challenged the practice of judicial resolution of custody, contending that litigation and judicial decision making are ill suited to establishing postdivorce child care arrangements. When divorcing couples enter a courtroom with their lawyers, it is said, rights are emphasized over feelings and needs, broken relationships become even more acrimonious, and the financial cost of breaking up the family becomes much higher. Moreover, these couples must put their relationships with their children in the hands of people – lawyers and judges – who have little or no expertise in child development and psychology, and the adversarial process is not well suited to supplying judges or GALs with the facts and understanding they would need to make decisions well.[7] In addition, the state does not supply the family court system with sufficient resources to make the kind of investigation or secure the kind of assistance needed to apply the test properly.[8] These criticisms certainly could also plausibly be raised with respect to judicial resolution of family matters other than custody, such as abuse or neglect of children.

Based on such negative views of judicial decision making, there has been strong support among scholars, and even among lawyers and judges, for channeling custody disputes into mediation and for limiting or elim- inating judges' authority to set aside agreements. In mediation, a social worker, family counselor, or specially trained lawyer aims to guide couples through a face-to-face, nonadversarial conversation, leading them toward the end of developing for themselves a mutually satisfactory parenting plan. Practice has in fact moved decidedly in this direction, with judges increasingly encouraging, and even mandating, that divorcing couples attempt to resolve custody disagreements in mediation before bringing the issue to court. Receptivity to mediation of family law disputes has not been universal, however. Many have expressed concern that media- tion presents the danger of a psychologically or financially weaker spouse, without the protection of a lawyer, being overpowered and taken advantage of in the negotiations. Overseers of mediation programs have responded by incorporating into training programs for mediators instruction on how to manage domineering individuals and level the playing field, but the concern lingers.

These positions as to the relative advantages and disadvantages of differ- ent decision-making processes, though, do not challenge the best-interests standard itself. Any decision maker could operate on the basis of that standard. Even a mediator, whose aim is to get the parties peacefully to fashion a plan of parenting themselves, should orient the discussion around what is best for the child, inform the parents that that must be their objective, and then rely on the parents to figure out, under such guidance, what is in their children's best interests. "Mediation" might even be an inappropriate way of characterizing or undertaking informal custody dispute resolution, insofar as it suggests a process in which negotiating parties fashion an agreement reflecting a compromise of their own interests and claims between themselves. A model more in line with the moral rights of children would be one in which parents meet with a person designated by the state as a representative of the child, a well-trained professional who performs an investigation of the child's situation (e.g., as custody evaluators do) and establishes, based on an assessment of the child's interests, the parameters within which parents must negotiate a plan for postdivorce parenting. Something like this already occurs informally in jurisdictions where courts appoint a GAL for children in disputed custody cases and where judges demonstrate a tendency to give much weight to the GAL's recommendation. A GAL will move parents toward an agreement by indicating to them what position she is likely to take as to the child's best interests and by suggesting to parents a range of outcomes consistent with that position.

The basic statement of children's moral entitlement to state decision making that aims at the best outcome for children is actually agnostic as to the optimal decision maker and procedural mechanisms. There are innumerable possibilities, including the traditional litigation approach and the modern innovation of mediation, but also variations on either of these – for example, judicial decision making without the participation of lawyers or closer judicial oversight of mediation – and approaches distinct from either of these – for example, ultimate decision making by GALs or parental negotiation directed by a representative of the child. Children's moral right would presumptively require selection of the decision-making entity and procedures, among those reasonably available, best suited to making a substituted judgment or determining their best interests, but which mechanism that is depends on the answers to many empirical questions. I do not undertake to provide such answers here. The upshot of the analysis of Chapters 4 through 6 is simply that children are the only parties to these proceedings whose interests should be the basis on which scholars and policymakers predicate arguments for one decision process or another. In particular, arguments predicated on fairness to mothers or fathers are out of place.

It is theoretically possible that the best-interests standard could be altogether rejected on process-related grounds. If it were the case that for every feasible individualized decision-making process some other substantive rule would better serve the interests of children, because of the nature of that process, then we should conclude that children's moral right must always be effectuated through some other substantive rule, which might vary from one type of decision to another. But no critic of the best-interests standard has shown this to be the case. At most, what some critics might have shown is that for one particular type of decision maker, because of the process its deliberations entail, the best-interests standard is not the norm best suited to serving children's welfare in some types of cases. Such a demonstration would support the conclusion that if and when that process is used in the real world for that particular type of case, where it might be politically infeasible to establish the optimal process, some criterion other than the best-interests standard should govern decision making. Perhaps, for example, judicial determination of postdivorce custody arrangements truly would, because of the current nature of judicial decision making, better serve children if governed by hard-and-fast presumptions, with no ultimate best-interests determination. I offer reasons below, however, for thinking that is not true.

If it is true, though, that one particular decision-making process, such as litigation, is not well suited to individualized best-interests determinations, this would not in and of itself undermine the conclusion that children are morally entitled to state decision making about their relationships, through a mechanism that is well-suited to the purpose, on the basis of an individualized assessment of their best interests. Such a mechanism might be, as suggested above, altogether different from judicial decision making, but it could also be a reformed judicial process, with greater investment in training and personnel and with introduction of special procedures designed to limit conflict, exclude consideration of adults' interests, and give a more prominent role to children's advocates. As a political matter, a failure to invest enough resources in creating a process that is good at substitute decision making for children is as foolhardy as a failure to invest adequately in children's education.

B) Vagueness Concerns

Critics also charge that best interests is too vague a concept. It provides too little guidance for making important decisions about families' intimate lives. It encourages highly case-specific and intuition-based judgments, leaving little role for precedent or appellate review to limit discretion and ensure consistency.[9] Presumably they would level the same charge against a substituted judgment dictate, as that approach will typically entail an assessment of children's interests. Though the charge usually contemplates that judges are the decision makers, the problems identified would also plague mediators directed to guide parties toward an agreement reflecting what their children would choose if able or that is in their children's best interests. The same would be true with any other decision makers, including GALs and parents themselves, whom the law instructed to act with such an aim in mind. And the charge would presumably also be pertinent in contexts other than divorce custody decision making and so would provide reason for objecting to extension of the standard to paternity, termination of parental rights, and other legal determinations concerning children's relationships.

One claimed consequence of this vagueness is that decisions are unpredictable, thereby increasing the rate of litigation, with all the harms that that inflicts on vulnerable families.[10] This concern should be distinguished from one about the state wielding excessive power over private life. As emphasized throughout the book, the state is, as a matter of practical necessity, critically involved in structuring children's relational lives, whether it does so through individualized and discretionary judicial decisions or by general and self-effectuating statutory rules. The pertinent question is how it will be involved in structuring family life, not whether it will be involved. Here the concern is with the state's involvement too often taking the form of protracted and destructive litigation.

The most often alleged consequence of the best-interests standard's vagueness, though, is simply bad decisions. In part, this is because it is said that decision makers do not know what to look for or how much weight to give to different facts. And in part it is because decision makers are set free to advance their own values or ideological agendas and to act, consciously or unconsciously, on the basis of their own biases and stereotypes.[11] With respect to postdivorce custody decisions, feminist critics assert that judicial bias is likely to include gender stereotypes that result in joint custody or paternal custody awards that effectively punish working women, lower-income-earning women, sexually active women, and lesbian women.[12] Advocates for fathers' rights likewise charge that gender stereotypes infect judicial exercise of discretion in custody cases but in ways unfair to men.[13] They find support in the prevailing view among legal practitioners – male and female – and even among judges that fathers do not usually receive fair consideration in custody decisions, because judges tend to operate on the basis of an assumption that children naturally belong with their mothers, and that it is usually futile for a father to seek primary custody.[14] In the child protective arena, where decisions are generally predicated on findings of particular behaviors rather than on a broad best-interests inquiry, some scholars express concern that shifting to greater use of a best-interests standard would result in more decisions being infected with bias against poor or minority-race parents. Martin Guggenheim warns that use of a best-interests standard for removing children from their homes would present "the danger of arbitrary enforcement," whereas "[o]ne virtue of tightly drawn statutes is the protection that they provide against wrongful intrusion."[15]

Significantly, though, no one who criticizes the best-interests test on vagueness grounds argues that, as a moral matter, children's welfare should therefore be entirely irrelevant to decision making about children's lives, that only adults have any moral claims in connection with children's relationships. It certainly does not logically follow from the premise that there are problems in applying a best-interests rule that the legal system morally ought to make decisions instead based on interests or preferences of adults. (Notably, reliance on adults' preferences is hardly a straightforward matter in family law, as evidenced by the large literature on the authenticity and reliability of women's choices as to such things as work/child-rearing trade-offs during marriage, agreement to joint custody at divorce, and continuing a relationship with an abusive partner.) Yet some scholars do appear to conclude from the premise that the best-interests test is plagued by unpredictability and bias that courts should focus, at least in part, on the adults involved and the claims they make to be deserving of parental status or custody. Martha Fineman has urged, in part on the basis of the allegedly arbitrary and biased nature of best-interests assessments, that custody decisions be used to reward the person who has sacrificed the most for the child in the past. Mary Becker goes farther, critiquing the best-interests standard solely in terms of its impact on women, and after finding "that gender-neutral custody standards, even the primary caretaker standard, do not adequately protect women," arguing for a "maternal deference rule," under which the mother would decide who gets custody.[16] Neither Fineman nor Becker presents an argument for this shift to a focus on rewarding and protecting mothers. Any argument would have to explain why, if a best-interests standard is not a workable tool for effectuating children's moral right, the appropriate thing to do is anything other than searching for an alternative substantive rule by which to effectuate their moral right, retaining an exclusive focus on children's well-being. We should be suspicious of any reasoning that takes the following form: "There is some problem with doing what is best for children, so let us instead focus on the interests of adults."

Most who focus on the vagueness of the best-interests standard, though, instead propose some "shortcut" rule, usually a presumption of greater or lesser stringency, on the grounds that it would better serve children's welfare. Here the familiar debate about rules versus standards plays out,[17] with some arguing that the greater determinacy and predictability of a single-fact-based rule make up for any loss of flexibility or accuracy. On the other side are people who are not so much fans of highly discretionary best-interests tests but rather opponents of particular alternative substantive rules. The alternative substantive rule for child custody that has been most popular among family law scholars in recent years is a primary caretaker presumption. Under this rule, courts award sole custody to the parent who provided more of the direct care of the child during marriage, absent a showing that this would be inappropriate (e.g., because that parent is now "unfit"). The ALI Principles, which are now taking center stage in the custody literature, adopt Professor Elizabeth Scott's "approximation rule," which resembles a primary caretaker presumption. Under that rule, in cases where the parents do not reach an agreement, courts presumptively would impose on them a postdivorce "parenting plan" in which the child's time is divided between the parents in roughly the same proportion as it was during the marriage. Also popular, principally among fathers' rights groups, has been a joint custody presumption.

In other areas of family law, the law already relies heavily on rules that make outcomes turn on specific facts – for example, basing paternity decisions ultimately on biological parenthood and basing termination of parental rights on particular types of conduct by parents. Those who bemoan the vagueness of the best-interests standard in discussing custody decisions in divorce might well think that extending it to other types of decisions would be a terrible mistake, bringing added costs to children and families without compensating benefits.

1) Predictability and litigation

To assess the strength of arguments for alternative decision rules based on the premise that the openness of the best-interests standard makes decisions too unpredictable and thereby increases litigation, one would have to make a comparative assessment of that standard and the alternatives. The comparison would need to take into account how much litigation each rule would generate, assess the effects of litigation on the children involved, estimate how well each rule serves the overriding aim of doing what is best for children, and arrive at some conclusion by combining and weighting those considerations – that is, the costs of conflict and the benefits of better decisions. It is not obvious how any of the proposed alternatives in the custody realm, or the existing rules in the removal and termination contexts, would fare against the best-interests standard in such a comparison, and no one has done such a comparison in a sufficiently rigorous way to give us confidence that any particular position is correct. I cannot undertake a full-blown comparison here, either, but can offer some reasons for finding unpersuasive the predictability rationale for abandoning or greatly curtailing the best-interests standard.

a) **The effects of uncertainty.** Uncertainty does not necessarily produce more litigation. Much depends on how risk-averse the parties are, how positively or negatively they view the prospect of bringing their grievances into a public forum, and how rationally they are behaving. Two highly risk-averse or conflict-averse disputants, particularly if they are in an emotionally fragile condition, might be led by the uncertainty of how a court would decide an issue to make more concessions to achieve an out-of-court settlement. As noted above, the reality in custody cases today, under the best-interests rule, is that roughly ninety percent of custody awards entail judicial ratification of an agreement between the parents. This suggests either that the uncertainty is actually not so great or that great uncertainty is not in fact producing a high rate of litigation. In the child protective context, it might be that a best-interests standard would lead more parents to capitulate to agency demands that they undertake counseling and parenting classes than do existing rules, which require the state to show particular types of conduct and concrete injury, and this might be better for children (and parents).

In contrast, if the applicable legal rule made one party confident that a judicial decision would be in her favor, she might be more comfortable going to court and might therefore decline to enter into any agreement, even one very close in terms to what she could expect to get by court order. Some people in that situation feel too much anger to negotiate or want the vindication of an official pronouncement. In divorce cases, the legal fees for both sides usually come out of the same pool – that is, the predistribution marital estate – so incentives to minimize one's own legal fees are reduced. Conversely, a high risk-taker with money to burn might be willing to drag the other party to court even under a rule that makes clear the unlikelihood of his succeeding, content to roll the dice and happy to have an opportunity to try to humiliate the other party in a public forum.[18] Another way of putting this is that for a significant percentage of individuals who divorce, there is intrinsic value in a court battle, and they will pursue it regardless of what the substantive rules of decision are. Some domestic relations judges observe that the people for whom mediation does not work are generally people who are deeply embittered and vindictive and that nothing a legislature or judge could do would prevent them from continuing to battle each other, in and out of court. Proponents of shortcut rules for custody decision making therefore seem overly optimistic about the prospect of reducing that ten percent litigation rate.

With respect to some other types of decisions, the picture might be significantly different. Maternity and paternity outcomes are today among the most certain and predictable in family law; the fact of giving birth is readily established and modern genetic testing can establish who the biological father of a child is with nearly absolute certainty. Only in a small minority of cases does more than one man seek paternity of a child, and the contest is almost always settled immediately by genetic testing. Making some portion of these outcomes turn on a less predictable and more judgmental best-interests determination rather than the simple fact of procreation could certainly invite more litigation. Most biological fathers of nonmarital children end up in court anyway under current practice, because they usually become legal fathers by court order and not automatically. But changing the basis of the court order from the results of genetic tests to an assessment of the biological father's preparedness to serve as a caretaker, as compared to other potential takers, would likely generate many more paternity challenges and require more involved proceedings to resolve.

However, the short-term costs to children that this might create, in terms of their parentage being unsettled for a while and the stress that litigation can cause their primary caretakers, would have to be balanced against the great potential long-term benefits for children of using an instrument superior to genetic matching to select a father for them, of forcing some people to think about what it takes to be a parent before assuming that role, and of sparing their mothers from the long-term stress of trying to co-parent with men they have no relationship with and who might be incompetent, uncooperative, and even malicious. Incidentally, unwed fathers who will make good social parents for their children might be better off if their status were elevated by the state's establishing a best-interests test for assumption of that role.

With respect to termination of parental rights, eliminating existing rules and substituting a best-interests test, with a list of relevant factors, could actually reduce litigation. Today, termination rules are extremely complicated, and many rely on amorphous concepts such as abandonment, abuse, neglect, injury, fitness, and inability to care for a child. Litigation of a termination case already typically involves extensive fact-finding, not only about the past conduct of the parents but also about the rehabilitative services offered by the social service agencies, the parents' efforts to become rehabilitated, and the child's best interests. Parents' past and present conduct and the rehabilitative efforts of the state would also be relevant in a straightforward best-interests analysis, but switching to a best-interests test would not increase the quantity of relevant facts and might actually simplify the analysis or produce quicker resolution of cases. For example, it is sometimes obvious to judges that termination would be best for a child, but existing rules nevertheless require them to hear all evidence about the state's and the parents' efforts at rehabilitation and sometimes require them to deny a petition for termination solely because the agency has not made substantial efforts to rehabilitate the parents, even though such efforts would clearly be futile. It might be that a simple best-interests rule would lead states to bring more petitions for termination, but it would not necessarily increase the number of families who are under state supervision or the number of children out of their parents' care. It might simply lead states to petition for termination sooner or in a greater percentage of the cases in which children are in state custody because of parental abuse or neglect. This in turn could mean fewer judicial and administrative hearings per child, as children spend less time in foster care and are removed fewer times from their homes.

The type of decision as to which the litigation concern might be most compelling is the third-party visitation decision, where nonparents seek to have a court override a parental decision to deny or limit contact with a child. This is an area where it might seem the state could stay entirely out of the business of individualized determinations without great cost to children. Several scholars have argued on this basis against application of the best-interests rule in this context, and even against giving nonparents standing to seek a visitation order under any substantive standard. There are simply too many situations, however, where parents are likely to be harming their children by refusing contact with third parties, to warrant an absolute bar. Many of these disputes arise in situations where the "third party" was actually the child's primary caretaker for a significant period of time while a very unstable or irresponsible parent was absent. There is good reason in such situations to presume that it is best for the child to have continuing contact with the nonlegal parent and to question the motives of the legal parent. Concerns about frivolous petitions can be dealt with by imposing a high burden of proof on nonparents and/or by requiring some threshold showing, such as having served as the primary caretaker for a certain period in the recent past, to obtain standing. Eliminating third-party visitation orders entirely is unwarranted.

b) Guided discretion. Prevailing best-interests rules are not so lacking in guidance as critics suggest. The standard itself is not boundless; it rules out consideration of the interests of persons other than the child. It thereby limits the types of evidence or assertions parties may advance and constrains a decision maker to justify any order exclusively in terms of how it will serve the child's well-being. In many contexts, that will simplify litigation, because the rules in some areas today invite courts to engage in a balancing of children's interests against other considerations. In addition, the prevailing custody rule today sets forth a substantial list of factors relevant to the best-interests decision. Legislatures do not tell judges how much weight to give each factor or how to prioritize them, but that makes sense, because the significance of any factor can vary considerably from one case to the next. The factors inform parties in advance what decision makers will inquire about and on what they will base their decision, and that should provide sufficient guidance to enable parties to predict in a substantial percentage of cases, perhaps most, who will get primary custody if joint custody is not awarded. Less predictable might be whether joint custody will be awarded.

Rules for approving adoptions also typically set forth a list of relevant considerations – in fact, a quite extensive and detailed list. Similar guidance could be provided for applying the standard in paternity and maternity cases where individualized decision making is in order. It is, after all, the same kind of decision – that is, who a child's legal parents will be in the first instance. The same is true for termination of parental rights cases, third-party visitation cases, and other situations, though certainly the list of factors could vary from one context to another. Proposals for alternative rules in all these areas typically rest on assumptions about what is best for children, and if those assumptions are well founded, they could provide the basis for developing guidelines and lists of factors.

It is worth considering in this context the great number of legal rules within and without the family law context that contain vague standards and concepts susceptible to very subjective interpretation, rules that have endured even though they might supply judges with less guidance for application than do typical custody statutes. To cite just a few examples: Laws aim to protect employees from sexual harassment, but "sexual harassment" is obviously susceptible to widely divergent interpretations, and biased judges can easily manipulate it to reach the results they desire. It does not necessarily follow from this that the law should eliminate this general term and instead prohibit only specific conduct. Many constitutional rules contain amorphous concepts and standards – for example, "undue burden," "state endorsement," "cruel," and "due process." Likewise with innumerable concepts and standards in the common law – "consideration," "reasonable person," "possession," and so on. Courts and legal scholars grapple with such rules on an ongoing basis, struggling to make them work better by improving understanding of what they mean and drafting guidelines for applying them, and by challenging decisions that appear based on aims or considerations that should be extraneous. Children are entitled to the same commitment in connection with the rules intended to protect their fundamental well-being.

c) Shortcomings of the alternatives proposed for custody. Last, the most popular alternatives today for custody rules are not obviously superior with respect to vagueness. In fact, almost any rule will leave substantial room for judicial discretion and interpretation. The ALI alternative mentioned above, in particular, does not appear well designed for predictability or reduced litigation. The substantive rule the ALI has proposed for judicial determination of the postdivorce parenting arrangement is for a court to "allocate custodial responsibility so that the proportion of custodial time the child spends with each parent approximates the proportion of time each parent spent performing caretaking functions."[19] Because this is the default rule, it would form the basis both for a court determination and for the parents' negotiation of an agreement, so in every case the parents would be asked to take a position on how much time each devoted to the children in the past. Could the ALI drafters really have believed that the outcome of a court inquiry into that fact would be highly predictable and that parents would be less likely to fight about who did what for or with the child and what counts as "caretaking functions" than they are to fight about what will be in their child's best interests in the future? As a general matter, encouraging divorcing couples to ruminate on the past is not a promising strategy for minimizing conflict. For most divorcing couples, a significant element in the marital breakdown was resentment and hostility surrounding their respective contributions to the family. How could it promote peaceful resolution of custody matters to make parents relive that?

The primary caretaker presumption suffers from this problem as well, but it at least calls for a simple either/or determination – did she do more of the caretaking or did he – rather than an estimation of percentages – was it fifty-five percent or sixty percent or sixty-five percent or...? The primary caretaker presumption too, though, invites renewed squabbling over what counts as a contribution to, or sacrifice for, the children's welfare. Feminist scholars and some courts emphasize the career and other sacrifices that women make to spend more time with their children and to manage the daily affairs of the household and downplay the role of primary-breadwinner fathers in children's lives,[20] but some fathers might believe that working a full-time job is also a contribution to, and sacrifice for, their children, that it amounts to "demonstrated care and concern for children," and they might want to argue the point. Insofar as a primary caretaker presumption rests as a normative matter on suppositions about relative degrees of commitment to children's well-being, or even on a (morally improper) view that custody decisions should reward parents for past sacrifices, that would seem a relevant point of contention. With respect to how much time was spent interacting with a child, some have observed that many primary caretakers view all the time they spend with their children as nurturing work but the time their spouses spend with the children as playtime that should not count as caretaking, and undoubtedly many "secondary caretakers" take exception to that. This is the sort of thing that produces family disharmony in the first place. All such points of disagreement could make settlement negotiations unravel and land divorcing couples in court.

A better way to minimize squabbling at divorce, it would seem, is to investigate directly those aspects of the current relationship between child and parent believed to be affected by time spent with and care devoted to a child in the past, such as the strength and quality of the emotional bond and familiarity with the child's characteristics and needs, and to make as realistic an estimate as possible of the time each parent will be willing and able to devote to the child in the parent's new life following divorce. In many cases, undoubtedly, the emotional bond with the past primary caretaker is so much greater than the bond with the other parent that this outweighs a primary parent's diminished availability in the future or the disruption that relocating would cause. But sometimes it will not be, and in all cases, getting parents to focus on what they can give their child in the future rather than on what they have given in the past could only redound to children's benefit.

A further problem with the ALI approach, in prescribing a presumptive postdivorce arrangement that approximates the predivorce arrangement, is that it might well cause an explosion of petitions for subsequent modification and result in a burgeoning of "round two" litigation, particularly because the presumption is a relatively strong one, overcome only by showing it would be harmful to a child. The situations of spouses, especially primary caretakers, commonly change dramatically after divorce. In particular, a homemaker spouse is typically compelled to begin full-time work soon after a divorce; long-term alimony is highly disfavored today. Many such spouses relocate after divorce to enter into an academic program or otherwise pursue a career or for the sake of a new relationship. At the same time, divorce sometimes induces a parent who previously spent less time than the other parent with the children to rearrange his or her work schedule to make more time for the children, and presumably the law should facilitate rather than forestall such a reorientation. In addition, children's needs change over time, such that a closer relationship with one parent might be best earlier in childhood and a closer relationship with the other parent best later in childhood. There are many reasons, therefore, to believe that the division of child-rearing responsibilities that worked during marriage will not work well for anyone in the family after divorce. Yet unlike a primary caretaker rule, which in practice would require judges simply to give the primary caretaker more custodial time than the secondary caretaker receives and therefore would allow for a broad range of possible allocations, the ALI proposal directs judges and parents to replicate the past, to allocate the child's time between them in approximately the same proportion as they had before divorce. It thus would straight-jacket families that are in a very fluid situation. In the quite likely event that the arrangement disserved everyone, couples would have to return to court to request modification of the parenting plan and, correspondingly, of child support. The assumption that replicating a past division of child-rearing responsibilities promotes stability for a child is therefore quite doubtful.

A joint physical custody presumption creates a similar problem, prescribing an outcome likely to generate a lot of modification petitions, only this presumption bases custody awards not on past behavior but rather on what might be supposed to be ideal behavior – namely a more or less equal devotion of time to parenting, which is usually not consistent with either parent's preferences in the long run. Joint legal custody – that is, shared authority to make larger decisions about a child's life – would appear practically easier for couples to manage, except that embittered couples are likely to end up back in court when they disagree, asking a judge to make decisions for them. Yet overcoming the presumption to avoid this requires demonstrating at the time of divorce that the couple will be unable to cooperate, which presents an obvious moral hazard.

The ALI drafters recognized that family situations are complex and that each one is unique, and for that reason created eight exceptions to the approximation rule, and that might mitigate concern about a flood of modification petitions. Several of these exceptions, though, exacerbate the vagueness problem, because they call for application of nebulous standards. They direct courts to take into account any "reasonable preferences" of a child, to keep siblings together when doing so is "necessary to their welfare," to "protect the child's welfare when the presumptive allocation under this section would harm the child because of a gross disparity in the quality of the emotional attachment between each parent and the child or in each parent's demonstrated ability or availability to meet the child's needs," to consider "the child's need for stability in light of economic, physical, or other circumstances," and to "avoid substantial and almost certain harm to the child." There is plenty of fodder there for litigation. Notably, there is no exception for cases in which children will, after the divorce, really need one parent to be more involved in their lives than he or she was during the marriage and in which that parent is prepared to become more involved. Some skepticism about the sincerity of parents who seek more time with a child after divorce than they gave during marriage is justified, in light of everyday experience in family court, but it stands to reason that many parents will devote more attention to their children after divorce than they did before, because they perceive that the children need more attention as a result of the divorce and because divorce is emotionally jarring for parents and so often causes a reordering of priorities.

For all the reasons adduced above, the ALI alternative does not appear to serve the aim of achieving the best results for children particularly well. Forcing a couple in the future, when their relationship and their daily lives are far different from what they were during marriage, to conform their lives in relation to their children to an arrangement they created in the past, is likely to result in inconvenience, stress, and deviation from the ordered schedule, with attendant instability and children spending time in daycare or with babysitters when they could be spending more time with a parent. Add to this the likelihood that during marriage many couples arrange their schedules not on the basis of what is best for their children but rather on the basis of financial pressures, the happenstance of who secured what kind of job, social convention, mistaken views of what is best for children, or any number of other possibilities, and such backward-looking rules look far inferior to the forward-looking best-interests test as a means of ensuring the best outcomes for children.

One advantage the ALI approach does have in terms of reducing conflict is its use of the terminology *parenting plan* rather than the traditional *sole custody, primary custody, visitation,* and *joint custody* terminology. This new terminology has the potential to mute desires and fears about winning and losing and to get the parties to focus on the practicalities of postdivorce parenting rather than on the labels applied to the arrangement. But that new terminology can be used along with the forward-looking best-interests standard; it characterizes the outcome, not the standard, of decision making. Decision makers in custody cases could craft parenting plans based on the best interests of the child, and statutes in some U.S. states now use that language.

As noted in the previous section, with respect to most other types of decisions, existing rules already rely on somewhat amorphous standards. Abuse and neglect findings turn on proof of physical or mental "injury." Termination of parental rights might occur as a result of a court finding abandonment based on "minimal contact" or finding that the state made "reasonable efforts" to rehabilitate abusive parents and that the parents failed "adequately" or "reasonably" to respond. Only maternity and paternity rules are substantially more definite than the best-interests standard, but they are a poor fit with children's moral right to the decision that is best for them. Tinkering with the existing rule in these other types of cases to make it closely track children's best interests might require so many presumption-shifting factual triggers and so many exceptions that the rule would lose its advantage in predictability, and so the preferable route would seem to be to shift to a clear best-interests standard with enumerated factors, as in custody decisions.

2) Bias

The bias concern might take two forms. One states that children are harmed because decision makers impute to them interests they do not actually have or perceive costs to them that they do not experience and on that basis reorder children's lives in ways that really are not best for them. An example might be a "dirty house" case in the child protective arena, where child protective workers remove children from a home simply because they are living in a messy house, perhaps sleeping on a mattress on the floor instead of on a regular bed and sharing space with a lot of pets. A novice agency worker might attributes injury to the children simply because the situation is so different from what he is used to. Judges, too, might know too little about child welfare or about how to assess input from those who purport to have expertise in child welfare. This form of the bias charge is child centered and clearly requires a response.

Where the problem is really ignorance, one response to it is to provide better guidance and training to state decision makers, whom we should assume want to make decisions based on accurate information about children's needs. The charge itself presupposes that we know better, so one solution is to convey our superior knowledge to decision makers. Family court judges and social services workers do receive some training already, and we have models of effective training programs that could be applied more extensively than they currently are – in particular, that for CASA (Court Appointed Special Advocate) volunteers.[21]

A "better training" answer is not likely, though, to satisfy those who are deeply cynical about the objectivity of state actors. Whether their cynicism is warranted would be difficult to establish; bias is in the eye of the beholder, and some people interpret any decisions they do not personally like as biased. Significantly, the harshest critics of family court judges tend collectively to cite as condemning evidence just a handful of court decisions, some quite dated. For example, in his recent book charging that advocacy for children's rights is misguided, Martin Guggenheim argues for strong parental rights on the grounds that any alternative legal regime, such as one requiring results that judges deem best for children, "empowers state officials to meddle in family affairs and base their decisions on their own values." "A best interests inquiry," he writes, "is not a neutral investigation that leads to an obvious result. It is an intensely value-laden inquiry." To demonstrate that this is a serious problem, Guggenheim cites a single judicial decision – from Iowa in 1966![22] The trial court in that case had decided to leave a child in the custody of his Iowan grandparents, with whom he had lived for over a year following his mother's death, rather than grant custody to his father, who lived in California. The state's Supreme Court upheld the decision, citing principally the boy's interest in stability and security while also referring to the father's bohemian lifestyle. Guggenheim does not claim that this decision was bad for the child. His objections to it are that it was not consistent with an Iowa law at the time dictating "that fit parents who did not abandon their children had a superior right to their children's custody over all others" and that the judges clearly applied values in the case that were not set forth in any law – in particular, regarding the value for a child of a "hippie" lifestyle in Berkeley relative to a more conventional midwestern lifestyle. For Guggenheim, the case "demonstrates that unless judges are constrained by principles, they will always be unleashing an unfettered, uncontrollable power."

This invective is not likely to convince anyone, in part because it is so poorly supported and in part because it so clearly reflects Guggenheim's own bias in favor of parental entitlement and his failure to appreciate that a legislative or judicial decision predicated on parental entitlement is also a value-laden intrusion of state power into family life. Moreover, even in applying a parents' rights rule, unless those rights are to be absolute, which almost no one would recommend, judges would have to make subjective judgments in close cases, defining the boundaries of the rights. Asking judges to decide how far parents' rights go does not seem less an invitation to them to inject personal values into a case than does asking them to decide what will be best for a child; it simply conjures up a somewhat different set of values. The same is true of other ostensibly more definite rules, such as a primary caretaker presumption or the approximation rule. In addition, Guggenheim's sweeping indictment of best-interests decision making as an exercise of unfettered power ignores the fact that legal rules today prescribing best-interests decision making typically contain a long list of factors to guide application of the basic standard, and many contain explicit warnings against value judgments unrelated to children's welfare – for example, using a custody decision to punish a parent for adultery or for what some might consider an immoral lifestyle after divorce.

I do not mean to suggest that bias on the part of state actors is not a problem. Indeed, in Chapter 2 I suggested at several points ways in which judges and other decision makers, such as adoption agency workers, appear to deviate from the written law because of prejudices that infect their reasoning. There are some recent reported decisions that one could cite as evidence of bias. What I am suggesting is that bias charges are often undersupported and therefore appear overstated, that no legal rule would eliminate the problem of bias, that no one has demonstrated that children are now being disserved in a substantial percentage of cases by application of a best-interests rule, and that legislatures can establish guidelines for application of a best-interests standard in every context, just as they do now in adoption laws and custody laws. Scholarly attention should be devoted to improving such guidelines rather than to developing new, adult-focused alternatives.

There is another kind of bias charge, however. This one states that certain adults are harmed by a best-interests standard, because background social conditions make it difficult for them to meet the legal system's expectations. This is true, for example, of feminist complaints about courts counting women's work commitments or relative lack of financial resources against them. It is also true of complaints that child abuse and neglect standards have a disparate impact on the poor, amount to blaming people for their poverty, and therefore are problematic even if there is injury to the children from an objective standpoint.[23] Strictly speaking, this is not an accusation of biased decision making, but rather a complaint about disparate impact from unbiased application of neutral rules and, in effect, a demand for a form of affirmative action or special treatment for those disadvantaged by social circumstances.[24]

On its face, this concern is not a child-centered concern; it is a concern about fairness as between adults. This is not to say that it is an illegitimate concern. There are good reasons to believe that we as a society should do all we can to eliminate poverty and barriers to social equality for women. Moreover, it could be restated in child-centered terms – namely as a concern that children's relationships with their parents suffer because of the economic hardship of their parents rather than because of any inherent deficiencies in their parents. Child welfare policy absolutely should be much broader than just taking children from their homes when parents harm them.[25] And if the child protective system in any individual case faces a choice between removing a child or giving poor parents resources that will enable them to succeed as parents, the latter is clearly preferable from a child-centered perspective. No family law scholar would argue to the contrary.

However, critics who advance this kind of bias complaint effectively, and in some cases explicitly, urge courts and other decision makers simply to disregard a mother's work commitments or lesser financial security and to apply lower parenting standards to poor parents in the cases that actually come before them in today's world.[26] Their position is to that extent not that the best-interests standard is inherently flawed, but rather that they do not like the results produced by doing what is best for children and would prefer that decisions instead protect the interests of certain adults. They offer no moral justification for sacrificing children's welfare in this way today, when poverty and gender inequality are entrenched, to ameliorate the suffering of adults. And their position is directly at odds with what the analysis of the preceding chapters showed to be the moral right of children. The impropriety of their position is made evident by considering an analogous claim in the context of adults' relationships among themselves. Poor people are also relatively disadvantaged in the pursuit of spouses and friends. Should the law therefore compel some adults to have relationships with poor people to ameliorate their suffering? The implicit willingness of some scholars and some advocates for women and the poor to use children's lives instrumentally to serve their causes represents a failure to give children the moral respect they are due as persons.

C) Epistemological Obstacles

Additional problems identified with best-interests decision making might be characterized as epistemological, relating to ineradicable cognitive limitations. They are obstacles to decision makers' having the knowledge necessary to a minimally rational application of the standard. One such problem is that the standard is forward looking, asking judges or other decision makers to speculate about the unknowable future under alternative dispositions and then select the one that appears best for a child.[27] Many supporters of a primary caretaker presumption or of the approximation rule for custody decision making rest their case in large part on this perceived problem, asserting that it is a virtue for a rule to be backward looking, the direction courts ordinarily look for facts on which to base decisions, because an inquiry into the past is inherently more determinate than a guess about the future. Fineman writes, for example, that an appropriate rule of custody decision making must "eliminate the need for predictions about the future psychological well-being of children or speculations about how best to ensure their developmental potential." At the same time, she insists that it "have at its core an appreciation of what we as a society agree will be in the 'best interests' of children." A great virtue of the primary caretaker test is that it "recognizes that no one can confidently predict the future and that the past may in fact be the best indication we have of future care and concern." A rule based on identification of the primary caretaker "is particularly susceptible to legal analysis because it involves past fact-finding, an inquiry traditionally performed by courts."[28]

Another aspect of the best-interests test said to create indeterminacy is that it calls for one person or group of people to make judgments about the character, disposition, and abilities of other persons (the parents) and to assess the welfare of another human being (the child). Yet no decision maker has direct, or particularly reliable indirect, access to the experience or inner nature of other persons, particularly not other persons whom they have never before met. Moreover, the great complexity and dynamic nature of human relationships, coupled with the biases or predispositions of decision makers, make it inevitable that fact investigators and fact finders will overlook or discount pertinent information in seeking insight into the lives and experiences of the parties. They cannot feasibly investigate every aspect of a family's life or rationally weigh all information. They must be selective in pursuing and giving salience to facts, and they are sure to have blind spots. In addition, it is sometimes claimed that we know too little about children's welfare in general to warrant giving state actors power to structure families on the basis of conclusions as to a particular child's future well-being. Becker states simply: "[W]e share no consensus about what is best."[29]

One could certainly challenge the empirical assumptions underlying these objections. The suggestion that an inquiry into the past is always more determinate than a prediction about the future is false. Which is more determinate depends on what the questions are. For example, family court judges likely can predict more reliably which couples will return to fight another day in court than they can determine which spouse was the primary instigator of conflicts in the past. Likewise, the suggestion that we always have better insight into our own welfare than into the welfare of others is false. Again, it depends on what the question is. Someone who has been through a particular experience many times might have a better sense for how it will impact another person who has never been through it than that other person has. That is a basic premise of parenting. And although there is much we do not know about human welfare, there is strong empirical support for some assumptions about what will best serve a child's needs.

Even if these factual assertions about the inherent limitations of best-interest decision making were true, though, the major premise implicit in the epistemological objection is doubtful – that is, the assumption that any decision making characterized by such weaknesses is inadequate in a relative or absolute sense and therefore should not be sanctioned. It is important to realize what other positions and principles would be ruled out if this premise were true, because the widespread faith placed in these other positions and principles suggests widespread rejection of the premise.

First, if that premise were true, then all of the proposed alternative rules for decision making about children's lives that purport to be designed on the basis of assumptions about what is best for children would also have to be rejected, because they too presuppose the ability to predict the future for another human being with some accuracy. How can Fineman consistently assert, in defending the primary caretaker rule, both that no one can predict the future and that the past is the best indication of the future? How can she suggest that "we as a society" know what custody outcomes are best for children and that legislatures should embody this knowledge in legal rules and at the same time renounce predictions and speculations about what custody arrangements will protect children's psychological and developmental interests? Her reasoning is self-contradictory. Likewise with Becker's unsupported claim that empowering mothers to decide custody will produce the best outcomes for children, a claim following soon after an argument against best-interests decision making that rested first and foremost on the premise that "we share no consensus about what is best."

This is a common mistake in criticisms of state decision making in many areas of family law. Scholars postulate that no one can predict or evaluate the results for children of receiving a particular sort of education or having particular persons as parents or being treated in a certain way by parents and then proceed to propose some legal rule that withdraws discretion from state decision makers and gives greater rights to certain adults, justifying their proposal by arguing that this will be best for children! The same is true with respect to the charges that state decision makers have blind spots and cannot have access to others' lives. The unstated, perhaps even unconscious, operative assumption for these scholars is that only they have powers of accurate prediction, that only they labor free of biases and blind spots, and that only they have access to knowledge of others' nature and well-being. Only if they know what is best for children can they say that others do not and cannot. And only if Fineman, Becker, and other proponents of shortcut rules know what the best results are for the children in family courts today can they justifiably claim that their proposal would best serve children's welfare. It would seem that they are not best-interests skeptics at all, but rather believe simply that they are better than anyone else at determining what is best for children.

It is no answer to this point to say that the alternative proposals, which are typically for the legislature to create a general rule curtailing the discretion of judges, rest on beliefs about the welfare of children in general, whereas the best-interests test calls for determination of the well-being of an individual child. Any beliefs about the welfare of children in general would have to be the product of inductive reasoning – that is, the result of aggregating judgments about how the lives of many individual children have gone better or worse because of certain decisions or actions. They must therefore presuppose the soundness of judgments about individual cases in the past and the validity of expecting similar results in future cases.

Moreover, to the extent that any generalizations arrived at inductively are well founded, judges can rely on them just as well as legislators can, and can apply them in individual cases, while at the same time – if allowed sufficient discretion – looking out for indications that the generalization does not hold true in the individual case. Such generalizations could relate not just to past caretaking – for example, a conclusion that children whose past primary caretaker receives sole custody at divorce fare better on average than those whose custody is shared or is given to the secondary caretaker. They could also relate to other facts – for example, if older boys on average do better after divorce when their fathers have primary custody or if children whose custodial parent is permitted to move them far away from the noncustodial parent fare worse on average than those whose custodial parent is refused permission to relocate them. (Note: I am not asserting the truth or falsity of any of these particular generalizations.)

Second, if the major premise implicit in the epistemological objection were true, competent adults' decision making about much of their own lives would also have to be judged inadequate and not deserving of legal protection. Our decision making about relationships is forward looking and so entails predicting the future. It, too, suffers from bias; we routinely make judgments about people after initial encounters, based on prejudices and stereotypes. Choosing friends or intimate partners calls for comparison of alternatives based on numerous potential costs and benefits, some quite difficult to comprehend. And in making many of our relationship choices, we have little information about the persons we choose; we certainly do not have direct or immediate access to their inner nature or experiences, and we cannot know what trajectory their future life will follow. The only aspect of the epistemological critique of best-interests decision making for children that does not also apply to our own decision making is the concern about assessing someone else's welfare, but it is also the case that we often have blind spots with respect to our own characteristics and needs.

In fact, there are reasons to believe that judicial decision making about the best interests of children in connection with their relationships is superior to adults' own self-determining relationship decisions. Adults often make relationship decisions for themselves with little experience of the type of relationship they are entering into, no training to prepare them for making the decisions, and little ability to stand back and assess the relationship objectively. This is clearly true of decisions to marry. And when adults make those decisions, they are often impervious to advice from others who have experienced those relationships or who are otherwise knowledgeable about such relationships. In contrast, any state-designated decision maker about children's relationships will have experienced parent–child relationships themselves, certainly as a child and in most cases also as a parent, and will also have had a relatively in-depth look at numerous other parent–child relationships, increasingly so as they accumulate experience in their jobs. So although the decision is about the future, it is about experiences in the future with which the decision maker is likely to have substantial familiarity and understanding. Persons who occupy a role within the legal system of routinely making choices about children's lives amass a great deal of experience, and they learn from the consequences of bad decisions, which frequently entail a return to court for child and parents. Family court judges and mediators are thus often able to warn parents about pitfalls with the choices they are contemplating, steering them toward decisions superior to ones they would have made on their own. Moreover, in making decisions under existing practices, judges receive and generally pay close attention to the input of many other parties, some of whom, such as family counselors, have substantial training and experience relevant to the decision. Increasingly, specialized judges with substantial training specifically in family matters are deciding family law disputes involving children. And presumably state decision makers are able to look at others' relationships more objectively than persons typically look at their own.

Imagine for a moment that young people contemplating marriage routinely enlisted lawyers, psychologists, and social workers to help them decide which choice to make among available options. Imagine that they were required to observe closely and evaluate the marriages of many other couples before they could enter into marriage themselves. And imagine that they were able to look at their relationship more or less objectively, with their judgment unclouded by ephemeral emotions, by the excitement of a wedding celebration and honeymoon, by the expectations and prejudices of family members, and by other factors that might prevent them from seeing the true nature of their feelings or from realistically assessing their long-term compatibility with the fiancé. They might do better than the current success rate for marriage, which is little more than fifty percent. Though it might be difficult to measure this, there is no reason to believe family court judges today have a worse record in their custody decision making, applying the best-interests standard, than adults have in their decision making about their own relationships. Of course, many marriages dissolve after working well for a number of years, and some marriages dissolve even though they were the best partnerships the people involved could have had at the time, given their personalities and inexperience. But it is also true of many custody arrangements that they work well for a while and then require adjustment, because a parent's weaknesses become salient only at a certain point in a child's life, because parents' circumstances change, and/or because a child's needs change. And it is true of custody that some children are destined for turmoil no matter what a judge does.

That the epistemological objection is overstated, or proves too much, also becomes apparent when we survey the full range of decisions that courts make on a daily basis. There are actually many legal rules that call for predictions of the future and judgments about the character, disposition, and experiences of others. The best-interests standard is not unique in this regard. Establishing the credibility of a witness in any sort of trial entails supporting a prediction of veracity and of ability to call on memory or expertise by referring to past behavior, character, and experience. Decisions as to preventive detention, bail, and sentencing in criminal cases likewise turn on predictions of future behavior and assessments of the character and disposition of other human beings. The rule for granting a preliminary injunction in civil cases requires courts to speculate as to the harm each party might experience if the injunction is or is not granted. Equitable relief to redress systemic wrongs such as school segregation often rests on predictions of future behavior and the consequences of that behavior.[30] In tort suits, awarding damages for pain and suffering, emotional harm, and lost income or enjoyment of life in the future would seem to present these same epistemological difficulties. The examples could be multiplied infinitely.

Further, although it is obviously true that making decisions in behalf of persons unable to decide adequately for themselves is a difficult enterprise, one in which we can rarely be certain we are doing the right thing, our moral obligation to those persons requires that we try to do so, and it is satisfied if we sincerely do the best we can. Numerous other areas of the law recognize this belief. The law governing decision making for incompetent adults entails many of the same problems,[31] yet the law insists that courts and guardians strive always to do what is best for those adults. Likewise, if persons are absent at a time when decisions need to be made about their property, either because they are in a distant location or because they are deceased, the law imputes choices to them, based on what is most in their interests and/or what they likely would have wanted, and insists on effectuation of those choices.[32] When an adult is not able to state his or her actual preferences, we do not eliminate that person from the equation and make decisions turn on others' preferences.

As a final note, we should be suspicious of arguments for abandoning the best-interests test that give no serious consideration to the possibility of improving its implementation. Some proponents of alternative rules ignore the possibility of refining statutory guidelines and factor lists for applying the standard, and of better training judges or other decision makers to enhance their knowledge and to counteract bias. One might justifiably suspect that the quick move from pointing out deficiencies in current statutes or in judicial expertise to a supposedly more determinate rule reflects some agenda other than doing what is best for children. As noted at the outset of the book, there is a tendency in debates about children's lives to use any indication of difficulty in doing right by children as an excuse to shift attention to the interests and agendas of adults rather than working harder to develop the best possible standard and process for advancing the welfare of children.

* * *

In sum, the standard objections to best-interests decision making are unpersuasive. They do not demonstrate that it works poorly or worse for children than proposed alternatives, rather than just imperfectly. They do usefully point to potential weaknesses in the process of substituted judgment or best-interests decision making in behalf of children, but they do not show that the proper response to this reality is to abandon a substituted judgment/best interests approach in favor of some other, rather than to take whatever steps are feasible to minimize these weaknesses.

III. What Sorts of Interests Should Be Imputed to Children?

Throughout the analysis of the book, I have assumed that the proper translation of "children's imputed choices" is what is best for the children all things considered. Yet when competent adults make choices about their relationships with others, they do not always do so solely on the basis of what might be called selfish interests – that is, to secure their own pleasures and gratification of their own preferences. They sometimes make altruistically motivated decisions and might be criticized when they do not. They might establish or maintain a relationship with another person out of a desire to be kind to the other person or to benefit the other person, even though they otherwise would not choose to have that relationship. The other person might be lonely or dependent on the relationship. Or they might feel a debt of gratitude to the other person for something he or she did for them in the past, such as offering friendship when the relative social needs of the parties were reversed. The law does not compel such decisions but it also does not interfere with them, even though they appear contrary to the decision maker's self-interest. This is so not simply because there is insufficient harm to those adults to warrant state action, nor simply because of the educative function of making good and bad decisions, but also or instead because such altruism is positively valued.

One can argue, of course, that altruistic decisions are in fact self-serving at a deeper level, that they gratify a need to feel good about oneself, to relieve guilt, or to be admired. Indeed, one might believe it impossible for human beings knowingly to choose against self-interest. It might be that what happens psychologically is that at some level persons decide that the benefits of feeling good about themselves outweigh the costs of maintaining a relationship they would otherwise avoid. Significantly, it is typically only more tangential relationships, such as friendships or casual ties with co-workers, in which interaction is not so great as to make the costs very pronounced, that people are willing to maintain out of sympathy for others or a sense of moral obligation. Few would enter into a family relationship such as marriage out of pity for the other person, and doing so would be unlikely to garner the kind of favorable regard from others that maintaining a less intimate relationship out of pity would. We would say such a person is not doing anyone a favor by establishing such an intimate relationship that is likely to go badly and that such a person is giving up too much, something too important objectively to his or her own life, for the sake of making someone else feel better.

Whether ostensibly altruistic relationship decisions are in reality necessarily or typically self-serving is significant, because it might inform a decision as to whether altruistic motives should be imputed to a nonautonomous person. If they are, and if a nonautonomous person is unable or unlikely to experience the psychological benefits of being altruistic, then an attempt to shape children's rights by analogy to competent adult rights would suggest that altruistic motivations should not be attributed to the nonautonomous person. Decisions for the nonautonomous person would then be based solely on what might be called the nonautonomous person's "self-regarding" interests.[33] And that is in fact true of current practice relating to incompetent adults.

But let us suppose for the sake of argument that competent adults engage in altruistic behavior and are motivated by altruism in making decisions about their relationships not because, or only because, this serves their own well-being in certain ways but instead or also because they are capable of and inclined toward genuine self-sacrifice or supererogatory moral action. If the appropriate model for decision making in behalf of children is to determine what they would choose for themselves if able to do so competently, should we include in the analysis not only self-regarding interests they would likely pursue if able but also "other-regarding" aims or motivations they might have if they had the capacity to evaluate a situation and to make an autonomous choice? In thinking about this, it might be helpful to have in mind some concrete cases where the question might arise.

One example might be the common case where a child is in foster care because a loving parent is addicted to drugs and repeatedly relapses despite participating in rehabilitation efforts. In many such cases, the child would on the whole be better off if the parent's rights were terminated. The child might be adopted into a good home, or even if the child is not likely to be adopted, permanent foster care might be arranged and then the child would have some certainty regarding future custody arrangements, which is quite important to children's development and bonding with others. At the same time, the child might suffer emotionally from the loss of the parent, if there is a substantial relationship between them, so there could be competing self-regarding interests. The state might determine at a certain point that the balance of the child's self-regarding interests has tipped in favor of termination, and the question could then be asked whether the state ought to attribute to the child the altruistic motive to spare the parent the anguish likely to result from terminating the parent–child relationship. Indeed, some older children manifest an actual desire to spare their parents from such suffering. Another example might be a custody decision where the allocation of postdivorce parenting that would be best for the child would give one parent much less time with the child than that parent would find bearable. That parent will be terribly distraught at that outcome and will have great difficulty adjusting to the diminished contact with the child. And in this context, too, older children sometimes actually express a preference relating to their custody that is motivated by a concern for the emotional well-being of a parent.

There might also be situations in which some think it reasonable to impute gratitude to a child. The clearest case might be a maternity decision. When a woman has chosen not to abort a child but instead to carry the child inside her until birth, giving the infinitely valuable gift of life, some might have the intuition that the child owes her a debt of gratitude and that this debt warrants some sacrificing of the child's future welfare. Another example might be in the third-party visitation context, where parents have presumably provided care for a child for an extended period after birth, and the question arises whether their desire just to be left alone deserves satisfaction as a way of repaying a moral debt the child might be thought to owe them. It is less clear that a gratitude argument of this sort could be advanced in paternity, adoption, or termination cases.

Last, we might ask whether decision making for children could incorporate consideration of societal aims, such as eliminating prejudice and advancing social equality, on the theory that some competent adults are influenced in their decision making about relationships by such progressive aims. Some adults make a special effort to interact with persons of other races, in part out of a desire to help generate more harmony among people of different races in our society. Some men, in choosing or maintaining relationships with women, might as a matter of principle discount the cost for them of a woman's relative unavailability for time together or for sharing of family responsibilities, where that unavailability stems from efforts to pursue a career, out of a sense that their own commitment to the ideal of social equality for women requires them to do so.

Significantly, although adults might also perceive that they would benefit personally from living in a society characterized by social equality and tolerance, any such benefit to them individually flowing from a single relationship decision consistent with that ideal is so slight that it could not rationally give rise to a material self-regarding motivation. And it is for that reason that the state, in making decisions for a child, should not make much of the fact that the child, too, would benefit from realization of the progressive aims on which some family law scholars and courts have focused.

There are several ways, then, in which non-self-regarding motivations sometimes enter into the relationship decisions of competent adults, and the question is whether the law should endeavor to replicate that phenomenon in formulating rules for surrogate decision making for children. Several possible responses to the question need to be distinguished and separately analyzed.

A) Actual Choices

As noted above, some children might have actual preferences to protect the feelings of a parent and might be consciously willing to sacrifice their own well-being to some degree to protect what they perceive to be the parent's well-being. The general theory dictates that children's choices be overridden only when demonstrably irrational, and sacrificing one's own selfish interests to benefit someone whom one loves is generally not regarded as per se irrational. Usually when a competent adult does this, we commend them and do not say they are being irrational. Thus, if the matter at hand is one as to which a particular child is sufficiently competent for her choice, rather than her interests, to be determinative, and if her choice to sacrifice her own interests for the sake of a parent is sufficiently independent and informed, then the state should respect her choice and not act in such a way as to preclude continuation of the relationship in a practical sense.

There are circumstances, though, where we do say it is irrational for a competent adult to remain in a relationship with someone else for altruistic reasons. For example, where the other person has been so uncaring or has behaved so badly that he or she is deemed unworthy of concern, or where the persons inclined to be altruistic would incur substantial harm or are driven by a psychological pathology (e.g., co-dependency), we urge such persons to change their minds and to free themselves of the relationship. We do not esteem the self-sacrificing choice in that situation. In a comparable situation with a child, if a parent has been utterly uncaring or if maintaining the relationship would be seriously detrimental to the child, then it would generally be irrational for the child to choose to maintain the relationship in order to benefit the parent. The child is likely in such circumstances to be misperceiving the parent's character or to be acting principally out of fear of such a dramatic change in his or her life, which would mean the child is not making a free and informed decision to be altruistic. The best rule might be one that allows children, upon demonstrating competence to understand the decision to be made, to choose on the basis of concern for a parent "within reason," or that allows children to do this so long as the decision does not put them at risk of substantial loss of physical, psychological, or emotional well-being. It might therefore be more likely to operate in the custody context than in the child protective context.

B) Best Interests

Even absent actual choices that should be respected, it might be that other-regarding considerations should factor into decision making. Decision makers might take into account any likelihood that a child will at some point become aware that a particular decision about his or her life was made and feel regret for the parent's suffering. Children in custody or child protective proceedings sometimes feel guilty about their role in occasioning suffering for a parent, even though it was a passive role. Children often feel responsible for things over which they have no control. Conceivably, children could come to have such feelings even about decisions made at the time of their birth, such as a decision to deny legal parenthood to their biological parents. Avoiding those feelings of regret or guilt down the road would presumably be in a child's long-term interests.

Should decision makers today be influenced at all by the possibility of children experiencing such negative feelings in the future? If decision makers were omniscient, the answer would likely be yes; there would not seem to be any reason to exclude consideration of this interest of children as a matter of principle. In actual practice, the answer would depend in part on how easy it is to predict which children will experience regret or guilt over their parents' suffering. If experience or studies suggest that only a small percentage of children have such feelings, that would counsel against attributing the interest to any particular child. The answer would also depend on how strong and enduring the feelings typically are; if they tend to be moderate and short-lived, that would counsel against making avoidance of the feelings a particularly significant consideration. With adults, who are fully aware of the situations in which relationship decisions are made and who themselves make the decisions, such feelings of guilt or regret appear usually to be not so strong as to override self-interest, at least not for long, in making decisions about more intimate relationships. We might expect such feelings to be more muted with children, who usually are not much aware of the situation at the time, find out about it long after the fact, and know that they themselves did not make the final decision. However, they are less able to sort it all out rationally.

These musings are obviously tentative; concrete empirical evidence of how many children experience these feelings and how pronounced they typically are should inform any final conclusion about whether state decisions should be influenced by this concern. Decisions should also take into account, however, available strategies for helping a child avoid unfounded feelings of guilt. For example, children old enough to be aware of a divorce or of abuse often see a counselor before, during, and/or after the process, and a counselor can help them work through their thoughts and feelings so that they recognize they are not responsible and so that they are able to deal with their parents' reactions to the situation. It seems more sensible to do what is best for a child independent of concerns about the child having such negative feelings and then take steps to prevent the feelings from arising than to choose what would otherwise be a worse outcome for the child on the assumption that the child will experience such feelings. This conclusion is bolstered by recognizing the danger inherent in considering such an interest – namely that decision makers would shift their focus to the well-being of parents under the guise of sparing the child from bad feelings later in life.

C) Imputed Morality

A third way of answering the question, though, would authorize direct consideration of the experience of parents, and of other affected adults, on the assumption that people in general should consider the welfare of others when they make decisions about personal relationships, and so a decision meant to mirror adult decision making should do so as well. Certainly we admire people who, in deciding whether to marry someone, consider not only what that person can give to them, and not only what is admirable about the person, but also what they can give to that person, what needs or desires they can satisfy. And we admire people who form friendships with a person who stands in need of a friend, who is lonely, and who might have qualities that make him or her unattractive as a friend to more self-regarding people. Some might contend that we all have a moral obligation to give of ourselves in this way, to enter into some relationships with the aim of giving more than, or at least as much as, we receive.

In addition, many believe that once we are in relationships with others, particularly in family relationships, we have an obligation to stick with the relationships and to sacrifice for the others even when things get rough because of the others' failings. We think we ought to be caring about and forgiving of, and be willing to sacrifice for, family members and to show gratitude for benefits they have bestowed on us in the past.[34] In particular, many believe that children owe a debt of gratitude to their parents for the care the parents have provided. If the basic idea behind constructing a theory of children's rights is to try to mimic adults' situation, one might think, then we should take the same moral stance toward children, in terms of what we would morally expect them to do if able, that we take toward adults – namely that some consideration should be given to the effects of decision on others and that gratitude should be shown for past beneficence by others.

One problem with this line of thinking is that whatever other private parties might think about or say to selfish adults, the law does not compel competent adults to be altruistic in their relationship decisions. The state does not impose such moral positions on people but rather leaves them free to make such moral decisions themselves. Allocation of legal rights and responsibilities is based on a balancing of persons' self-regarding interests or on equal respect for persons' autonomy, but morality goes beyond the legal requirements and calls for a somewhat other-regarding attitude. In fact, one might think genuine moral action impossible if the law compelled every action deemed desirable or admirable. So how should we view the state's deciding as agent for a child in part on the basis of altruistic motives? Would that amount to the state's compelling someone to be "moral," or would it just be a matter of the state's doing its best to imitate what a person would likely do voluntarily if able, given the moral expectations in our society?

Significantly, the law in other contexts reflects an aversion to imputing morally correct decisions to incompetent persons. For example, with respect to incompetent adults, courts have held that public officials may not be appointed as guardians for such persons if the government entity they represent has a conflict of interest with the incompetent person. I mentioned earlier the example of an incompetent adult in a health care facility, subsidized by government welfare programs, who becomes entitled to a significant amount of private wealth, perhaps by inheritance. Although the morally appropriate thing for competent persons receiving public assistance to do in that situation might be to accept the inheritance and use it to start paying their own way, or to repay the government for past assistance, courts have held that an official of the social services agency, which would ultimately receive that wealth, may not serve as guardian for an incompetent person in that situation. Rather, a disinterested agent, who might ensure that the wealth passes to other family members instead, by renouncing an inheritance, must be appointed. Another example is the law concerning gift giving by guardians from a ward's assets; guardians are generally prohibited from doing so, absent evidence that making the gift would be in the ward's interests (e.g., because part of a rational estate or tax-avoidance plan) or that the ward expressed while competent a wish to make a gratuitous transfer.[35]

There are ostensibly exceptions to this practice of exclusively self-regarding surrogate decision making for incompetent persons. One is for cases where a once competent, but now incompetent, person previously expressed a desire to give a gift to someone else. The terms of a trust, for example, continue to be carried out even if the grantor becomes incompetent after execution. In those cases, however, the law is not imposing morality, but rather just effectuating earlier actual choices, choices that are not necessarily altruistic. The law in some jurisdictions goes further in attempting to effectuate what it is believed an incompetent person would choose if able insofar as it allows guardians for incompetent adults to give gifts to charity or to family members out of a ward's estate. But authorization to make such gifts is closely circumscribed; they generally must either serve the overall interests of the ward – for example, because they are part of a sound tax-planning strategy – or they must be predicated on evidence of intent prior to incapacity, such as a prior pattern of gift giving or competent statements of intention, and must not significantly impact the ward's financial situation. The law regarding organ transplants from incompetent persons is not well developed, but courts generally focus here also on benefits that the donor would experience – for example, from the survival of a sibling with whom the ward has a close relationship – and on evidence about a particular individual's personality that suggests he would have consented if he had remained competent.

Laws regarding disposition of property at death arguably do not compel other-regarding results at all. The law of wills strives assiduously to effectuate the intent of testators with respect to distribution of their wealth after death, whatever that intent might have been. The usual intent – that is, to pass on all one's wealth to one's family – arguably is not altruistic; because "you can't take it with you," arguably the most self-serving thing one can do from an anthropological perspective is to bequeath one's wealth to one's blood relatives. Intestacy law, which applies in the absence of a will, effectuates an assumption that, in the absence of an expression of contrary intent, such a "self-serving" choice is what the decedent wanted; it directs that a decedent's wealth be distributed to family members. A truly moral or altruistic action might be to give all or most of the wealth either to the state, to support social welfare programs, or to private charities, at least if family members are otherwise financially secure.[36] Yet intestacy rules go to extreme lengths to direct a decedent's wealth to relatives rather than having it escheat to the state, preferring quite distant relatives – whom scholars and practitioners sometimes refer to as "laughing heirs" – that the decedent likely never knew, over the state. These rules are based on an assumption that most people have no interest in sacrificing for the sake of public programs, but rather, given that they can no longer enjoy the wealth themselves, would selfishly prefer their kin to have it whether they need it or not.

The general aversion in the law to imputing moral choices to incompetent adults reflects several precepts, all of which hold in the case of children as well. One precept is that the moral obligation to be altruistic or to show gratitude arises from being blessed with abilities and resources that allow one to be magnanimous. We would not expect a competent adult who labors under great physical disabilities, disadvantages, and misfortunes to be as magnanimous as one who has a very comfortable and secure life.

As mentioned earlier, many ascribe to the principle that "to whom much is given, much is expected," and its converse would be "to whom little is given, little is expected." Incompetent persons are under a rather great disability or disadvantage, so we do not expect altruism or self-sacrifice on their part even if they are capable of choosing to be altruistic or self-sacrificing, and we do not impute altruism or self-sacrificing choices to them when they are not capable of actually choosing. We think it fitting that their self-regarding interests be satisfied to the greatest extent possible. Such persons should be the beneficiaries, not the givers, of altruism. Similarly, there is not much intuitive appeal to the claim that a newborn child owes a moral obligation of concern or gratitude to a drug-addicted birth mother, the claim that a six-year-old ought to care about the happiness of his divorcing parents, or the claim that a ten-year-old should put up with further abuse or neglect or prolonged foster care to spare her parent the anguish of losing parental rights. Any intuitive appeal would vanish in situations where the adults seeking a relationship have given little or nothing to the child – for example, a disengaged biological father seeking paternity or a legal parent who has mostly left a child in the care of others.

Another operative precept is that moral obligations exist only for rational moral agents, so persons who are incompetent in such a way as to be incapable of rational moral agency are seen as not having any moral obligations. As such, persons who are not now rational moral agents but later become such are not likely, even if they turn out to be very magnanimous persons, to believe that they had moral obligations earlier or to feel remiss that altruistic decisions were not made in their behalf. Another way to look at this assumption is as holding that only rational moral agents can fulfill moral obligations, because part of the fulfillment lies in the agent's recognizing himself or herself to be under the obligation. We should not impute to persons moral obligations they are incapable of fulfilling. This problem is not avoided by saying that the adult in question has a right to expression of gratitude or concern from someone and that an agent for the child can bear the duty corresponding to that right, because the sacrifice being demanded still falls on the child, and so the question remains why the child should bear that sacrifice, a question that demands a response in terms of the moral position of the child. Society as a whole might owe an obligation to help parents avoid suffering, but it must find some way to fulfill that obligation other than sacrificing the welfare of children; we may not use children instrumentally to salve the wounds of adults' misfortunes.

A third operative assumption is that great danger lies in acting for incompetent persons on the basis of imputed altruism, a danger that decision makers will transfer their concerns entirely to other persons – in particular, to competent adults who are able to make forceful demands in their own behalf or to make a sympathetic plea to state decision makers. In a culture that for most of its history did not treat incompetent individuals as persons deserving of equal respect, but in fact did treat them instrumentally in many ways, the law should guard diligently against slippage back into that way of thinking. This is certainly true of children as well as of incompetent adults.

These three assumptions together support a conclusion that decision makers for all incompetent persons, including children, should not impute moral choices to them on the grounds that people in general ought to act morally. I would add that, in the case of parents, it is not as clear as many suppose that parents are owed gratitude for giving a child life or for providing caretaking, however extensive. Gratitude generally arises from receiving gratuitous benefits, and as suggested in discussing a hypothetical bargain between parents and children in Chapter 6, children actually provide great benefits in return to parents. It might actually be we parents who owe a debt of gratitude to someone, for having been given the opportunity to share in our children's lives, a debt that would be so much larger if we enjoyed that opportunity even though it was not best for our children that we do so. Someone whose parental status must be terminated because she has proven unfit to raise a child should be thankful she was given a chance. Her child owes her nothing.

D) Attributing Hypothetical Choices

A final way of answering the question, though, would be to attribute a hypothetical choice to a child. Even if there is no actual choice, even if ascribing an interest in avoiding regret or guilt in the future is too speculative, and even if it is improper to impose a moral decision on children, it might be reasonable to act on the basis of an assumption that a child most likely would now voluntarily choose to act altruistically if competent to make the decision. One basis for attributing such a hypothetical choice might be evidence concerning a given child's propensities to altruism and/or devotion to a parent. Imagine a child who cares deeply about his or her parent, despite serious abuse or neglect, and who, it seems reasonable to suppose, would, if able, choose to maintain the relationship, as an act of love for the parent. The child might be incapable of understanding the legal situation sufficiently to actually make an informed decision on the legal issue of termination, or a judge might determine that it would be deleterious to the child to ask the child to decide. It might be reasonable in such a situation to maintain the relationship, precisely because of a conclusion of what the given child would now choose, based on knowledge of his individual characteristics.

An alternative means of attributing a hypothetical choice, in the absence of convincing evidence as to the individual child's inclination to altruism, might be on the basis of probabilities, which in turn might be based on facts about what most competent adults do. This option would have the state say that if most competent adults *do* act altruistically in analogous situations, then courts should attribute altruistic motives to every child, unless a particular child expresses a contrary choice that warrants respect. Courts should do so not because altruisitc action is morally correct but rather because the state is trying to guess what the child would choose if able, and the rates of altruism among adults support (let us suppose, for the sake of argument) a guess that the child would choose altruistically. On that basis, courts could create or maintain parent–child relationships even when they are otherwise not in children's best interests, so long as the loss of welfare for the child is not too great (as determined by examining how much adults are willing to sacrifice in the cause of altruism).

The first means of attributing hypothetical choices is consistent with the general theory, as it endorses a substituted judgment approach. The state must be careful, though, not to make too much of an inclination to altruism. Competent adults have their breaking point as to when they are no longer willing to sacrifice for others, even those whom they love deeply. Reliance on inclination to altruism, if done at all, should be limited to cases where the costs and benefits for a child are otherwise close to being evenly balanced. Because the choice here is hypothetical rather than actual, and therefore entails some guesswork on the part of state actors, the choice should be more readily overridden on the basis of a showing that it is irrational than in the case of actual choices.

The second means of attributing hypothetical choices is also consistent with the general theory, insofar as it attempts to determine, as best it can, what the child would choose if able to make a free and fully informed choice, in the absence of a controlling actual choice by a child. Under this approach, the state would not by design impose a particular morality on people but rather would try to implement what any given child most likely would want if able to choose independently. The state would thus be respecting the child's personhood. In fact, one might think it would disrespect a child's personhood to ignore the fact that she likely would, if able, choose to act altruistically.

This second means of attributing hypothetical choices, however, is problematic in certain respects. Imputing motivations on the basis of probabilities, or what motivations most competent adults actually have, is significantly different from extrapolating from actual characteristics of a nonautonomous person. As to any given individual, it makes little sense to say that she herself is likely to act a certain way because most members of a class to which she does not now belong, and whose members possess a critical characteristic that she lacks – namely the capacity to recognize, develop, and choose to act on the motivation at issue – act in that way. When we impute choices based on self-regarding interests (which can be future oriented, as in the case of education, as well as present oriented) and/or known characteristics, we begin with something actual about the individual and simply impute instrumental rationality to them, a capacity they would necessarily have if they belonged to the class of persons who make legally effective choices themselves. We do not impute values and beliefs – the stuff of personality, which can vary greatly among competent persons. Imputing aspects of personality to those who could never have actually possessed them, based on probabilities, is a metaphysical exercise and glosses over human individuality. Thus, in the absence of evidence as to a particular individual's propensity for altruism or actual caring for another person, the state should not impute altruistic motivations to a child and should instead decide based solely on a child's "self-regarding" interests.

In any event, any probability transported from the adult population to children might not be that great; it might be that most people able to make relationship decisions themselves are not willing to sacrifice their own welfare to avoid causing suffering to others who want an intimate relationship, so there would not in any case be a strong basis for imputing an altruistic choice. This is especially true of more intimate, family relationships; it would be a rare person, and not someone we would deem rational, who chose to marry another despite recognizing that the marriage would make him or her worse off or who chose for altruistic reasons to remain married to someone who was very abusive and indifferent. And in the case of children's relationships, there clearly is a reason to impute a contrary preference – namely to protect their self-regarding interests.

* * *

To summarize: A child's actual, free, and independent choice to act altruistically toward a parent should be controlling unless it is clearly and substantially irrational. In the absence of an actual choice by the child, the state might place some weight on a perceived inclination in the child to be altruistic and on a perception that the child feels love for the parent in question, and on that basis attribute to a child a hypothetical choice to act altruistically. But it should not be a lot of weight. And state decision makers should not be influenced by the possibility that a child might someday regret or feel guilty about what happened to a parent. Nor should the state sacrifice a child's welfare for the sake of a parent simply because the legislature or a judge believes family members ought to sacrifice for each other, thus imposing a moral choice on a child. And state decision makers should not impute a hypothetical altruistic choice to children on the grounds that many adults make self-sacrificing decisions in connection with their personal relationships.

Conclusion

The theoretical analysis is now complete. I have constructed a positive theory of children's relationship rights by articulating the normative underpinnings of adults' relationship rights and then extending them to children. I have considered numerous objections to that theory and given content to the basic prescription for a substituted judgment or best-interests approach to state decision making about children's relationships. It remains now just to give greater concreteness to the theoretical conclusions by suggesting how they might play out in a few areas of actual practice – that is, how they might be embodied in specific legal rules. That is the task of the final chapter.

8 Applications

Having developed a general theory of children's moral rights in connection with state decision making about their relationships, and having worked out a number of details and answered a number of objections, I proceed now to consider concrete ways in which the law might be reformed to conform to children's moral rights. Explaining the specific proposals I offer below will help to reiterate theoretical points made in earlier chapters. The proposals are tentative, because my aim was not to amass all the empirical information relevant to the legal issues I discuss but rather to develop a theoretical framework for addressing them. A fuller investigation of all the empirical issues relevant to a child-centered reformation of the law would help to refine the proposals.

I do not attempt a comprehensive code of children's relationships rights here. I focus on three particular areas of the law to illustrate the conclusions of the normative analysis. Parentage laws in many countries now pay little or no heed to the welfare of children, and they are the ultimate cause of so much suffering for children and of so many societal problems that they cry out for reform. Legal rules for responding to inadequate parenting (i.e., abuse and neglect laws) are, in the United States and elsewhere, a quagmire of standards and tests that reflect an improper balancing of parents' interests and children's interests. The law governing children's relationships with persons who are not legal parents causes significant suffering to children in a significant number of cases, principally where it denies standing to third parties other than grandparents, and it is now very much on the minds of scholars and on the agendas of legislatures and courts in many jurisdictions.

Many existing rules governing children's relational lives, as described in Chapter 2, are so far removed from an ideal set of rules that proposing adoption of something even close to an ideal rule will appear radical, politically unrealistic, and unworkable in practice. For example, the idea of all adults needing to "qualify" to parent their biological offspring is, despite the widespread practice of adults having to qualify to parent children who are not their biological offspring, unthinkable to most people in the western world. To avoid having the proposals dismissed out of hand as utopian, I offer what might be characterized as better rather than ideal rules, rules that would bring us closer to effectuating children's moral rights without necessarily getting us all the way. Thus, rather than espousing the mandatory parental licensing idea that some philosophers and social scientists have promoted,[1] I suggest reworking parentage laws just to spare children from the state's assigning them to the worst parents. This scaled-down approach is also responsive to legitimate concerns about the potential for governmental misuse of authority over family life. The proposals I offer might still be politically unrealistic in some respects, and inconsistent with constitutional doctrine in some countries, but I have tried to stay within the bounds of what is practicably workable, in light of existing institutions and established patterns of life.

I. Reforming Parentage Laws

Existing rules for creating parent–child relationships are inconsistent. The best-interests standard controls the process of approving nonbiological parents for parenthood, but the interests of children and the preparedness of adults to care for children are irrelevant to the process of bestowing legal parenthood on biological parents. Few would seriously maintain that a biological connection with a parent is so important to a child's well-being that this disparity can be justified on purely child-centered grounds. Moreover, legal parenthood is an exclusive status, preventing other persons from occupying a legally protected care-giving role and, in most jurisdictions, carrying with it an automatic right to at least partial custody of the child. Thus, the state largely dictates who will care for a child throughout his or her life up to adulthood and does so with no regard for the character or capacities of the persons it places in that role.

In addition to violating the moral rights of newborn children, absolute deference to biological parents is bad public policy, and so there should be substantial public support for revising parentage laws to screen out those most unprepared to raise a child well. States now expend enormous resources intervening in dysfunctional families, providing for the care of children who must be removed from their homes, giving remedial education to children who come from bad homes, dealing with youth from dysfunctional families who commit crimes,[2] and otherwise cleaning up after bad parents. The costs for society continue when children who were abused and neglected or who were unable to bond with a permanent caregiver in the earliest stages of development become dysfunctional adults, less able to be productive members of society, requiring social services of many kinds to help them function, and likely themselves to abuse and neglect children. Moreover, we do not do biological parents any favor when we set them up for failure, when they are manifestly unprepared to care for a child and yet we place the mantle of parenthood on their shoulders anyway. The lives of many children and of many biological parents would go better, and many societal problems would be ameliorated, if we reformed parentage laws so as to confer legal parenthood in the first instance only on adults who are at least minimally prepared to take on the enormous responsibility of raising a child.

At the same time, modifying parentage laws to exclude manifestly unfit parents at the outset would not be a radical departure from current practice in terms of its impact on adults and so would not be terribly upsetting of settled expectations. The state is already taking custody of many children immediately after birth, because their birth mothers have previously engaged in conduct that makes them unfit to parent or are currently unfit because of drug addiction, mental illness, or imprisonment. Only now, the state is sticking those children in costly and sometimes dangerous foster care while it undertakes costly and usually unsuccessful rehabilitative efforts until it can complete the costly process of terminating parental rights, after which the children are typically already permanently harmed and less attractive to potential adoptive parents.[3] The state is already imposing protective orders against biological fathers who have previously engaged in bad conduct that makes them unsuitable to parent and then undertaking the costly process of terminating the parental rights of those men. Moreover, the state is removing many children from the custody of mothers and fathers after the children have been in their care for a time, when child protective agencies become aware that parents are abusing and/or neglecting the children, and ultimately is terminating the parental rights of some of those parents, again after extensive and intrusive measures are taken to reform the parents and after children have spent lengthy periods in foster care. In addition, the state is already conducting court proceedings soon after birth to adjudicate the parental rights and responsibilities of biological fathers for a substantial percentage of the children whose biological parents are not married to each other, and in a significant percentage of those cases is severely restricting and monitoring the contact that the fathers have with the children. My proposal entails denying legal parenthood in the first instance only to a small percentage of biological parents, those who are highly likely to lose custody of their children anyway, while leaving the rules largely unchanged for the great majority of births. The real impact of the proposal would be on children, and it should be on the whole quite positive. It would aim to create in the first instance for every child a parent–child relationship that can begin immediately upon birth, that is likely to be nurturing, and that is likely never to be disrupted by parental departure or state intervention.[4]

What is more difficult than making the policy case for screening out the worst parents is identifying the precise substantive bases on which the state would deny legal parenthood and prescribing a process for applying the substantive rule. Social scientific research does reveal some readily observable parental characteristics that correlate highly with poor outcomes for children. These include drug or alcohol abuse, being of a very young age, criminality, past abusiveness toward children or adults, and mental illness.

Maternal drug addiction, and the underlying psychological problems that addiction typically reflects, damage children both before and after birth, particularly in communities where poverty and violence are prevalent, and the success rate for rehabilitative efforts with drug addicts is quite low.[5] Elizabeth Bartholet explains how dismal the prospects are for children born to drug addicts as follows:

> Anyone familiar with child abuse and neglect issues knows that parental substance abuse is an overwhelmingly important issue. The statistics say a lot here. Somewhere in the range of 70–90% of all parents identified as maltreating their kids are abusing illegal drugs or alcohol or both. The conflicting time clocks of parent and child are a major piece of the problem: for parents the road to rehabilitation for most who get there is long and tortured, with many false starts and relapses, and many will never even get on that road, and many who do will never make it to the end; for children, parenting is something they need today and tomorrow, and if too many months go by without adequate nurturing, irreparable damage can be done.[6]

Alcohol abuse is similarly damaging to fetuses and children.[7] There is also a high correlation between substance abuse and domestic violence, and domestic violence turn is both psychologically damaging to children who witness it and highly correlated with child abuse by perpetrators of interadult violence and by adult victims.[8] As Bartholet suggests, there is little chance that parents of newborn children can overcome addiction or escape the pathology of domestic violence quickly enough to become nurturing and protective parents for children during the crucial years of infancy.[9] Further, drug addicts are also at high risk of being imprisoned and therefore entirely unavailable to their children, either for using illegal substances or for committing crimes to secure drugs.[10] Empirical research also shows that children of teenage mothers are significantly more likely to grow up in poverty and in single-parent households (which in turn are highly correlated with child abuse and neglect),[11] to perform poorly in school, to be abused and neglected, to end up in prison, and to become teen parents themselves.[12] Susan Apel observes: "The specter of such teen-aged children attempting, and often failing, to provide even the rudiments of basic child care to their infants is a horrible one. Virtually everyone recognizes the problems generated by the infliction of parenthood on young and poor women. We ache for the babies that are ill-cared for and often severely neglected and abused."[13] Other studies demonstrate adverse impacts on children of having a parent who is imprisoned[14] or who has a serious mentally illness,[15] the high rates of repeated abuse and neglect by parents after a first finding of abuse or neglect,[16] and the toll that foster care takes on children's health and development.[17]

One approach might therefore be to amend parentage laws so that people below a certain age, people who have committed certain crimes, and so forth simply may not become the legal parent of a newborn child. However, for none of the characteristics listed above is there a one hundred percent correlation with poor parenting or poor outcomes for children, and there would be much public resistance (however misguided) to a rule that categorically excluded some people because of their current situation, especially if that situation were viewed as unchosen or undeserved, or because of their past behavior, if they have worked hard to overcome past problems. Such a rule would also result in entirely too many children needing adults other than their biological parents to become their legal parents.[18] Moreover, categorically excluding some people, leaving them with no hope for retaining the children they conceive, would likely induce some in those categories who do conceive a child to abort the child or to engage in behaviors harmful to the child, such as foregoing prenatal care and giving birth in secret, so as to avoid detection of their circumstances/behavior or of the pregnancy (though there is some tendency among scholars who express this concern to exaggerate the extent to which pregnant women are indifferent to the welfare of their unborn child). My proposal therefore does not absolutely disqualify anyone from parenthood, but rather requires certain categories of biological parents – that is, biological parents manifesting certain characteristics or circumstances – to petition for legal parenthood as to particular children and to demonstrate that making them the legal parents of their offspring is likely to be better on the whole for the child than would be bestowing legal parenthood on any other available persons (e.g., applicants for adoption). The characteristics and circumstances are ones that we most clearly would want to avoid if we were going to be born again and got to choose our parents.

A final point before presenting the model statute: The response many would have to any proposal to deny parenthood to persons possessing certain characteristics, if some of those characteristics might be changed or ameliorated with public provision of financial assistance and services, is to contend that society should instead provide the assistance and services. I fully embrace that position as a conclusion of ideal theory. However, children are born today into a real world in which we do not collectively provide sufficient assistance and services,[19] and it is indefensible and irresponsible to dismiss efforts to spare children from bearing the costs of inhospitable parental circumstances on the grounds that in an ideal world those circumstances would not exist. Similarly, it would be wrongheaded to eliminate programs designed to assist women to exit abusive relationships on the grounds that in an ideal world all women would receive an education that prepares them well for independence and men would be taught to treat women with respect. And it might be that denying parenthood to adults in dire circumstances would highlight and generate sympathy for their plight, sufficiently so to produce greater public and private assistance for them. Here is the proposal:

Code of Everystate

Chapter 1 – Family Formation

Part I. Creation of parent–child relationship. When a child is born, a legal parent–child relationship shall arise between the child and one or more adults as follows:

A. In the case of a child born to a woman who is married at the time of birth:
   1) The birth mother shall become a legal parent of the child automatically by operation of this statute if:
      a) the birth mother signs a Parental Vow as described in Subsection 2 below within two days after the child's birth,[20] and

b) the state does not, upon petition filed within seven days after the child's birth, demonstrate by clear and convincing evidence that the birth mother falls into one of the categories of persons identified in Section C below as being required to petition for legal parenthood.

2) The birth mother's spouse shall become a legal parent of the child automatically by operation of this statute if:

   a) the birth mother becomes a legal parent,

   b) the birth mother's spouse signs a Parental Vow as described in Subsection 2 below within two days after the child's birth,

   c) the birth mother executes a Consent to Spouse's Parenthood, and

   d) the state does not, upon petition filed within seven days after the child's birth, demonstrate by clear and convincing evidence that the birth mother's spouse falls into one of the categories of persons identified in Section C below as being required to petition for legal parenthood.

3) If and only if the birth mother or her spouse does not become a legal parent automatically by operation of this statute, as prescribed in Paragraphs 1) and 2) of this Section, then any person, including the birth mother and her spouse, may petition under this Part for legal parenthood of the child within thirty days of the child's birth. The child shall be made a party to the proceeding and a guardian *ad litem* shall be appointed to represent the child. The court shall make a substituted judgment for the child as to which, if any, of those petitioners should be chosen at that time to serve as a legal parent of the child, taking into account the factors identified in Section D below. If, upon being selected for parenthood, a petitioner signs a Parental Vow, the court shall confer legal parenthood on that petitioner.

B. In the case of a child born to a woman who is not married at the time of birth:

   1) The birth mother shall become a legal parent of the child automatically by operation of this statute if:

      a) the birth mother executes a Parental Vow within two days after the child's birth, and

      b) the state does not, upon petition filed within seven days after the child's birth, demonstrate by clear and convincing evidence that the birth mother falls into one of the categories of persons identified in Section C below as being required to petition for legal parenthood.

2) Any person, including the birth mother if she does not become a legal parent automatically by operation of this statute as provided in Paragraph 1) of this Section, may petition for legal parenthood within thirty days of the child's birth. The child shall be made a party to the action and a guardian *ad litem* shall be appointed to represent the child. The court shall make a substituted judgment for the child as to which, if any, of those petitioners should be chosen at that time to serve as a legal parent, taking into account the factors identified in Section D below. If, upon being selected by the court for parenthood, a petitioner signs a Parental Vow, the court shall confer legal parenthood on that petitioner.

C. A biological parent or spouse of a birth mother must petition for legal parenthood, rather than having legal parenthood conferred automatically by operation of this statute, if she or he:

1) is below eighteen years of age at the time of the child's birth;

2) at the time of the child's birth is imprisoned or has been sentenced to serve a prison term following the birth;

3) has harmed the child before birth through voluntary conduct, including but not limited to committing acts of violence toward the gestational mother during pregnancy and ingesting [specified illegal drugs or legal drugs in excessive quantities] or [a specified quantity of alcohol] while knowing one is pregnant;

4) has previously been found by a state child protective agency or court to have abused, neglected, or committed a crime against any child;

5) has previously allowed a child to suffer substantial pain or die by willfully failing to secure medical care when it was needed;

6) has previously been found in a civil or criminal legal proceeding to have committed acts of violence toward or sexual offenses against any person;

7) is already a legal parent to four or more children and is receiving [specified forms of public assistance];

8) has been diagnosed with a mental illness that would, even with treatment then being received, endanger the safety of a child in his or her care; or

9) has an IQ of less than 70.[21]

D. The family court shall consider all petitions for legal parenthood properly filed under this Part and shall make a substituted judgment for the child as to which, if any, of the petitioners shall become the child's legal parents, based on the following factors:

1) the nature and extent of any existing personal relationship between the petitioner and the child;

2) the nature and extent of any personal relationship between the petitioner and any other petitioner or legal parent, including any expected positive or negative impact on a child arising from the nature of that relationship, and the likely future duration of that relationship;

3) the age and maturity of the petitioner;

4) any interest previously shown by the petitioner in the child, as evidenced by such behavior as providing material support to the mother during pregnancy, securing prenatal medical care, and preparing to care for the child after birth;

5) the attitudes of the petitioner's family members, of any copetitioner, or of any existing legal parent toward the child and toward the petitioner's participation in the child's life, and their willingness to support the parenting of the petitioner;

6) any special needs of the child;

7) the parenting abilities and knowledge of the petitioner;

8) the mental and physical health and abilities of the petitioner, taking into account, in the case of illness or disability, treatment or compensatory measures that are currently available and that the petitioner is willing to use;

9) the living circumstances of the petitioner, including home environment, financial resources, the petitioner's ability and desire to spend time with the child, other personal relationships of the petitioner insofar as they might enhance or inhibit the petitioner's ability to parent, and threats to the child's welfare that might exist in or around the petitioner's residence;

10) any past conduct by the petitioner that suggests a potential for harm to the child, including but not limited to any prior acts of violence against family members or other persons and any prior findings of a state child protective agency or court that the petitioner abused or neglected any child;

11) the petitioner's level of commitment to securing a good education, health care, and positive socializing experiences for the child;

12) any biological relationship between the petitioner and the child;

13) the desire of other adults to serve as legal parents; and

14) any other considerations relevant to the welfare of the child.

E. There shall be a presumption that it is in the best interests of the child to have no more than two legal parents. This presumption may be overcome only by clear and convincing evidence. However, restriction of legal parenthood to one or two persons shall not preclude legal protection of relationships between children and nonparents, as provided for in [sections of the code governing nonparent visitation].

Part II. Parental vow. The state department of social services shall draft a standard Parental Vow, which all persons must sign before they may become legal parents for a child. The Parental Vow shall state the name of the executing parent and of the child. The Parental Vow shall contain statements committing the parent, at a minimum, to devote substantial time to direct care for the child, to provide love and emotional support for the child, to secure and devote to the child adequate financial resources to provide for the child's physical needs, to ensure that the child attends school and receives appropriate preventive and remedial medical care, to refrain from acts of violence toward the child and toward other family members, to support the positive caregiving efforts of any co-parent, to respect the bodily and psychological integrity of the child, to facilitate a healthy social life for the child, including relationships with persons outside the immediate family, and to view themselves as caretakers rather than owners of the child.

Part III. Facilitating assignment of parenthood to biologically unrelated person. All public and private providers of services to pregnant women or to persons employing reproductive technologies shall report to the [state child protective agency] at the earliest feasible time any evidence they perceive that any persons pursuing parenthood possess any of the characteristics listed in Section C of Part I.[22] All hospitals and other providers of birth-related services shall immediately report the birth of any child, along with the names and ages of the birth mother and of any man claiming to be the biological father of the child, to the [state child protective agency], which shall then immediately consult [a computerized registry that combines information about the agency's own operations with information supplied by other state agencies to generate a list of all persons who: are convicted criminals; are current prison inmates; have previously committed domestic violence, child abuse or neglect, or a sexual offense; are receiving specified forms of public assistance and claim already to have four or more children; have been involuntarily committed to a psychiatric facility; or have been assessed as having an IQ below 70], to determine if a biological parent appears in the registry. Upon receiving evidence that a person who is a biological parent of or who is pursuing legal parenthood of a newborn child has any of the characteristics listed in Section C of Part I, the [state child protective agency] shall immediately file a petition in the local family court for an order requiring that person to petition for legal parenthood and shall immediately notify of its petition all public and private agencies that accept applications for parenthood from biologically unrelated persons.

* * *

This is a moderately demanding statute, in terms of what it expects of biological parents who wish to become legal parents. Good arguments could be made for weakening certain of the provisions that preclude automatic conferral of legal parent status. For example, with respect to age considerations, a minimum age of sixteen for automatic parenthood, rather than eighteen as I have it, would trigger an individualized review only for those more clearly too immature to be good parents, allowing older and more mature minors to become parents automatically. But this might implicitly send a message that sixteen-year-olds are ready to be parents and so encourage some minors to conceive a child. A minimum age of eighteen for automatic conferral of parenthood is still much less demanding than the age restriction found in most adoption laws, which entirely precludes persons under age twenty-one from seeking legal parent status. Most teen births are nonmarital and result in legal paternity proceedings anyway. And children born to teens are, on average, more "adoptable" than children born to women manifesting some of the other characteristics that trigger review under this proposal. With respect to past conduct, a less demanding statute might deny automatic parenthood only to those who have previously had parental rights terminated, not to all as to whom there has been a finding of abuse or neglect. But the rules for terminating parental rights now are quite onerous, so today a substantial number of unfit parents retain their parental status. Making the statute more demanding makes it all the more important that denying persons automatic legal parenthood does not, in and of itself, amount to denying them parenthood. Under this proposal, it means simply that one must demonstrate to a court that it is in the child's best interests that one become the legal parents of a newborn child, all things considered and in light of available alternatives.

Reasonable arguments could also be made for making the proposal more demanding. Perhaps would-be parents should be required not only to sign a Parental Vow but also to take parenting classes and (as occurs with adoption) agree to a probationary period during which their parenting would be monitored. In addition, one could certainly imagine other potential bases for denying automatic parenthood. I offer a relatively modest proposal (though one still certain to trigger strong opposition) both in recognition of political realities and with an eye to the likely number of available biologically unrelated parents.

Even this statute, though, would likely result in a substantial increase in the number of newborn children available to biologically unrelated applicants for parenthood (i.e., those who now apply for "adoption").[23] And so the following question naturally arises: "Where will all these children go?" A more finely tuned statute might reflect estimates of how many children are born to persons who possess certain problematic characteristics, estimates of how many adults are currently waiting to adopt a child, and estimates of how many more adults would wish to become legal parents of children who are not their biological offspring if more newborns were available and if the process for doing so were made somewhat easier by eliminating the need to terminate the rights of a prior parent. Currently, the number of applicants for adoption of newborns in North America and western Europe far exceeds the number available domestically for adoption, as evidenced by the great number of applicants who ultimately adopt from abroad.[24] This is in large part because of the dramatic decline in the rate of single mothers' relinquishing their newborn children for adoption, as the stigma attached to single motherhood has diminished. In addition, there is a great number of people who consider adopting but never apply, and a great number who apply but never adopt at all, and it might be that a greater availability of newborns and simplified legal proceedings (i.e., without the need to terminate a prior parent's rights) would encourage a portion of them to go through with an adoption. However, the demand is principally for healthy white babies, so the prospects currently are not as great for nonwhite children or for those born with health problems, such as those stemming from maternal drug or alcohol abuse, and simplifying the legal process for adoption might not change this appreciably.

Numerical fine-tuning of the statute is actually not needed, however, to spare children from ending up parentless, because the consequence of being denied automatic parenthood is simply that one must appear in court to request legal parent status, as a substantial percentage of biological fathers already must do today. If no biologically unrelated persons wish to become the legal parent of a particular child, then the court would confer legal parent status on one or both of the child's biological parents, if that is better for the child than not conferring parental status on anyone at that time; the biological parents simply would have no competition in their pursuit of legal parenthood. And in the process, the biological parents might be forced to think seriously about the responsibility they are undertaking and about what they need to do to fulfill that responsibility well, and the court might direct them to a public or private agency that can assist them in various ways in doing so. Those benefits might well outweigh the incremental cost to the legal system and to the private parties of conducting the hearings.

Several particular things are noteworthy about the substantive provisions of the statute: First, it preserves the marital presumption of parenthood that has long been a feature of paternity laws in most countries. Much research supports the proposition that, on average, children raised by two parents living together in a stable relationship do better in many aspects of welfare than do children raised in other arrangements.[25] Adoption law generally reflects an assumption that this is the case, with clear favoritism shown to married couples. This model rule does not treat same-sex partners the same as married couples in jurisdictions where marriage is not available to same-sex partners, but it establishes a mechanism for conferring legal parenthood on both members of a same-sex relationship that is more straightforward than that provided by existing rules, which in some jurisdictions provide no mechanism at all. In the case of nonmarital births, a person who is not a biological parent may petition for legal parent status, and the factors for making a substituted judgment include the nature of the petitioner's relationship with an existing parent or copetitioner.

Second, the proposed law treats birth mothers differently from biological fathers. Men can become legal parents automatically, without petitioning, only if they are married to the birth mother and the mother consents to their parenthood. This approach treats the mother–child relationship as presumptively the core relationship for a newborn child, on the assumption that being the birth mother of a child creates a psychological bond with the child even before birth and, on average (though not always), generates greater dedication to the welfare of a newborn child than does being the biological father of a child per se. The law throughout western society has long reflected, in parentage rules and in custody rules, to varying degrees at different times, an assumption that a child's first attachment is to his or her mother, and current social practice in the western world is almost uniformly consistent with that assumption. The proposed law protects what is presumed to be a child's crucial primary first attachment and adds additional relationships insofar as they are supportive of that core relationship.[26] Such support is very likely with a man who is married to the mother, who wishes to serve as the child's legal parent (as evidenced by his signing the Parental Vow), and whom the mother wants to serve as her co-parent (as evidence by her signing a consent to her husband's becoming a legal parent). Making such a man the legal parent even if he is not the biological father might better serve a child's interests than would denying him a legal relationship and giving legal parent status to a biological father who is an outsider to the family in a practical sense. Being a biological parent should be a relevant factor in a court's consideration of a man's petition for legal parenthood, if a petition is allowed, but it should not by itself be controlling or give rise to an entitlement.

The rule thus recognizes what other family law scholars and what most social scientists have been saying for some time – namely that although a biological connection has some relevance to the welfare of a child, it is not so important as to override all other considerations relevant to the selection of parents, and particularly not the benefits for a child of being raised by adults who are nurturing and who are supportive of other caregivers, in an environment protected from harmful outside interference.[27] Thus, where the birth mother and her husband accept legal parenthood, the rule does not allow a man claiming to be the biological father, or anyone else, to petition for legal parenthood. The same might result from a court's assessment of competing petitions where the birth mother marries a man after giving birth. In contrast, where a birth mother refuses to consent to her husband's becoming a legal parent of the child she has just delivered, it is likely that the marriage is in jeopardy (perhaps because the child is not his biological offspring), and so conferring legal parenthood on the husband could mean giving a child a legal parent who is neither a biological parent nor likely to be in a supportive relationship with the mother going forward.

Importantly, the proposal treats the mother–child relationship as the core relationship only presumptively and this rule only applies at birth; it allows for exclusion of the birth mother from parenthood altogether in certain cases and it is not incompatible with having a rule governing decisions that typically occur later in a child's life, such as custody decisions at divorce, reflecting the possibility that a child will eventually develop an equal or greater attachment to a father. Because it makes fatherhood turn on choices made by the mother and her husband at the time of birth, as current law does to a significant degree as well, it might be wise to supplement the rule with a requirement that genetic testing be done routinely at the time of birth (or marriage, if that comes later) to determine whether the husband is the child's biological father, so that those choices are made on the basis of full information, as June Carbone and Naomi Cahn have proposed.[28] For although the rule would diminish the weight given to biology as a legal matter, the reality is that it matters subjectively to many people, and so in recent years an increasing number of men have sought to disestablish their paternity after acting for years as a father under the false belief that they were biological father.

Third, the rule makes no provision for notifying biological fathers of the existence of a child. It assumes that a man so disconnected from the birth mother as to be unaware of the pregnancy or unaware of his biological tie to the child is not a good candidate for parenthood of that child, if for no other reason than he likely has no relationship with the mother. Thus, a man who finds out well after a birth that he is the biological father of the child would have no claim to the child on the basis of failure to give notice. This would avoid "botched adoption" tragedies of the Baby Richard variety. At best, such a biological father could petition for parenthood, in cases where the provision for a birth mother's husband is not controlling, at the point when he learns the facts, either under the provision in this proposed statute for nonmarital children or under separate adoption laws, and seek to convince the court to make a substituted judgment for the child in his favor. He would have a particularly good chance of doing so where the birth mother does not become or remain a legal parent, he comes forward before others establish a social parent–child relationship with the child, and he is otherwise in a good position to raise a child.

Fourth, the proposed rule contemplates there being instances when a child will have only one legal parent at the outset, most often a legal mother but no legal father. This might seem contrary to children's welfare, given the well-documented fact that children raised by single mothers are worse off on average on many measures of well-being. However, much of the detriment to such children stems from economic hardship, and the proposed rule in and of itself does not worsen children's economic situation. Child support obligations could still be imposed on biological parents, even if they do not become legal parents, though it is not clear that non-marital children actually benefit much today from child support orders.[29] In the United States, most people currently think of the financial support obligation as linked to parental status and rights, but this is morally and practically unsound, and most family law scholars today favor a revision of the law to disconnect the support obligation from parental rights. A financial obligation can be justified solely on the grounds of making people take responsibility for the consequences of their past actions. If this were not the case, the state would not currently foist parenthood on biological parents who do not want to be social parents and impose a support obligation on them regardless of whether they seek custody or visitation. There is therefore no need to compensate biological parents for their financial burden by giving them parental rights as well, and doing so unjustifiably sacrifices the welfare of the child. Separating responsibilities and rights in this way, which England already does to some degree and which some other European countries, such as Germany and the Netherlands, do to the same degree that I propose, would only enhance the deterrent effect of the child support obligation, which is now muted when the state confers, along with the obligation, an exclusive privilege that even most initially unwilling biological parents come to see as a benefit.

Children in single-mother households also suffer from the lack of a second parent in their lives, research suggests,[30] but conferring legal parenthood on men who are not in a relationship with the mother is unlikely to redress this problem, because other research shows a high rate of parental drop out among men who are not married to or living with the mother of their offspring.[31] The proposed rule prevents the state from foisting exclusive legal fatherhood on a man who does not want it or vesting it in a man who now wants it but is unlikely to serve as the kind of nurturing, permanent co-parent that can be very beneficial for children. As a result, it leaves the door open to another man later becoming the first legal father, which is likely only where the birth mother enters into a committed long-term relationship with another man. For many mothers, that will never happen,[32] but if and when it does, the child would receive both the added financial support and the psychosocial benefits that stem from having both a mother and a father in the full sense. Unless and until that happens, the mother could receive from the biological father whatever financial support he is able to provide but would not incur the psychosocial costs of being forced to negotiate a child's life with an unsupportive and unhelpful, and perhaps dangerous, biological father.

The mother would, however, be free to permit, encourage, and facilitate contact between the child and the biological father if and insofar as she believed that beneficial for the child, within the bounds of her legal obligation to protect the child from harm. And any unwed father who is disposed and prepared to be a good co-parent to a child can petition for legal parent status and make the case that it would be in the child's interests on the whole for that to occur. In that case, there would be a paternity hearing in which a court addresses a request for visitation or even custody, just as there commonly is today, only this proposal would require a biological father to say more than "it's my kid" to receive legal parental status and an attendant right to involvement in the child's life; he would have to express his motivation to act as a parent, explain what he has to offer as a parent, and sign a document vowing his commitment to being as good a parent as he can be throughout the child's life. The proposal is therefore not a prescription for even greater fatherlessness than already exists but rather is designed to avoid fatherlessness.

Fifth, legal parenthood is always voluntary; persons must willingly sign a Parental Vow before they become invested with legal parenthood. The rule thus implicitly makes a desire to be a parent prerequisite to being made a legal parent. Even for the most qualified parents, signing the prescribed Parental Vow could have salutary effects, impressing on them the important responsibilities they are undertaking and their great fortune in enjoying the privilege of parenthood. The terminology is obviously intended to suggest an analogy to marital vows, which all adults are expected to make when they marry and which are intended to impress on them the essential nature of the relationship and what commitments they are making by entering into it. The Parental Vow is also analogous to the oath that persons must take when courts appoint them as guardians for incompetent adults.[33] Parents would, of course, be free to supplement the prescribed vow with a more personalized one that they draft themselves and give to their child. Some religious faiths have their own prescribed vows for parents to affirm in religious ceremonies following a birth, such as baptism. As with marital vows, this civil Parental Vow would not be directly enforceable – in particular, the pledge to devote substantial time to caring for one's child would not authorize the state to physically force a parent to spend time with a child. Rather, separate legal rules specifying parental responsibilities would govern as they do now and, consistent with the idea of making children's rights no less nor no more than adults' rights in relationships with each other, in the case of parental abandonment the legal remedy would be severance of the relationship, not forced association (though, of course, as a policy matter we would want to encourage parents to be devoted to their children and give them any assistance they might need to do so). Significantly, the proposed rule does not authorize the state ever to petition to establish a legal parent–child relationship. The state may only seek to prevent legal parenthood from vesting in a particular person, based on a showing that the person is not minimally qualified. As just explained, however, that legal parenthood must be voluntary would not preclude the state from imposing a financial support obligation on any biological parent.

To give some sense of how this proposed parentage statute would apply in practice, I offer two different scenarios in which men petitioning for paternity would get different results and two in which outcomes for birth mothers would be different. First, suppose I have recently become a biological father. I am not married to the mother of my offspring, but neither is anyone else, and I want to have a parent–child relationship with the baby. I have been conscientiously preparing myself for fatherhood, and I really care about the child's well-being. I would be able to petition for legal fatherhood but would have no presumption in my favor. That I am the biological father would simply count in my favor, as would my efforts to make myself a good candidate for parenthood. None of the things that make a person presumptively not minimally qualified to parent apply to me, and I have an amicable relationship with the birth mother. I am mentally and physically healthy, I have a good understanding of the basic needs of children, and I am able to provide material and emotional support for the child. In this scenario, it is unlikely that any other petitioner would be a better candidate, and I would likely become the legal father. A judge could reasonably conclude that the child would, if able, choose to have a parent–child relationship with me, rather than any other available person, because a parent–child relationship with me is best for her, all things considered.

Now suppose instead that I, as the biological father, have been uninvolved with the pregnancy, my life is in turmoil, and I am seeking paternity principally because the mother told me to get lost and I want to get back at her or I hope she will take me back. I do not care much about the baby and that is evident. In those circumstances, a judge should conclude that the child would, if able, not choose me to be her legal parent, because, all things considered, having a parent–child relationship with me would not be in her best interests. Family law practitioners see innumerable cases of this sort, which typically result in years of turmoil for the mother and her family, which in turn adversely affects the infant, before the father fades out of the picture. The proposal reflects a view that the child has a right to be free of that sort of biological father and that such a man has no more right to a relationship with the child than he has a right to a relationship with the child's mother. Accordingly, a court should deny my petition for legal parent status. It might still be beneficial to the child to know who her biological father is and to collect information about me for medical or other purposes, but I would have no basis for demanding any greater role in the child's life than what the mother voluntarily chooses to give me.

Imagine now a single woman who is homeless and addicted to drugs and who supports her addiction through prostitution, an activity that entails danger of disease, physical attack, and imprisonment. She becomes pregnant and a service provider – for example, a welfare office, a health care worker dispensing clean needles, or a doctor providing prenatal care – becomes aware that she is pregnant and is using illegal drugs. The service provider would have a legal obligation to alert a child protective agency of this situation, as is the case today in many jurisdictions. The child protective agency would in turn have a legal obligation to take custody of the child at birth, as commonly occurs today in such situations. What follows today, however, is usually an extended period of foster care for the child so that the mother can have more time (presumably she has already had years) to try to overcome her addiction and to establish a stable and safe home, usually followed by legal proceedings to terminate the mother's parental rights when she fails to become rehabilitated. Instead, under this proposed rule, this birth mother would likely never be vested with legal parent status and so the state would never have an obligation – at least, none stemming from parental status – to provide rehabilitative services (most likely she has always had such services available to her anyway). The mother could still petition for parenthood, and this possibility might prevent her from concealing the pregnancy and birth or otherwise harming the child, but she would have no presumption in her favor and she would have to compete with others who wish to become the child's legal parents, including persons on waiting lists at local adoption agencies. Her biological connection with the child would count in her favor, but this would almost certainly be outweighed by the likelihood that a child's life would go very poorly if put in her hands.

This approach seems consistent with what rules we would want to apply to our own situation if we went through the thought experiment described in Chapter 5 and we imagined that we were about to be born again. It is not plausible, to my mind, to say that if one were going to be born tomorrow to a woman in circumstances like those just described, one would want to be placed in a temporary home for a couple of years to give one's birth mother every last chance to become a minimally fit parent, before being adopted or sent to live with her in whatever sort of home she has established, rather than being placed in the first instance in a permanent parent–child relationship with adults who are not one's biological parents but who are prepared to be good parents and to provide a safe and nurturing home. One might also want there to be a legal requirement that one be informed about the identity of one's biological mother later in life, and perhaps even that contact with her must be arranged if she and the child are both willing. But no one would want for themselves or for anyone they care about the sort of life that comes from being raised by a biological parent in the circumstances just described.[34] Those who would reject the proposed rule on the grounds that it is insufficiently sympathetic to birth mothers who have had difficult lives, or that it will have a disproportionate impact on poor and minority-race parents, are simply wrong to think such sentiments or concerns are pertinent to the state's decision in behalf of a child. The right we adults possess to avoid family relationships that we deem not to be in our best interests also has a disparate impact on adults who have had difficult lives and who as a result are addicted to drugs or are poor, but no one would suggest that the proper response to this inequity is to force some adults into family relationships with such unfortunate persons. The equal moral standing of children precludes our treating them in such an instrumental fashion, using their lives to ameliorate the suffering of certain adults, however unjust that suffering might be. Liberals must stop viewing children as consolation prizes for victims of social injustice.

There are, however, circumstances in which under the proposed rule even a birth mother with an addiction problem might be likely to end up being a child's legal parent. For example, imagine a woman who is an alcoholic and who drinks a considerable amount of alcohol while pregnant, but who is married to the child's father and in an otherwise stable and financially secure household. A service provider, such as an obstetrician, would have a legal obligation to report to the state child protective agency evidence of fetal alcohol poisoning, and that agency would notify the local adoption agencies of the child's potential availability. Assuming the fact of excessive alcohol consumption is proved, this woman would not become a legal parent automatically after the birth of the child. In addition, her husband would not become a legal parent automatically unless the birth mother succeeds in a petition to become a legal parent. Both would be able to petition for legal parenthood, but would then have to compete with any biologically unrelated petitioners. In reviewing their petition, a court would count the wife's alcoholism against both of them, but that might be so outweighed by a combination of the biological connection they have with the child and such things as the husband's willingness and ability to take on a primary role in parenting, the mother's entry into a treatment program, the presence of extended family to assist them, and other positive qualities either of them possesses, that it would still be better for the child to have them as legal parents rather than other persons who might petition. It might be that the father alone would be successful in becoming a legal parent initially, in which case, if the mother overcomes her alcoholism, she might at a later date be able to secure legal parenthood herself, by showing then that it is in the child's best interests that she become a legal parent.

The rule as a whole should not greatly increase the number of individualized decisions about parent–child relationships and might actually reduce the overall caseload of family courts. Most of the characteristics listed in Section C of Part 1 are things that now trigger involvement by child protective agencies anyway, and changing from a practice of putting children in foster care and trying to rehabilitate parents to a practice of excluding patently unqualified persons from parenthood in the first instance should reduce from many to one the number of court proceedings that must take place with respect to a given child. In addition, there is reason to believe that the model statute would reduce the number of children who ever become the subject of legal proceedings. Legal reform effectively "raising the bar" for parenthood could effect some change in prevailing social attitudes toward conceiving children, impressing on the public generally that parenthood is a difficult undertaking that not just anyone is able to do successfully and so might discourage some people who are unqualified to parent from deciding to procreate. In particular, many teenage girls today intentionally become pregnant because being a mother raises their social status. If fourteen-year-old girls knew that they were unlikely to be able to serve as the parent to any child they conceived, and that if they became pregnant the baby would most likely become the legal child of other people, they should be less likely purposely to become pregnant.

Of course, teenagers, drug addicts, and women who have had other children taken away sometimes get pregnant unintentionally, and even though they would, under the model statute, be able to petition for parenthood, the possibility of not succeeding in keeping their child might have the unfortunate consequence alluded to earlier – namely that they will choose to have an abortion or will carry the child to term but hide the pregnancy by not seeking prenatal care and giving birth without medical assistance. Thus, even from a purely child-centered perspective, there are competing considerations in formulating ideal rules for maternity. This topic requires extensive empirical investigation, but I will first suggest that making prenatal care a relevant factor in a court's decision whether to grant a birth mother's petition for legal parenthood creates a countervailing inducement to seek such care. Second, an additional countervailing inducement can be created by imposing criminal liability on women who at any point are discovered to have failed to secure proper medical attention for their child before, during, or after birth.[35] The prospect of a greater number of abortions is not a happy one for anyone, though views would diverge as to whether "children" are harmed by abortion. What effects the proposed statute would have on the behavior of pregnant women is too complicated a question to address fully here, so I will simply point out that analysis of the question should take into account that there might be ways other than guaranteeing them legal parenthood to make it seem worthwhile to pregnant women to carry a fetus to term and to secure adequate medical care. Many do so now even when they do not intend to keep the child, having enough concern for the welfare of the child they have created to give the child the best outcome they can.

What would be the likely impact from the perspective of the court system? First, it would expand dramatically the family courts' parentage docket. They would hear many more paternity cases than they now do, and they would begin to have a significant maternity docket. And in those parentage cases, they would not just be ordering genetic tests and establishing a visitation schedule; they would be conducting an inquiry similar to the one they undertake today in child protective proceedings and in step-parent adoption proceedings, only the inquiry would concern the future for a newborn child with no established parent–child relationships rather than for an older child who already views the biological parents as his or her parents. The "adoption" docket would also be substantially expanded. (Some other term might be used, though, for cases in which persons who are not biological parents petition to become the first legal parents.) At the same time, however, family court judges should begin to see a marked drop in the most depressing and difficult part of their dockets – namely child protective proceedings, including removal hearings, adjudications of abuse and neglect, foster care reviews, and petitions to terminate parental rights. My guess is that most family court judges would be happy with that trade-off. Critics of the current child protective and foster care system should welcome the change as well; if the state is not especially successful at fixing bad parents (who could be?) or at providing temporary substitute care for children, then the sensible thing to do is to prevent the need to do either from arising in the first place, and the only way to do that in today's world, where poverty, drug addiction, teen pregnancy, and other social ills are entrenched, is for the state not to assign children in the first place to parents who are beset by those ills. We might also expect to see a reduction in the criminal courts' caseload, as sparing children from assignment to the very worst parents should go some way toward breaking the cycle of intergenerational dysfunction that exists in some families and communities today.

Is this proposal politically viable? As emphasized earlier, the proposal aims principally to exclude only the worst candidates for parenthood rather than pushing for a universal parental licensing scheme as some scholars have proposed, so will adversely impact only a small percentage of adults. Many legislators might find attractive the proposal's more hard-nosed approach toward people who conceive children they are not prepared to care for or who engage in criminal conduct, might find the proposal consistent with calls for strengthening families and (apart from facilitating co-parenting by same-sex couples) with the "traditional values" sentiment that has influenced elections in recent years, and might be influenced by constituents who want to adopt undamaged children. In addition, legislators in the United States, England, and elsewhere have become increasingly troubled by the phenomenon of children being placed in foster care for long periods, and the proposal furthers a clear trend toward moving children of unfit parents more readily to adoption.[36]

Nevertheless, several of the specific provisions would be quite controversial, because they conflict with supposed rights of adults and adult-centered liberal sentiments. The provision regarding ingestion of drugs or alcohol might encounter resistance from those who are generally opposed to any legislation that operates to inhibit women's control over their own bodies. The provisions regarding securing of medical care might disqualify a significant number of adherents to certain religious faiths – namely those that oppose medical care on theological grounds, if they are unwilling to adapt to generally applicable legal requirements for parenting. One provision denies automatic parenthood to some people on the basis of their financial situation, which obviously would have a disparate impact on poor people, implicitly declaring that poor people should be less free to have very large families than wealthy people, which will trouble some people. A morally proper perspective on the issue, however, requires excluding consideration of the adults' desires and interests and denying that adults have any rights in the matter that could justify sacrificing the welfare of children. Any legitimate objections to these bases for disqualifying persons for parenthood must rest on concerns for the welfare of children. My proposal allows biological parents in each such situation the opportunity to

show that their becoming legal parents is best for a child despite the facts
that require them to petition for parenthood, so a child-centered objection
would have to allege that the children of those biological parents would
be better off if legal parenthood were conferred on their biological parents
automatically, without the individualized review and without considering
alternative potential parents.

Still, some will object to the proposal as a whole as social engineering
and an increase in the power of the state over children's lives, something
that existing foster care systems suggest the state is not very adept at. It will
therefore be necessary to point out to those objectors, again and again if
necessary, that the state is already determining children's lives, that existing parentage laws are as much social engineering as is my proposal, that
there is no avoiding state selection of legal parents, and that its current
approach to doing that harms far more children than does the foster care
system. It will also be necessary to point out the illogic of concluding from
an assumption that the state is not particularly good at reforming parents
and at providing temporary substitute care for abused and neglected children that the state cannot do anything adequately or of concluding that
the state should assign children to biological parents, regardless of any
indications that they are likely to be very bad at parenting, and then wash
its hands. Although complaints about the child protective system are often
exaggerated, tending to extrapolate too much from highly publicized individual incidents or from pervasive problems in particular locales, there is
no denying that foster care is not a good situation for children. But the
most sensible conclusion to draw from that fact, it seems plain, is that
the state should do whatever it can to avoid the need for any direct state
involvement in families' lives. By no means am I suggesting that state decision making under this proposed parentage law would be flawless, but I
would suggest that the state is likely to be much better at identifying the
worst parents in advance than it is at transforming the worst parents into
good parents or at raising children itself.

Whether this proposal would be "constitutional" under existing interpretations of fundamental rights documents is a separate matter and would
vary among nations. In the United States, the Supreme Court in the early
1970s transformed parentage law by holding that an unwed biological
father who had provided substantial care for his offspring for many years
had a constitutional right against the state denying him legal parenthood
and custody, after the children's mother died, absent a showing that he was
unfit.[37] That ruling could conflict in some cases with the best-interests
standard for deciding petitions for parenthood, at least if efforts before

birth count as "care" for constitutional purposes and could be substantial, both of which are uncertain. The Court in a later decision appeared to endorse an even more robust constitutional right for unwed fathers, suggesting in dictum that biology in and of itself gives rise to a right to the opportunity to provide care.[38] Such a right would more clearly conflict with the proposal, insofar as the proposal would deny some biological parents such an opportunity. However, in a still later decision, *Michael H. v. Gerald D.*, the Court upheld a California law denying unwed biological fathers legal parenthood and any right to spend time with a child even where they had cared for a child in the past in situations where the mother was married at or around the time of the child's birth and the husband wished to serve as a father to the child.[39] Some U.S. states today have a conclusive marital presumption, not allowing a putative biological father to petition for legal parenthood. The marital predicate for parenthood in my proposal, and the correlative exclusion of any putative father from a child's life, would therefore appear to be constitutional. Significantly, in none of the Court's unwed father decisions did the fathers at issue have any of the characteristics that under my proposal preclude anyone from obtaining legal parent status automatically, which the Court might accept as reasonable bases for ascribing unfitness. As noted in Chapter 2, the laws of all states, under mandate of federal law, now authorize termination of parental rights immediately after birth in certain cases, on the basis of egregiously bad prior conduct by a biological parent, which would be functionally equivalent from the parent's perspective to denying legal parenthood in the first place, and there has been no successful constitutional challenge to date regarding that practice.

The constitutional rights picture in Europe appears similar to that in the United States. Article 8 of the European Convention on Human Rights guarantees a substantive right to protection of family life. With respect to mothers, the European Court of Human Rights has interpreted Article 8 to require that legal motherhood be bestowed on unwed mothers as automatically as it is bestowed on married mothers, based on the premise that family life exists between a child and any birth mother, whether married or not, at the moment of birth.[40] My proposal, too, treats married and unmarried mothers equally. The ECHR has not held that there is no basis on which states could deny legal parent status to a married or unmarried birth mother. With respect to fathers, the ECHR has stated that a family life protected by the Convention exists from the moment of birth between a child and a biological father who is married to or cohabiting with the child's mother.[41] My proposal ensures legal parenthood to fathers who are married to the birth mother, if she becomes a legal parent, provided these fathers sign a Parental Vow and do not have a characteristic that triggers individualized review. My proposal does not extend the same protection to unwed, cohabiting fathers; they must undergo a best-interests review, and an important aspect of that review would likely be an inquiry into the stability of the father's relationship with the mother.

The Convention rights of biological fathers who are neither married to nor cohabiting with the mother appear to depend on the degree to which they have attempted to develop a relationship with their offspring and on whether the mother is married to another man, as in the United States. In *Nekvedavicius v. Germany*, the ECHR stated the following:

> Article 8 cannot be interpreted as only protecting "family life" which has already been established but, where the circumstances warrant it, must extend to the potential relationship which may develop between a natural father and a child born out of wedlock. Relevant factors in this regard include the nature of the relationship between the natural parents and the demonstrable interest in and commitment by the natural father to the child both before and after the birth.[42]

At the same time, the ECHR cited approvingly a prior decision of the European Commission of Human Rights holding that a man claiming to be the biological father of a child born to a woman who was married to another man had no right to demand genetic tests to establish his paternity.[43] My proposal does not guarantee legal parent status for any unwed fathers, regardless of their efforts or of the mother's marital status; all must petition for legal status and convince a court to impute to the child in question a choice to have a family relationship with the biological father, though the biological tie, their efforts to care for the child, and the mother's relationship situation would all be relevant. In any event, it appears that the ECHR interprets Article 8 to require only that rather weak substantive rights attach to an unwed father's legal parent status once conferred, rights weaker than ordinarily attach to legal parenthood in the United States. In *Nekvedavicius*, the ECHR upheld a decision of German courts denying a biological father access to his offspring, even after his paternity was established and even after the ECHR determined that he had a "family life" with the child, where the German courts' basis for denying access was simply that it would be contrary to the best interests of the child. The effect of the unwed father's right to legal parent status thus appears limited to an ongoing right to petition for access – that is, to be considered for a relationship with a child – and to receive access where he can show it would be in the child's best interests. My proposal allows unwed fathers to petition where the birth mother is not married and imposes no time limit.

Stepping back from existing constitutional doctrine, we might ask what fundamental, constitutional right *should* be attributed to a biological parent who wishes to be a legal parent. Significantly, a putative father seeking a declaration of parenthood is not demanding that the state not involve itself at all in formation of intimate relationships; the claim is not an antistatist one for freedom of private action. Rather, the putative father is demanding that the state place another human being into an intimate relationship with him, which is a state action as invasive in private life as one can imagine. So the question is whether such a demand should have legal purchase in any form it might take. The theoretical analysis of this book shows that it should have purchase when it takes the following form: "I have a right to state creation and protection of a legal and social relationship with this child because it is a relationship the child would choose to have if able to choose, insofar as the relationship would be in the child's long-term best interests." In that case, there is the mutuality that we require before we say that an adult has a right to protection of a relationship with another adult, as discussed in Chapter 3. The proposed statute is consistent with this conclusion. The putative father's demand should not have purchase, however, when it takes the following form: "I have a right to a relationship with this child because we are biologically related." A state decision to place a child in an intimate relationship for that reason alone would be as arbitrary as an adult deciding to marry someone for the sole reason that the person is from the same hometown, a fact that can generate some benefits for a couple (e.g., similar background and convenience in visiting family) but surely not enough for it properly to be the sole consideration. Biology alone is not a sufficient basis for imputing a mutuality of choice. And no one can have a fundamental right to arbitrary state action benefiting them. In fact, everyone, including a newborn child, has a fundamental right *against* arbitrary state action affecting them adversely.[44]

II. Reforming Child Protection Law

Throughout the western world, a person in the kind of relationship closest to a parent–child relationship in terms of intimacy – a marriage – is entitled to suspend the social aspect of the relationship at will if he or she perceives that to be in his or her best interests and is entitled to terminate the relationship permanently either at will or after making some showing to a state actor – typically, a judge – that the relationship is dysfunctional. To the extent any obstacles are put in the way of permanent termination, they are usually justified on paternalistic grounds or as a means to avoid harm to third parties – children of the marriage – rather than to protect supposed rights or interests of the other person in the relationship or to serve collective interests of a larger community.

Putting greater legal obstacles in the way of suspending or terminating a parent–child relationship than the law does with respect to marriage might be justifiable on the grounds that there is greater potential for harm to the child from being separated from a parent than there is potential for harm to an adult from being separated from a spouse. Existing legal obstacles to termination of parental rights are so great, however, that they cannot be fully explained on those grounds. They clearly also reflect a pervasive and mistaken adherence to the idea that parents have an entitlement, a proprietary claim even, to retain custody of children, one that does not depend on the continued custody's being best for the child, all things considered. The law might much better serve children's welfare, and so their moral rights, by simplifying the basic rules for removal and terminations considerably, to state that the ultimate standard and sole relevant general consideration is the best interests of the child. Whatever specific facts are pertinent to evaluation of a child's welfare but might otherwise be overlooked by judges or child protective workers can be set forth in a statute as factors subsidiary to that ultimate standard. Here is one such approach:

Code of Everystate

Chapter 2 – Child Protection

Part I. First response to abuse or neglect. Parental custody is predicated on a commitment to satisfying the physical, psychological, emotional, and cognitive needs of a child and refraining from conduct harmful to the child. Accordingly, upon receipt of a report that a parent is neglecting or abusing a child or will soon become unable to care for a child, the child protective agency shall investigate the child's situation and, if the investigator finds reasonable grounds to believe neglect or abuse has occurred or is likely to occur, the child protective agency shall act diligently to protect the child's welfare. If the child appears to be in imminent danger of significant harm, the child protective agency shall place security personnel in the home until the agency can secure a protective order against the offending parent. A court hearing a petition for a protective order shall, upon finding reasonable grounds to believe that the parent presents a danger to the child, order the parent to stay away from the child. If feasible, the court shall order that the child remain in the home, with proper supervision by another parent or by another responsible adult. If it is in the child's best interests, even in light of available assistance, to leave the home, the court shall order a suitable placement with a relative or in foster care.[45]

Part II. Foster care. A child placed in foster care has a right to reside with qualified and trained foster parents and to continue to have contact with family members when and to the extent that is in the child's best interests. The child protective agency shall encourage a nurturing relationship between foster parents and children placed in their care and shall not move a child from one foster home to another on grounds that the child is forming a close bond with foster parents. A child in foster care shall be returned to the custody of his or her parent only upon a finding by a preponderance of the evidence that this is in the child's best interests. If foster care is terminated, the child protective agency shall arrange ongoing visitation between the child and the foster parents if and to the extent that the foster parents wish to have visitation and visitation is in the best interests of the child.

Part III. Termination of the parent–child relationship. Every child has a right to the termination of a parent–child relationship when that would be in his or her best interests, all things considered. A state child protective agency, a parent, a representative of the child, or persons seeking to become substitute parents may petition for termination at any time in behalf of the child. Upon presentation of substantial evidence that termination would be in the child's best interests, the court shall place that petition on its docket.

When a petition to terminate a parent–child relationship filed in behalf of a child is placed on its docket, the court shall ensure that a guardian *ad litem* (GAL) has been appointed to represent the child and shall direct the GAL to investigate fully the child's situation. The GAL's investigation shall include making a home visit, reviewing records for any relevant prior legal proceedings relating to the child, ordering mental health evaluations for the child and the parent as to whom termination is sought, and interviewing parties with knowledge of the child's situation. The GAL shall thereafter prepare a written report, summarizing the findings, making a recommendation as to the child's relationship with the parent, and presenting the reasons for that recommendation. The parent shall be a party to the proceeding and may present evidence and arguments.

The court shall terminate the parent–child legal relationship upon finding clear and convincing evidence that this is in the child's best interests. In reaching this judgment, the court shall consider:

1) the nature and severity of any abusive or neglectful behavior toward this child by the parent;
2) the likelihood of any such behavior recurring in the future, taking into account:
   a) the parent's past behavior toward other children,
   b) any pattern of relationships between the parent and other adults that fosters the abusive or neglectful conduct,
   c) the parent's manifest commitment to eliminating the causes of the abuse or neglect, including any causes stemming from mental health problems or disabilities;
3) the nature of the child's existing relationship with the parent, considering among other things the length of time the child has spent in the parent's custody and the impact that any abuse or neglect has had or is likely to have on the relationship;
4) the nature of the child's relationship to other members of the immediate and extended family;
5) the extent to which the child has formed a positive identity within the parent's family, community, or culture;[46]
6) the parent's ability to satisfy the child's current and future needs, as reflected by:
   a) the parent's desire to continue in the role of parent,
   b) the parent's availability to care for the child, taking into account any drug addiction, imprisonment, or other absence on the part of the parent,
   c) any criminal history of the parent,
   d) the parent's mental and physical health, and
   e) the parent's material circumstances, including employment, income, residential environment, and support system;
7) any past efforts by any public or private agency to rehabilitate an abusive or neglectful parent;
8) the likelihood that future efforts to rehabilitate the parent would be successful, taking into account the degree of commitment to rehabilitation that the parent has demonstrated;

9) the availability of substitute parents or alternative residential placements and the extent to which they can meet all of the child's needs; and

10) any other considerations relevant to the child's welfare.

Upon ordering termination of the parent–child relationship, the court shall consider whether it would be in the child's best interests to have periodic visitation with the former parent and/or with other members of the family of birth, taking into account the ability and willingness of any substitute parents to assume custody if facilitating such visitation were a condition of their becoming parents.

* * *

Part I of this provision reflects a view that, where consistent with the child's welfare, the abuser rather than the victim should be forced out of the family home, as is common today in the case of spousal abuse. However, it requires removal where that is best for the child, rather than following the currently prevailing rule and removing only upon showing of imminent danger of substantial harm, though this change might not make a significant difference in practice, given the strong interest a child has in not being removed from his or her home. Part II reflects a rejection of the view that foster parents should keep an emotional distance from children in foster care,[47] which in turn rests on a rejection of the view that a reunited dysfunctional family must exclude all other parentlike figures. A bond with foster parents should not make reintegration with the family difficult for the child if the child is allowed continuing contact with the foster parents. This approach has the incidental benefit of improving a child's chances for adoption if return to the legal parents proves unsuccessful, because a bond with foster parents often leads to adoption. That such an approach is not unworkable is suggested by the fact that it is essentially what happens when parents leave their children with relatives for a time or when a children protective agency places a child in relative foster care. If an agency places a child with grandparents as foster parents, it does not try to ensure that there is no bonding with the grandparents, and the agency does not regard it as bad for the child if the bond develops and the child later returns to the parents, even if there is hostility between the parents and grandparents. A proper set of rules for foster care might effectively make foster parents members of the extended family, should they wish to become such.

Part III simplifies the rule for termination considerably while incorporating as factors many of the considerations that are now treated in most jurisdictions as prerequisites to termination. For example, under existing rules in most jurisdictions, courts may terminate on the basis of abuse if and only if the state has provided rehabilitative services. The proposed rule reflects an understanding that in some instances it is in a child's best interests to try to rehabilitate the parents, rather than terminating immediately, just as you and I might conclude that it is best to give a spouse or a friend a chance to reform and redeem herself or himself before we sever the relationship. But it also reflects a rejection of the idea that parents are entitled to rehabilitative efforts.

That this is the appropriate approach is reinforced by comparing societal treatment of child abuse and societal treatment of spousal abuse. Elizabeth Bartholet writes that, in the distant past, American society reacted to spousal abuse and child abuse in much the same way.[48] With respect to both, the state emphasized family preservation, privacy, and paternal authority. Like children, women were generally unable as a practical matter, and perhaps as a legal matter as well, to escape from an abusive situation. Today, however, domestic violence laws aim to liberate women instead of trying to rehabilitate their abusers. Criminal statutes prohibit any assault and in many states impose mandatory arrest policies and "no-drop" prosecution policies. Civil provisions for protective orders empower women to have abusive partners removed from the home and ordered to stay away rather than requiring the women to move out of their homes. Today, Bartholet writes as follows:

> [n]o one argues that the appropriate response to wife battering is to redouble efforts to keep the wife in the home and her marriage intact. . . . [Yet parents] who abuse and neglect children are treated largely as victims in need of services and treatment, not perpetrators in need of incapacitation and deterrence. Families are to be preserved not separated. Children victimized by their parents are described as children "at risk of removal," rather than children in need of liberation. . . . While women press for criminalization of male violence against women, "Community Partnership" advocates argue that we should avoid stigmatizing parents as perpetrators by investigating them for maltreatment, or listing their names on child abuse registries.[49]

Bartholet does not claim that parent–child relationships are identical to spousal relationships. As noted above, there might be greater costs to a child in severing a parent–child relationship than there are for an adult abuse victim leaving his or her partner. But this does not justify taking an altogether different approach to terminating relationships in the two cases; with respect to both we can say that the law should facilitate exit for the vulnerable party when that is best for him or her rather than aiming to secure for the other party every opportunity to preserve the relationship for his or her own sake. In addition, in many cases, such as those involving children who have little psychological connection to the deficient parent, either because the child is very young or because of the parent's neglect or absence, the costs of severing the relationship might well be less for the child than is typically true for adults seeking to exit an intimate partnership. The proposed statute implicitly directs the court to assess the likely costs for the child, if any, of ordering termination of parental status.

Last, the proposal contemplates that preservation of some tie with the birth family might be beneficial for a child. Particularly with noninfants, complete severance of an existing parent–child relationship, even though it is insufficiently nurturing, can leave a child bewildered and with a lifelong sense of loss and uncertain identity.[50] Some jurisdictions have moved in the direction of facilitating or even ordering posttermination contact, but there are obviously competing child-welfare considerations that must be balanced.

III. Reforming the Rules for Relationships with Nonparents

Last, I offer up a rule for affording legal protection to children's relationships with nonparents. One way to protect such relationships is to confer parenthood more broadly. The proposed rule for parentage above allows that in some circumstances immediately after birth, and adoption laws might also allow for addition of a third legal parent. Then, if a legal parent left a child in the custody of grandparents for an extended period of time, such that the grandparents came to assume a parental role and formed a close bond with the child, the grandparents might themselves become legal parents. Though I have not drafted a model rule for allocating custody and visitation among legal parents, that status would certainly entail standing to petition for custody or visitation and a presumption in one's favor.

Assuming that extended family members or other nonparents do not become legal parents, the question remains as to what rule should apply when they or a representative of a child seek to ensure contact between them and the child. Even if one takes a purely child-centered approach to this issue, decision making necessarily differs in important ways from that in the other contexts discussed. This is the one area in which state decision makers are not deciding who a child's legal parents will be but rather whether they should override a particular child-rearing decision by persons who are and will continue to be the immediate caregivers for a child. State decision making in this context presupposes an ongoing parent–child relationship. This fact changes the analysis in at least two critical ways.

First, state decision makers must take into account the effect of their decision on the child's presupposed, primary family relationship. Second, state decision makers must ask not only what effects their decisions will have on children, whose circumstances and personalities are diverse and complex, but also whether they, the state actors, are in the best position to make decisions, given that there is in this context a private party to whom decision-making authority could be entirely entrusted. There are, that is, questions about the decision makers' relative competence that arise more clearly in this context than in any other. In the other relationship contexts, the state typically must make the decision, because what is in doubt is who should be in a parentlike role and so be in a position to make day-to-day decisions about such things as visits with grandparents.

In recognition of these differences, some scholars urge a pragmatic, case-by-case approach. Professor David Meyer, for example, recommends "highly nuanced and fact-sensitive" decision making, taking into account the extent to which a visitation order disrupts life within the nuclear family and the degree of unity or division within the family as to the issue at hand.[51] The former consideration reflects the importance for children of secure family relationships largely insulated from outside interference. The latter consideration might be indicative of the legitimacy of the parents' motivations and the soundness of their judgment; if we assume that most members of an extended family have a child's well-being at heart and have an accurate sense of whether the child would benefit from contact with the third-party petitioners.

Another position some scholars take, in recognition of the crucial fact that in this context the children are in a parent–child relationship that is not itself under review, is that parents should have strong rights to make the decisions about their children's relationships, because in most cases this will be best for the children. The illogic of this reasoning is apparent. Rather than establishing the best interests of the child as the legal standard, with whatever subsidiary rules – presumptions, procedural requirements, evidentiary standards, and so on – are necessary to ensure adherence to that standard, these scholars adopt a rule that substitutes for the child's interests the rights of other people. That is nonsensical. If parents usually make the best decision in this context – and no one contends that they always do, then a legislature can codify a presumption that a parent's choice is in the child's best interests and place the burden of overcoming that presumption – however heavy a burden the legislature deems appropriate, in light of the strength of the presumption and in light of the limitations on courts' powers of judgment – on third parties seeking to override the parents' choice. If a constitutional mandate is necessary to make legislatures get it right, the mandate can rest on substantive due process rights of children, a right against the state that it not issue orders that are contrary to children's relationship interests, but also a right against the state that it not give any private party power to prevent social interactions that are good for the child. There is no theoretical or practical advantage to imputing control rights to parents, and doing so generates the cost for children of diverting judicial attention away from their welfare and toward the interests of parents.[52]

In this context, there is little need for novel drafting (in either sense of *novel!*), because some states have actually had laws that appear entirely consistent with the rights of children and with the considerations alluded to above. The provision below is an adaptation of the Washington State provision challenged in *Troxel*,[53] which the U.S. Supreme Court did not find unconstitutional on its face, but rather only when applied without any presumption that the parents' assessment of the child's welfare was correct. It favors grandparents, as the laws in most jurisdictions do, but it also recognizes that many other nonparents can play an important role in children's lives.

Code of Everystate

Chapter 3 – Children's Relationships with Nonparents

Children have a right to a healthy social life and to maintain relationships with nonparents when that is consistent with their best interests.

Part I. Visitation with grandparents. Grandparents may petition for a court order of visitation with a child at any time, upon showing that the child's parents have denied them significant time with the child. If the child is fourteen years of age or older and wishes to visit with the grandparents, the court shall order the parents not to obstruct the efforts of grandparents and child to spend time with each other. If the child is less than fourteen years of age, the court shall appoint a guardian *ad litem* for the child and shall order visitation if it finds that it would be in the child's best interests. Visitation with a grandparent shall be presumed to be in the child's best interests when the grandparent has previously served as the primary caretaker for the child for six months or more. Parents may rebut this presumption by demonstrating by a preponderance of the evidence that visitation would be contrary to the child's best interests, taking into account the considerations listed in Part III below. Where grandparents have not previously served as primary caretaker for the child for at least six months, the parents' judgment shall be presumed correct, and the grandparents carry the burden of showing by a preponderance of the evidence that visitation would be in the best interests of the child.

Part II. Visitation with other nonparents. Any other person may petition for an order of visitation with a child. Upon a showing by the petitioner that a significant relationship exists between the child and the petitioner, the court shall place the matter on its docket and appoint a guardian *ad litem* for the child. The court shall presume that the parents' judgment regarding the child's best interests is correct and shall order visitation only if and insofar as the petitioner demonstrates by a preponderance of the evidence that this would be in the child's best interests, taking into consideration the factors listed in Part III below.

Part III. Best interests factors. In determining what is in the child's best interests regarding visitation with nonparents, the court shall consider:

1) The extent of any existing relationship between the child and the petitioner;
2) The relationship between each of the child's parents and the petitioner;
3) The nature of and reason for parental objections to granting visitation;
4) The effect that granting visitation is likely to have on the relationship between the child and the child's parents;
5) The residential time-sharing arrangements between parents who are not residing together;
6) The good faith of the petitioner;
7) Any criminal history or history of physical, emotional, or sexual abuse or neglect by the petitioner or by the parents;
8) The wishes of the child, if known; and
9) Any other factor relevant to the child's best interests.

* * *

This provision differs from the Washington statute in creating a presumption in favor of grandparents only where they have served as a primary caretaker for the child rather than where they show simply that they have a significant relationship with the child. Relationships with grandparents are special for most children, but as is true of parents, grandparents are not always acting solely out of concern for the child when family disputes of this nature arise, so a significant relationship seems too slender a basis for putting the burden of proof on parents. Where a parent has left the child in the care of the grandparent for six months or more, however, there is good reason to question the competence and good intentions of the parents and there is good reason to suppose that the relationship with the grandparent is important for the child. Where grandparents have not been primary caretakers for a long period, they may still petition for visitation, even if they have no prior relationship with the child. The burden of proof as to what choice should be imputed to a child simply shifts from the parents to them in that case.

The threshold requirement of an already existing relationship with the child in the case of persons other than grandparents, for them even to have standing to seek a visitation order, seems justified by the fact that severing existing relationships carries a potential for harm or unhappiness for the child not present with persons with whom the child has no prior relationship. Some danger of harm ought to be present to justify even bringing parents into court. It is difficult to imagine a danger of harm to children flowing from being denied an opportunity to form relationships in the first place with particular third parties other than grandparents. There is a danger to a child's emotional well-being if a parent endeavors to isolate a child completely from the outside world, but an appropriate definition of neglect in child protective statutes would create an independent basis for legal action against parents where they deprive children of all or nearly all contact with outsiders, so that the children are unable to form significant relationships with any nonparents.

Conclusion

The law governing children's relationships can and should strive for consistency with our practices and beliefs regarding adults' relationship rights. Doing so would enhance the likelihood of children being treated in a principled rather than arbitrary way and being treated with the respect they are owed as persons. Consistency would mean, as this book has shown, that all decisions concerning children's relationships would be based either on children's own choices or, where appropriate, on a substituted judgment for them, which usually will mean what some other decision maker determines is in their best interests, all things considered. The decisions would never be based solely on any adult's unilateral desire to have a relationship, nor even on a balancing of children's interests against the interests of adults or against diffuse societal aims. Likewise, children's rights would not operate – as they do not operate now – to force any unwilling adult to have a relationship with them. But they would prevent anyone else from forcing a relationship on a child, against the child's expressed wishes or contrary to the child's welfare.

This conclusion shows the need for a wholesale reformation of that large share of family law pertaining to children's relationships. Perhaps the greatest need for reform is in connection with parentage laws, which now show the least consideration for the interests of children yet are most vital to the lifelong happiness and prospects for success for every human being. Nothing is more important to individual well-being and societal well-being than in whose care the state places each newborn child. The model statutory provisions I have proffered in this chapter are meant to be merely suggestive. Efforts far more extensive than I can apply to the task need to be devoted to fashioning the set of rules most consistent with the best available social scientific and psychological research. My aim in this chapter has been only to show how differently we might approach certain legal issues if our sole concern were for the rights and welfare of children, as it should be.

The Conceptual Possibility of Children Having Rights

There is a long-standing debate among philosophers about the purpose and conceptual content of rights that has direct implications for the law's treatment of children. It is a somewhat esoteric debate, and one that few people need resolved before they are willing to attribute rights to children, and for that reason I have not addressed it in the main text. But for the sake of any readers for whom the idea of nonautonomous persons having rights seems conceptually confused, I offer here an account and assessment of that debate with a focus on the implications for children, something that the main participants in the debate generally have not done.

The debate has to do with the connection between rights and autonomous choosing. An objection to ascribing rights to children in the contexts addressed in this book would come from those who deny that nonautonomous persons can or should be bearers of rights at all. One might think this debate long rendered moot by actual practice; the law throughout western society has for some time explicitly attributed various sorts of rights to nonautonomous persons, including children, and legal scholars and lawmakers have for some time spoken unhesitatingly about children's rights. Yet some philosophers persist in arguing against this practice, and occasionally some academics and nonacademics who do not regularly focus on the situation of nonautonomous persons assert or take for granted that rights are things only autonomous persons have. Some people appear simply to assume that having a right always means being empowered to choose what one wants to do, and so would find it odd to talk about ascribing rights to newborn children in connection with formation of legal parent–child relationships.

The philosophical objection that, as a conceptual matter, children are incapable of possessing rights rests on what is most commonly known as the Will Theory of rights, a theory that draws a necessary connection between rights and exercise of an autonomous will. What exactly that connection is, however, is not always clear. There are several possibilities: The connection could relate to (1) the function of rights – that is, what basic aim rights are supposed to serve; (2) the structural content of rights – that is, what conceptual bundle of legal advantages rights essentially embody; and (3) the moral foundation of rights – that is, why it is that anyone has rights.

As to the first of these possible connections, concerning the function of rights, some legal philosophers appear to take the view that the concept of a right is or should be limited to protection of persons' exercise of will. For some or all Will Theorists, a right is solely something that guarantees the effectiveness of choices within, or confers sovereignty over, some domain of human activity.[1] This understanding of rights appears to underlie the assumption of many nonphilosophers that talk of children's rights must be about letting children make decisions for themselves.

This idea of rights as only protection of choices is itself ambiguous, though, and differing interpretations have different implications for the second connection – that is, for what one takes to be the inherent structural content of a right. One thing this idea could mean (though it is not clear that any Will Theorists do mean this) is that the only duties others owe to me are duties to respect my choices – in other words, that the only claims (legal theorists refer to these correlates of duties as "Hohfeldian claims," after the great cataloger of legal concepts Wesley Hohfeld) I have against others under the rubric of rights are claims that they not interfere with activities I choose to pursue or otherwise act against my expressed preferences.[2] On this view, no Hohfeldian claims would protect interests independent of choices, and there would be no duties to promote the interests of specific other persons or to refrain from injuring others independently of their making and expressing choices about those interests.

The implication of that view for children would be that they should possess rights only to the extent that it is morally appropriate to guarantee the effectiveness of certain of their choices, to give them decision-making authority over some aspect of their daily lives. Correspondingly, on this view children cannot possess any rights if they are incapable of making any choices, which might be thought true of newborns, and even after they develop the capacity for making choices as to some matters, they cannot possess rights with respect to any aspects of their life as to which they remain incapable of making choices in any meaningful sense. A two-year-old might, for example, be capable of choosing between breakfast cereals but not between religions. Indeed, Will Theorists might go further and say that Hohfeldian claims protect not merely any choices but rather only choices made in a fairly sophisticated way – for example, with sufficient means–ends rationality, foresight of consequences, and self-control, in which case they might deem minors incapable of possessing any rights until adolescence or even until they are no longer minors but rather adults.

The main competitor to the Will Theory, sometimes called the Benefit Theory but more often the Interest Theory of rights, however, clearly takes the position that Hohfeldian claims can and do include protections of persons' important interests, independently of any choices they make. Among the human interests that these claims can protect are interests in being free and in having one's choices be effective and uncoerced, but that is only a subset of all the interests humans have and, according to the Interest Theory, all other interests are also potential candidates for receiving the protection of Hohfeldian claims and for being the subject of duties that others owe one.[3] Which interests should receive such protection depends on which substantive normative standard for attributing rights one adopts – for example, a standard by which some interests are judged more important or more closely connected to happiness or human perfection than others – rather than on anything inherent in the concept of a right. It follows from this position that children are not precluded from possessing Hohfeldian claims; they could have rights tied to any of their interests, including interests in having or not having close relationships with particular other persons, whether by their choice or not. Which of children's interests should receive the protection of rights would depend on the outcome of an independent normative analysis, such as that contained in this book.

Another interpretation of the idea that the only function of rights is to protect persons' exercise of free will, though, is that rights guarantee ultimate authority over some aspects of one's life; they put one in a position to decide whether and how others' duties to one will be carried out. This view is more clearly a component of the Will Theory, and its main implication for the structural content of rights is that the concept of a right entails not just having a Hohfeldian claim – that is, being the object of others' duties – but also holding the legal power either to demand performance of the duties or to waive the claim.[4] On this view, it makes no sense for us to attribute a legal right to a person unless we are prepared to say not only that others owe a duty to that person but also that that person should herself possess the legal power to decide whether the duty-holder must perform or will instead be absolved from the obligation.[5] For the very purpose of rights, it is said, is to make a right-holder sovereign over some domain of social existence, and sovereignty necessarily entails control over enforcement of one's claims on others, the ability to insist that some duties be fulfilled or to decide on reflection that one will forego such insistence.

Theorists who adhere to this view could accept that Hohfeldian claims protect interests, including but not limited to interests in having one's choices be effective, and in fact many Will Theorists do so explicitly. They simply deny that a person whose interests are the subject of a claim has a "right" unless that person also possesses a power with respect to the claim – that is, the legal authority to demand or waive compliance with the claim. Proponents of the Will Theory generally go on to point out that it is nonsensical to attribute to any being a power of enforcement or waiver unless that being has the practical capacity to decide, in a meaningful way, whether a duty should be enforced or waived.[6] Insofar as children do not have that capacity, they are not proper holders of "rights." This view might preclude attribution of rights not only to very young children but even to adolescents, if they are presumed to be lacking in the reasoning capacities necessary for this seemingly higher-order decision making. It would depend on how stringent the standards are for satisfactory exercise of such power. What the alternative is is not always clear; it might be that any duties concerning children's welfare must be owed to whomever is given the power to enforce those duties – for example, parents – or that those duties are owed to the children themselves but the "right" is held by the power-holders.

On the other side of this debate is the view, generally held by proponents of the Interest Theory, that to have a right, conceptually, means simply having a Hohfeldian claim or, correlatively, simply that others owe one certain duties and that the power to demand or waive enforcement of the duties is a separate matter.[7] On this view, as long as it makes sense to say that others can owe duties to children, then it makes sense to say that children can possess rights, and parents or guardians *ad litem* are in no way confused or misspeaking when they enter a courtroom and assert the "rights" of a young child. So the debate seems to boil down to whether the concept of a right necessarily includes a power of enforcement or whether the word *right* can connote a claim standing alone.

Last, there is some debate as to the normative basis on which rights should be attributed. The principal positions are the view that the moral impetus for according rights on any being derives from rational agency and, standing in opposition, the view that the moral trigger or foundation for assigning rights is simply having welfare interests that can be frustrated or fulfilled. The former position has a close affinity to that strand of modern moral theory, typically traced to eighteenth-century philosopher Immanuel Kant, that reposes ultimate moral value in auton-omy. The latter is more consistent with a competing strand, utilitarianism, that reposes ultimate moral value in welfare or happiness. For some theo-rists, this question is conceptually prior to the two discussed above; their answers to the other questions are driven at least in part by their views on this third issue, and they might even contend that answers to the two questions discussed above necessarily depend on substantive moral or political considerations.[8] Others, though, view the first two questions as resolvable on purely conceptual grounds or on the basis of which theory best fits with accepted usage of the term *right*.

From a Kantian perspective, one might think that only rational or "moral" agents properly possess rights, because rights are tied to matters of ultimate moral value, and what is of ultimate moral value to human life is the realization of moral personhood and exercise of moral faculties.[9] From a utilitarian view, in contrast, any sentient being can be a right-holder, because what is ultimately valuable is simply well-being, under-stood as happiness or experiencing more pleasure of various kinds and less pain. On this latter view, some moral theorists have argued that even non-human animals have moral rights and should have legal rights.[10] Other views predicate rights, or at least moral status of some kind, on other bases, such as simply being alive, or being a "subject of a life," or occupying an important role in a biological or social community, but rational agency and sentience or possession of interests predominate as bases for ascribing rights in most ethical theory and moral discourse.

The common element in these three debates is cognitive capacity. With respect to all three issues, philosophers on one side valorize rational or moral agency and draw conclusions about the object, content, and moral foundation of rights with an eye to that ultimate value. The emphasis on agency might be explained as a historical matter by the origination of the concept of a natural right in the Middle Ages.[11] In its origin, a right was understood as a legal power to control the world in some way or a claim to do something, and therefore as a legal protection for the freedom of rational moral agents, as against control of their lives by a monarch. By way of justification for these new claims of individual right, it was said that humans have a special dignity among sentient creatures because of their unique capacity for moral agency, which makes them in God's image. According to James Griffin, this conceptual link between the unique human capacity for self-determination and a dignity that gives rise to moral entitlement was presupposed by political thinkers for centuries.[12] Thus, it has exerted a great influence on rights discourse and on the development of legal systems.

Contemporary proponents of the Will Theory might not appeal to natural rights or natural law per se or speak of human participation in divine nature, but they are likely to claim special moral significance for human moral agency.[13] As much as anything else, though, these theorists appeal to historical fidelity and conceptual tidiness, and in fact those who concede that Hohfeldian claims can protect interests independent of choices appear committed to granting that aspects of human experience or human nature other than exercise of rational agency have moral significance. Some Will Theorists rest their position on the premise that words and concepts should retain their initial or predominate meaning absent some compelling reason for altering or extending the meaning, warning that if the meaning of *right* is stretched beyond its origins, there is no way to cabin its use. Using the concept of a right to encapsulate protections against suffering would allow for any sentient beings, including the humblest members of the animal kingdom, to possess rights. Using it to encapsulate protections of mere interests might allow for even greater dispersion of rights, to encompass any and every entity in the universe, even trees and rocks, if it can plausibly be said that they have interests. Such a proliferation of rights, these theorists contend, would dilute their significance, cheapen their currency, and confusingly transform the meaning of the term *right*, and would also conflict with widespread intuitions as to the moral standing of nonhuman entities.

One need not deny that moral agency has special normative significance, however, to reject all three of the positions I have associated with the Will Theory. Indeed some theorists argue against the Will Theory on the grounds simply that its moral vision is too narrow, that not only current exercise of moral agency but also individuals' interests in receiving or possessing the material preconditions for present and future exercise of moral agency – for example, life, sustenance, and education – and even their interest just in avoiding suffering warrant the protection that rights provide. This argument cuts most clearly against the Will Theory position on the third, normative issue discussed above – that is, that only current possession and exercise of autonomy is a proper normative basis for attributing rights, but at the same time it accepts that moral agency does have some special significance.[14]

However, one could also challenge the assumption that rational agency is of greatest moral value, an assumption underlying the claim that the singular moral foundation for rights is the appropriateness and necessity of protecting individuals' exercise of autonomous will. One might think the assumption inherently suspect, in light of the fact that it is so clearly self-serving for us who are autonomous agents, and who control moral discourse, to assert that characteristic as a basis for elevating our moral status above all other beings.[15] Those who revere it should therefore provide an argument for the claim that it alone or it more than anything else gives rise to moral entitlements, and an argument that differentiates autonomy from other characteristics to which those in power historically have accorded special significance, with the result of elevating their own moral status, but that we now view as irrelevant to moral standing, such as race or gender. Kant's attempt to provide such an argument is widely regarded as a failure,[16] and neo-Kantians have not much improved the arguments.[17] In fact, it proves quite difficult to show that human rationality has any inherent value, rather than simply being instrumentally valuable to the pursuit of other values, such as happiness and avoidance of suffering. Moreover, one might think that possession of such a useful capacity more naturally gives rise to responsibilities than to rights; the adage "to whom much is given, much is expected" encapsulates a widespread moral intuition.

In addition to the instability of any presupposition that exercise of an autonomous will is of greatest, even exclusive, moral importance, the Will Theory suffers from problems with the other, conceptual connections between rights and choosing. The first potential connection between rights and choosing discussed above is clearly inconsistent with widespread and long-standing practice, so reliance on it could not be justified in terms of historical fidelity or contemporary usage. A view that all Hohfeldian claims and their correlative duties relate only to choices is simply untenable, and, as suggested above, it is not clear that any Will Theorists actually maintain it. The view would be untenable because it would appear to entail attributing claims only in a radically lesser set of circumstances than we now do and for centuries have done, even with respect to autonomous adults. This is so because, under this view, before any duties could arise on the part of others, such that one could be said to have a claim, one presumably would have to make and communicate a choice to the world. An essential feature of the rule of law is that people know in advance what their legal obligations are; imposing on someone a duty not to interfere now with whatever choices another person will make in the future would be patently unfair, because it is impossible to fulfill. Yet most of the Hohfeldian claims that the law currently bestows even on competent adults are protections of interests, fully effective without our having expressed any preferences. The law confers on us claims with respect to our property and person that impose duties on others not to interfere with our interests even if we have not expressed a wish that they not interfere with our interests.

Now many such claims that we have might be said to be based on "imputed choices" – that is, legislative or judicial assumptions about what any given individual would be likely to choose if asked before the fact about another person's proposed actions. But imputed choices are not actual choices, and imputed choices would usually be hypothesized on the basis of interests – that is, lawmakers would infer from assumptions about what interests people generally have what choices they would be likely to make with respect to others' actions. They assume people want to maximize their welfare and would make choices accordingly if able to do so. So most existing claims are ultimately protections of interests. Moreover, as adherents to the Interest Theory have pointed out, many of the claims we possess today protect our interests even against our choices. We cannot opt out, for example, from our rights not to be killed, maimed, or enslaved.

Certainly this has been true of claims since their origination. Undoubtedly the concept was extended from the outset, as a matter of practical necessity, beyond actual choices, because those in a position to influence the law would have wanted their interests protected regardless of whether they had actually made any decisions about a particular matter in question. For example, property owners would have been deemed to have a right against novel forms of trespass, even though it had never occurred to the property owner to make a decision not to allow such trespass. And they would have had rights respecting their property even if they were abroad or otherwise indisposed to make decisions about their estate, or if they were unaware that they had inherited some property. Gentlemen would have been deemed to have a right against any sort of physical attacks out in public, regardless of whether they first made a choice whether to allow the attack. The history of Anglo-American common law is essentially characterized by judicial extension of rights in cases where a claimant was harmed by unanticipated actions and events.

Undoubtedly, then, the law of western societies in the late Middle Ages, when the idea of a right emerged, immediately accommodated the idea of imputed choices in its creation of legal claims, based on assumptions about what people generally prefer in certain situations, regardless of the particular choices, attitudes, or values of a given individual. Indeed it likely incorporated early on the idea that rights protect interests independently of choices, where no choices had been made. From the beginning of their use of the term *right*, western societies must have recognized as entirely unworkable an understanding of rights that limited them to protection of prior, expressed preferences, and therefore must have extended them beyond their core function of protecting rational agency and respecting the dignity of persons thought to flow from their being moral agents to encompass also protection of interests independently of choices. Children certainly have interests even before they become rational agents, and the idea of imputing choices to generate rights can coherently be extended to them. Law and popular discourse in the West today in fact clearly reflect an understanding that duties are owed to children to protect certain of their interests; it is well established that even to the youngest children we owe legal and moral duties – for example, as individuals to refrain from acts of violence toward them and collectively as the adult members of society to ensure that they receive the means for healthy development, including food, shelter, and education. And we do not understand those duties to be limited to responding to choices children make – for example, to instances when children ask us not to assault them or decide that they want to go to school.

That leaves the second possible connection between rights and exercise of autonomous agency, which is the real heart of Will Theorists' conceptual argument. This is the view that the best conceptual understanding of a right, by which seems typically to be meant the understanding that is most consistent with prevailing practices or discourse, is one by which the concept of a right entails not just a claim but also a power to demand or waive enforcement of the claim. A Will Theorist could concede that Hohfeldian claims are protections of interests, including but not limited to interests in not being interfered with in making and effectuating choices, and could concede that exercise of a mature, rational will is not the only thing that gives rise to moral status and to moral obligations, but insist that the term *right* should be reserved for cases where persons having claims also possess the power of enforcement, so that the law preserves for them the ultimate decision about how others will treat them. In fact, Will Theorists generally acknowledge that the law should protect the welfare of incompetent humans but insist that such protection should not be viewed as conferring rights on those beings, because they are incapable of exercising powers, of wielding final authority over important aspects of their lives.

Such a view is not unworkable in the way that a view resting on the first possible connection between rights and choices would be. Although it is impractical for any of us to express preferences in advance as to every possible interference with our interests, it is not impractical for competent adults always to make choices after the fact – that is, after someone has breached duties owed to us or has asked for a waiver of a duty – as to whether we will demand enforcement of our claims, through a demand for specific performance, compensation for harm done, or punishment, or will instead waive our claims. Still, it is problematic in many respects.

First, this view, too, is inconsistent with widespread use of the concept of a right even in relation to competent adults by legal systems in the western world today and, most likely, since the concept originated. It has undoubtedly always been the case that many competent adults delegated to others – for example, to financial managers and legal advocates – the power to act to enforce certain of their claims, without anyone understanding this to mean that they transferred the right to the agent. Agents for original right-holders are not understood to possess the rights at all. Rather, they are understood to be asserting rights of their principals, and they articulate demands in those terms. Significantly, this is true even after principals become incompetent or otherwise incapable of exercising the power themselves; their rights do not expire and are not transferred to their agents when they begin to lose their mental faculties or are in a location where they cannot be contacted. Thus, rights per se are commonly held by persons even though the power of enforcement is held by someone else, additionally or exclusively. The concept of a trust, one might add, with trustees protecting the "rights" of trust beneficiaries, is centuries old.

In most instances where competent adults delegate power to an agent, it is true, they retain the power themselves; agent and principal become joint possessors of the power. And the principal also possesses the power to withdraw the powers bestowed on the agent. However, common usage of the term *right* today suggests that competent adults have many rights as to which they never have a power of enforcement themselves. The criminal law is understood to confer rights on individuals – for example, rights against murder, maiming, and theft. Yet the power over enforcement of those rights typically resides ultimately in state officials, not the individuals themselves. Prosecutors have the power to demand or waive enforcement of duties imposed by the criminal law, insofar as they wield discretion whether to prosecute rights-violators (which is not always the case). But it would strike most people as very odd to conclude from this that we have no right arising from the criminal law against being killed or maimed or robbed.[18]

Less familiar are civil law contexts in which only government agencies are empowered to assert the claims of individuals harmed by violation of some law. Many federal statutes in the United States, ranging from consumer protection laws to labor laws to public access laws, effectively confer rights on private individuals by prohibiting conduct of other private parties that would harm them in certain ways, yet reserve the power of enforcing those rights to state agencies. There is a substantial body of doctrine in American law concerning when statutes should be interpreted to confer a "private cause of action" – that is, to authorize private parties who are harmed by violations to bring suit themselves against the entities that denied them the benefits to which they were entitled, or instead should be interpreted to authorize only some administrative agency to take legal action to punish infractions, at its discretion.

In addition, and crucially, it is well settled in the law and popular discourse today that infants and incompetent adults have "rights," even though they do not possess the power to demand or waive enforcement. Legal codes throughout the West (though less so in the United States than in most other nations) attribute "rights" to incompetent persons – adults and children – even though such persons are incapable of making decisions about enforcement of their claims. References in judicial opinions to children's constitutional or common law rights are also very common (again, more so outside the United States). The view that children and incompetent adults cannot and do not have any "rights" would strike the vast majority of people as preposterous, and their perplexity would not diminish on being reassured that people do owe duties with respect to children and incompetent adults, only the duties are owed to persons other than the children and incompetent adults. It is a well-accepted practice that certain competent adults – typically, parents or guardians *ad litem* – act as agents to enforce rights of children and of adults who are mentally disabled or mentally ill, and do not themselves become right-holders by virtue of exercising that power.

It should be plain, then, that Will Theorists who insist that rights exist only where a claim-holder also holds a power of enforcement are urging that the legal system adopt an understanding of rights and a usage of the term *right* that is patently inconsistent with established usage and settled expectations in a large and important area of the law.[19] On the further assumption that it would be unjustifiably confusing and disruptive, or simply futile, for the legal system suddenly to insist on a much more restrictive understanding of rights, one must conclude on pragmatic grounds that the legal system should not adopt and implement the view that only claims coupled with powers are "rights" and that, therefore, only those capable of exercising a power of enforcement or waiver can be "right"-holders.

There is also the political concern to which the emphasis on rational agency gives rise, discussed further below, that persons who do not operate at the requisite level of rational agency will not receive the legal protection they need or deserve. Will Theorists might protest that they do not claim such persons should not receive protection for their important interests, but only that such protection should come in some form or go by some name other than "rights." They might insist that they are making a point simply about terminology, not about the substance of legal protections. Their contention might be convincing if there were some alternative legal concept providing protection equal to or greater than that provided by "rights." But the reality is that there is none. Persons of lesser capacity require and deserve greater protection from the legal system, not less. Yet there is no assertion that an agent for an infant or incompetent adult could present to a legislature or court today that has force even approaching that of the assertion that such persons have a "right" to protection of their interests. Asserting that a particular decision would be good or bad for such persons, or appealing to a decision maker's sense of moral responsibility or sympathy, is simply much less effective; it commands much less attention from legislators and very little indeed from judges. Perhaps western societies could invent a new term or concept, such as *child-claim*, or *first-order need*, or *ultimate guarantee*, and imbue it with gravitas equal to or greater than that which *right* now carries. But unless and until that happens, our moral responsibility to dependent and vulnerable persons would appear to require that we use the best legal and rhetorical tools at hand. Rights are the currency of recognition and respect in our legal and political culture today. To withhold that currency entirely from some class of persons should require compelling justification, and Will Theorists offer none.

Some proponents of the Will Theory, such as Hillel Steiner, attempt to evade this objection by contending that the law could simply attribute rights to the agents for any persons incapable of exercising powers. And, in fact, American judges have sometimes justified their resort to parents' rights to resolve legal disputes over children's upbringing by explaining that parents possess rights because this is conducive to the welfare of children. Steiner contends that there is no analytical or practical difference between, on the one hand, construing the rights that protect incompetent persons as rights held by the persons who would seek enforcement of the duties – for example, a parent or guardian – and, on the other hand, construing them as rights held by the incompetent persons themselves.[20] This contention is plainly wrong.

As an analytical matter, if an agent for an incompetent person is deemed the holder of the rights that are correlates of duties to assist or forbear from adversely affecting the incompetent person, then the prevailing understanding of rights would deem those duties to be owed to the agent rather than to the person whose welfare is at stake and whose needs are supposedly the moral basis for the duties. The established understanding of rights is that the person to whom a duty is owed is the bearer of the corresponding right and, conversely, that the bearer of a right is the person to whom the corresponding duty is owed. Accepted usage does not contemplate a division between the holder of a right and the person to whom the corresponding duty is owed. Even those judges and other persons who defend parental child-rearing rights do not assert that the duties corresponding to those rights are owed to children rather than to parents. And outside the context of child rearing, accepted usage also generally does not contemplate designating as the object of duties someone other than the person whose welfare is the moral basis for, and protected through the establishment of, the duties. This is true in the case of agents acting for competent adults as well as in the case of incompetent adults. Thus, analytical confusion is clearly one result of Steiner's move.

There is an important practical difference as well. As any legal practitioner could attest, legal decision makers instinctively focus on the interests and wishes of the persons before them who are understood to be the holders of rights, precisely because the common understanding is that the corresponding duties are owed to the right-holder and are founded upon the interests of the right-holder. So unless there were a perfect unity of interests between the agents and the persons in whose behalf they are supposed, by the agency arrangement, to be acting, which arguably is never the case, attributing the rights to the guardian would inevitably lead in practice to some sacrifice of the interests of the dependent person for whose sake the duties and rights were actually established. When parents go to court and claim that their rights relating to child rearing are being violated, judges focus on the (often self-regarding) desires of the parents and on the parents' feelings, experience, and interests. Such claims do not induce judges to focus on the welfare of the child and in fact create an obstacle to judges' doing so. Although attributing the rights instead to a nonfamily member who is trained to serve in a fiduciary role, such as a guardian *ad litem*, might create less danger of misdirected judicial concern, it would not avoid the danger entirely. Thus, the premise that it makes no practical difference whether rights are attributed to agent or principal, a premise Steiner says is crucial to a defense of the Will Theory, is belied by everyday experience in the legal system.

H. L. A. Hart adopted a somewhat different stance under the guise of favoring the Will Theory, and his approach might salvage the Will

Theory from the charge that it is inconsistent with a large body of law. In criticizing what he termed the Benefit Theory of rights, as implausibly identifying rights in situations where intended beneficiaries of certain laws had no control whatsoever over whether the laws would be enforced – for example, the criminal law – Hart insisted, as Will Theorists generally do, that a right must contain both a claim and a power. However, he suggested in a footnote, discussing the situation of children in particular, that the power need not be held by the right-holder. It is proper, Hart contended, to say that children have rights, even though it is their parents or some other adult who would enforce their claims, so long as "what such representatives can and cannot do by way of exercise of such power is determined by what those whom they represent could have done if sui juris."[21] So on this variation of the Will Theory, there is no obstacle to attributing rights, legal or moral, to children. We would simply only do so when some private party holds a power with respect to their claims and so can act in the child's behalf to enforce the child's claims.

What Hart's view reflects is less an assumption that exercise of autonomous will is the only aspect of human life that commands moral consideration or can be tied conceptually to rights and more an assumption that the concept of a right entails the possibility of enforcement for the sake of the right-holder. Where a law generally benefits an individual but no one acting in behalf of that individual can insist on enforcement, many would join with Hart in saying that the individual has no right but rather only a hope to be benefited. The benefit seems too uncertain and the protection too weak to put one in the strong position that having a right is ordinarily assumed to do.

Even this assumption is questionable, though, for in some contexts the prevailing view is that laws confer rights even when there is no mechanism for enforcing them. Some international human rights documents, for example, have announced explicitly that all humans or particular humans have a right to one thing or another, without there being any means for anyone to assert a claim in a legal forum on the basis of that pronouncement. Even some individual countries have passed laws purporting to establish rights but providing no means of enforcement. For example, some countries have declared in their laws that children have a right not to be hit, even for purposes of discipline by parents, but have not created the possibility of a civil, criminal, or administrative action against any parent who engages in corporal punishment. The more common description of such laws is that they create unenforceable or very weak rights rather than that they create no rights at all.

What is utterly essential to the concept of a right, it seems, is just that there be a relational component to duties held by some persons or institutions – that is, that the obligations are owed to someone in particular. A legal obligation held by a government employee, such as a legislator or judge, does not appear to give rise to a right for any particular individual if there is no reason to view the obligation as owed to that individual, but it does where there is reason to view the obligation as owed to that individual. That the individual benefits from the obligation and has a power to enforce the obligation, a power exercisable by himself or by an agent, is a good reason to view the obligation as owed to the individual. But it is not the only reason. Another would be that the law imposing the obligation says explicitly that the individual has a corresponding right. Still another might be that the law makes clear, by some means other than speaking of rights, that the sole purpose for imposing the obligation is to benefit the individual, as might be the case, for example, where the duty is something like "do whatever is in the best interests of" that individual.

In short, what appears to trouble Will Theorists is that some people benefit from the performance of duties even when the duties are not understood to be owed to those people, and Will Theorists think the Interest Theory must nevertheless attribute rights to those people in those instances. But that is not the case. The Interest Theory holds simply that being owed a duty amounts to having a right and that the duty can be one other than noninterference with choices. It does not hold that whenever one benefits from performance of a duty that the duty must have been owed to one. And insofar as Will Theorists maintain that the only way to know if a duty is owed to a particular person is to determine whether that person has a power to enforce the duty, they are likewise mistaken. For there are other indicia that one is the object of a duty, and, moreover, sometimes people possess powers, as agents, without themselves being the object of the duties they are empowered to enforce.

Finally, though, something more must be said about tidiness, for it cannot help but trouble one to be told that one's view of rights entails a commitment to the proposition that, for example, certain sentient but base creatures, such as ants, can possess rights or even that a grain of sand can possess rights. Such a commitment is at odds with prevailing intuitions. And were rights to be so widely dispersed, it might well occur, as the Will Theorists warn, that rights lose much of their value.

One response to this concern that proponents of the Interest Theory could make is that current realities belie the fears. The legal systems of western nations are already operating and have long operated on the basis of an assumption that nonautonomous beings can possess rights, yet rights still have substantial force. We have not much extended rights beyond human beings; the animal rights movement has made some inroads in behalf of higher-order animals, but calls for recognition of trees' rights have fallen unheard. And as to no group of human beings is there a good moral or pragmatic argument to be made for withdrawing rights altogether. So things are more or less as they should be, with no need of a Will Theory to keep rights within manageable bounds. Conferring new rights on children would amount to mere tinkering with the moral apparatus of the universe.

Another response Interest Theorists can and do make is that the Interest Theory does not commit its proponents to any position as to which particular beings or entities should have rights. It simply broadens the category of those entities who are potential right-holders.[22] Even if one accepts the Interest Theory, one could take the position that legal systems should not confer any rights on nonhuman entities on several possible grounds, some more plausible than others, including (1) that no other beings can properly be said to possess interests; (2) that even if some non-human entities have interests, none have interests sufficiently compelling to warrant the protection of rights; (3) that even if some nonhuman entities have pronounced interests, none have some other characteristic that the best normative theory of rights requires; and (4) that nonhumans are not members of our moral community and only members of our moral community are entitled to anything from the community. An Interest Theorist could also arrive at some intermediate position, such as that higher-order nonhuman animals should have rights but no other nonhuman entities should.[23]

Put somewhat differently, an Interest Theorist might say that if Will Theorists were to identify what really underlies the widespread intuition that, for example, trees and rocks should not be accorded rights, it likely would not be the fact that trees and rocks are not moral agents, because there is near universal acceptance of the belief that humans who are not now moral agents should have rights. Many people also take the position that certain nonhuman animals, such as all mammals, should be viewed as having some rights with respect to how they are treated, even though they believe that members of many or all mammal species are not moral agents. Most likely, what underlies the intuition that trees and rocks should not be accorded rights would be a sense that beings that appear incapable of anything approximating the human experience of pain and suffering do not trigger in us the feelings of empathy or sympathy that would move us to say they are entitled to anything from us or that we owe them any obligations. It might also contribute to this intuition that these entities can have no awareness of us or of our treatment of them.[24] It might also be that there is no potential for these things to change about trees and rocks; they do not have the potential to develop into creatures that experience pain and suffering or have conscious awareness of other beings. All of these beliefs are consistent, incidentally, with a belief that it is morally wrong to destroy a particular animal or tree or rock or to destroy too many members of some species of animal or plant. The perceived wrong in such a case might be a violation of a duty, but one owed to other humans (because of harm to them), or to the Creator (based on religiously grounded obligations), or even to oneself (based on some perfectionist moral outlook).

Ultimately, it is difficult to perceive much merit in the Will Theory and so to any objection on conceptual grounds to attributing rights to children in connection with state decision making about their relationships. The Will Theory is inconsistent with widespread legal and popular discourse about nonautonomous persons, so it cannot claim fidelity to accepted usage for its side of the debate. It cannot claim an advantage in conceptual nicety, for one can easily distinguish the situation of autonomous and nonautonomous persons without denying rights to the latter; one could simply say, for example, that although all humans can possess rights, only autonomous persons can be appropriate holders of powers with respect to rights. And in any event, the practical cost to nonautonomous persons of withholding "rights" from them would outweigh considerations of etymological consistency and conceptual nicety. Newborn children in particular need a rights banner waved in their behalf to alert state actors to the children's claims against them when they undertake to create legal families.

Notes

Introduction

1. For an analysis of this normative question, see Peter Vallentyne, "Rights and Duties of Childrearing," *William & Mary Bill of Rights Journal* 11 (2003), 991–1010.

2. Cf. Thomas Hurka, "Normative Ethics: Back to the Future," in Brian Leiter, ed., *The Future for Philosophy* (Oxford: Clarendon Press, 2005), 251 ("In my view an anti-theoretical position is properly open only to those who have made a serious effort to theorize a given domain and found that it cannot succeed. Anti-theorists who do not make this effort are simply being lazy . . . ").

3. See Immanuel Kant, *Groundwork of the Metaphysic of Morals*, trans. H. J. Paton (New York: Harper & Row, 1964), 96 (setting forth the Formula of the End in Itself, requiring moral agents to "[a]ct in such a way that you always treat humanity, whether in your own person or in the person of any other, never simply as a means, but always at the same time as an end"). Some philosophers would limit the term *person* and some incidents of personhood to autonomous adult human beings. I critique this view in a forthcoming work, but for present simply stipulate what is almost universally accepted, that children are persons and as such are morally entitled to equal consideration of their interests in state decision making that impacts their lives.

4. See Elizabeth S. Scott and Robert E. Scott, "Parents as Fiduciaries," *Virginia Law Review* 81 (1995), 2418 (there is "an emerging

sense that the primary objective of state regulation of this relationship should be to advance the interests of children whenever they conflict with those of their parents"); Jane C. Murphy, "Rules, Responsibility and Commitment to Children: The New Language of Morality in Family Law," *University of Pittsburgh Law Review* 60 (1999), 1128 (noting "an emerging consensus about the centrality of protecting children as, perhaps, the core value that should be promoted in family law" and citing public surveys supporting that observation).

1. Why Rights for Children?

1. In Hohfeldian terms, what I refer to as *rights* against certain state actions will largely be, strictly speaking, immunities – that is, protections against the state altering one's legal relations to others, because the state action at issue will principally be its creating, maintaining, or dissolving legal relationships between children and others or its decisions to give or not give legal protection to social relationships between children and others. But in everyday discourse, we commonly use *rights* to connote such immunities, so my analysis will be more intelligible if I adhere to that usage. We also commonly refer to the state's position in these situations as one of owing duties to individuals and groups not to pass laws or take other institutional actions that adversely affect the legal position of those individuals or groups. We do not much use Hohfeld's term

disability to characterize the state's position. Thus, Hohfeld's immunity/disability pairing could easily and intelligibly be recharacterized as a right/duty pairing of a special sort.

2. See, e.g., Mary Ann Glendon, *Rights-talk: The Impoverishment of Political Discourse* (New York: Free Press, 1991), 9–15; Mary Midgley, "Rights-Talk Will Not Sort out Child-Abuse: Comment on Archard on Parental Rights," *Journal of Applied Philosophy* 8 (1991), 107; Lynn D. Wardle, "The Use and Abuse of Rights Rhetoric: The Constitutional Rights of Children," *Loyola University – Chicago Law Journal* 27 (1996), 321 (arguing not for elimination of, but greater constraint on, talk about children's rights).

3. See Barbara Bennett Woodhouse, "Hatching the Egg: A Child-Centered Perspective on Parents' Rights," *Cardozo Law Review* 14 (1993), 1818 ("Courts and philosophers writing about parental rights often trace the legitimacy of those rights to the role parental authority plays in the exercise of parental responsibility. Rights rhetoric, however, has tended to obscure this foundation of adult power. Our focus on these adjunct rights rather than on their basis has distracted us from carefully examining the nature of responsibility itself."). See also Katharine Bartlett, "Re-Expressing Parenthood," *Yale Law Journal* 98 (1988), 298. Bartlett also identifies, and objects to, an "exchange view" of parenthood, under which parenthood is viewed as something to which adults are entitled in exchange for having accepted certain responsibilities. That is certainly a common view. Also common today, however, is an "ownership view" of parenthood that has deep historical roots, under which parenthood is something to which adults are entitled simply by virtue of having biologically generated a child, not something arising from having assumed responsibilities, any more than ownership of a shoe entails or arises from assuming responsibilities to the shoe. See Barbara Bennett Woodhouse, "Who Owns the Child?: Meyer and Pierce and the Child as Property," *William & Mary Law Review* 33 (1992), 995.

4. Many adults also do not have forceful advocates in family law and other legal proceedings. But the adults, unlike the children, are usually present at court proceedings and the law encourages judges to focus on parents' interests and rights.

5. Ferdinand Schoeman, "Rights of Children, Rights of Parents, and the Moral Basis of the Family," *Ethics* 91 (1980), 9.

6. Michael Freeman, *The Moral Status of Children: Essays on the Rights of the Child* (Amsterdam: Marinus Nijhoff, 1997), 16. See also id., 15 ("In societies that make rights the coin of the realm, a critique of rights that reduces the availability of rights does nothing to assist the excluded or the disadvantaged."), 17 ("Rights are . . . valuable commodities [and] weapons to undermine power"), 23–9 (providing a fuller response to objections to children's rights).

7. Tom D. Campbell, "Really Equal Rights? Some Philosophical Comments on 'Why Children Shouldn't Have Equal Rights' by Laura M. Purdy," *The International Journal of Children's Rights* 2 (1994), 259, 263.

8. Cf. Freeman, *Moral Status*, 60 (distinguishing having equal rights both from having unequal rights and from having the same rights).

9. Schoeman, "Rights of Children," 9.

10. Barbara Arneil, "Becoming versus Being: A Critical Analysis of the Child in Liberal Theory," in D. Archard and C. MacLeod, eds., *Moral and Political Status of Children* (Oxford: Oxford University Press, 2002), 75–6.

11. See, e.g., *Hansen v. Turkey*, (2004) 39 EHRR 18, ¶ 97 (in holding that state officials in Turkey had not taken sufficient steps to enforce a visitation order in favor of a mother, the Court stated: "There are in addition positive obligations inherent in an effective 'respect' for family life. In this context, the Court has repeatedly held that Art. 8 includes a right for parents to have measures taken that will permit them to be reunited with their children and an obligation on the national authorities to take such action."); *Mikulic v. Croatia*, (2004) ECHR 53176/99, ¶ 57 (holding that state officials had taken insufficient steps to determine the paternity of a man alleged to be the biological father of the applicant child).

12. (2000) ECHR 32346/96, ¶¶ 63, 65.

13. *Kutzner v. Germany*, (2002) ECHR 46544/99, ¶ 76; *Hansen v. Turkey*, (2004) 39 EHRR 18, ¶ 97.

14. The legal codes of many nations other than the United States do contain explicit references to children's rights. The Russian Family Code, for example, contains an entire chapter on "The Rights of Underaged Children," which establishes, among other rights, the right to be nurtured in a family, the right to live with one's parents except when this is contrary to the child's interests, the right to defense against abuses by parents, and "the right to express his or her opinion when deciding any question in the family affecting the child's interests." Kodeks Zakonov o Brake, Semie i Opeke RF (Family Code of the Russian Federation), arts. 54, 56, and 57. The South African Constitution contains a detailed listing of the rights of children. South African Constitution of 1996, ch. 2, §§ 28 (children's rights), 29 (education). The United Nations Convention on the Rights of the Child, Nov. 20, 1989, 28 I.L.M. 1448, has been ratified and thereby incorporated into domestic law by nearly every government other than the United States, and it accords to children a "right to know and be cared for by his or her parents," id. art. 7; "the right of the child to preserve his or her . . . family relations as recognized by law," id. art. 8; "the right of the child who is separated from one or both parents to maintain personal relations and direct contact with both parents on a regular basis, except if it is contrary to the child's best interests," id. art. 9; "the right to maintain on a regular basis . . . personal relations and direct contacts with both parents" when the parents live in different countries, id. art. 10; "the right to express [his or her] views freely in all matters affecting the child," id. art. 12; the right "to freedom of association," id. art. 15; "the right to the protection of the law against . . . interference" with his or her privacy or family, id. art. 16.

15. See Neil MacCormick, "Rights in Legislation," in P. M. S. Hacker and J. Raz, eds., *Law, Morality, and Society* (Oxford: Clarendon Press, 1977), 191–2. The concept of standing is different from that of having a power of enforcement. In law, to have standing means that one's interests are a proper basis on which a claim can be stated in court, and this could be true of a person deemed incompetent to present such a claim himself or herself. Thus, a newborn child can have standing in court, even though he or she cannot possess a power of enforcement. Cf. *Kingsley v. Kingsley*, 623 So.2d 780 (Fla. Dist. Ct. App. 1994) (holding that a minor lacked legal capacity to initiate termination of parental rights proceeding himself, while indicating that a guardian, attorney, or next friend could do so in the minor's behalf and stating that in such a case the minor is nevertheless the party in interest, not his agent, and that the minor's "lack of capacity due to nonage is a procedural, not substantive, impediment which minimally restricts his right to participate as a party in proceedings").

16. I elaborate on the idea of implicit rights and provide a taxonomy of such rights in James G. Dwyer, "A Taxonomy of Children's Existing Rights in State Decision Making about Their Relationships," *William & Mary Bill of Rights Journal* 11 (2003), 847–54. For an explanation of why it makes sense to look at whose interests a law actually protects rather than at whom the lawmakers intended to benefit, see H. L. A. Hart, "Bentham on Legal Rights," in A. W. B. Simpson, ed., *Oxford Essays in Jurisprudence* (Oxford: Clarendon Press, 1973), 188–9.

2. The Existing Relationship Rights of Children

1. This chapter's presentation of U.S. law is largely a distillation of a 145-page conceptual and descriptive account of children's existing rights in the United States presented in a law journal article. James G. Dwyer, "A Taxonomy of Children's Existing Rights in State Decision Making about Their Relationships," *William & Mary Bill of Rights Journal* 11 (2003) 845–990. The reader should consult that work for citations to the specific laws that form the basis for the summary account that follows here. For the corresponding legal rules in England, I rely principally on Jonathan Herring, *Family*

Law (London: Pearson Education, 2001). For legal rules in other European countries, I rely largely on Carolyn Hamilton and Alison Perry, eds., *Family Law in Europe* (2nd ed.) (London: Butterworths, 2002).

2. For an outline of the components of rigorous comparative law scholarship, see John C. Reitz, "How to Do Comparative Law," *American Journal of Comparative Law* 46 (1998), 617. But see also Shirly S. Abrahamson and Michael J. Fischer, "All the World's a Courtroom: Judging in the New Millennium," *Hofstra Law Review* 26 (1997), 285–8 (extolling the benefits of even a casual comparative inquiry).

3. See also U.N. Convention on the Rights of the Child, Article 3(1); Charter of Fundamental Rights of the European Union, Article 24(2); Hamilton and Perry, *Family Law in Europe*, 651 (describing custody rule in Sweden), 462 (Netherlands); Children Act 1995 (Scotland) § 11(7). But see Michael Freeman, *The Moral Status of Children: Essays on the Rights of the Child* (The Hague: Marinus Nijhoff Publishers, 1997), 105–10 (explaining that England's Children Act of 1989 actually reflects and is used to advance values other than the welfare and rights of children).

4. John Eekelaar, "Children between Cultures," *International Journal of Law, Policy and the Family* 18 (2004) 178, 186–7. See also Jane Fortin, *Children's Rights and the Developing Law* (2nd ed.) (London: Butterworths, 2003), 253–4 (endorsing the view that Article 8 of the European Convention requires a balancing of children's and parents' interests), 248–51 (discussing the similar view of other scholars).

5. See, e.g., *Kosmopoulou v. Greece*, (2004) ECHR 60457/00, ¶¶ 42–47 (access rights of noncustodial parent); *Hansen v. Turkey*, (2004) 39 EHRR 18, ¶ 98 (same); *EP v. Italy*, (2001) 31 EHRR 17, ¶ 62 (removal from custody of abusive parent); *Nuutinen v. Finland*, (2000) ECHR 32842/96, ¶¶ 128–129 ("Where contacts with the parent might appear to threaten [the child's] interests or interfere with [the child's] rights, it is for the national authorities to strike a fair balance between them.").

6. See Herring, *Family Law*, 266 (England and Wales); Irish Children Act 1997, s. 5;

European Convention on the Legal Status of Children Born Out of Wedlock, Article 2, 1138 U.N.T.S. 303 (1975) (twenty-one state signatories); Claire Archbold, "Family Law-Making and Human Rights in the United Kingdom," in Mavis Maclean, ed., *Making Law for Families* (Oxford: Hart, 2000), 199–200 (describing 1979 decision of the European Court of Human Rights holding that Belgium's law requiring unmarried mothers to petition for legal parent status violated Articles 8 and 14 of the European Convention for the Protection of Human Rights and Fundamental Freedoms, to which over forty countries are parties); Hamilton and Perry, *Family Law in Europe*, 85 (Denmark), 311 (Germany), 389 (Ireland), 461 (Netherlands), 687 (Switzerland); W. Pintens, ed., *International Encyclopedia of Laws, Volume I: Of Family and Succession Law* (2002), 79 (Germany), 94 (Denmark), 110–11 (Greece), 122 (Czech Republic); *Martindale-Hubbell International Law Digest* 2004, 24 (Bulgaria), 27 (Alberta, Canada); French C. Civ., ch. 2, art. 319–21; Status of Children Act (Northern Territory of Australia) 2004, ss. 4A, 5C.

7. See D. Marrriane Blair and Merle H. Weiner, *Family Law in the World Community: Cases, Materials, and Problems in Comparative and International Family Law* (Durham, NC: Carolina Academic Press, 2003), 24.

8. See Herring, *Family Law*, 292.

9. Satoshi Minamikata et al., "Japan," in W. Pintens, ed., *International Encylopedia of Laws, Volume II: Of Family and Succession Law* (1999), 133.

10. See Blair and Weiner, *Family Law in the World Community*, 556 ("The concept that a child belongs to the father's family is common to many of the patrilineal societies in sub-Saharan Africa"); Pintens, *International Encyclopedia*, Vol. II (Botswana), 58. Blair and Weiner suggest that there might be a child welfare justification for this practice, where a child's material well-being depends on being in the care of the father, who can provide support and an inheritance in a very poor society where men generally own what little wealth there is. Blair and Weiner, *Family Law in the World Community*, 557.

11. *In re Bobbijean P.*, 784 N.Y.S.2d 919, 2004 N.Y. Slip Op. 50286U, *5 (Monroe County Fam. Ct. 2004). See also "Court Orders Couple to Stop Having Children and to Attend Family Planning Sessions," *New York Law Journal* 94 (May 17, 2004), 20; Tarek Tannous, "'Born to a No-Parent Family': The Troubling Case of Baby Bobbijean," *City Newspaper* (Rochester, NY), May 19, 2004; Janice G. Inman, "How Will It Play in New York?" *New York Family Law Monthly* 5(9), 1 (June 2004) (describing similar orders by trial courts in other states).

12. See Inman, "How Will It Play in New York?"

13. *In re V.R.*, 2004 N.Y. Slip Op. 51706U (Monroe County Fam. Ct. 2004).

14. Id., 4, 8.

15. See Brief of Amici Curiae in Support of Respondent Stephanie P's Motion to Vacate, in *In re Bobbijean P.* (Monroe County Family Court Docket No. NN-03626-03), dated October 18, 2003; *In re Bobbijean P.*, 2005 N.Y. Slip Op. 50031U (Monroe County Fam. Ct.) (denying the motion to vacate).

16. Dorothy Roberts, *Shattered Bonds: The Color of Child Welfare* (New York: Basic Books, 2002), 155. Instead Roberts quickly shifts focus to older children who have already lived with an unfit parent for some time, making the well-known points that there are not enough people wanting to adopt such children and that such children typically identify with and have a conscious bond with the parent despite the parent's shortcomings, which makes termination more costly for the child. Id., 157–61. See also Twila Perry, "Race Matters: Change, Choice, and Family Law at the Millenium," *Family Law Quarterly* 33 (1999), 461; Dorothy E. Roberts, "Punishing Drug Addicts Who Have Babies: Women of Color, Equality, and the Right to Privacy," *Harvard Law Review* 104 (1991), 1419; Mary L. Shanley, "Reflections on Unwed Fathers' Rights and Sex Equality," in Patrice DiQuinzio and Iris Marion Young, *Feminist Ethics and Social Policy* (Bloomington, IN: Indiana University Press, 1997), 95–120, 111 (arguing that mothers should be entitled to place their children with adoptive parents without interference from biological fathers, because otherwise the

mothers might be upset, and stating: "It is important, however, to ascertain just what the drug-dependent mother is guilty of, and whether punishment or taking away her right to be heard concerning custody of her child is an appropriate response to her behavior.")

17. French Civil Code, Art. 341–1; Blair and Weiner, *Family Law in the World Community*, 24.

18. For description of the history of French law and recent developments in other European countries, see *Odievre v. France*, (2003) ECHR 42326/98, in which the European Court of Human Rights upheld France's regime of confidential births against the claim of a person whose mother had requested confidentiality that denying her knowledge of her mother's identity violated her rights respecting private life under Article 8 of the Convention on Human Rights. Safe haven and anonymous birth laws are typically justified as conducive to lower rates of abortion and infanticide and as making the adoption process easier, and these considerations formed part of the Court's reasoning in *Odievre*.

19. On the history of, and rationales for, the marital presumption in English and American law, see Jane Murphy, "Legal Images of Fatherhood: Welfare Reform, Child Support Enforcement and Fatherless Children," *Notre Dame Law Review* 81 (2005), 101; June Carbone and Naomi Cahn, "Which Ties Bind? Redefining the Parent–Child Relationship in an Age of Genetic Certainty," *William & Mary Bill of Rights Journal* 11 (2003), 1017–20. See also Martin Guggenheim, *What's Wrong With Children's Rights* (Cambridge, MA: Harvard University Press, 2005), 57–62 (explaining that the correlative exclusion of unwed fathers from parenthood reflected in part the aim of protecting the property and reputation of those men).

20. See, e.g., Hamilton and Perry, *Family Law in Europe*, 86 (Denmark), 280 (France), 311–12 (Germany), 687 (Switzerland).

21. See Fortin, *Children's Rights*, 394–5 (discussing rights of biological fathers in England and Wales); Hamilton and Perry, *Family Law in Europe*, 139 (discussing paternity rules in England and Wales); Gillian Douglas, *An Introduction to Family Law*

(Oxford: Oxford University Press, 2001), 118 (England); Irish Status of Children Act 1987, s. 38; Family Law Act 2001 (Northern Ireland), ss. 2, 3; Status of Children Act (Northern Territory of Australia) 2004, ss. 11, 16.

22. See, e.g., id., s. 11 ("the Court may refuse to hear an application for a declaration of paternity if it is of opinion that it is not just or proper to do so"); Carbone and Cahn, "Which Ties Bind?" 1056–60, 1064 (citing court decisions in Pennsylvania and New York).

23. *Michael H. v. Gerald D.*, 491 U.S. 110, 123 (1989).

24. Irish Status of Children Act 1987, ss. 10, 12. Many U.S. states have retained in their laws other bases of presumed fatherhood, such as the man's having taken a child into his home and treated the child as his, but these are less commonly invoked today and can be rebutted with genetic evidence. England has also retained some such presumptions. See Herring, *Family Law*, 267–8.

25. Irish Children Act 1997, s. 6.

26. Susanne Storm et al., "Denmark," in Pintens, *International Encyclopedia*, 94.

27. Hamilton and Perry, *Family Law in Europe*, 317–18; *Nekvedavicius v. Germany*, (2004) 38 EHRR CD1 (stating that under German law since 1998, "parents of a minor child born out of wedlock jointly exercise custody if they make a declaration to that effect (declaration of joint custody) or if they marry" and that "a child is entitled to have access to both parents").

28. See Murphy, "Legal Images of Fatherhood," (U.S.); Herring, *Family Law*, 308–10 (England and Wales).

29. For discussion of the social scientific literature on the value for a child of being raised by his or her biological parents, see Fortin, *Children's Rights*, 383–93. Further references are noted in Chapter 8.

30. See Nancy E. Dowd, *Redefining Fatherhood* (New York: New York University Press, 2000), 30 (noting that only one fourth of nonmarital children are born to a cohabiting couple).

31. (2000) ECHR 32842/96.

32. See David L. Hudson, Jr., "A Dad Is as a Dad Does: Child's Best Interests Trump Father's Biological Connection," *ABA Journal E-Report* 3(10), 4.

33. See Inman, "How Will It Play in New York?" (describing cases).

34. Cf. *Frette v. France*, (2002) ECHR 36515/97, ¶ 32 ("the [European Human Rights] Convention does not guarantee the right to adopt . . . the right to respect for family life presupposes the existence of a family and does not safeguard the mere desire to found a family").

35. This rule is embodied in Article 8 of the European Convention on the Adoption of Children, 634 U.N.T.S. 255 (1967), to which eighteen states, including the United Kingdom, are parties. See also Adoption and Children Act 2002 (England), ss. 1–(2), (6); Herring, *Family Law*, 538 (England and Wales); Irish Adoption Act 1974, s. 2 ("welfare of the child . . . the first and paramount consideration"); New South Wales Adoption of Children Act 1965, ss. 17, 21. This standard applies to international adoptions as well as domestic adoptions. See Convention on Protection of Children and Co-operation in Respect of Intercountry Adoption, Article 4, S. Treaty Doc. No. 105–51, 32 I.L.M. 1134 (1993), to which more than fifty states are parties.

36. Herring, *Family Law*, 529, 535; New South Wales Adoption of Children Act 1965, s. 21.

37. See Alastair Bissett-Johnson, "Recent Developments and Problems in Scottish Children's Law," in Gareth Miller, *Frontiers of Family Law* (Burlington, VT: Ashgate, 2003), 62 (indicating age of consent to adoption is twelve in Scotland and seven in Ontario, Canada); Children and Family Services Act S.N.S. 1990 (Nova Scotia), Art. 74 (twelve); Herring, *Family Law*, 542 (indicating that there is no legal requirement in England and Wales that an older child consent but that as a matter of practice courts are unlikely to order an adoption over the objection of an older child); Adoption of Children Act (Northern Territory of Australia) 1994, s. 10(2).

38. See Robin Fretwell Wilson, "A Review of From Partners to Parents: The Second Revolution in Family Law, by June Carbone," *Family Law Quarterly* 35 (2002), 841

(summarizing studies); Herring, *Family Law*, 527 (citing sources).

39. Herring, *Family Law*, 533; Adoption and Children Act 2002 (England), s. 50; Irish Adoption Act 1991, s. 10-(5)(a).

40. See French Civil Code, Arts. 343, 343–1.

41. See, e.g., European Convention on the Adoption of Children, Article 9, 634 U.N.T.S. 255 (1967) (eighteen state parties); Herring, *Family Law*, 529 (discussing examination of would-be adopters by local "adoption panels"); Adoption and Children Act 2002 (England), ss. 42–45.

42. Herring, *Family Law*, 529, 535–6.

43. See Adoption and Children Act 2002 (England), s. 19. In Ireland, such placements are restricted to relatives of the child. Adoption Act 1998 (Ireland), s. 7.

44. See Herring, *Family Law*, 537; Adoption and Children Act 2002 (England), ss. 32, 52; Application of A and B, 2000 NSW Lexis 172, *10, 20–21 (Supreme Court of New South Wales, 2000) (arguing that the interests of surrogate mothers should be a prominent consideration in public policy analysis of adoption petitions predicated on a surrogacy contract). In Ireland, the High Court has authority to approve an adoption despite a birth parent's revocation of consent, on the grounds that doing so would be in the child's best interests, but the governing statute does not mandate that action. Adoption Act 1974 (Ireland), s. 3.

45. In Europe, the Convention on the Adoption of Children, in Article 6, precludes both members of a same-sex couple from adopting unless they are "married" to each other, which presently could occur only in the Netherlands, Belgium, and Spain. See also Herring, *Family Law*, 533–4 (to adopt together in England, a couple must be married); Adoption Act 1991 (Ireland), s. 10 (court may not order adoption by more than one person except in the case of a married couple).

46. See Herring, *Family Law*, 541 (noting court decision holding that homosexuality is not a bar to individual adopting).

47. See *Lofton v. Secretary of Dept. of Children and Family Services*, 358 F.3d 804 (11th Cir. 2004); *Frette v. France*, 36515/97 (2002) ECHR 156 (upholding the law in France against challenge under Articles 8 and 14 of the Convention on Human Rights).

48. The law in Ireland is unclear on this matter. An applicant ordinarily must be of the same religion as the birth parents. Adoption Act 1952 (Ireland), s. 12.

49. Herring, *Family Law*, 541.

50. Adoption and Children Act 2002 (England), s. 1 – (5).

51. See Elizabeth Bartholet, "The Challenge of Children's Rights Advocacy: Problems and Progress in the Area of Child Abuse and Neglect," *Whittier Journal of Child and Family Advocacy* 3 (2004b), 223–5 (citing a federal government report on a county in Ohio); Herring, *Family Law*, 527.

52. See Bartholet, "Challenge of Children's Rights Advocacy," 224–6 (citing a government report finding numerous such cases in one county and citing a recent study showing the willingness of a substantial percentage of white applicants for adoption to adopt African-American children from the child protective system).

53. See, e.g., Dorothy Roberts, *Shattered Bonds*, vii, ix.

54. See Wilson, "Review of Partners to Parents," 841–84; Robin Fretwell Wilson, "Children at Risk: The Sexual Exploitation of Female Children after Divorce," *Cornell Law Review* 86 (2001), 251.

55. Adoption laws generally provide that adoption of a child by someone other than an existing parent's spouse works a termination of the existing parent's rights with respect to the child. See Michael T. Morley et al., "Developments in Law and Policy: Emerging Issues in Family Law," *Yale Law & Policy Review* 21 (2003), 200.

56. Adoption and Children Act 2002 (England), ss. 46-(3), 51. Section 68 of the Act makes explicit reference to same-sex couples adopting.

57. See *K.M. v. E.G.*, No. S125643 (Cal., 2005) (birth mother and partner who supplied the ova both legal parents); *Elisa B. v. Emily B.*, No. S125912 (Cal. 2005) (conferring legal parenthood on both birth mother and partner, who supported artificial insemination of birth mother, agreed to raise the child jointly, and received child into her home and

held child out as her own); *Kristine H. v. Lisa R.*, No. 126945 (Cal. 2005) (birth mother and partner both parents because birth mother estopped from attacking validity of stipulation she agreed to during pregnancy).

58. See Canadian Divorce Act 1985, s. 18-(8); Ontario Children's Law Reform Act, R.S.O. 1990, ch. C.12, Art. 24; Hamilton and Perry, *Family Law in Europe*, 245 (Finland).

59. Fortin, *Children's Rights*, 247–8; Australian Family Law Act 1975, s. 68F; Ontario Children's Reform Act, Art. 24(2). With at least one exception, Finland, states' laws generally do not require children's consent per se to a custody arrangement at any age. Fortin, *Children's Rights*, 253.

60. See, e.g., Australian Family Law Act 1975, s. 65E; Irish Guardianship of Infants Act 1964, s. 3.

61. In a 1970 decision involving a dispute between natural parents and long-term foster parents, the English House of Lords clarified that treating the child's welfare as paramount means that other considerations operate only insofar as two alternative courses of action are equally good for the child and should not be balanced against the child's interests. See Douglas, *Introduction to Family Law*, 146–7. One might wonder, though, whether it occurs often enough that two alternatives are equally good for a child such that it makes sense to invite consideration of others' interests.

62. *Gordon v. Geortz*, (1996) 2 SCR 27, ¶ 19.

63. See, e.g., Martha Fineman, "Dominant Discourse, Professional Language, and Legal Change in Child Custody Decisionmaking," *Harvard Law Review* 101 (1988), 773 ("if we value nurturing behavior, then rewarding those who nurture seems only fair").

64. An example found in most family law textbooks is *Burchard v. Garay*, 724 P.2d 486, 494 (Cal. 1986) (Bird, J., concurring) ("Typically, it is the mother who provides most day-to-day care, whether or not she works outside the home. A presumption which ignores this fact is likely to lead to erroneous and unfair decisions.").

65. David L. Chambers, "Rethinking the Substantive Rules for Custody Disputes in Divorce," *Michigan Law Review* 83 (1984), 501.

66. Malcolm C. Kronby, *Canadian Family Law* (8th ed.) (Stoddart, 2001), 88–90. See also id., 92 (describing decision of Saskatchewan court stating that a custodial mother must be permitted to move a child away from the noncustodial parent unless doing so would be clearly detrimental to the child's long-term well-being); *Hollandsworth v. Knyzewski*, 109 S.W.3d (Ark. 2003) (describing the array of positions on the relocation issue among U.S. courts). The MacGyver court also relied in its reasoning on a false assumption, shared by many family law scholars, that an asymmetry exists between custodial parents and noncustodial parents in terms of freedom to move. The reality is that custody rules do not prohibit custodial or noncustodial parents from moving themselves and that a modification rule permitting a change of custody on the basis of a custodial parent's relocation would not create an asymmetry in the time-with-child costs for the two parents in choosing to move themselves. If a noncustodial parent moves a substantial distance and that makes the existing visitation schedule impractical, then the custodial parent can petition for a reduction of the noncustodial parent's time with the child. So either parent's moving could result in his or her having less time with a child. In fact, there is an asymmetry in existing rules that disadvantages noncustodial parents, insofar as they have no basis for seeking to move a child. A custodial mother who wants to relocate has a very good chance of being authorized to move the child with her. A noncustodial father who wants to relocate for career advancement or a new relationship has no chance of getting a court to order that the child move to his new locale.

67. *Gordon v. Geortz*, (1996) 2 SCR 27, ¶ 37. The ECHR and courts in England appear to have adopted a muddled middle ground, by which they posit that all persons affected by a relocation decision have rights at stake that must be balanced and that a custodial parent's rights include both a right to protection of his or her family life and a right to liberty of movement and choice of residence, but then assert that the child's interests must

be treated as primary or paramount, meaning that they override parents' interests and rights. See, e.g., *Payne v. Payne*, (2001) EWCA Civ. 166, (2001) 2 FLR. 1052, ¶¶ 26, 40, 82, 84, 85. Balancing and paramountcy are mutually exclusive approaches to resolving these situations. Balancing entails a willingness to compromise the interests and rights of any party involved where they conflict with weightier interests or rights of others. If children's welfare is assumed always to have greater import, therefore requiring paramountcy, then there is no balancing to be done; you identify the solution(s) consistent with the child's best interests and only if you cannot decide between two potentially best options on child-centered grounds do you give any thought to the interests of others.

68. See, e.g, Fathers & Families website, http://www.fathersandfamilies.org/site/ballot.php, for description of the organization's efforts to pass legislation mandating joint custody between divorcing parents unless one parent is found to be unfit.

69. See, e.g., *Vitek v. Jones*, 445 U.S. 480 (1980) (holding unconstitutional a state statute authorizing transfer of a prisoner to a mental hospital based solely on a physician's finding that the prisoner suffered from a mental illness or defect that could not be properly treated in the prison, citing the stigma of placement in a mental hospital); *Addington v. Texas*, 441 U.S. 418 (1979) (recognizing the absence of stigma as an essential element of the constitutional liberty interest of persons being treated involuntarily for mental health problems); *Loving v. Virginia*, 388 U.S. 1 (1966) (striking down a state ban on interracial marriage, based primarily on a finding that the ban communicated a message of minority-race inferiority); *Brown v. Bd. of Education*, 387 U.S. 483, 494 n. 11 (1954) (holding unconstitutional racial segregation in schooling, based in part on a finding that separation per se had a harmful stigmatizing effect on African-American children). Conversely, the U.S. Supreme Court has also said in other contexts, as it did in *Palmore*, that the law should not give effect to private biases. See, e.g., *City of Cleburne, Texas v. Cleburne Living Center*, 473 U.S. 432, 448 (1985) (rejecting

fears and prejudices of community regarding mentally disabled persons as a legitimate basis for imposing a special use permit requirement only on group homes for such persons).

70. *Van de Perre v. Edwards*, (2001) 2 SCR 1014, ¶¶ 38, 40, 42–3.

71. 899 So.2d 904, 911 (Miss. App. 2005) ("For over a century, our courts have considered a parent's involvement in the 'moral and religious training' to determine custody.... In this case, the record shows that Coit regularly takes the children to church. Thus, there was evidence to support the chancellor's decision to weigh the moral fitness factor in his favor").

72. *Hoffmann v. Austria*, (1993) 225 ECHR (ser. A).

73. Herring, *Family Law*, 413–14; Canadian Divorce Act 1985, s. 16-(9); Ontario Children's Law Reform Act, Art. 24(3); Family Relations Act, R.S.B.C. 1996 (British Columbia), § 24(3) ("If the conduct of a person does not substantially affect a factor set out in [subsection listing best interests considerations], the court must not consider that conduct").

74. See, e.g., 899 So.2d at 911 ("It is well settled that the court can consider a homosexual lifestyle as a factor relevant to the custody determination of the child, as long as it is not the sole factor").

75. Ex parte H.H., 830 So. 2d 21, 37 (Ala. 2002). See also *Hertzler v. Hertzler*, 908 P.2d 946 (Wyo. 1995) (affirming a trial court decision based on similar sentiments).

76. Herring, *Family Law*, 414 (discussing *Da Silva Mouta v. Portugal*).

77. Kronby, *Canadian Family Law*, 66.

78. See, e.g., Hamilton and Perry, *Family Law in Europe*, 87 (noncustodial parent in Denmark has a right to visitation), 280–1 (same in France).

79. *Glaser v. United Kingdom*, (2000) ECHR 32346/96, ¶ 66 ("Where contacts with the parent might appear to threaten [children's] interests or interfere with [children's] rights, it is for the national authorities to strike a fair balance between them"), ¶ 70 ("Their decision-making process must inevitably involve a balancing of the respective interests, as coercive measures may in themselves present a risk of damage to the

children concerned"). See also *Kosmopoulou v. Greece*, (2004) ECHR 60457/00, ¶¶ 45, 46. Cf. *Nekvedavicius v. Germany*, (2004) 38 EHRR CD1 (upholding a decision of German courts to deny access to an unwed father on the grounds that this would be contrary to the child's best interests).

80. Herring, *Family Law*, 427–8; Hamilton and Perry, *Family Law in Europe*, 389–90, 397 (welfare of child controls resolution of unwed father's petition for custody or access in Ireland); Irish Children Act 1991, s. 9 (applying this standard to all parent requests for custody or access). But see Liz Trinder, "Contact after Divorce: What Has the Law to Offer?" in Miller, *Frontiers of Family Law*, 23 (stating that courts applying the Children Act 1989 in England have made a presumption of contact with a noncustodial parent into a legal rule).

81. Hamilton and Perry, *Family Law in Europe*, 317 (Germany), 245–6 (Finland).

82. *Nekvedavicius v. Germany*, (2004) 38 EHRR CD 1. See also Herring, *Family Law*, 432–3 (referring to earlier decisions of the Court).

83. Kronby, *Canadian Family Law*, 67–8.

84. In Switzerland, by way of contrast, the standard order provides, according to one source, shockingly little time with the noncustodial parent – "between half a day and one day per month." Hamilton and Perry, *Family Law in Europe*, 693.

85. See Herring, *Family Law*, 386–7; Freeman, *Moral Status of Children*, 158 (finding no precedent in any common law country for a court ordering a parent to spend time with a child); Solangel Maldonado, "Beyond Economic Fatherhood: Encouraging Divorced Fathers to Parent," *University of Pennsylvania Law Review* 153 (2005), 941 (discussing U.S. law). Maldonado contends that it would be good social policy to encourage parents who do not have physical custody of a child after divorce to spend time with their children and suggests a presumption of joint legal custody as a way to do this, but stops short of suggesting compulsory visitation.

86. See Katharine T. Bartlett, "Rethinking Parenthood as an Exclusive Status: The Need for Legal Alternatives When the Premise of the Nuclear Family Has Failed," *Virginia Law Review* 70 (1984), 879.

87. See Herring, *Family Law*, 283, 285, 286 (England and Wales); Hamilton and Perry, *Family Law in Europe*, 143 (England and Wales); Canadian Divorce Act 1985, ss. 16-(1), (3) (requiring leave of the court for a nonparent to petition for custody); Australian Family Law Act 1975, s. 65C (authorizing "any other person concerned with the care, welfare or development of the child" to apply for a parenting order).

88. See *V.C. v. M.J.B.*, 748 A.2d 539 (N.J. 2000) (applying this standard and citing statutes in other states); Canadian Divorce Act 1985, s. 16; Australian Family Law Act 1975, ss. 65C, 65E. Malcolm Kronby asserts, however, that in Canada, a nonparent will, in practice, not receive custody unless the legal parents have abandoned the child or otherwise behaved very badly. Kronby, *Canadian Family Law*, 64.

89. Fortin, *Children's Rights*, 382.

90. See Irish Guardianship of Infants Act 1964, s. 10 (announcing entitlement of "guardians" to custody of a child as against nonguardians), s. 16 (allowing guardian to recover custody after leaving child in care of another so long as parent is "fit").

91. Herring, *Family Law*, 280. But see Hamilton and Perry, *Family Law in Europe*, 143 (stating that the child's welfare is the paramount concern for courts in England deciding any petition for a residence order).

92. See Barbara Bennett Woodhouse, "Horton Looks at the ALI Principles," *Journal of Law and Family Studies* 4 (2002), 162:

[G]ood foster parenting ripens into real parenthood. Our past policy of asking care-givers to raise a child over many years, while precluding them from forming a parent-child relationship, placed bureaucratic convenience and parents' abstract rights of possession above continuity and stability for children. This detached stance simply does not work for kids – especially young kids. . . . After fifteen months, a foster mother has often become simply Mother.

Constitutional challenges in the United States to disruption of the foster parent–child relationship have generally failed, because courts deem de facto caregiver–child social relationships less deserving of constitutional protection than natural parents' claims on their offspring. See, e.g., *Smith v. Organization of Foster Families*, 431 U.S. 816, 844–47 (1977) (concluding, in addressing foster parents' challenge to procedures for returning children to legal parents, that foster care relationships give rise only to a very limited "liberty" interest under the U.S. Constitution, much less than that to which legal parent–child relationships give rise).

93. Herring, *Family Law*, 479–86; Children and Young Persons Act 1968 (Northern Ireland), ss. 93, 95; Irish Child Care Act 1991, ss. 12, 13, 18. Some jurisdictions require simply "harm" or specified abusive acts. See, e.g., Child and Family Services Act 1990 (Ontario), ss. 37.(2), 51.(3).

94. Va. Code Ann. § 16.1-252(E) (2005).

95. See, e.g., *L. v. Finland*, (2000) ECHR 25651/94, 31 EHRR 737 (2000), ¶ 122 ("a fair balance has to be struck between the interests of the child in remaining in public care and those of the parent in being reunited with the child . . .). See also id., ¶ 122 ("the parent cannot be entitled under Article 8 of the Convention to have such measures taken as would harm the child's health and development"); *Kutzner v. Germany*, (2002) ECHR 46544/99, ¶ 69 ("the fact that a child could be placed in a more beneficial environment for his or her upbringing will not on its own justify a compulsory measure of removal from the care of the biological parents").

96. Child and Family Services Act 1990 (Ontario), s. 61.(6).

97. *L. v. Finland*, 31 EHRR 737 (2000), ¶ ¶ 113–14.

98. Hamilton and Perry, *Family Law in Europe*, 317.

99. See Melanie B. Jacobs, "Micah Has One Mommy and One Legal Stranger: Adjudicating Maternity for Nonbiological Lesbian Coparents," *Buffalo Law Review* 50 (2002), 341; Nancy D. Polikoff, "This Child Does Have Two Mothers: Redefining Parenthood to Meet the Needs of Children in Lesbian-Mother and Other Nontraditional Families," *Georegetown Law Journal* 78 (1990), 459.

100. *Heltzel v. Heltzel*, 638 N.W.2d 123, 135 (Mich. Ct. App. 2001).

101. See, e.g., Herring, *Family Law*, 543 (citing decision of English court in *Re E* (1989)

and statutory provision); *Quilloin v. Walcott*, 434 U.S. 246, 255 (1978) ("We have little doubt that the Due Process Clause would be offended '[i]f a State were to attempt to force the breakup of a natural family, over the objections of the parents and their children, without some showing of unfitness and for the sole reason that to do so was thought to be in the children's best interest'"). But see 434 U.S. at 255 ("Whatever might be required in other situations, we cannot say that the State was required in this situation [i.e., a step-parent adoption where the objecting biological father had never had custody of the child] to find anything more than that the adoption, and denial of legitimation, were in the 'best interests of the child'").

102. See, e.g., Dorothy Roberts, *Shattered Bond*; Martin Guggenheim, "Somebody's Children: Sustaining the Family's Place in Child Welfare Policy," *Harvard Law Review* 113 (2000), 1734; Jane C. Murphy, "Legal Images of Motherhood: Conflicting Definitions from Welfare 'Reform,' Family, and Criminal Law," *Cornell Law Review* 83 (1998), 702–23; Kathleen A. Bailie, "The Other 'Neglected' Parties in Child Protective Proceedings: Parents in Poverty and the Role of the Lawyers Who Represent Them," *Fordham Law Review* 66 (1998), 2285.

103. See Anne Griffiths and Randy F. Kandel, "Legislating for the Child's Voice: Perspectives from Comparative Ethnography of Proceedings Involving Children," in Maclean, ed., *Making Law for Families* (Hart, 2000), 164 (discussing Scotland).

104. See Patrick Parkinson, "Child Protection, Permanency Planning and Children's Right to Family Life," *International Journal of Law, Policy and the Family* 17 (2003), 147. Parkinson criticizes ASFA and the efforts to replicate it in Britain and Australia, but on grounds that do not go to the heart of ASFA. He points out the potential harm to older children of severing all their ties to the birth family, which suggests a need simply to consider children's interests in continuity when courts make an individualized assessment of whether termination is in a child's best interests, as ASFA allows. It also suggests a policy of encouraging or even sometimes requiring open adoption, and ASFA does not

rule that out. Parkinson also points out that for some children an option other than adoption or return to parents might be best, but ASFA does not rule out such things as special guardianship or permanent foster care. He notes that a proadoption stance might deter parents from seeking help when they have problems, but he does not explain how the prospect of adoption would be more of a deterrent to self-initiated remediation than the prospect of removal and long-term foster care under existing law. It might be if adoption entails complete severance of ties, although foster care typically does not, but then the response to the concern about children's identity above would apply – namely an existing tie is a reason not to terminate, and a proadoption policy is not inconsistent with a pro-open-adoption policy. He also notes that adoptive parents receive less financial support than foster parents for dealing with the special needs of abused and neglected children. The cure for that problem, though, would be to change the rules for such support, and it would be cost-effective for the state to do that if doing so facilitates more adoptions. Last, Parkinson notes the objection of some in Australia that the proadoption legislation proposed in New South Wales was insensitive to the history of forced removal of children from aboriginal and Torres Strait Islander communities, given that today children from those communities are overrepresented in the foster care population. But that is not, at least as described by Parkinson, a child-centered concern. One valid criticism Parkinson offers in closing is that aggregate state outcomes mandated by ASFA and England's Adoption of Children Act, tying top-down assistance to meeting targets for number of adoptions per year, could induce termination and adoption in some cases when it is not best for children. One might add that the targets create a financial disincentive to implementing policies aimed at reducing the need for termination and adoption and that state agencies already have a large financial incentive to reduce their foster care roles (i.e., the cost of foster care) and so do not need the extra inducement. But the targets are incidental to the law, not essential.

105. Herring, *Family Law*, 544–7; Adoption Act 1998 (Ireland), s. 4 (requiring, except in limited circumstances, "consultation" of the biological father before approving an adoption and authorizing any father who objects to the adoption to apply to a court for an order preventing the adoption and granting him custody) and Adoption Act 1988 (Ireland), s. 3 (court must first find parent has failed to fulfill duties for over a year, parent is likely to continue to fail to do so for the rest of the child's minority, and failure amounts to abandonment, before considering whether adoption would be in child's best interests); Hamilton and Perry, *Family Law in Europe*, 321 (German law requires "either grave or consistent violations of parental duties, or callousness by the natural parents"); Kronby, *Canadian Family Law*, 85 (Canada); Children and Family Services Act S.N.S. 1990 (Nova Scotia), Art. 75(4). In England and in a few U.S. states, there is a possibility for dispensing with consent that is "unreasonably withheld," and the predominant interpretation of that standard in England is the peculiar one that consent is unreasonably withheld where a hypothetical reasonable parent in the shoes of the parent in question would consent to the adoption, a conclusion arrived at by giving some, but not necessarily great, weight to the welfare of the child. A recent alternative that surfaced would have courts consider whether the benefits of adoption for the child are great enough to justify overriding the interest of the objecting parent. Herring (2001), 544–6.

106. See Archbold, "Family Law-Making," 199 (citing and describing decision).

107. Woodhouse, "ALI Principles," 153.

108. See Ellen Marrus, "'Where Have You Been, Fran?': The Right of Siblings to Seek Court Access to Override Parental Denial of Visitation," *Tennessee Law Review* 66 (1999), 977.

109. See, e.g., Hamilton and Perry, *Family Law in Europe*, 320.

110. See William Wesley Patton, "The Status of Siblings' Rights: A View into the New Millenium," *DePaul Law Review* 51 (2001), 1.

111. See Beaudry, Simard, Drapeau, and Charbonneau, "What Happens to the Sibling Subsystem Following Parental Divorce?" in

C. Violato, E. Oddone-Paulucci, and M. Genuis, eds., *The Changing Family and Child Development* (Aldershot: Ashgate, 2000), 105–16.

112. For discussion of state decision making regarding removal, see Ellen Marrus, "Fostering Family Ties: The State as Maker and Breaker of Kinship Relationships," *University of Chicago Legal Forum* 2004 (2004), 319.

113. I argued that this is the proper characterization of the moral foundation of parental legal authority in a prior work. See James G. Dwyer, *Religious Schools v. Children's Rights* (Cornell University Press, 1998), ch. 3.

114. See, e.g., Ontario Children's Law Reform Act, Art. 20(2).

115. Hamilton and Perry, *Family Law in Europe*, 650.

116. See Hamilton and Perry, *Family Law in Europe*, 28 (grandparents and other third parties in Austria), 279 (grandparents and, in more limited circumstances, other third parties, in France), 317 (grandparents and other third parties in Germany if the latter previously lived with the child for substantial period); Irish Children Act 1997, s. 9 (any relative or any person who has acted *in loco parentis* to the child may petition if granted leave to do so by a court); Canadian Divorce Act 1985, s. 16 (any party, with leave of the court).

117. 530 U.S. 57 (2000).

118. See Hamilton and Perry, *Family Law in Europe*, 279 (courts in France may refuse grandparent request for access to grandchildren only for "grave cause").

119. See *Marckx v. Belgium*, (1979) ECHR 6833/74, ¶ 45.

120. Herring, *Family Law*, 287.

121. See Hamilton and Perry, *Family Law in Europe*, 279 (France), 317 (Germany). The statutory rule in Ontario contains no such restrictions. Ontario Children's Law Reform Act, Art. 21.

3. Paradigmatic Relationship Rights

1. Arguably all normative reasoning is coherentist at some level. Even one attempting a "foundationalist" moral theory must begin by taking as given some one or more beliefs with normative significance and then exploring the implications of those beliefs and the consistency of those beliefs with others that people hold. And for the theory to be at all plausible, the taken-as-given beliefs must be ones that are widely held. Cf. Thomas Hurka, "Normative Ethics: Back to the Future," in Brian Leiter, ed., *The Future for Philosophy* (Oxford: Clarendon Press, 2005), 256 (noting that foundationalists, like nonfoundationalists who prefer structural analysis, use coherentist reasoning, relying on the consistency of abstract ideas with intuitive judgments about particular issues as evidence for the validity of those ideas). I use the term *coherentist* here to signify an approach that makes no attempt to establish a connection between ultimate conclusions or general principles and bedrock moral "truths" but rather aims only to show that certain general moral beliefs that happen to be widely held and that are clearly reflected in some areas of law commit those who hold those beliefs to accepting certain conclusions in another area of law, conclusions that might be at odds with their existing views about the latter area of law. This approach bears close resemblance to the "wide reflective equilibrium" method of ethical analysis, which is the dominant mode of ethical philosophizing today. For explanation and defense of this sort of methodology, see John Rawls, "Justice as Fairness: Political Not Metaphysical," *Philosophy and Public Affairs* 14 (1985), 228–31; Allen Buchanan, Dan W. Brock, Norman Daniels, and Daniel Wikler, *From Chance to Choice: Genetics and Justice* (Cambridge, UK: Cambridge University Press, 2000), 371–8; Michael R. DePaul and William Ramsey, *Rethinking Intuition: The Psychology of Intuition and Its Role in Philosophical Inquiry* (Lanham, MD: Rowman & Littlefield, 1998); and Hurka, "Normative Ethics," 261–3. It does not entail an assumption that the ultimate basis for moral beliefs can only be intuition; rather, it treats that meta-ethical issue as irrelevant. Cf. Hurka, "Normative Ethics," 262 ("Whatever metaethics decides, the practice of making moral judgments will continue essentially as before"). Consistent with the reflective equilibrium approach, I accept that more

general principles, as well as specific beliefs, are subject to revision, if it turns out that some more specific beliefs that are inconsistent with widely held general principles have too great a rational or intuitive hold on us to abandon them. As demonstrated in Chapter 2, in the case of children's relationships, the specific legal rules and underlying moral beliefs I challenge are relatively unstable; they are frequently criticized in the scholarly literature concerning, and in public debate over, highly publicized controversies.

2. See, e.g., American Declaration of the Rights and Duties of Man, O.A.S. Res. XXX, Ninth International Conference of American States, 43 Am. J. Int'l L. 133 (1948), Article VI ("Every person has the right to establish a family, the basic element of society, and to receive protection therefore."); Charter of Fundamental Rights of the European Union, 2000 O.J. (C.364) 1 (2000), Article 9 ("The right to marry and the right to found a family shall be guaranteed . . . ").

3. See, e.g., American Convention on Human Rights, S. Exec. Doc. F, 95–2, 1144 U.N.T.S. 123 (1969), Article 17(3) ("No marriage shall be entered into without the free and full consent of the intending spouse").

4. This principle operates, of course, against a historical and cross-cultural context in which some societies at some points in their histories have allowed the practice of arranged marriages, by which young people were forced into intimate associations not of their choosing. International condemnation of this practice dates back at least to 1962, when the Convention on Consent to Marriage, Minimum Age for Marriage and Registration of Marriages, 521 U.N.T.S. 231, to which fifty nations are parties, was promulgated.

5. The closest the law comes to creating an exception is in the criminal context, where the state takes custody of persons accused and/or convicted of criminal acts and forces them to reside with other such persons. But the compulsion does not extend beyond living together. The state cannot force inmates to socialize or form friendships with other inmates. It might condition certain privileges or promises of early release on having conversations with other people – for example, a

psychologist or a support group. However, it cannot impose additional penalties on them for declining to speak with others, such conversations do not really amount to personal relationships, and in any event, the criminal context is anomalous and not equivalent to the situation of children.

6. The U.S. Supreme Court, in *Roberts v. United States Jaycees*, 468 U.S. 609 (1984), upheld against constitutional challenge by the Jaycees (a social/business organization) a state law prohibiting gender discrimination in public establishments. Significantly, the Court, in holding that the organization had no right under the Due Process Clause that could provide a basis for objecting to the state law and for continuing to refuse membership to women, relied on the fact that the organization did not embody the sort of intimate relationships that characterize the family.

7. Before the 1960s, governments closely regulated marriage dissolution. A divorce was allowed only where a spouse had clearly engaged in an act defined by the state to constitute fault. But in the early 1960s, distaste for public intrusion into the marital relationship led to the decline of the fault system throughout the common-law world and elsewhere. See Laura Bradford, "The Counterrevolution: A Critique of Recent Proposals to Reform No-Fault Divorce Laws," *Stanford Law Review* 49 (1997), 607. Today the divorce statutes of the United States and most other western nations contain some type of no-fault provision that allows either spouse to secure a divorce on the ground simply that the couple is not getting along, which is typically captured by a standard of "irreconcilable differences" or "irretrievable breakdown" or by a period of living separately that could be six months or a few years. Matthew Butler, "Getting Divorced: Grounds for Divorce: A Survey," *Journal of Contemporary Legal Issues* 11 (2000), 164; Carolyn Hamilton and Alison Perry, eds., *Family Law in Europe* (2nd ed.) (London: Butterworths, 2002), 115 (discussing irretrievable breakdown rule in England and Wales and easy evasion of a prescribed two-year waiting period); Canadian Divorce Act 1985, s. 8 (divorce granted upon showing of marital breakdown, which can be evidenced by living

apart for one year). Irreconcilable differences/ irretrievable breakdown as a reason for divorce was not initially expected or intended to result in divorce on demand but rather to reform divorce law so that scrupulous trial courts, not impulsive couples, would determine the right to a divorce. Reformers did not wish that a couple's consent to dissolve their marriage would itself constitute the required establishment of irreconcilable differences. See Elizabeth S. Scott, "Rational Decision-making about Marriage and Divorce," *Virginia Law Review* 76 (1990), 17. But the vision of no-fault conceived by the reformers never materialized and trial courts simply refused to deny divorces under any circumstances. See id., 17–19; J. Herbie DiFonzo, "No-Fault Marital Dissolution: The Bitter Triumph of Naked Divorce," *San Diego Law Review* 31 (1994), 519.

8. Jonathan Herring, *Family Law* (London: Pearson Education, 2001), 82–3.

9. Canadian Divorce Act 1985, s. 9; Herring, *Family Law*, 90.

10. Scott, "Rational Decisionmaking," 17. Of course, many people are critical of this development and urge legal reform to make divorce more difficult to obtain. See id., 10–11.

11. Elizabeth S. Scott and Robert E. Scott, "Parents as Fiduciaries," *Virginia Law Review* 81 (1995), 2464.

12. Id.

13. See Scott, "Rational Decisionmaking," 27 ("That parents have a 'right to divorce' without regard to the possible detriment to their children is taken for granted."); id., 25–37 (describing the harms to children from divorce); Scott and Scott, "Parents as Fiduciaries," 2465. The principal legal mechanism for protecting children in this context is a longer waiting period for divorcing couples with children than for childless couples.

14. See *Goodridge v. Department of Public Health*, 798 N.E.2d 941, 957 n.14 (Mass. 2003) (citations omitted).

15. One restriction in the criminal context is the unavailability of individuals in solitary confinement in prisons. Another is judicial orders against convicted criminals that they not associate with former partners in crime or

that they stay away from individuals or classes of persons whom they have victimized in the past. However, in *Turner v. Safley*, the Supreme Court struck down a prohibition against prisoners marrying other inmates or noninmates, on the grounds that even prisoners have a constitutional right to marry, absent a showing that this would interfere with prison operations. 482 U.S. 78 (1987). In the domestic violence context, civil protective orders will issue in most jurisdictions only if the victim petitions for one, which thereby extinguishes the mutuality of the relationship. In England and Wales, however, a court may issue a protective order on its own initiative. Herring, *Family Law*, 228. Once an order issues, police and prosecutors generally enforce the order regardless of any later change of heart by the victim, unless she successfully petitions the court to terminate the order. In a "first of its kind" case in the United States, prosecutors in Ohio recently charged a victim of domestic violence herself with violating a protective order by inviting her abuser to their child's birthday party. See Adam Liptak, "Ohio Case Considers Whether Abuse Victim Can Violate Own Protective Order," *New York Times*, May 30, 2003.

16. See *Dudgeon v. United Kingdom*, 45 ECHR (ser. A) at 54 (1981).

17. See, e.g., Hamilton and Perry, *Family Law in Europe*, 67 (minimum age of eighteen in Denmark), 102 (sixteen in England and Wales), 258 (fifteen for females and eighteen for males in France), 296 (eighteen in Germany), 363 (eighteen in Ireland), 443 (eighteen in the Netherlands), 525 (sixteen in Portugal), 549 (sixteen in Scotland), 593 (eighteen in Spain), 624 (eighteen in Sweden); Age of Marriage Act 1951 (Northern Ireland), s. 1 (sixteen). In several of these countries, exceptions can be made in certain cases, such as when a girl is pregnant and her parents consent. In Canada, the age of consent varies from sixteen to nineteen, but younger minors who are at least fourteen generally may marry with parental consent. Malcolm C. Kronby, *Canadian Family Law* (8th ed.) (Toronto: Stoddart, 2001), 4.

18. See, e.g., Hamilton and Perry, *Family Law in Europe*, 68 (Denmark). However, the

European Convention on Human Rights does not appear capable of serving as a vehicle for making such recognition uniform throughout Europe, as it reflects a conventional understanding of the family and "leaves signatories a wide margin of appreciation as regards which family forms are accepted as legitimate." Claire Archbold, "Family Law-Making and Human Rights in the United Kingdom," in Mavis Maclean, ed., *Making Law for Families* (Oxford: Hart Publishing, 2000), 192.

19. In nine U.S. states, the court may order counseling on its own initiative, upon petition by one or both parties or upon petition by counsel for a minor child. Ariz. Rev. Stat. § 25–381 (2005), Ind. Code § 31-15-4 (2005), Iowa Code § 598.16 (2005), Conn. Gen. Stat. § 46b–53 (2005), Ohio Rev. Code Ann. § 3105.091 (2005), Utah Code Ann. §§ 30-3-16.2, 30-3-16.7 (2005), Mont. Code Ann. §§ 40-3-111, 40-3-127 (2003), Wash. Rev. Code § 26.09.030 (2005), Neb. Rev. Stat. § 42-360 (2004). In Ohio, if the court orders counseling, the court may refuse to enter a divorce ruling until the couple attends the ordered counseling. Ohio Rev. Code Ann. § 3105.091 (2005). In Vermont, a court has no authority to order but may "suggest" marital counseling. Vt. Stat. Ann. tit. 15, § 552 (2004). In Indiana, the court may "order" the parties to seek marital counseling, but both parties must consent to the counseling, making the court order more of a suggestion than an order. Ind. Code § 31-15-4 (2005).

20. In Connecticut, if the court orders counseling and a party refuses to attend, the court may refuse to act on the divorce action for six months (otherwise the waiting period is ninety days). Conn. Gen. Stat. § 46b–53 (2005). In Utah, Arizona, and Montana, a statutory bar to further divorce proceedings begins when the jurisdiction of a special conciliation court is invoked or when the parties are ordered to attend marital counseling. If a party refuses to attend ordered counseling, divorce proceedings may nevertheless proceed upon expiration of the statutory bar or sooner if the court so orders. The statutory bars are thirty days in Montana and sixty days in Utah and Arizona. Utah Code Ann. §§ 30-3-16.2, 30-3-16.7 (2005), Ariz. Rev. Stat. § 25-381

(2005), Mont. Code Ann. §§ 40-3-111, 40-3-127 (2003).

21. See John Parry and F. Philips Gilliam, *Handbook on Mental Disability Law* (Washington, DC: ABA Commission on Mental and Physical Disability Law, 2002), 3, 59.

22. Uniform Probate Code § 5-103(7).

23. See, e.g., Mich. Comp. Laws § 700.5314 (2005), Va. Code Ann. § 37.1-134.6 (2005) ("'Guardian' means a person appointed by the court who is responsible for the personal affairs of an incapacitated person, including responsibility for making decisions regarding the person's support, care, health, safety, habilitation, education, and therapeutic treatment, and, if not inconsistent with an order of commitment, residence").

24. See, e.g., Va. Stat. § 37.2-1020 (2005); Minn. Stat. § 524.5-313 (2005).

25. See, e.g., Mich. Comp. Laws § 700.5314 (2005); Minn. Stat. § 525.56(3.2), (4.3) (2005).

26. The absence of litigation would be consistent either with a reality that practice almost always conforms to formal rules or with a reality that states make little effort to enforce the rules despite frequent violations. My focus here is on formal rules, which is sufficient for the purpose of uncovering prevailing moral attitudes toward incompetent adults. Admittedly, it is not sufficient for the purpose of determining the feasibility of implementing for incompetent persons a set of rights equivalent to those afforded competent adults. For the latter purpose, we would want to know the rate of compliance and to what extent the state could effectively police noncompliance. I am not aware that anyone has studied these matters with anything approaching scientific rigor. Some observers of the adult guardian system have, however, expressed the view that noncompliance with the legal rules is common. See Parry and Gilliam, *Handbook*, 7; P. B. Tor and Bruce D. Sales, "Research on the Law and Practice of Guardianship," in Bruce D. Sales and Saleem A. Shah, eds., *Mental Health and Law: Research, Policy, and Services* (Durham, NC: Carolina Academic Press, 1996).

27. Tor and Sales, "Guardianship," 81, 93. See, e.g., Alaska Stat. §§ 13.26.113, 47.30.700

(2004); Ariz. Rev. Stat. § 14-5304 (2005); N.Y. Mental Hyg. Law § 81.02 (2005); Ohio Rev. Code Ann. § 2111.01(D) (2005); Va. Code Ann. § 37.1-134.6 (2005).

28. *In re Doe*, 696 N.Y.S.2d 384, 387 (Nassau County 1999).

29. Peter G. Guthrie, "Priority and Preference in Appointment of Conservator or Guardian for an Incompetent," *American Law Reports* 65 (2004), 991, § 14. See, e.g., N.Y. Mental Hyg. Law §§ 81.17, 81.19(b) (2005).

30. Guthrie, "Priority and Preference," §§ 2, 12, 13, 15. See, e.g., 755 Ill. Comp. Stat. § 5/11a-12(d) (2005); N.M. Stat. Ann. § 45-5-311(C)(1) (2005); N.Y. Mental Hyg. Law §§ 81.02, 81.19(c) (2005); *In re Kustka*, 622 N.Y.S.2d 208 (Queens Cty. 1994) ("The court usually gives great weight to the desires of the alleged incapacitated person over whom to appoint as guardian . . . .").

31. See, e.g., Iowa Code § 633.552 (2005); Mich. Comp. Laws §§ 700.5303(1), 700.5404(1) (2005); Neb. Rev. Stat. § 30-2619 (2004); N.J. Stat. § 3B: 12-25 (2005); N.M. Stat. Ann. § 45-5-303 (2005).

32. Guthrie, "Priority and Preference," §§ 6, 7. See, e.g., Ariz. Rev. Stat. § 14-5307 (2005); Ark. Code Ann. § 28-65-204 (2005); N.J. Stat. Ann. § 3B:12-25 (2005).

33. Guthrie, "Priority and Preference," § 9.

34. See, e.g., Ohio Rev. Code Ann. § 2111.01 (2005) (defining "parent" as "a natural or adoptive parent").

35. Guthrie, "Priority and Preference," §§ 2, 4.

36. See, e.g., Ala. Code § 26-2A-104 (2005); Ark. Code Ann. § 28-65-204 (2005); N.Y. Mental Hyg. Law § 81.19(a) (2005); R.I. Gen. Laws § 33-15-6 (2004).

37. N.Y. Mental Hyg. Law § 81.19(d) (2005). Illinois defines the term simply to require that a candidate for guardian be "capable of providing an active and suitable program of guardianship for the disabled person." 755 Ill. Rev. Stat. 5/11a-5(a) (2005).

38. N.Y. Mental Hyg. Law § 81.39(a) (2005).

39. N.Y. Mental Hyg. Law § 81.09(c)(5) (2005).

40. Guthrie, "Priority and Preference," § 6(b). See, e.g., Ariz. Rev. Stat. § 14-5311 (2005); N.M. Stat. Ann. § 45-5-311(C) (2005).

41. See, e.g., N.Y. Mental Hyg. Law § 81.39(b) (2005).

42. Guthrie, "Priority and Preference," §§ 2, 3, 5, 8, 10, 11. See, e.g., Ala. Code § 26-2A-104 (2005); Mass. Gen. Laws Ann. ch. 201, § 6A (2005); N.J. Stat. § 3B:12-25 (2005); N.M. Stat. Ann. § 45-5-311(C) (2005).

43. Ohio Rev. Code Ann. § 5905.05 (2005).

44. 626 N.Y.S.2d 298 (App. Div. 3rd Dept. 1995).

45. See, e.g., *In re Wogelt*, 646 N.Y.S.2d 94 (App. Div. 1st Dept. 1996) (second cousin); In re Bessie C., 639 N.Y.S.2d 234 (App. Div. 4th Dept. 1996) (son and Commissioner of Department of Social Services); 622 N.Y.S.2d at 208 (granddaughter).

46. Parry and Gilliam, *Handbook*, 3, 7, 141–3. See, e.g., Alaska Stat. §§ 13.26.090, 116 (2004); Ark. Code Ann. § 28-65-105 (2005); Idaho Code §§ 15-5-303(a), 15-5-304(a) (2005); Minn. Stat. § 525.56(2) (2005); Mont. Code Ann. § 72-5-312 (2003); N.Y. Mental Hyg. Law §§ 81.01, 81.16(c) (2005); Ore. Rev. Stat. § 125.300(1) (2005). W.V. Code § 44a-1-8 (2005).

47. N.D. Cent. Code § 30.1-26-01 (2003).

48. John Parry, *Mental Disability Law: A Primer* (5th ed.) (Washington, DC: ABA Commission on Mental and Physical Disability Law, 1995), 99–100.

49. *In re M.R.*, 638 A.2d 1274, 1282 (N.J. 1994).

50. N.J. Stat. Ann. § 3B:12-57 (2005). See also Ariz. Rev. Stat. § 14-5312 (2005); Idaho Code § 15-5-312(a) (2005); Mich. Comp. Laws § 700.5314(a) (2005); Mont. Code Ann. § 72-5-321 (2003); N.J. Stat. Ann. §§ 3B: 12-49, 3B: 12-56 (2005); N.M. Stat. Ann. § 45-5-312 (2005); N.Y. Mental Hyg. Law § 81.22(a) (2005); S.C. Code Ann. § 62.5.312 (2004); Va. Code Ann. § 37.1-134.6 (2005).

51. Parry, *Mental Disability Law*, 101–2.

52. See, e.g., Minn. Stat. § 525.56(3.1) (2005); N.J. Stat. Ann. § 3B:12-36 (2005).

53. Tor and Sales, "Guardianship," 96. See, e.g., N.Y. Mental Hyg. Law §§ 81.20(a)(4), 81.31(b)(6) (2005).

54. Cf. Mich. Comp. Laws § 333.20201 (3)(e) (2005) ("A home for the aged resident may be transferred or discharged only for medical reasons, for his or her welfare or that of other residents, or for nonpayment of his or her stay . . . ").

55. N.Y. Mental Hyg. Law § 81.22(a)(9) (2005).

56. *O'Connor v. Donaldson,* 422 U.S. 563 (1975). In connection with this decision, then, the state acts in a *parens patriae* role and/or in a police power role, depending on whom a person of diminished capacity might harm if not committed. Michael L. Perlin, *Mental Disability Law: Civil and Criminal* (2nd ed.) (Charlottesville, VA: LEXIS Law, 1998), 157. In *Addington v. Texas,* 441 U.S. 418 (1979), the Court added that a state must establish the need for institutionalization on grounds of mental illness by "clear and convincing" evidence, rather than the less demanding "preponderance of the evidence" standard that is more common in civil proceedings.

57. *Olmstead v. L.C.,* 527 U.S. 581 (1999).

58. *Youngberg v. Romeo,* 457 U.S. 307, 324 (1982). Significantly, the Supreme Court has held that minors are entitled to much less protection against institutionalization when their parents seek to commit them. *Parham v. J.R.,* 442 U.S. 584 (1979). And lower courts have held that minors are entitled to less than adults in terms of the restrictiveness of their treatment and environment. See, e.g., *Doe v. Public Health Trust of Dade County,* 696 F.2d 901 (11th Cir. 1983). Minors receive the same legal protections as adults, however, when the state seeks to institutionalize them without parental consent.

59. Parry and Gilliam, *Handbook,* 181.

60. See id., 206–7.

61. Id., 176–80; Perlin, *Civil and Criminal,* 159–65, 417–26.

62. Parry and Gilliam, *Handbook,* 59, 166, 202; Michael L. Perlin, *The Hidden Prejudice: Mental Disability on Trial* (Washington, DC: American Psychological Association, 2000), 276–9.

63. *In re Schmidt,* 429 A.2d 631, 636 (Pa. 1981).

64. See Peter Bartlett and Ralph Sandland, *Mental Health Law: Policy and Practice* (London: Blackstone Press, 2000), 52–74.

65. See, e.g., Ala. Code § 26-2-55 (2005); Alaska Stat. §§ 13.26.113(h), 13.26.125 (2004); Ariz. Rev. Stat. § 14-5307 (2005); Mich. Comp. Laws § 700.5310(2) (2005); Neb. Rev. Stat. § 30-2623 (2004); N.J. Stat. Ann. § 3B:12-64 (2005); N.Y. Mental Hyg. Law § 81.36 (2005).

66. See, e.g., Mich. Comp. Laws § 700.5310(1) (2005); N.J. Stat. Ann. § 3B:12-64 (2005); N.Y. Mental Hyg. Law § 81.37 (2005).

67. See, e.g., Mich. Comp. Laws § 700.5312(2) (2005); Minn. Stat. § 525.56(3.2) (2005); N.Y. Mental Hyg. Law § 81.35 (2005).

68. See, e.g., Mich. Comp. Laws §§ 330.1931, 700.5310(2) (2005); Neb. Rev. Stat. § 30-2623; N.J. Stat. Ann. § 30:4-165.15(c) (2005); N.Y. Mental Hyg. Law § 81.35 (2005).

69. See, e.g., Ala. Code § 26-2A-110 (2005); Ariz. Rev. Stat. § 14-5307 (2005).

70. *In re Maher,* 621 N.Y.S.2d 617 (1994).

71. Perlin, *Civil and Criminal,* 417–25; Michael L. Perlin, *Mental Disability Law: Cases and Materials* (Durham, NC: Carolina Academic Press, 1998), 33–5, 74–5.

72. See, e.g., 696 N.Y.S.2d at 387 ("A bad attitude and a fickle nature may not make for an attractive personality, but they do not warrant the deprivation of constitutionally protected rights and liberty").

73. See, e.g., N.Y. Mental Hyg. Law § 81.22(a) (2005).

74. Perlin, *Cases and Materials,* 74–5; Tor and Sales, "Guardianship," 91.

75. Ore. Rev. Stat. § 125.300(1) (2005). See also Alaska Stat. § 13.26.117 (2004); Ariz. Rev. Stat. § 14-5312 (2005); Ark. Code Ann. § 28-65-105 (2005); Ky. Rev. Stat. Ann. § 387.660 (2005); N.Y. Mental Hyg. Law § 81.20 (2005).

76. N.Y. Mental Hyg. Law § 81.20(a)(7) (2005).

77. Parry, *Mental Disability Law,* 99.

78. N.Y. Mental Hyg. Law § 81.20(a) (2005). See also Mass. Gen. Laws ch. 201, § 6A(g) (2005) ("The guardian of a mentally retarded person shall act to protect the welfare of such person . . . "); Mich. Comp. Laws § 700.5314(d)(ii) (2005).

79. See, e.g., Minn. Stat. § 525.56(1) (2005).

80. See, e.g., Mich. Comp. Laws § 700. 5314(e) (2005); N.Y. Mental Hyg. Law §§ 81. 20(a)(4), 81.31(b)(6) (2005).

81. 39 N.W.2d 87 (Mich. 1949).

82. Parry and Gilliam, *Handbook*, 200; Perlin, *Cases and Materials*, 34-6, 128-30.

83. See, e.g., N.J. Stat. Ann. §§ 30:4-24.2(e)(2); 30:4-27.11d(b)(2) (2005).

84. See, e.g., Alaska Stat. § 47.30.840 (2004); Ariz. Rev. Stat. § 36-507 (2005); Ga. Code Ann. § 31-8-114 (2005); Idaho Code §§ 15-5-304(a) (2005); Mich. Comp. Laws § 333.20201(2)(d) (2005); N.J. Stat. Ann. §§ 30:4-24.2(e)(1); 30:4-27.11d(b)(1) (2005).

85. Minn. Stat. § 144.651(19) (2005).

86. Parry and Gilliam, *Handbook*, 200; Perlin, *Cases and Materials*, 130-1, 398–405. See, e.g., Ariz. Rev. Stat. § 36-514 (2005); Fla. Stat. § 394.459 (2005); Haw. Rev. Stat. §§ 334E-2(21), (22) (2004); 410 Ill. Comp. Stat. 50/3.2 (2005); Minn. Stat. §§ 144.651(21), (26), 253B.03(2), (3) (2005); N.J. Stat. Ann. §§ 30:4-24.2(e)(5)–(7), 30:4-27.11d(b)(5)–(7) (2005); Wis. Stat. § 146.95(2)(a) (2005). See also 42 U.S.C. § 9501 (1983) (Federal Mental Health Systems Act, encouraging states to guarantee associational rights to patients in mental health facilities).

87. Mich. Comp. Laws § 333.20201(2)(k) (2005). See also id., § 333.20201(3) (providing detailed rights of visitation for persons in a nursing home or home for the aged).

88. See Perlin, *Cases and Materials*, 398–9, 401–5.

89. *Olmstead v. L.C.*, 527 U.S. 581, 597 (1999).

90. See *Foy v. Greenblott*, 141 Cal. App. 3d 1 (1983); Mont. Code Ann. § 53-21-142(10) (2003); N.J. Stat. Ann. §§ 30:4-24.2(e)(10), 30:4-27.11d(b)(10) (2005); Ohio Rev. Code Ann. §§ 5122.29(I), 5123.62(K) (2005).

91. See, e.g., Ct. Gen. Stat. § 45a-598 (2005); Fla. Stat. § 394.459 (2005); Haw. Rev. Stat. § 334E-2(21) (2004); Minn. Stat. §§ 253B.03(2),(3) (2005); N.J. Stat. Ann. §§ 30:4-24.2(g), 30:4-27.11d(c) (2005); Wis. Stat. § 146.95(2)(b) (2005).

92. See, e.g., id., § 146.95(2)(b)(4).

93. Parry and Gilliam, *Handbook*, 160–1.

94. See, e.g., Ariz. Rev. Stat. § 36-514 (2005); Ct. Gen. Stat. § 45a-598 (2005); Idaho Code § 66-346 (2005).

95. See, e.g., Ct. Gen. Stat. § 45a-598 (2005).

96. See, e.g., Fla. Stat. § 394.459 (2005).

97. See, e.g., Ct. Gen. Stat. § 45a-598 (2005).

98. See, e.g., *Schmidt v. Schmidt*, 459 A.2d 421 (Pa. Super. 1983).

99. See, e.g., Minn. Stat. § 525.56(3.6) (2005).

100. See, e.g., *Murray v. Murray*, 426 S.E.2d 781 (S.C. 1993).

101. David E. Rigney, "Power of Incompetent Spouse's Guardian or Representative to Sue for Granting or Vacation of Divorce or Annulment of Marriage, or to Make Compromise or Settlement in Such Suit," *American Law Reports* 32 (2004), 673, § 5.

102. Id., § 3(b).

103. See, e.g., *Nelson v. Nelson*, 878 P.2d 335 (N.M. App. 1994).

104. Rigney, "Incompetent Spouse's Guardian," §§ 3(a), (c), (d).

105. See, e.g., *Ruvalcaba v. Ruvalcaba*, 850 P.2d 674 (Ariz. App. 1993); *McRae v. McRae*, 250 N.Y.S.2d 778 (1964).

106. Rigney, "Incompetent Spouse's Guardian," §§ 3(a), (c), 4.

4. Why Adults Have the Relationship Rights They Do

1. John Tomasi, *Liberalism beyond Justice: Citizens, Society, and the Boundaries of Political Theory* (Princeton, NJ: Princeton University Press, 2001), 3.

2. See Samuel Freeman, "Illiberal Libertarians: Why Libertarianism Is Not a Liberal View," *Philosophy and Public Affairs* 30 (2002), 111 (noting as the principle contenders for a liberal account of basic rights and liberties persons' "capacities for happiness or desire (as liberal utilitarians may say)," persons' "capacities for reason and freedom (as Kantians claim)," and the supposed fact that "all are created equals by God (as Locke and natural law

theorists contend)"). Cf. Hugo Adam Bedau, "Why Do We Have the Rights We Do?" *Social Philosophy and Policy* 1 (1984), 71 ("The best explanation for the human rights we have must take its cue from the role these rights play in our lives ... Human rights, like other rights, are themselves not ends or intrinsic goods; rather they are instruments or conditions of such goods ... "). Of course, any given theory might assign importance to both of these values, welfare and autonomy, as well as to others. For example, Mill's utilitarianism, discussed immediately below, assigned ultimate value to welfare but viewed exercise of the higher human capacities, including those we would understand as constituting autonomy, as a large component of human welfare. See Freeman, "Illiberal Libertarians," 106.

3. I gloss over here points of contention among rival versions of utilitarianism. For a more nuanced description of utilitarianism, and of its various iterations and difficulties, see Will Kymlicka, Contemporary Political Philosophy (2nd ed.) (Oxford: Oxford University Press, 2002), 10–48. Kymlicka contrasts what he regards as a more plausible understanding of utilitarianism, as a procedure for fairly advancing the interests and preferences of existing members of society, with what he deems an implausible theory often attributed to utilitarians by their critics, under which the aim is to maximize utility per se – that is, to create a state of affairs in which there is as much happiness or preference-satisfaction in the world as there can possibly be, regardless of how it is distributed and regardless of the effect on particular individuals.

4. John Stuart Mill, *On Liberty* (1859) (Cambridge, MA: Hackett, 1978), 9.

5. Id., 12.

6. E.g., id., 75 (right to refuse association), 102–3 (freedom of childless couples to divorce, wives' self-determination), 107.

7. Neil MacCormick, *Legal Right and Social Democracy: Essays in Legal and Political Philosophy* (Oxford: Clarendon Press, 1982), 162. See also Mill, *On Liberty*, 55, 64–5, 74–5, 81 ("the strongest of all the arguments against the interference of the public with purely personal conduct is that, when it does interfere, the odds are that it interferes wrongly and in the wrong place"), 95.

8. Gerald Dworkin points out that even many utilitarians have criticized Mill's assumption that most adults are the best judges of their own interests. See Gerald Dworkin, "Paternalism," in Richard A. Wasserstrom, ed., *Morality and the Law* (Belmont, CA: Wadsworth, 1971), 15.

9. See Gerald Dworkin, "Consent, Representation, and Proxy Consent," in Willard Gaylin and Ruth Macklin, eds., *Who Speaks for the Child: The Problems of Proxy Consent* (Plenum, 1982), 207. There is a tension in this respect between Mill's political philosophy and his moral theory, as the latter held that individual moral agents are always under an obligation to act so as to advance aggregate welfare rather than (just) their own welfare, a position often criticized as being too demanding.

10. See Elizabeth Scott, "Rational Decisionmaking about Marriage and Divorce," *Virginia Law Review* 76 (1990), 9, 12, 20–2.

11. See Samantha Brennan, "Children's Choices or Children's Interests: Which Do Their Rights Protect?" in David Archard and Colin M. Macleod, eds., *The Moral and Political Status of Children* (Oxford: Oxford University Press, 2002), 64; James Griffin, "Towards a Substantive Theory of Rights," in R. G. Frey, ed., *Utility and Rights* (Minneapolis: University of Minnesota Press, 1984), 141, 148; Mill, *On Liberty*, 108. Mill believed this sort of pleasure to be of a different, and higher, kind than physical pleasures and pedestrian amusements. John Stuart Mill, *Utilitarianism* (1861), (New York: Macmillan, 1957), ch. 2. Immanuel Kant in his early writings emphasized this gratification as the basis of the value of autonomy. See Paul Guyer, "Kant on the Theory and Practice of Autonomy," in E. Paul, F. Miller, and J. Paul, eds., *Autonomy* (New York: Cambridge University Press, 2003), 81–5.

12. See Griffin, "Substantive Theory," 150 ("We value our status as persons and want to live recognizably human lives, and liberty is an indispensable condition for that. But then liberty, like autonomy, can be fitted into the scheme of our preferences, and its

value explained by its place there."); Dworkin, "Consent, Representation, and Proxy Consent," 203.

13. Mill, *On Liberty*, 56. There is also a perfectionist strain in Mill's defense of liberty, particularly in discussing freedom of thought and expression, suggesting that Mill assigned intrinsic value to this sort of personal growth. Mill might be read to argue that affording humans ample liberty will better allow them to realize their higher natures and to pursue human excellence. E.g., id., 56, 60–1, 75.

14. E.g., id., 54, 61–2, 67, 108.

15. Id., 108–13.

16. Mill, *On Liberty*, 103.

17. Colin M. Macleod, "Liberal Equality and the Affective Family," in David Archard and Colin M. Macleod, eds., *The Moral and Political Status of Children* (Oxford: Oxford University Press, 2002), 215–16.

18. *Roberts v. United States Jaycees*, 468 U.S. 609, 618–20 (1984) (citations omitted).

19. Paul H. Wright, "The Essence of Personal Relationships and Their Value for the Individual," in George Graham and Hugh LaFollette, eds., *Person to Person* (Temple University Press, 1989), 18.

20. Wright, "Essence of Relationships," 20.

21. See Neera K. Badhwar, "Love," in Hugh LaFollette, ed., *The Oxford Handbook of Practical Ethics* (Oxford: Oxford University Press, 2003), 42–69.

22. Wright, "Essence of Relationships," 25.

23. See, e.g., European Convention on Human Rights, Article 8 (establishing a right to respect for family life); *Stanley v. Illinois*, 405 U.S. 645 (1972) (giving constitutional protection to a social parent–child relationship); *Loving v. Virginia*, 388 U.S. 1, 12 (1967) ("The freedom to marry has long been recognized as one of the vital personal rights essential to the orderly pursuit of happiness").

24. Macleod, "Liberal Equality," 216.

25. Barry McCarthy, "Adult Friendships," in Graham and LaFollette, *Person to Person*, 32–45.

26. See Peter Singer, *Practical Ethics* (Cambridge, UK: Cambridge University Press, 1979), 83 ("There is a strand of ethical thought, associated with Kant but including many modern writers who are not Kantians,

according to which respect for autonomy is a basic moral principle."). As widespread is the view that autonomy is inherently valuable, rather than merely instrumentally valuable in achieving some other end such as happiness, it proves rather difficult to justify the view rationally. Donald Regan concludes that it is not possible to justify assignment of ultimate value to autonomy in the abstract – that is, independent of some standard of value, some idea of what is good and what is bad between which an autonomous agent can choose. Donald H. Regan, "The Value of Rational Nature," *Ethics* 112 (2002), 267–91. Thomas Hurka attempts to defend the intuition that autonomy is intrinsically good "by connecting it to deeper values, in this case the values of agency," behind which is "a more general value of relation-to-the-world." Thomas Hurka, "Why Value Autonomy?" *Social Theory and Practice* 13 (1987), 371. It is not clear, though, whether this in fact makes autonomy only instrumentally valuable, because it serves such other, deeper values, or whether instead Hurka is contending that autonomy is a component or manifestation of agency and of relation-to-the-world, in which case we might expect him to establish why agency – by which he means "causal efficacy" or "making a causal impact on the world and determining facts about it," id., 366 – and a particular way of relating to the world that entails altering it, are intrinsically valuable.

27. Steven Wall, "Freedom as a Political Ideal," in E. Paul, F. Miller, and J. Paul, *Autonomy*, 307–8.

28. Isaiah Berlin, *Four Essays on Liberty* (Oxford: Oxford University Press, 1969), 131.

29. See, e.g., Thaddeus Metz, "Respect for Persons and Perfectionist Politics," *Philosophy and Public Affairs* 30 (2002), 418 ("The Kantian perspective is probably the most influential and promising motivation for liberalism"), 420 ("Kantian liberals at bottom claim that any nonliberal state is disrespectful, which means that such a state treats people's capacity for reasoned decision-making as having less than the highest value in the world. To treat disrespectfully is to express the judgment or attitude that their ability to make voluntary choices has less than a superlative

worth."); S. Freeman, "Illiberal Libertarians," 110 ("For Kant, our humanity consists in our capacities for freedom and reason. Having these capacities, persons have dignity, a kind of value 'beyond all price.' Having dignity, persons are due respect whatever their status or situation."). For a fuller summary of Kant's ethics, see Warner A. Wick, ed , *Immanuel Kant· Ethical Philosophy* (Cambridge, MA: Hackett, 1983), xi–lxii.

30. See Guyer, "Kant on Autonomy," 72–3; Regan, "Value of Rational Nature," 268–9. Cf. Berlin, *Four Essays on Liberty*, 132 (describing the "two selves" of human personality – the "real" or "dominant" self that is "identified with reason, with my 'higher nature,'" and the "'empirical' or 'heteronomous' self, swept by every gust of desire and passion").

31. Sir William Blackstone, *Commentaries on the Laws of England, Vol. 1: Of the Rights of Persons* (1765) (Chicago: University of Chicago Press, 1979), 121.

32. Cf. Berlin, *Four Essays on Liberty*, 157 ("Paternalism is despotic, not . . . merely because it ignores the transcendental reason embodied in me, but because it is an insult to my conception of myself as a human being, determined to make my own life in accordance with my own (not necessarily rational or benevolent) purposes, and, above all, entitled to be recognized as such by others."). Gerald Dworkin finds this idea in Mill's *On Liberty* as well. See Dworkin, "Paternalism," 117.

33. See Immanuel Kant, *Groundwork of the Metaphysic of Morals*, trans. H. J. Paton (New York: Harper & Row, 1964), 108; *Katrin Flikschuh, Kant and Modern Political Philosophy* (Cambridge, UK: Cambridge University Press, 2000), 85–7; Christine M. Korsgaard, *The Sources of Normativity* (Cambridge, UK: Cambridge University Press, 1996), 97–8.

34. Cf. Marina Oshana, "How Much Should We Value Autonomy?" in E. Paul, F. Miller, and J. Paul, *Autonomy*, 119 ("Requiring that the autonomous individual be ideally rational, disposed to sublimate her empirical nature for her dispassionate side, and making this the locus of individualism and personal freedom countenances a state of affairs potentially hostile to the negative species of freedom espoused in Mill's liberalism. It also severely limits the class of people whom we call autonomous. The idea that there is a particularly correct way of life, and a correct set of creeds that sustain the rationalist vision, invites intolerance and the suppression of opinions. No longer is autonomy an ideal associated with individual responsibility and self-mastery but, ironically, autonomy becomes a species of self-perfection."); Thomas E. Hill, Jr., *Autonomy and Self-Respect* (Cambridge, UK: Cambridge University Press, 1991), 34 (noting that being autonomous entails simply having some values beyond personal gratification), 47 (stating that under the modern conception of autonomous living: "No one is urged to live with his or her eyes fixed on abstract moral principles, still less with concentration on their justification from an impartial perspective. . . . Impartiality has its important place, but its place is not that of a model for moral sainthood."). Kant himself appears to have adopted a conception of autonomy along these lines in his political writings. See Flikschuh, *Kant and Modern Political Philosophy*, 88–91. Today, both philosophers and nonphilosophers speak of individuals being autonomous even when they make seemingly grossly irrational choices; this is precisely what vexes contemporary philosophers who address the question of when paternalism is justified with competent adults – that is, the perceived conflict between respecting such persons' autonomy and the impulse to prevent them from taking actions that could undermine their autonomy in the long run. See, e.g., Hill, *Autonomy and Self-Respect*, 34 ("We do not hold that persons have a right to make their own decisions only so long as they will decide in a perfectly rational way, and that therefore we may interfere with any predictably irrational decision."), 49 ("The right of autonomy, as I see it, is not rooted . . . in the optimistic faith that people will use their opportunity to make the best possible choices. All the more, I would not want to say that people have a right of autonomy only to the extent that we expect they will make rational choices. Within limits, people should be allowed to make their own choices even if the choices are likely to be foolish.").

35. See, e.g., Korsgaard, *Sources of Norma-tivity*, 120–4 (contending that exercising prac-tical reason entails valuing one's own human-ity), 131–45 (arguing that valuing one's own humanity and seeing one's own needs and desires as reasons for others, logically entail valuing the humanity of others and viewing the needs and desires of others as reasons for oneself). Cf. Regan, "Value of Rational Nature," 287–8 (arguing that it is not possi-ble to generate a moral requirement of self-restraint for the sake of other autonomous persons without assuming the objective value of a rational nature); Alan Gewirth, *Reason and Morality* (Chicago: University of Chicago Press, 1978), 102–5 (attempting to show that any purposeful action by a moral agent logi-cally entails a recognition of the moral obli-gation to respect the rights of others to freedom).

36. See Hill, *Autonomy and Self-Respect*, 45–6. This does not entail that morality always requires impartial behavior; it means that moral conclusions should be arrived at by a process of reasoning that gives equal consid-eration to all persons, rather than being self-serving, but among the conclusions arrived at could be ones authorizing or even requir-ing moral agents, as a general principle, to have special regard for particular other per-sons, such as members of their family, or even for themselves – for example, a duty to give affection to one's spouse and a duty to care for one's own health. See Brian Barry, *Jus-tice as Impartiality* (Oxford: Oxford University Press, 1995), §§ 31, 37 (distinguishing "first-order impartiality" and "second-order impar-tiality").

37. See John Rawls, *A Theory of Justice* (Cambridge, MA: Harvard University Press 1971), 11–13; John Rawls, "Kantian Construc-tivism in Moral Theory," *Journal of Philosophy* 77 (1980), 515. Rawls later came around to the position that a liberal state should be based on a political conception of justice and not a conception of justice embedded in a compre-hensive moral doctrine such as that of Kant. He did not, however, jettison the social con-tract ideal of requiring that the basic principles of society be ones that all reasonable persons could embrace. For a discussion of the ways in which Rawls incorporated Kantian ideas into his work at different stages in his evolution, see Onora O'Neill, *Bounds of Justice* (Cambridge, MA: Cambridge University Press, 2000), 65–73. For discussion of Kant's own social con-tract theory, see, e.g., Elisabeth Ellis, *Kant's Politics: Provisional Theory for an Uncertain World* (New Haven, CT: Yale University Press, 2005), 126–34.

38. Milton C. Regan, Jr., *Alone Together: Law and the Meanings of Marriage* (Oxford: Oxford University Press, 1999), 16.

39. Blackstone, *Laws of England*, 121.

40. See Kymlicka, *Contemporary Political Philosophy*, 62–3. Cf. John Rawls, *Justice as Fairness: A Restatement* (Cambridge, MA: Harvard University Press, 2001), 93–4 (on problems with actual consent).

41. See David Hume, "Of the Original Con-tract," (1748), in Robert Stewart, ed., *Read-ings in Social and Political Philosophy* (2nd ed.) (Oxford: Oxford University Press, 1996), 44.

42. See Metz, "Respect for Persons," 424 ("the deep problem that a Kantian has with nonliberal governments in the real world: perfectionist states have dissenters who can avoid the perfectionism only with a substan-tial cost"). In this article, Metz argues that the Kantian objection to a perfectionist state would drop out if exit could be made costless.

43. See Rawls, *Justice as Fairness*, 14–18, 81–2; Rawls, "Kantian Constructivism," 542 ("Justice as fairness tries to construct a con-ception of justice that takes deep and unre-solvable differences on matters of fundamen-tal significance as a permanent condition of human life.").

44. Rawls, *A Theory of Justice*, 180.

45. Rawls, *Justice as Fairness*, 18, 87. See also Kymlicka, *Contemporary Political Philosophy*, 61.

46. Rawls, *A Theory of Justice*, 18–19; Rawls, *Justice as Fairness*, 15.

47. See T. M. Scanlon, "Rawls' Theory of Justice," in Norman Daniels, ed., *Read-ing Rawls* (Stanford, CA: Stanford University Press, 1975), 172, 177.

48. Rawls, *A Theory of Justice*, 12. Kant similarly wrote of ideal moral legislators "abstracting from personal differences" in order to arrive at general principles for

governing interactions among persons. Kant, *Groundwork*, 101.

49. Rawls, "Kantian Constructivism," 526. See also Rawls, *Justice as Fairness*, 16–18, 80–1, 85–9.

50. Rawls, "Kantian Constructivism," 526–8. See also Robert S. Taylor, "Rawls's Defense of the Priority of Liberty: A Kantian Reconstruction," *Philosophy and Public Affairs* 31 (2003), 246, 256–61; Scanlon, "Rawls' Theory of Justice," 178. As noted above, in his later writings Rawls disavowed reliance on a comprehensive moral doctrine and any ideal of the person that such a doctrine might entail. But he still justified assigning priority to liberties on the grounds that they ensure the opportunity "for the adequate development and full and informed exercise of the two moral powers." Rawls, *Justice as Fairness*, 58. He asserted in this last statement of his position that he is acting on only a "partial conception of the good that citizens, who affirm a plurality of conflicting comprehensive doctrines, can agree upon." Id., 60. See also John Rawls, *Political Liberalism* (Cambridge, MA: Harvard University Press, 1993), 77–8, 98, 199–200. The idea seems to be that autonomy is a basic value for all persons, regardless of their comprehensive moral doctrines, and so a value that would be a component of an overlapping consensus in a pluralistic society and that may properly be assumed in developing a purely political theory of justice. For a pessimistic assessment of the likelihood of an overlapping consensus on Rawls's equal liberty principle and the emphasis on autonomy underlying it, see Taylor, "Rawls's Defense," 266–70.

51. Rawls, *Justice as Fairness*, 42. This is a revised version of the first principle, more modest than the original version, which guaranteed every person "an equal right to the most extensive basic liberty compatible with a similar liberty for others." Rawls, *A Theory of Justice*, 60.

52. Rawls, *Justice as Fairness*, 45. See id., 104, 112–13; Freeman, "Illiberal Libertarians," 134 ("Liberals give priority to... liberties crucial to maintaining a person's status as a responsible and independent agent.")

53. Rawls, *Justice as Fairness*, 18–19.

54. Id., 45.

55. Id.

56. See id., 46, 104.

57. See Taylor, "Rawls's Defense," 254–7.

58. Rawls, *Justice as Fairness*, 45. See also Scanlon, "Rawls' Theory of Justice," 174, 178. In ranking liberties and other goods, Rawls appears to operate on the basis of both welfarist and Kantian impulses and assumptions. He is driven in part by a sense of what goods are basic to human well-being – what he terms *primary goods*. Rawls, *Justice as Fairness*, 88. The basic liberties are essential to our welfare because they protect our most fundamental interests. Id., 46. So there seems some convergence with utilitarianism in justifying basic freedoms. Hurka in fact suggests that the intrinsic value of autonomy cannot alone support a strong liberalism but that that value in combination with instrumental arguments for autonomy and with values not tied to autonomy might be sufficient. Hurka, "Why Value Autonomy?" 380. Rawls was predominantly driven, though, at least in his original articulation of the theory, by Kantian precepts as to what it means to be human and to realize one's humanity, which is essentially to develop one's powers as a free and equal moral agent and to build a life upon one's conception of the good, one's beliefs about what is of ultimate value in life. One cannot have a "good" life without the freedom to think and speak and interact freely with other persons of one's choosing. It is this special, metaphysical significance attributed to autonomy in the original position, as well as the basic social contract approach (i.e., the foundational requirement that all reasonable persons should be able to endorse the principles emerging from the original position as just, because that decision-making heuristic encapsulates widely held beliefs about what personal characteristics are relevant to moral deservingness), that distinguish the early Rawlsian argument for liberty from utilitarian arguments.

59. See Taylor, "Rawls's Defense," 259–61; Scanlon, "Rawls' Theory of Justice," 178; Rawls, *A Theory of Justice*, 261–5. T. M. Scanlon remarks that this is a conception of the person "that has a particularly deep hold

on us and is not a matter of great controversy." Scanlon, "Rawls' Theory of Justice," 178.

60. Rawls, *Justice as Fairness*, 104–5.

61. Id., 104.

62. Id., 44, 105.

63. See, e.g., Rawls, *A Theory of Justice*, 543 (referring to "the free internal life of the various communities of interests in which persons and groups seek to achieve, in modes of social union consistent with equal liberty, the ends and excellences to which they are drawn" and "the desire of human beings to express their nature in a free social union with others"); Rawls, *Justice as Fairness*, 45 ("liberty of conscience and freedom of association enable citizens to develop and exercise their moral powers in forming and revising and in rationally pursuing (individually or, more often, in association with others) their conception of the good").

64. See, e.g., Susan Moller Okin, *Justice, Gender, and the Family* (New York: Basic Books, 1989); James G. Dwyer, *Religious Schools v. Children's Rights* (Ithaca, NY: Cornell University Press, 1998), ch. 6.

65. Scanlon, "Rawls' Theory of Justice," 185.

66. On the value of having more rather than fewer options, from the standpoint of aiming to advance autonomy, see Hurka, "Why Value Autonomy?" 361–3, 368–70.

67. Taylor, "Rawls's Defense," 261.

68. Id.

69. Metz, "Respect for Persons," 435–6. One weakness some might perceive in a Kantian outlook, relative to a utilitarian or other moral outlook, is that the tremendous emotional and psychological satisfactions a person can derive from intimate association are for a Kantian, as suggested by this passage, not inherently valuable but rather are valuable only instrumentally, insofar as they enhance a person's ability for rational and independent choice.

70. Hurka contends that "some autonomous choices...have more intrinsic worth" than others, because they involve establishing over-arching goals for one's life, and "[b]y organizing all a person's activities, these goals sit atop immense hierarchies" of

intentions. Hurka, "Why Value Autonomy?" 373.

71. Wright, "Essence of Relationships," 25.

72. Badhwar, "Love," 53.

73. Katharine Baker, "Property Rules Meet Feminist Needs: Respecting Autonomy By Valuing Connection," *Ohio State Law Journal* 59 (1998), 1537.

74. Regan, *Alone Together*, 15–22.

75. Id., 22–8.

76. Id., 24 (quoting Jeffrey Blustein, *Care and Commitment* (Oxford: Oxford University Press, 1991), 231).

77. Id., 27–8 (quoting Charles Taylor, *The Ethics of Authenticity* (Harvard University Press, 1991), 38).

5. Extending the Theoretical Underpinnings

1. Joseph H. Carens, "Aliens and Citizens: The Case for Open Borders," *The Review of Politics* 49 (1987), 268.

2. See Barbara Arneil, "Becoming versus Being: A Critical Analysis of the Child in Liberal Theory," in David Archard and Colin MacLeod, eds., *The Moral and Political Status of Children* (Oxford: Oxford University Press, 2002), 72–5.

3. See Susan M. Turner and Gareth B. Matthews, eds., *The Philosopher's Child: Critical Essays in the Western Tradition* (University of Rochester Press, 1998), 1. This book is an excellent source of information and analysis concerning philosophical treatment of children historically.

4. See generally James G. Dwyer, "Changing the Conversation about Children's Education," in *NOMOS XLIII: Moral and Political Education* (New York: New York University Press, 2002). As an example of statist thinking, see Rawls, *Justice as Fairness*, 156–7, 166 ("The state's concern with [children's] education lies in their role as future citizens, and so in such essential things as their acquiring the capacity to understand the public culture and to participate in its institutions, in their being economically independent and self-supporting members of society over a complete life, and in their developing the political virtues, all this from within a political point of view.").

5. See Will Kymlicka, *Contemporary Political Philosophy* (2nd ed.) (Oxford: Oxford University Press, 2002), 3–4 ("A theory is egalitarian in this sense [of treating people as equals] if it accepts that the interests of each member of the community matter, and matter equally. Put another way, egalitarian theories require that the government treat its citizens with equal consideration; each citizen is entitled to equal concern and respect.").

6. See id., 4 ("[I]f a theory claimed that some people were not entitled to equal consideration from the government, if it claimed that certain kinds of people just do not matter as much as others, then most people in the modern world would reject that theory immediately. Dworkin's suggestion is that the idea that each person matters equally is at the heart of all plausible political theories."); *Bennett v. Jeffreys*, 40 N.Y.2d 543, 546 (1976) (noting "the modern principle that a child is a person, and not a subperson over whom the parent has an absolute possessory interest").

7. John Stuart Mill, *On Liberty* (1859) (Cambridge, MA: Hackett, 1978), 9.

8. Id.

9. Colin M. Macleod, "Liberal Equality and the Affective Family," in David Archard and Colin Macleod (eds.), *Moral and Political Status*, 215–16.

10. Id., 222–3.

11. For a presentation and critique of the common arguments for parental control rights, see James G. Dwyer, "Parents' Religion and Children's Welfare: Debunking the Doctrine of Parents' Rights," *California Law Review* 82 (1994), 1371.

12. See David D. Meyer, "Self-Definition in the Constitution of Faith and Family," *Minnesota Law Review* 86 (2002), 791.

13. See, e.g., Naomi Cahn, "Reframing Child Custody Decisionmaking," *Ohio State Law Journal* 58 (1997), 1.

14. John Harris, "The Right to Found a Family," in Rosalind Ekman Ladd, ed., *Children's Rights Re-Visioned: Philosophical Readings* (Belmont: Wadsworth, 1996), 80. See also Ferdinand Schoeman, "Rights of Children, Rights of Parents, and the Moral Basis of the Family," *Ethics* 91 (1980), 17 ("society cannot determine and should not try to determine who may have intimate relationships with whom").

15. See Martin Guggenheim, "Somebody's Children: Sustaining the Family's Place in Child Welfare Policy," *Harvard Law Review* 113 (2000), 1742.

16. Marina Oshana, "How Much Should We Value Autonomy?" in E. Paul, F. Miller, and J. Paul, eds., *Autonomy* (New York: Cambridge University Press, 2003), 103.

17. See Bernard Berofsky, "Identification, the Self, and Autonomy," in E. Paul, F. Miller, and J. Paul, *Autonomy*, 220 ("[O]ne cannot be counted autonomous unless one is actually guided by values and principles endorsed by autonomous reflection. The demands of autonomy will go unrealized if professed ideals do not find sufficient mooring in the self.").

18. Cf. Mary Ann Warren, *Moral Status* (Oxford: Oxford University Press, 1997) (describing the views of other theorists who predicate moral status on a criterion other than autonomy and advancing her own multicriterial theory of moral status).

19. John Rawls, *A Theory of Justice* (Cambridge, MA: Harvard University Press, 1971), 505. See also John Rawls, *Justice as Fairness: A Restatement* (Cambridge, MA: Harvard University Press, 2001), 163, 165 (discussing children's "moral development and education into the wider culture" and claims children have on society as its future citizens); H. J. McCloskey, "Respect for Human Moral Rights versus Maximizing Good," in R. G. Frey, ed., *Utility and Rights* (Minneapolis: Minnesota University Press, 1984), 127 ("Infants evidently possess the right to life by virtue of their potentiality to be full persons.").

20. Rawls, *A Theory of Justice*, 509. See also Emily R. Gill, *Becoming Free: Autonomy and Diversity in the Liberal Polity* (Lawrence: University Press of Kansas, 2001), 3 (asserting that a liberal society will "encourage in all individuals the development of the capacity for autonomy as rational deliberation, critical scrutiny, and reflection on the projects and goals that we adopt"); Thomas E. Hill, Jr., *Autonomy and Self-Respect* (Cambridge, MA: Cambridge University Press, 1991), 37 (referring to "[t]he ideal of developing the psychological capacities associated with autonomy").

21. This move leaves the problem that widely held beliefs also attribute moral standing to human beings who have neither autonomy nor the capacity to become autonomous – for example, anencephalic infants, permanently mentally disabled children, and adults who either never have been or have been but will never again be autonomous. It is not my purpose here, though, to defend a view that assigns highest or exclusive moral significance to autonomy. My aim is only to determine the implications for children's associational rights of a moral outlook that places ultimate value on autonomy.

22. Kant suggested that adults owe a duty to themselves to foster and maintain their autonomy. See Immanuel Kant, *Groundwork of the Metaphysic of Morals*, trans. H. J. Paton (New York: Harper & Row, 1964), 97–8; Paul Guyer, "Kant on the Theory and Practice of Autonomy," in E. Paul, F. Miller, and J. Paul, *Autonomy*, 90–4; Donald H. Regan, "The Value of Rational Nature," *Ethics* 112 (2002), 276–7. Rawls seems to have shared this view. See John Rawls, "Kantian Constructivism in Moral Theory," *Journal of Philosophy* 77 (1980), 527 ("we expect and indeed want people to care about their liberties and opportunities in order to realize [their moral] powers, and we think they show a lack of self-respect and weakness of character in not doing so").

23. Kant suggested we have a duty to assist all humans, or at least all other rational beings, in advancing toward greater autonomy. See Kant, *Groundwork*, 98 (describing a duty to make others' ends our own); Onora O'Neill, "Between Consenting Adults," *Philosophy and Public Affairs* 14 (1985), 264–5 (interpreting these passage in Kant). See also Oshana, "How Much Should We Value Autonomy?" 103–4 (discussing the ways in which persons might be nonautonomous or unable to exercise autonomy despite having the mental powers and freedom from external compulsion that are requisite to autonomy).

24. A collective duty owed to all children and an individual duty owed to a specific child are both "perfect duties" and therefore correlate with rights; the persons to whom the duty is owed are specified in each case and the occa-

sion for fulfillment of the duty is determinate – namely during each child's minority. As is true of other perfect duties, such as a contractual obligation to provide a particular service to another adult, some discretion is left to the duty-holder in this case as to the precise means and timing of fulfilling the duty.

Rawls notes an additional motivation for assisting children in becoming autonomous. As citizens, he pointed out, we view our aim in political deliberations to be deciding upon basic principles and rules to govern our society not only for the sake of coordinating our lives and aims presently but also to establish a basis for social cooperation over the long run, for subsequent generations as well as our own. This entails fostering in children the capacities for individual and collective self-governance that we value in ourselves. In discussing specifically the role of the family in maintaining a just society, Rawls wrote that "a political society is always regarded as a scheme of cooperation over time indefinitely; the idea of a future time when its affairs are to be wound up and society disbanded is foreign to our conception of society." Rawls, *Justice as Fairness*, 162. Such a self-regarding collective aim would not, though, give rise to moral rights on the part of children.

25. Onora O'Neill, *Bounds of Justice* (Cambridge, UK: Cambridge University Press, 2000), 49.

26. For a fuller account of how children might be accounted for in a Rawlsian analsyis, see Samantha Brennan and Robert Noggle, "John Rawls's Children," in Susan M. Turner and Gareth B. Matthews, eds., *The Philosopher's Child: Critical Essays in the Western Tradition* (Rochester, NY: University of Rochester Press, 1998), 203–32; James G. Dwyer, *Religious Schools v. Children's Rights* (Ithaca, NY: Cornell University Press, 1998), ch. 6. As Brennan and Noggle point out, Rawls's statements in *A Theory of Justice* that we should assume the "parties" in the original position are in possession of the full moral powers are inessential and can be ignored; we need not think of any actual bargaining going on among multiple parties but rather can simply reason through what principles we would adopt after imagining that we could turn out to be persons

occupying any of the possible positions in our society or having any of the characteristics common to our society, which could include nonautonomous persons. It is an interesting question whether one should reach back farther in time in representing "persons" in the original position, to incorporate children not only after birth but also before birth, but I bracket such questions about the state's proper treatment of potential autonomous persons before birth.

27. Scanlon's version of contractualism explicitly prescribes such a comparative evaluation of the objections different persons could make to different rules of social governance. See Thomas Scanlon, *What We Owe to Each Other* (Cambridge, MA: Harvard University Press, 1998).

28. Rawls, *A Theory of Justice*, 249.

29. Id.

30. Id.

31. Id., 152, 246–7, 542–3. Kant and Mill expressed a similar view. See Warner A. Wick, ed., *Immanuel Kant: Ethical Philosophy* (Cambridge, MA: Hackett, 1983), lvi; Mill, *On Liberty*, 9–10.

32. Id., 248 ("I have assumed that it is always those with the lesser liberty who must be compensated. We are always to appraise the situation from their point of view").

33. See Gerald Dworkin, "Paternalism," in Richard A. Wasserstrom, ed., *Morality and the Law* (Belmont, CA: Wadsworth, 1971), 119 ("Parental paternalism may be thought of as a wager by the parent on the child's subsequent recognition of the wisdom of the restrictions. There is an emphasis on what could be called future-oriented consent – on what the child will come to welcome, rather than on what he does welcome"); Gerald Dworkin, "Paternalism," *The Monist* 56 (1972), 78; Isaiah Berlin, *Four Essays on Liberty* (Oxford: Oxford University Press, 1969), 132–4.

34. Dworkin, "Paternalism," 119. See also id., 120 ("We may argue for and against proposed paternalistic measures in terms of what fully rational individuals would accept as forms of protection").

35. John Tomasi, *Liberalism beyond Justice: Citizens, Society, and the Boundaries of Political Theory* (Princeton, NJ: Princeton University Press, 2001), 3 (emphasis added). See also id., 16 ("Liberal theorists, in everything they write, can be thought of as providing answers to questions that might reasonably be asked by would-be citizens. In response to their citizens' questions, liberal theorists owe arguments that the citizens themselves can accept").

36. Peter O. King, "Thomas Hobbes's Children," in Susan M. Turner and Gareth B. Matthews, eds., *The Philosopher's Child: Critical Essays in the Western Tradition* (Rochester, NY: University of Rochester Press, 1998), 75. I note that the textual evidence King cites for Hobbes's having relied on a notion of hypothetical consent by infants is quite scant and readily interpreted otherwise. I would also point out that the substance of Hobbes's reasoning as King presents it is flawed insofar as it considers only two options for a child, death or the dominion of biological parents. In western society today, at least, parenting of children who are not one's biological offspring is very common and a model of hypothetical choosing by newborn children must include that option.

37. Cf. Brian Barry, *Justice as Impartiality* (Oxford: Oxford University Press, 1995), 55–6 (defending Rawls's reliance on the notion of hypothetical consent for his basic theory of justice).

38. Rawls devoted a great deal of attention to children's moral development in *A Theory of Justice*, but principally for the purpose of showing how a just society could be preserved from generation to generation, rather than for the purpose of discerning what children are entitled to as a matter of justice. See Dwyer, *Religious Schools*, ch. 6. At the same time, Rawls did respond, in his discussion of stability and moral instruction, to the potential objection that his just society would have to engage in coercion of the young to ensure conformity to the ideals governing the society, an objection that might rest on beliefs about the rights of persons as children. Rawls argued that moral education in a well-ordered society would appeal as far as possible to each child's reason and that the aim of developing in children a sense of justice is not inconsistent with their collective well-being as future

adults, who will do best if they get along with each other in harmonious communities and if they, too, enjoy the benefits of a just society that is embraced by a critical mass of reasonable persons. Rawls, *A Theory of Justice*, 515–16; T. M. Scanlon, "Rawls' Theory of Justice," in Norman Daniels, ed., *Reading Rawls* (Stanford, CA; Stanford University Press, 1975), 176. This is consistent with, and reinforces, the earlier treatment of children as beings with a moral standing equal to that of fully autonomous persons, insofar as it requires that they be able ultimately to see the rules governing their early life as fair to them and as conducive to their well-being and their realization of their full human potential.

39. Rawls, *Justice as Fairness*, 42–3.

40. See, e.g., Rawls, *A Theory of Justice*, 224–6. See also Samuel Freeman, "Illiberal Libertarians: Why Libertarianism Is Not a Liberal View," *Philosophy and Public Affairs* 30 (2002), 117–18 (characterizing this position as a "basic tenet of high liberalism," and finding support for it in Kant's writings).

41. Rawls, *Justice as Fairness*, 44.

42. See Rawls, *A Theory of Justice*, 62 (including "health and vigor, intelligence and imagination" among the "natural" primary goods whose possession "is influenced by the basic structure [of society, but] not so directly under its control"), 178 and 544–6 (discussing the importance of self-respect). See also James Griffin, "Towards a Substantive Theory of Rights," in R. G. Frey, ed., *Utility and Rights* (Minneapolis, Minnesota University Press, 1984), 138–9.

43. Rawls, *A Theory of Justice*, 440.

44. Milton C. Regan, Jr., *Alone Together: Law and the Meanings of Marriage* (Oxford: Oxford University Press, 1999), 25–7.

45. Rawls, *A Theory of Justice*, 181.

46. Id., 74.

47. See, e.g., Freeman, "Illiberal Libertarians," 117.

48. See Kymlicka, *Contemporary Political Philosophy*, 76–9, 97.

49. The argument is more often made that state regulation of education violates the rights of parents to control their children's upbringing. I addressed that argument in an earlier book. See Dwyer, *Religious Schools*, ch.

3. And sometimes the argument is made that state control over children's upbringing violates rights of communities. I also addressed that argument in the earlier book. See id., ch. 4.

50. For an argument that having access to one's culture should be treated as a primary good in modern liberal theory, see Will Kymlicka, *Multicultural Citizenship* (Oxford: Oxford University Press, 1995), 86.

51. See Brennan and Noggle, "John Rawls's Children," 216–23 (discussing theories of children's moral development).

52. Many legal scholars have considered this question in considerable depth in connection with decisions about particular aspects of young people's lives. See, e.g., Elizabeth S. Scott, "The Legal Construction of Adolescence," *Hofstra Law Review* 29 (2000), 547; Emily Buss, "The Adolescent's Stake in the Allocation of Educational Control between Parent and State," *University of Chicago Law Review* 67 (2000), 1233; Catherine J. Ross, "An Emerging Right for Mature Minors to Receive Information," *University of Pennsylvania Journal of Constitutional Law* 2 (1999), 223. Many have also explored the moral case for empowering young people. See, e.g., Michael Freeman, *The Moral Status of Children* (Amsterdam: Martinus Nijhoff, 1997).

53. Willard Gaylin, *Who Speaks for the Child: The Problems of Proxy Consent* (New York: Plenum, 1982).

54. See *Gillick v West Norfolk and Wisbech Area Health Authority* (1985) 3 All ER 402 (HL)

55. Jane Fortin, *Children's Rights and the Developing Law* (2nd ed.) (London: Butterworths, 2003), 267.

56. S. Day Sclater, *Families* (London: Hodder & Stoughton, 2000), 80. See also Fortin, *Children's Rights*, 254, 260–6 (discussing various circumstances where asking children to choose could be detrimental to them).

57. See, e.g., Carolyn Hamilton and Alison Perry, eds., *Family Law in Europe* (2nd ed.) (London: Butterworths, 2002), 280 (thirteen in France), 463 (twelve in the Netherlands), 613–14 (twelve in Spain), 651 (twelve in Sweden). In Germany, children's wishes are relevant at any age, and children fourteen and

older must be heard from personally rather than through a representative such as a GAL. Id., 320.

58. John Eckalaar takes such a view, in "The Interests of the Child and the Child's Wishes: The Role of Dynamic Self-Determinism," *International Journal of Law and the Family* 8 (1994), 42. See also Fortin, *Children's Rights*, 255.

6. Rebutting Defenses of the Status Quo

1. John Robertson, "Procreative Liberty and the Control of Conception, Pregnancy, and Childbirth," *Virginia Law Review* 69 (1983), 410.

2. Mary Midgley, "Rights-Talk Will Not Sort Out Child-Abuse: Comment on Archard on Parental Rights," *Journal of Applied Philosophy* 8 (1991), 107. As is apparent from the title of this article, Midgley is among those who object to arguments for expanded rights for children on the basis of a premise that rights-talk is not fitting for resolving morally and empirically complex family law issues, yet she is also entirely comfortable endorsing rights for parents despite the inconsistency with that premise.

3. John Eekelaar, "Beyond the Welfare Principle," *Child and Family Law Quarterly* 14 (2002) 237.

4. *Frette v. France*, (2002) ECHR 36515/97, ¶ 32.

5. Id., ¶ 42.

6. See *Planned Parenthood of Southeastern Pennsylvania v. Casey*, 505 U.S. 833 (1992) (invalidating provision in state law requiring married women merely to notify their husbands of a plan to have an abortion and stating that it "is an inescapable biological fact that state regulation with respect to the child a woman is carrying will have a far greater impact on the mother's liberty than on the father's").

7. Some have also argued against limiting the rights of parents within established parent–child relationships, for the sake of children's relationships with other persons, by speaking of the autonomy of the "family unit." See, e.g., Martha Albertson Fineman, "What

Place for Family Privacy?" *George Washington Law Review* 67 (1999), 1223–4. This sort of talk is simply incoherent, because families with children are not a cognitive or existential "unit." They are groupings of ontologically and experientially distinct persons whose interests and views can conflict, in which parents typically enforce their will regarding their children's lives even when their children disagree or have interests to the contrary. Talk of family autonomy is just a mask for parental power.

8. Ferdinand Schoeman, "Rights of Children, Rights of Parents, and the Moral Basis of the Family," *Ethics* 91 (1980), 17.

9. John Stuart Mill, *On Liberty* (1859) (Indianapolis: Hackett Publishing, 1978), 9, 11.

10. Id., 76.

11. Thomas E. Hill, Jr., *Autonomy and Self-Respect* (Cambridge, UK: Cambridge University Press, 1991), 32. See also id., 48 ("autonomy is not freedom to control others' lives in matters that mainly affect them, for example, a friend's choice of companions, jobs, and hairstyle. On the contrary, a person's right of autonomy protects certain decisions that deeply affect that person's own life . . . "); Thomas Hurka, "Why Value Autonomy?" *Social Theory and Practice* 13 (1987), 370 ("We call a person autonomous when he can make choices about his own life; it is something beyond this to make choices about other people's lives, or about the material world. A person has autonomy if he can decide whether or not he eats a banana; he has something more – call it external power – if he can decide whether someone else eats a banana.").

12. I develop this point further in an earlier book. See James G. Dwyer, *Religious Schools v. Children's Rights* (Ithaca, NY: Cornell University Press, 1998), ch. 3. See also James G. Dwyer, "Children's Interests in a Family Context – A Cautionary Note," *Santa Clara Law Review* 39 (1999), 1063–4.

13. Elizabeth S. Scott and Robert E. Scott, "Parents as Fiduciaries," *Virginia Law Review* 81 (1995), 2401.

14. See id., 2440 ("It is unlikely that, in a hypothetical bargain over the terms of their performance, parents would agree to

undertake the responsibilities desired by the state without assurance that their investment would receive legal protection").

15. Id., 2474. This articulation of the point is inherently circular, insofar as it presupposes that thwarting a child's relationship with third parties is consistent with satisfactory performance of parental responsibilities, when the very question they address is whether that is the case. They might restate the point, however, to say that extensive authority and rights are necessary compensation for fulfilling substantial caretaking responsibilities toward a child.

16. Id., 2404. At other points, their analysis suggests the weaker conclusion that parents simply should not be held to so high a standard as "absolutely no self-dealing." See, e.g., id., 2437. That conclusion is consistent with a recommendation for much greater regulation than currently exists and with legislative authorization for court-ordered third-party visitation.

17. This is one possible reading of this passage:

> The significant [parental demoralization] costs entailed in enforcing legal rules that trump informal norms implies that preemptive conflict of interest rules would be specified only when a societal consensus about the impact of the regulated conduct on children dictates a particular choice. These same concerns argue for retaining parental discretion whenever "reasonable" parents are likely to differ about what choice promotes the interest of children.

Id., 2438.

18. Id., 2434 ("the role of parent is among the most important in defining personal identity for both men and women"), 2472 ("the role of parent is intrinsically desirable ... personal fulfillment is linked to having children and rearing them successfully").

19. Id., 2440, 2456 ("parental authority and discretion are the necessary quid pro quo for parents undertaking the responsibilities of parenthood").

20. For a thoughtful analysis along these lines, see Katharine Bartlett, "Re-Expressing Parenthood," *Yale Law Journal* 98 (1988), 298.

21. See *Grutter v. Bollinger*, 539 U.S. 306, 328 (2003) (rejecting the argument that "remedying past discrimination is the only permissible justification for race-based governmental action" and holding that creating a diverse student body is also an adequate justification for an affirmative action policy).

22. Katharine T. Bartlett, "Comparing Race and Sex Discrimination in Custody Cases," *Hofstra Law Review* 28 (2000), 877, 880–1.

23. See id., 879.

24. Id., 886.

25. See *Ashcroft v. Free Speech Coalition*, 535 U.S. 234, 263 (2002) (O'Connor, J., concurring) ("The Court has long recognized that the Government has a compelling interest in protecting our Nation's children"); *New York v. Ferber*, 458 U.S. 747, 756–7 (1967) (upholding state statute criminalizing distribution of printed material depicting sexual performance by minors) ("It is evident beyond the need for elaboration that a State's interest in 'safeguarding the physical and psychological well-being of a minor' is 'compelling'").

26. *Palmore v. Sidoti*, 466 U.S. 429, 433 (1984).

27. According to Samuel Freeman, within liberal theory the state always acts in a fiduciary capacity, rather than being the bearer of basic rights itself. "Political power is held in trust, as a fiduciary power; those who occupy political offices act in a representative capacity, for others' benefit." Samuel Freeman, "Illiberal Libertarians: Why Libertarianism Is Not a Liberal View," *Philosophy and Public Affairs* 30 (2002), 121–2. Freeman asserts that "since political power is public, it is to represent everyone, and therefore is to be impartially exercised and only for the common good." Id., 122. But the point of this statement is to contrast legitimate government with government that systematically favors some groups in society over others and/or whose officials use their power for self-serving reasons. Freeman appears simply not to have been mindful of the fact that sometimes the state properly acts for less than all members of society – most significantly, in its *parens patriae* role.

28. "Developments in the Law – The Constitution and the Family," *Harvard Law Review* 93 (1980), 1199.

29. 639 N.Y.S.2d 234 (1996).

30. Elizabeth Scott, "Sterilization of Mentally Retarded Persons: Reproductive Rights and Family Privacy," *Duke Law Journal* 1986 (1986), 821.

31. See, e.g., *Cruzan v. Director, Missouri Department of Health*, 497 U.S. 261, 286 (1990) (upholding state law allowing for withdrawal of life support only upon a showing by clear and convincing evidence that the patient while competent desired that this would be done if such circumstances arose) ("[W]e do not think the Due Process Clause requires the State to repose judgment on these matters with anyone but the patient herself. Close family members may have a strong feeling – a feeling not at all ignoble or unworthy, but not entirely disinterested, either – that they do not wish to witness the continuation of the life of a loved one which they regard as hopeless, meaningless, and even degrading. But there is no automatic assurance that the view of close family members will necessarily be the same as the patient's would have been had she been confronted with the prospect of her situation while competent."); *In re Quinlan*, 355 A.2d 647 (1976) (rejecting parents' claim grounded in religious freedom to be entitled to decide whether their daughter would remain on life support).

7. Implementing Children's Moral Rights in Law

1. I am not suggesting that adolescents' values or moral views should always be determinative or even that they should always be given some weight. Though I cannot undertake a full analysis of the issue here, it is plausible to think a state decision maker should ignore or attempt to counteract certain values or views of an adolescent in ordering his or her relationships, based on a judgment that it is contrary to the youth's long-term well-being to hold those values or views. For example, a youth might tell his guardian *ad litem* in a divorce proceeding that he wants his father to have primary custody, because his father and he both believe in the violent overthrow of the government, whereas his mother opposes violent means of achieving legal reform. Some kinds of values could present very difficult questions for a state decision maker trying to act as surrogate for a youth – for example, racist, sexist, or homophobic views or a youth's own religious conviction that members of other faiths are damned or that one should never resort to conventional medical care.

2. See, e.g., Emily Buss, "Children's Associational Rights, Why Less Is More," *William & Mary Bill of Rights Journal* 11 (2003), 1101; Martha Albertson Fineman, "What Place for Family Privacy?" *George Washington Law Review* 67 (1999), 1222–3.

3. ALI (2002), 1.

4. Mill's perfectionist distinction between higher pleasures (e.g., poetry) and lower pleasures (e.g., "pushpin," a mindless amusement) might be an exception, but that is not a kind of distinction the best-interests term is meant to capture.

5. See, e.g., Goldstein, Solnit, and Freud, *Before the Best Interests of the Child* (New York: Free Press, 1979), 6.

6. Mary Becker, "Maternal Feelings: Myth, Taboo, and Child Custody," *Southern California Review of Law and Women's Studies* 1 (1992), 133, 172.

7. Janet Weinstein presents all of these challenges in "Weinstein, and Never the Twain Shall Meet: The Best Interest of Children and the Adversary System," *University of Miami Law Review* 52 (1997), 79.

8. See, e.g., David L. Chambers, "Rethinking the Substantive Rules for Custody Disputes in Divorce," *Michigan Law Review* 83 (1984), 482–3; Robert Mnookin, "Child-Custody Adjudication: Judicial Function in the Face of Indeterminacy," *Law & Contemporary Problems* 39, Summer (1975), 226.

9. See Mnookin, "Child-Custody Adjudication," 253–4; Becker, "Maternal Feelings," 172–4.

10. See, e.g., Chambers, "Substantive Rules for Custody Disputes," 479; Becker, "Maternal Feelings," 174.

11. See Jane Fortin, *Children's Rights and the Developing Law* (2nd ed.) (London: Butterworths, 2003), 248 (discussing such criticisms among British family law scholars); Katharine T. Bartlett, "Comparing Race and Sex Discrimination in Custody Cases," *Hofstra Law Review* 28 (2000), 877, 883–4 ("The best-interests test is an empty vessel, to be filled by the subjective views of judges about what is good for children, including views about sex and race."); Twila Perry, "Race and Child Placement: The Best Interests Test and the Cost of Discretion," *Journal of Family Law* 29 (1990/1991), 51.

12. See Naomi Cahn, "Reframing Child Custody Decisionmaking," *Ohio State Law Journal* 58 (1997), 12–13 (summarizing feminist critiques); Becker, "Maternal Feelings," 175–83. Survey evidence contradicts some of these assertions. See Douglas Dotterweich and Michael McKinney, "National Attitudes Regarding Gender Bias in Child Custody Cases," *Family and Conciliation Courts Review* 38 (2000), 208, 213–14 (reporting results of survey of 4,579 attorneys and judges from four states, showing that only 3.2 percent of judges and 5.9 percent of attorneys perceived that the relative financial standing of parents always or usually influences custody decisions and that only around 1 percent of attorneys and judges perceive that employment outside the home always or usually influences custody decisions).

13. See June Carbone, *From Partners to Parents: The Second Revolution in Family Law* (New York: Columbia University Press, 2000), 191 (describing the conflicting perspectives on custody decision making of feminists and fathers' rights groups).

14. See Dotterweich and McKinney, "Gender Bias," 213 "[f]ewer than half of the judges (45.5%) feel that courts 'always or usually' give fair consideration to fathers" and that "[f]ewer than one third of all attorneys (31.1%) hold the view that fathers are always or usually given fair consideration"); Katherine Hunt Federle, "Looking for Rights in All the Wrong Places: Resolving Custody Disputes in Divorce Proceedings," *Cardozo Law Review* 15 (1994), 1537–8.

15. See, e.g., Martin Guggenheim, "Somebody's Children: Sustaining the Family's Place in Child Welfare Policy," *Harvard Law Review* 113 (2000), 1734. See also Dorothy E. Roberts, "The Genetic Tie," *University of Chicago Law Review* 62 (1995), 267–8 (regarding racial prejudice); Perry, "Race and Child Placement"; Douglas E. Cressler, "Requiring Proof beyond a Reasonable Doubt in Parental Rights Termination Cases," *University of Louisville Journal of Family Law* 32 (1994), 809–11 (regarding race, social class, and other bias factors).

16. Becker, "Maternal Feeling," 203. Becker makes some effort to justify this rule on child welfare grounds, asserting that "mothers, as a group, have greater competence and standing to decide what is best for their children after a divorce than judges, fathers, or adversarial experts." Id., 204. She cites no empirical research to support this bald claim as to competence, and it stands in tension with her plea for sympathy for mothers on the grounds that most mothers find "the possibility of separation [from their children] terrifying," which suggests that most mothers are overcome by self-protective emotion at the time of divorce. In elaborating on this assertion, Becker actually focuses principally on the "standing" part of it, by which she means that "mothers earn their authority" through the sacrifices they make.

17. See Richard A. Posner, *The Problems of Jurisprudence* (Cambridge, MA: Harvard University Press, 1990), 42–52.

18. See Brian Bix, "State Interest and Marriage – The Theoretical Perspective," *Hofstra Law Review* 32 (2003), 104 ("family matters are notorious for being an area where angry parties will bring and maintain lawsuits even when the law is clearly against them").

19. ALI (2002): § 2.08.

20. See, e.g., Fineman, "Dominant Discourse," 773; Katharine K. Baker, "Taking Care of Our Daughters," *Cardozo Law Review* 18 (1997) 1495, 1512. Oddly, Baker herself treats waged work as selfless caring for children when mothers do it. See id., 1510 ("today's working-class women and women without parenting partners who can work, often do so as a means of caring for their children").

21. See Michael S. Paraino, "Lay Representation of Abused and Neglected Children," *Journal of the Center for Children and the Courts* 1 (1999), 63; Laurie K. Adams, "CASA: A Child's Voice in Court," *Creighton Law Review* 29 (1996), 1467. For a constructive discussion of how to give judges guidance in assessing expert testimony and reports, see Sarah H. Ramsey and Robert E. Kelly, "Social Science Knowledge in Family Law Cases: Judicial Gate-Keeping in the Daubert Era," *University of Miami Law Review* 59 (2004), 1.

22. Martin Guggenheim, *What's Wrong with Children's Rights* (Cambridge, MA: Harvard University Press, 2005), 38–41.

23. See, e.g., Martin Guggenheim, "Somebody's Children," 1734, 1737, 1741, 1744, 1746–7.

24. Significantly, it is not, at least in the case of feminists, a complaint against disparate impacts of child welfare rules in general. Feminists are generally untroubled by the fact that ostensibly gender neutral rules such as the primary caretaker and approximation rules would result in mothers getting primary custody in a far higher percentage of cases than fathers do and would effectively "penalize" fathers for working. See, e.g., Fineman, "Dominant Discourse," 773.

25. Guggenheim, "Somebody's Children," 1749.

26. See, e.g., Chambers, "Substantive Rules for Custody Disputes," 540 (urging that courts disregard the relative economic circumstances of divorcing parties, arguing as follows: "The problem with giving substantial weight to resources or income potential is that, in this country today, the effect of doing so is to disadvantage mothers in two ways that many people would consider unfair"); Michael Wald, "State Intervention on Behalf of 'Neglected' Children: Standards for Removal of Children from Their Homes, Monitoring the State of Children in Foster Care, and Termination of Parental Rights," *Stanford Law Review* 28 (1976), 623 (urging that courts excuse neglect by parents to some degree where it reflects a lack of personal or financial resources rather than a deliberate disregard for their children's welfare).

27. See, e.g., Mnookin, "Child-Custody Adjudication," 251–2.

28. Fineman, "Dominant Discourse," 770–2.

29. Becker, "Maternal Feeling," 172.

30. Chambers, "Substantive Rules for Custody Disputes," 481.

31. For discussion of the difficulties inherent in implementing legal protections for incompetent adults, see Tor and Sales, "Guardianship."

32. This is true, for example, of many aspects of trusts and estates law. The rules for passing property by intestate succession are designed to replicate what most people choose to do with their property when they make express decisions. The rules for recognizing and revoking wills when statutory formalities are not observed are designed to effectuate presumed intent as well. Likewise, rules for "pretermitted" spouses and children, setting aside part of a decedent's estate for persons who became members of the decedent's family after execution of a will, are based on an assumption that most people in such circumstances have simply forgotten to amend their wills and would have intended to include these later additions to the family.

33. Ordinarily "self-regarding" is used to characterize interests of competent adults, who are able subjectively to have regard for self or others, and it is a little out of place in discussing incompetent persons. But no alternative comes readily to mind to capture the distinction, in the case of incompetent persons, between interests that make reference only to the interest-holder and those that make reference to the welfare of others, so I import the terminology to the context of children.

34. For discussion of the duty of gratitude, see A. John Simmons, *Moral Principles and Political Obligations* (Princeton, NJ: Princeton University Press, 1981), ch. VII; Fred Berger, "Gratitude," *Ethics* 85 (1975), 298; and A. D. M. Walker, "Political Obligation and the Argument from Gratitude," *Philosophy and Public Affairs* 17 (1988), 191. I am grateful to Emile Lester for suggesting this line of reasoning to me.

35. See, e.g., *In re Keri*, 853 A.2d 909 (N.J. Sup. Ct. 2004) (authorizing guardian to

transfer assets from his incompetent mother's estate to hasten her eligibility for Medicaid benefits); Carolyn L. Dessin, "Financial Abuse of the Elderly: Is the Solution a Problem?" *McGeorge Law Review* 34 (2003), 376 (citing other court decisions).

36. Of course, the state has for some time taken a share of a small percentage of estates, the largest ones, in the form of estate taxes. Existing law phases out the estate tax in the next half dozen years, motivated by popular belief that it is unfair to tax wealth that was already taxed once when it was first received as income. In any event, the estate tax has never been justified on the grounds that wealthy people ought to give their money to the state but rather on the grounds that property ownership ends at death and that no living persons are morally entitled to wealth they themselves have not earned. The argument, then, is that the wealth of a decedent is up for grabs, and the state lays some claim to all unowned property.

8. Applications

1. The genesis of the idea is often attributed to Hugh LaFollette, "Licensing Parents," *Philosophy and Public Affairs* 9 (1980), 182–97. One can imagine some benefits to children from requiring even the best parents to demonstrate their competence and dedication, and there are innumerable analogies one can draw to other practices or professions for which one must secure a license from, or undergo evaluation by, the state – including, most tellingly, parenthood by adoption. But the very idea of state licensing of every parent would be so offensive to so many people that it is politically pointless to push it.

2. On the connection between adolescent violence and poor parenting, see Doriane Lambelet Coleman, *Fixing Columbine: The Challenge to American Liberalism* (Durham, NC: Carolina Academic Press, 2002), chs. 3 and 4.

3. See Ellen Marrus, "Crack Babies and the Constitution: Ruminations about Addicted Pregnant Women after Feguson v. City of Charleston," *Villanova Law Review* 47 (2002), 318–20 (explaining that "crack babies" are

commonly placed in foster care, that prospects for rehabilitation of drug-addicted mothers are very poor, that babies placed in foster care commonly suffer from attachment disorder and therefore "have difficulty forming normal relationships and [are] likely to have impaired social development," but that babies born with crack cocaine "who are brought up in nurturing environments, with consistent, caring caretakers, can catch up developmentally with children who are born drug-free"); id., 328 (discussing laws allowing for immediate state removal of child born to a drug abusing woman); id., 331 (noting that usual reaction of courts to finding that mother caused illegal drugs to enter child's body is to require the mother to enter a drug treatment program, after completion of which the court will consider returning the child to her custody); Elizabeth Bartholet, "The Challenge of Children's Rights Advocacy: Problems and Progress in the Area of Child Abuse and Neglect," *Whittier Journal of Child and Family Advocacy* 3 (2004b), 227 (stating: "Research, including the most recent research, demonstrates that even well-funded, model family preservation programs have not succeeded in transforming dangerous family environments into ones that are safe and nurturing," and citing sources).

4. On the crucial importance for children of early attachment to a permanent, loving caregiver, see Elizabeth Bartholet, "Guiding Principles for Picking Parents," *Harvard Women's Law Journal* 27 (2004a), 323; Eleanor Willemsen and Kristen Marcel, "Attachment 101 for Attorneys: Implications for Infant Placement Decisions," *Santa Clara Law Review* 36 (1996), 439.

5. See, e.g., Nora D. Valkow, "Drug Related Damage That Begins before Birth," NIDA Notes (2004), available at: http://www.nida.nih.gov/NIDA_notes/NNvol19N4/ (impact of drug/alcohol abuse during pregnancy on unborn child); "The Relationship between Parental Drug and Alcohol Abuse and Child Maltreatment" (1999), available at http://www.childabuse.com/fs14.htm (statistics and facts on child neglect and abuse as resulting from parental drug/alcohol abuse); Jain Mukti Campion, *Who's Fit to Be a Parent?* (London: Routledge, 1995), 169–72 (noting

various problems associated with drug addiction, such as HIV, depression, prostitution, and general lack of self-control); Douglas J. Besharov, ed. *When Drug Addicts Have Children: Reorienting Child Welfare's Response* (Washington, D.C.: Child Welfare League of America Press, 1994), ix ("The plain fact is that – even with the best treatment services available – most crack addicts cannot be totally freed of their addiction. Instead, drug addiction must be seen as a 'chronic, relapsing disorder'..."), xi–xii, xiv, xix [describing "a perverse cycle of opening, closing, and reopening (child abuse and neglect) cases" involving drug addicted parents]; Marrus, "Crack Babies," 334–5 (explaining that drug treatment programs generally take at least a year to complete, that it may take considerable time before a birth mother is even able to get into such a program, and that the likelihood of success in such programs is low).

6. Bartholet, "Challenge of Children's Rights Advocacy," 228–9. See also Barbara A. Babb and Judith D. Moran, "Substance Abuse, Families, and Unified Family Courts: The Creation of a Caring Justice System," *Journal of Health Care Law and Policy* 3 (1999), 1–9; "The Relationship between Parental Drug and Alcohol Abuse and Child Maltreatment," (1999), available at http://www.childabuse.com/fs14.htmin.

7. See National Exchange Club Foundation, "Fetal Alcohol Syndrome," available at http://www.preventchildabuse.com/fas.htm; Jonathan G. Tubman, "Family Risk Factors, Parental Alcohol Use, and Problem Behaviors among School-Age Children," *Family Relations* 42(1) (1993), 81–6.

8. Jane C. Murphy and Margaret J. Potthast, "Domestic Violence, Substance Abuse, and Child Welfare: The Legal System's Response," *Journal of Health Care Law and Policy* 3 (1999), 88. See especially id. at 92–3 (referring to a survey finding "that when wife abuse was severe, seventy-seven percent of the children also suffered physical abuse at some time during their lives"). See also "The Relationship between Domestic Violence and Child Abuse," (1999), available at http://www.childabuse.com/fs20.htm (statistics and facts on child abuse as

related to other domestic abuse/spousal abuse).

9. See Murphy and Potthast, "Legal System's Response," 117–18 (noting "the complexity and profound difficulty of protecting children in homes where poverty, domestic violence, and substance abuse are routinely present" and concluding that "the short time frames imposed by ASFA may be inadequate to provide meaningful services to parents experiencing multiple problems, particularly domestic violence and substance abuse"). See also Jane C. Murphy, "Legal Images of Motherhood: Conflicting Definitions from Welfare 'Reform,' Family, and Criminal Law," *Cornell Law Review* 83 (1998), 742–4, 747–8 (describing the threats to children's welfare when their mothers are victims of domestic violence and the great obstacles battered women face to escaping abusive relationships).

10. See, e.g., Christopher J. Mumola, "Bureau of Justice Statistics Special Report: Incarcerated Parents and Their Children" (1997), available at http://www.ojp.usdoj.gov/bjs/pub/pdf/iptc.pdf (reporting that eighty-five percent of inmates in state prisons were using drugs immediately before committing their crimes and that one third of mothers in state prisons committed the crimes for which they were imprisoned to get drugs).

11. See, e.g., Murphy and Potthast, "Legal System's Response," 108 (reporting on study of child abuse cases in four Maryland jurisdictions, finding that all the mothers involved who were themselves victims of family violence lived at or below the poverty level). But see also id., 116 [finding that the average age of the women in the study was thirty-one, which is "inconsistent with the stereotype of the CINA (child in need of assistance) parent as a young single mother"].

12. Planned Parenthood, "Pregnancy & Childbearing Among U.S. Teens," available at http://www. plannedparenthood. org/pp2/portal/files/portal/ medicalinfo/teensexual-health/fact-pregnancy-teens-us.xml; R. A. Maynard, ed., *Kids Having Kids: A Robin Hood Foundation Special Report on the Costs of Adolescent Childbearing* (New York: Robin Hood Foundation, 1996), 181–203;

R. H. Haveman, B. Wolfe, and E. Peterson "Children of Early Childbearers as Young Adults," in R. A. Maynard, ed., *Kids Having Kids: Economic Costs and Social Consequences of Teen Pregnancy* (Washington, DC: The Urban Institute Press, 1997), 257–84; B. Wolfe and M. Perozek, "Teen Children's Health and Health Care Use," in Maynard, ed., *Kids Having Kids* (1997), 181–203; R. M. George and B. J. Lee, "Abuse and Neglect of Children," in Maynard, ed., *Kids Having Kids* (1997), 205–30; House Democratic Committee on Ways and Means, "Steep Decline in Teen Birth Rate Significantly Responsible for Reducing Child Poverty and Single-Parent Families" (2004), available at http:// www. teenpregnancy. org/about/announcements/pdf/Ways&Means Report.pdf. (finding that twenty-six percent of the decrease in the child poverty rate for children under age six, and eighty percent of the decrease in the number of children under six in single mother homes, have been caused by the decline in teenage birth rates); Annie E. Casey Foundation, Kids Count Data Book 2004 (2004), 35 (showing a fifty percent greater infant mortality rate); Sara McLanahan, "The Consequences of Single Motherhood," *American Prospect* 18 (Summer 1994), 48–58 (showing worse outcomes for children from single-parent households even after controlling for socioeconomic status). One cause for skepticism about some of these findings is that children of teenage mothers have lower average birth weights, and it might be that low birth weight, rather than bad parenting, is the primary cause of some adverse outcomes, such as poorer school performance. One organization estimates that teen pregnancy costs the United States at least seven billion dollars annually. See http://www.teenpregnancy.org/ resources/data/genlfact.asp [citing National Campaign to Prevent Teen Pregnancy, Whatever Happened to Childhood? The Problem of Teen Pregnancy in the United States (Washington, DC: 1997)].

13. Susan B. Apel, "Communitarianism and Feminism: The Case against the Preference for the Two-Parent Family," *Wisconsin Women's Law Journal* 10 (1995) 1, 8.

14. See, e.g., Cynthia Martone, Loving through Bars: Children with Parents in Prison (Santa Monica, CA: Santa Monica Press, 2005) (describing the author's experience with one family and citing other sources); Urban Institute Justice Policy Center, "Families Left Behind: The Hidden Costs of Incarceration and Reentry," (2003) available at www.urban.org/ UploadedPDF/ 310882_families_left_behind. pdf; Cynthia Beatty Seymour, *Parents in Prison: Children in Crisis* (Washington, D.C.: Child Welfare League of America, 1999); Cynthia Beatty Seymour, "Children with Parents in Prison: Child Welfare Policy, Program and Practice Issues," *Child Welfare Journal of Policy, Practice & Program* (1998), available at http://www.cwla.org/ programs/incarcerated/ so98journalintro.htm; Mumola, *Incarcerated Parents and Their Children* (reporting that sixty percent of parents in state prisons have served multiple prison terms); K. Gabel and D. Johnston (eds.), *Children of Incarcerated Parents* (New York: Lexington Books, 1995); B. Bloom and D. Steinhart, *Why Punish the Children? A Reappraisal of the Children of Incarcerated Mothers in America* (San Francisco, CA: National Council on Crime and Delinquency, 1993). Most studies, though, look at all children with a parent in prison, without differentiating those who had a relationship with the parent prior to incarceration and those whose parent was in prison at their birth. For purposes of initial assignment to parents at birth, it would be desirable to have studies of children whose parents were in prison at the time of birth. Careful attention should also be paid to the ability of studies to separate out the effects of prison per se from the effects of other circumstances that frequently accompany a parent's imprisonment, such as a home environment marked by poverty and drug use by adults in the home and neighborhood.

15. Krista A. Gallager, "Mentally Ill Parents and the Impact of Illness on Their Children," *Family & Conciliation Courts Review* 38 (2000), 234; Richard Green, "Mentally Ill Parents and Children's Welfare" (NSPCC Practice Development Unit, February 2002), available at http://www.nspcc.org.

uk/inform/Info_Briefing/Mentally IllParents. asp (summarizing research).

16. See Elizabeth Bartholet, *Nobody's Children: Abuse and Neglect, Foster Drift, and the Adoption Alternative* (Beacon Press, 1999), 97, 109–10, 120–1, 263 n.130, 266 nn.20–23, 269–70 nn.11–15; "Prevention of Child Abuse and Neglect Fatalities," (1999), available at: http://www.childabuse.com/fs20.htm (fatality rates of children who had previously been in contact with CPS).

17. See Claudio Violato and Clare Russell, "Effects of Nonmaternal Care on Child Development: A Meta-Analysis of Published Research," in C. Violato, E. Oddone-Paulucci, and M. Genuis, eds., *The Changing Family and Child Development* (Aldershot:Ashgate, 2000), 268–301 (finding that even placing infants in daycare, with return to "normal" parents each day, has significant deleterious effects on children's cognitive, social-emotional, and behavioral development and on maternal attachment); Besharov, *When Drug Addicts Have Children*, xvii (describing children "mired in the child welfare system" who ultimately cannot be placed in an adoptive home).

18. See, e.g., Babb and Moran, "Creation of a Caring Justice System," 8–9 (citing study estimating "that there are twenty-eight million children of alcoholics in the United States and 'several million children of drug addicts and abusers'").

19. See, e.g., Murphy, "Legal Images of Motherhood," (describing the gross inadequacy of the legal and social service systems' current responses to the situation of mothers who are addicted to drugs and/or victims of domestic violence).

20. As to this and all other time limits in the statute, provision might be made for extending time limits for good cause, such as the temporary incapacity of the birth mother after delivery.

21. Mental retardation is generally defined, in part, as having an IQ score below seventy to seventy-five. See Martha A. Field and Valerie A. Sanchez, *Equal Treatment for People with Mental Retardation: Having and Raising Children* (Cambridge, MA: Harvard University Press, 1999), 29. For discussion of and

references to studies concerning the inability of persons with mental retardation to care for children, see Campion, "Who's Fit," 157, 159. As with other of the listed criteria, this characteristic would not automatically disqualify a person from parenthood but rather would obviate any presumption they would otherwise have in their favor and would invite a holistic analysis of the person's preparedness to care for a child.

22. Such a reporting requirement would not violate constitutional rights of parents under U.S. law. See Marrus, "Crack Babies," 306, 308 n. 44, 313–14. In fact, the federal Keeping Children and Families Safe Act of 2003 now requires states to compel medical professionals to report discovery of illegal drug use by pregnant women. Public Law No. 108-36, 117 Stat. 800 (2003).

23. See U.S. Department of Health and Human Services, How Many Children Were Adopted in 2000 and 2001 (Washington, DC: National Adoption Information Clearinghouse, 2004), 4–5 (showing that roughly 127,000 adoptions took place in 2000 and 2001, 50,000 or so from the public child protective system); Jane Lewis, "Adoption: The Nature of Policy Shifts in England and Wales, 1972–2002," *International Journal of Law, Policy and the Family* 18 (2004), 237 (showing that only 4,317 adoptions took place in England and Wales in 1999, compared to over 21,000 in 1975, and that only 196 of the 1999 adoptions were of children under age one) . Currently, only one percent of teens in the United States who become pregnant place their children for adoption. National Adoption Information Clearinghouse, "Voluntary Relinquishment for Adoption: Numbers and Trends," (2005) available at http://naic.acf.hhs.gov/pubs/s_place.cfm.

24. See Lewis, "Adoption: Shifts in England," 235 (noting that the vast majority of adoptions in continental European countries are transnational); *Frette v. France*, (2002) ECHR 36515/97, ¶ 20 (noting that in 1999 in France there were eleven thousand five hundred applications for authorization to adopt, only two thousand children in state care waiting to be adopted, and four thousand visas issued to foreign children to allow for their

adoption by French applicants), ¶ 42 (noting, as partial justification for France's excluding homosexuals from adoption, that "there are not enough children to adopt to satisfy demand"); Virginia Senate Joint Resolution No. 331 (2005) (citing "the reduction in children available for adoption in the United States" as a rationale for revising adoption laws to facilitate foreign adoptions). Of course, this raises questions about the fate of children in the (typically poor) countries from which westerners now adopt, should many more newborns within western nations become available for adoption, questions I cannot adequately address here. I will just say that there clearly are many people in the West who are interested in adopting domestically but not internationally and that in thinking about what is just in this realm as between newborn children in wealthy countries and newborn children in poor countries, analogizing to the case of marriage might again be useful. No one would argue, I assume, that adults in the third world who would like to marry an American are treated unjustly by any U.S. policies that make it more likely that Americans will choose to marry other Americans. There might also be an impact in the short run on children in state care waiting for adoption, but the long-term result should be to lessen dramatically the number of children who must enter state care, or in other words to place with alternative parents now children who will otherwise be in the next cohort of children in foster care waiting for adoption.

25. See Solangel Maldonado, "Beyond Economic Fatherhood: Encouraging Divorced Fathers to Parent," *University of Pennsylvania Law Review* 153 (2005), 925; Kristin Anderson Moore and Susan M. Jekielek, "Marriage from a Child's Perspective: How Does Family Structure Affect Children, and What Can We Do about It?" (Washington, DC: Child Trends, 2002), available at www.childtrends.org; June Carbone, *From Partners to Parents: The Second Revolution in Family Law* (New York: Columbia University Press, 2000), 111–22.

26. For an explanation of parent–child attachment and a defense of an "attachment-centered" approach to legal parenthood, based on a review of empirical literature on child development, see Willemsen and Marcel, "Attachment 101." Cf. Karen Czapanskiy, "Interdependencies, Families, and Children," *Santa Clara Law Review* 39 (1999), 957–8 (advancing an "interdependency theory" of state intervention into established families, under which the aim of state actions relating to family life "should be to respect the caregiver's commitment, hard work, and knowledge and understanding of the child by according him or her maximum autonomy, authority, and assistance," and "to encourage and support people and institutions that provide help to the caregiver").

27. See Bartholet, "Picking Parents," 323; June Carbone and Naomi Cahn, "Which Ties Bind? Redefining the Parent–Child Relationship in an Age of Genetic Certainty," *William & Mary Bill of Rights Journal* 11 (2003), 1022–39 (assessing the relevance of biology to child-centered selection of parents); Barbara Bennett Woodhouse, "Horton Looks at the ALI Principles," *Journal of Law and Family Studies* 4 (2002), 157 (noting that substantial psychological harm can befall a very young child as a result of an early caregiver's departure, something that happens with alarming frequency with fathers after their relationship with a child's mother ends); Moore and Emig, "Marriage from a Child's Perspective"; Nancy E. Dowd, *Redefining Fatherhood* (New York: New York University Press, 2000), 24 (noting that across societies, fathers' involvement in child-rearing correlates highly with their relationship to a child's mother), 157–80 (urging that legal fatherhood be predicated principally on a man's interconnectedness and mutual support with a child's mother); David Archard, "Child Abuse: Parental Rights and the Interests of the Child," in Rosalind Ekman Ladd, ed., *Children's Rights Re-Visioned: Philosophical Readings* (Belmont: Wadsworth, 1996), 113 ("Natural parents do abuse and neglect their children. They have done so throughout history and continue to do so such numbers that talk of rare exceptions to a general rule appears naïve at best and dangerously misguided at worst."); David Archard, "What's Blood Got to Do with It? The Significance of Natural Parenthood,"

Res Publica 1 (1995) 91; Elizabeth Bartholet, *Family Bonds: Adoption, Infertility, and
the New World of Child Production* (Boston,
MA: Beacon Press, 1993), 51–61, 164–86;
Barbara Bennett Woodhouse, "Hatching the
Egg: A Child-Centered Perspective on Parents'
Rights," *Cardozo Law Review* 14 (1993), 1747
(arguing for placing greater weight on nurturing than on biology in defining parenthood).

Some theorists have reasoned, illogically,
that because biological relationship has some
cultural meaning and is conducive to intimacy, that it should be given great weight. See,
e.g., Ferdinand Schoeman, "Rights of Children, Rights of Parents, and the Moral Basis
of the Family," *Ethics* 91 (1980), 18. But this
does not follow. It is clearly not the only factor determining the quality of parent–child
relationships, and so there must be an assessment of the importance of other factors. The
prevailing view among developmental psychologists today is that parents' personality,
motivation, and abilities are more significant.
Increasingly, scholars are emphasizing the
importance to individuals' sense of personal
identity of knowing their biological origins,
and this counsels in favor of identifying and
informing a child at some point about the biological parents, which can be done without
making the biological parents a child's legal
parents.

28. Carbone and Cahn, "Which Ties
Bind?" Carbone and Cahn would not force
men to undergo such testing, but would give
them a choice between submitting to testing
or being estopped thereafter from challenging
their paternity.

29. See Jane Murphy, "Legal Images of
Fatherhood: Welfare Reform, Child Support
Enforcement and Fatherless Children," *Notre
Dame Law Review* 81 (2005) 101 (explaining
that a substantial portion of unwed fathers
have too little income for their child support
obligation to make any difference in single-
mother households and that bringing legal
proceedings against unwed fathers, after compelling mothers to reveal their identity, often
generates psychological costs for the mothers – for example, because the fathers become
hostile toward them and demand unhelpful

involvement in the child's life – that indirectly
harm the child).

30. See David Blankenhorn, *Fatherless
America: Confirming Our Most Urgent Social
Problem* (New York: Basic Books, 1995) (relating the impact of father involvement on children's emotional well-being, performance in
school, and relationships as adults); James
A. Levine, with Edward W. Pitt, *New Expectations: Community Strategies for Responsible
Fatherhood* (New York: Families and Work
Institute, 1995), 26–7 (1995) (describing benefits for children's cognitive and social development of having involved fathers during
infancy).

31. See Maldonado, "Beyond Economic
Fatherhood," 925. For an extended critique
of the assumption that two parents are always
better than one, see Apel, "Communitarianism and Feminism."

32. See June Carbone, *From Partners to Parents*, 81–3 (discussing reasons why a great
percentage of African-American women are
unable ever to form stable marriages).

33. See, e.g., Va. Stat. § 37.2-1011 (2005)
("A guardian or conservator appointed in
the court order shall qualify before the clerk
upon the following: 1. Subscribing to an oath
promising to faithfully perform the duties of
the office in accordance with all provisions of
this chapter; 2. Posting of bond . . . ; and 3.
Acceptance in writing . . . of any educational
materials provided by the court").

34. Journalistic and ethnographic accounts
of life for children in neighborhoods where
drug addiction, prostitution, violence, and
poverty abound are quite telling. See, e.g.,
Adrian Nicole LeBlanc, *Random Family: Love,
Drugs, Trouble, and Coming of Age in the Bronx*
(New York: Scribner, 2003); Jonathan Kozol,
*Amazing Grace: The Lives of Children and the
Conscience of a Nation* (New York: Crown,
1995); Alex Kotlowitz, *There Are No Children
Here: The Story of Two Boys Growing up in the
Other America* (New York: Doubleday, 1991).

35. Doing so would appear permissible
under current constitutional doctrine in the
United States. See Marrus, "Crack Babies,"
306, 314 n. 81. Professor John Robertson
explains why punishing women for harming a

fetus is also just, even from a perspective that assumes a right to abort is a proper component of procreation rights as follows:

> The mother has, if she conceives and chooses not to abort, a legal and moral duty to bring the child into the world as healthy as is reasonably possible. She has a duty to avoid actions or omissions that will damage the fetus and child, just as she has a duty to protect the child's welfare once it is born until she transfers this duty to another. In terms of fetal rights, a fetus has no right to be conceived – or, once conceived, to be carried to viability. But once the mother decides not to terminate the pregnancy, the viable fetus acquires rights to have the mother conduct her life in ways that will not injure it.

John A. Robertson, "Procreative Liberty and the Control of Conception, Pregnancy, and Childbirth," *Virginia Law Review* 69 (1983), 438. See also id., 444–5, 451–3, 456, 464 ("One sees here, as elsewhere, the bittersweet nature of freedom, which provides meaning only through the acceptance of constraint."). Robertson points out that persons other than the mother are subject to legal sanction if they harm a fetus and contends that the mother should have no greater immunity from such sanctions than others have. Id., 439. He also explains why criminal sanctions for harming a fetus, by act or omission, would not conflict with women's recognized constitutional rights. Id., 442–3, 449–52.

36. See generally Lewis, "Adoption: Shifts in England" (describing political developments in England and the influence on them of developments in the United States that led to the Adoption and Safe Families Act, discussed in Chapter 1). Id., 248–9 (quoting a conservative member of the House of Commons who decried "'the living hell of institutional care or serial fostering arrangements'").

37. *Stanley v. Illinois*, 405 U.S. 645 (1972). For a fuller and more nuanced review of U.S. constitutional doctrine concerning the rights of biological fathers, see David D. Meyer, "Family Ties: Solving the Constitutional Dilemma of the Faultless Father," *Arizona Law Review* 41 (1999), 753.

38. *Lehr v. Robertson*, 463 U.S. 248 (1983).

39. 491 U.S. 110 (1989) (plurality decision).

40. *Marckx v. Belgium*, (1979) ECHR 6833/74.

41. With respect to marital births, see *Berrehab v. The Netherlands*, (1988) ECHR 10730/84, ¶ 21 ("It follows from the concept of family on which Article 8 is based that a child born of such a [marital] union is ipso jure part of that relationship; hence, from the moment of the child's birth and by the very fact of it, there exists between him and his parents a bond amounting to 'family life,' even if the parents are not then living together."). The Court reiterated this position in *Gul v. Switzerland*, (1996) ECHR 23218/94, ¶ 32, and more recently in *Kosmopoulou v. Greece*, (2004) ECHR 60457/00, ¶ 42. With respect to births to unmarried couples cohabiting at the time of conception, see *Nekvedavicius v. Germany*, (2004) 38 EHRR CD1:

> [T]he notion of "family life" in Art. 8 is not confined solely to marriage-based relationship and may encompass other de facto "family" ties where the parties are living together outside of marriage. A child born out of such a relationship is ipso iure part of a "family" unit from the moment of his birth by the very fact of it. There thus exists between the child and his parents a bond amounting to family life even if at the time of his or her birth the parents are no long cohabiting or if their relationship has then ended.

42. (2004) 38 EHRR CD1. Cf. *Mikulic v. Croatia*, (2002) ECHR 53176/99, ¶ 52 (finding that "no family tie has been established" between a child and a putative father who resisted DNA testing to establish his paternity). The European Charter of Fundamental Rights, Article 9, more explicitly guarantees "the right to found a family," but only "in accordance with the national laws governing the exercise of these rights," which suggests that it is essentially a procedural due process or equal protection type of right.

43. The earlier decision was *M.B. v. United Kingdom*, App. No. 22920/93, Comm. Dec. 06.04.1994. See Jane Fortin, *Children's Rights and the Developing Law* (2nd ed.) (London:

Butterworths, 2003), 393. In M.B., the Commission noted that the relationship between unmarried fathers and their children "varies from ignorance and indifference to a close stable relationship indistinguishable from the conventional family-based unit." But see *Mikulic v. Croatia*, where the Court held that states must provide some mechanism for establishing who a child's biological father is, as a matter of the right of children "to establish details of their identity as individual human beings," including the fact of who their biological parents are, stating that for a child "such information is of importance because of its formative implications for his or her personality," (2002) ECHR 53176/99, ¶ 54. See also id., ¶ 64 (stating that children "have a vital interest, protected by the Convention, in receiving information necessary to uncover the truth about an important aspect of their personal identity."), ¶ 65 (referring to "the right of the [child] to have her uncertainty as to her personal identity eliminated without necessary delay").

44. See *Hansen v. Turkey*, 39 E.H.R.R. 18 (2004) Par. 97 ("the essential object of Art. 8 [protecting family life] is to protect the individual against arbitrary action by the public authorities").

45. The evidentiary standard for initial intervention in this section mirrors that in common statutory provisions for issuance of temporary protective orders in cases of domestic violence against a spouse. See, e.g., Maryland Family Act s. 4-505 (2005) (authorizing issuance of temporary protective order, including an order that the offender stay away from the victim's residence regardless of who owns it, upon finding "reasonable grounds to believe" abuse has occurred); Wisconsin Statutes s. 813.12(3) (2005) (same).

46. On the importance of this consideration, see Patrick Parkinson, "Child Protection, Permanency Planning and Children's Right to Family Life," *International Journal of Law, Policy and the Family* 17 (2003), 147, 157–60.

47. On the need to respect emotional bonds that develop between foster parents and children, see Woodhouse, "ALI Principles," 158–62.

48. Bartholet, *Nobody's Children*, 50–5.

49. Id., 52–3.

50. See Barbara Bennett Woodhouse, "'Are You My Mother?': Conceptualizing Children's Identity Rights in Transracial Adoptions," *Duke Journal of Gender Law & Policy* 2 (1995), 125–8.

51. See David D. Meyer, "Constitutional Pragmatism for a Changing American Family," *Rutgers Law Journal* 32 (2001), 725–30.

52. For an extended critique of the argument for parental rights as a means of serving children's welfare, see James G. Dwyer, "Parents' Religion and Children's Welfare: Debunking the Doctrine of Parents' Rights," *California Law Review* 82 (1994), 1371.

53. Wash. Rev. Code § 26.09.240 (2005).

Appendix: The Conceptual Possibility of Children Having Rights

1. Hillel Steiner, "Working Rights," in Matthew H. Kramer, ed., *A Debate over Rights* (Oxford: Oxford University Press, 1998), 238.

2. See, e.g., L. W. Sumner, *The Moral Foundation of Rights* (Oxford: Clarendon Press, 1987), 46 (describing the "control account of claims" as follows: "Central to this conception is the idea of the right-holder having the freedom to choose among a set of options, and of this freedom being protected by a set of duties imposed on others. The choice in question may be provided by a full liberty, in which case its protection will include claims of non-interference against others."). By duties here, I intend to speak only of "perfect duties." Imperfect duties more clearly include duties to further interests rather than just not to interfere with choices.

3. Neil MacCormick, *Legal Right and Social Democracy: Essays in Legal and Political Philosophy* (Oxford: Clarendon Press, 1982); Matthew H. Kramer, "Rights without Trimmings," in Kramer, ed., *A Debate over Rights*, 61–2; Sumner, *The Moral Foundation of Rights*, 96 ("Because autonomy can be treated as a particular component of individual welfare, anything which counts as a right under the choice conception will also count as

such under the interest conception. But the reverse will not be true, since there are ways of protecting welfare without protecting autonomy.").

4. See Steiner, "Working Rights."

5. H. L. A. Hart, *Essays on Bentham: Studies in Jurisprudence and Political Theory* (Oxford: Oxford University Press,1982), 183–4. Onora O'Neill makes the related assertion that talk of children's rights is wasted rhetoric, because children cannot become empowered by it, being in a condition of natural powerlessness. See, e.g., Onora O'Neill, "Children's Rights and Children's Lives," *Ethics* 98 (1988), 463. That assertion falsely presupposes that the only utility of rights-claims derives from the inspiration they give to those for whom rights are claimed.

6. E.g., Steiner, "Working Rights," 261.

7. E.g., Matthew Kramer, "Getting Rights Right," in Matthew Kramer, ed., *Rights, Wrongs, and Responsibilities* (New York: Palgrave, 2001), 28–9.

8. E.g., N. E. Simmonds, "Rights at the Cutting Edge," in Kramer, ed., *A Debate over Rights*, 116.

9. As discussed in Chapter 5, however, most contemporary Kantians take the position that adults owe a duty to children and incompetent adults to assist them in becoming autonomous; they do not limit moral value to current autonomy but rather extend it also to the potential for autonomy.

10. See, e.g., Peter Singer, *Practical Ethics* (Cambridge, UK: Cambridge University Press, 1993).

11. See James Griffin, "Do Children Have Rights?," in David Archard and Colin M. Macleod, eds., *The Moral and Political Status of Children* (Oxford: Oxford University Press, 2002), 19–20.

12. Id., 20.

13. See, e.g., H. L. A. Hart, "Bentham on Legal Rights," in A. W. B. Simpson, ed., *Oxford Essays in Jurisprudence* (Oxford: Clarendon Press, 1973), 197; Sumner, *The Moral Foundation of Rights*, 97–8. Sumner argues directly against natural rights and natural law reasoning. Id., 92–128. He also offers a peculiar alternative normative argument for adopting the Will Theory, or what he calls the "choice con-

ception" of rights. He suggests that limiting rights to protections of autonomy will remind philosophers and the public that there is basic disagreement between utilitarians and Kantians about what is of ultimate moral value. Id., 98. What other consequences might follow from limiting "rights" to protection of autonomy – for example, that nonautonomous persons would no longer have any "rights" – appears not to have concerned Sumner.

14. Samantha Brennan, "Children's Choices or Children's Interests: Which Do Their Rights Protect?," in D. Archard and C. Macleod, eds., *Moral and Political Status*, 65–6.

15. Cf. Daniel M. Weinstock, "Review of Robert R. Louden, *Kant's Impure Ethics: From Rational Beings to Human Beings*," *Ethics* 112 (2002), 386 ("Kant in his 'pure' moral philosophy provides us with a picture of the kind of moral agency which, in his more 'empirical' works, constitutes the end toward which human history tends. Should it not give us pause that Kant also happened to think that white European males just happened to be closest to that end?").

16. See Christine M. Korsgaard, *The Sources of Normativity* (Cambridge, UK: Cambridge University Press, 1996), 220–1; Thomas E. Hill, Jr., *Autonomy and Self-Respect* (Cambridge, UK: Cambridge University Press, 1991), 30 (noting that Kant's autonomy-based moral theory is "embedded in a metaphysical framework and surrounded by specific moral opinions which most philosophers today, quite rightly, reject"), 45.

17. See Donald H. Regan, "The Value of Rational Nature," *Ethics* 112 (2002), 267–91 (critiquing Kantian and neo-Kantian arguments for the inherent value of human rational agency).

18. Some Will Theorists take the peculiar view that state officials are the holders of rights created by the criminal law. See, e.g., Steiner, "Working Rights," 248–55. They arrive at this conclusion by presupposing the thesis they aim to establish – namely that the true rightholder in any situation is the person possessing the power to waive or enforce duties – rather than by appealing to any example of ordinary usage of the term *right*. It would be shocking,

surely, for a prosecutor to assert that a rapist violated his (the prosecutor's) rights or the state's rights.

19. Will Theorists contend that their view better explains certain existing practices relating to competent adults, but they are unpersuasive. Their chief example is that in connection with contracts created for the benefit of a third person, the contracting parties, whom Will Theorists say derive no benefit from the contract, are deemed to have rights, but the third-person beneficiary is not. See, e.g., Hart, "Bentham on Legal Rights," 195–6. This example does not, however, make their point. In reality, the contracting parties do benefit from performance of the contract. In particular, the party whose wish it was to benefit the third party gets the satisfaction of benefiting the third party. That such a satisfaction is a benefit concrete enough to ground a right is evident from the law of wills and trusts, which is replete with references to the right of the testator or grantor to have carried out his or her intentions to effect gratuitous transfers, and judicial precedent treating the power to make gratuitous transfers as having economic value for the transferor. See, e.g., *Hodel v. Irving*, 481 U.S. 704 (1987). In addition, it is not the case that the law never confers on third-party beneficiaries a right against the contracting party who agreed to provide the benefit. Estate law again presents an example; in most U.S. jurisdictions, an intended will beneficiary can in his or her own right sue the drafting attorney for botching the bequest. And even if it were the case, that would not be a problem for the Interest Theory. This is in part because Interest Theorists could take the position that

the rules for third-party beneficiaries are simply anomalous; Will Theorists suppose that these rules are correct in some sense, but they themselves recognize that actual practice as to "rights" is in some ways not rationally consistent. It is also in part because the Will Theorists reason circularly when they suppose that legal rules do not ascribe a right to third-party beneficiaries because the rules do not give them the power to demand enforcement of contracts. And it is in part because the Interests Theory does not entail that whenever a person benefits from a legal duty that person must be said to have a right. Rather, it holds that a person's benefiting from a duty is sufficient basis for perceiving a right held by that person so long as the duty is owed to that person, which is not always the case when someone benefits from performance of a duty; sometimes we benefit incidentally. Thus, it is necessary to find some basis in addition to a person's benefit for concluding that the duty is owed to a particular person. Contrary to the Will Theory, however, possession of a power is neither a necessary nor a sufficient condition for establishing that a particular person is the object of a duty.

20. Steiner, "Working Rights," 261.

21. Hart, "Bentham on Legal Rights," 192–3, n. 86.

22. Kramer, "Getting Rights Right," 32–7.

23. See Brennan, "Children's Choices," 66; Kramer, "Getting Rights Right," 41.

24. This likely would not be, on its own, a sufficient explanation for the intuition, given that most people believe humans who are comatose or in a persistent vegetative state have rights.

Index

paternity, 1
    custody disputes and, 40, 46–50
    genetic testing for, 31–32, 138–139, 222,
        274, 278–279, 349–350
    interest-protecting rights and, 161
    parentage laws and, 270–271
paternity rules, 31–35
    abuse/neglect and, 34, 35
    best interests and, 60, 209, 220
    for custody and visitation, 33, 34–35, 47
    ECHR on, 34–35, 349–350
    financial support and, 33, 35, 267–269
    for unwed fathers, 32–34, 268–269, 277
patriarchy, 28, 312
perfectionism, Kant on, 331
personal v. impersonal relationships, 105, 117
pleasures
    autonomy, liberty and, 101–102
    Mill on, 328, 340
police power role, state in, 195–199, 203
poverty
    best interests bias and, 232–233
    parentage laws and, 256–257
    teenage parents and, 345
    termination rules and, 54
    violence and, 344, 348
primary caretaker
    custody and, 40, 41–42, 214, 220, 225–227,
        231, 233, 236, 342
    feminists on approximation rules and, 342
primary goods, 145
    cultural access as, 337
    Rawls on, 112, 116–118, 332, 337
    self-esteem as, 116–118, 145
    self-respect as, 154
prison. See also crimes
    ending legal parent–child relationships and,
        54, 55–56
    parents in, 345
    prisoner's rights, 323
pro-choice, women and, 174
procreation rights, 4, 76
property, children as, 15, 179
property rights
    state on, 19–20, 199–200, 238
    trespass and, 298
proxy decision making, 130–133, 160, 172,
    205–210
public/private destriction, 19

race. See also minorities
    adoptions and, 3, 38–39, 190, 264, 313
    constitution, society and, 188–194, 199,
        201–203

custody disputes and, 2–3, 43–44, 189, 199
    gender, competence and, 69
    interracial relationships, 3, 317
    prejudice and, 137, 317
rational agency, 295–299, 301
Rawls, John
    on autonomy, 335
    on contractualism, 150–152, 181
    on hypothetical consent, 150–152
    on justice, 113, 114–115, 142–143, 146–155,
        157–158, 336–337
    Kant and, 110, 112–114, 147, 153, 331–332
    on liberty and self-respect, 153–156
    on original position, 112–114, 146–150,
        153–154, 184–185
    on primary goods, 112, 116–118, 332, 337
    social contract theory and, 110–116, 332
reform, 4
    of child protection laws, 279–285
    of parentage laws, 253–279, 290
Regan, Milton
    on autonomy, 118–119, 155, 158, 329
    on social contract theory, 110
    on trust, 155, 156
relatives. See also specific relatives
    blood, marriages to, 76
    relationships with, 60, 62, 66
religion, 123–124
    adoptions and, 38, 190
    constitution, society and, 188, 190–192, 194,
        199–200, 201–203
    cults, 64
    custody disputes and, 44–45
    freedom of, 97, 98–99, 114, 188, 190–192,
        194
    medical care and, 190, 275
    visitation for noncustodial parent and, 49
relocation, custody disputes and, 42–43, 172,
    175, 190, 227, 316–317
rights. See also specific rights
    absolute, 70, 84
    children as holders of, 11–23, 291–307
    duties and, 12, 14, 17, 22–23, 132, 181–182,
        299–305, 309–310, 352
    within families, 12, 15–17, 71, 72–73, 92
    implicit, 311
    interests, choices and, 11–12, 125, 126–127,
        129–133, 160–167, 172–173, 292–302
    natural, 295–296, 351
    negative and positive, 17–22
    use/understanding of term, 11–12,
        295–307
rights discourse, children's lives and, 12–17
Roberts, Dorothy, 30, 189